GREEK IS GREAT GAIN

A Method for
Exegesis and Exposition

GREEK IS GREAT GAIN

A Method for
Exegesis and Exposition

By
William J. Larkin

foreword by Andreas J. Köstenberger

WIPF & STOCK · Eugene, Oregon

GREEK IS GREAT GAIN
A Method for Exegesis and Exposition

Copyright © 2008 William J. Larkin
All rights reserved. Except for brief quotations in critical publications or reviews, no part of this book may be reproduced in any manner without prior written permission from the publisher. Write: Permissions, Wipf & Stock, 199 W. 8th Ave., Eugene, OR 97401.

ISBN 10: 1-55635-345-6
ISBN 13: 978-1-55635-345-1

Unless otherwise indicated, the Scripture quotations are the author's translation.

The Greek text of the New Testament is taken from *Bibloi CD-ROM*. Silvermountain Software Version 8.0. Cedar Hill, TX: Silvermountain Software, 2004. Used with permission.

Contents

Foreword		vii
Preface		ix
Abbreviations		xiii
1.	Using Greek in Ministry	1
2.	Definitions and Presuppositions	15
3.	Greek Reading and Computer Resources	27
4.	Finished Translation and Mechanical Layout	39
5.	Survey	57
6.	Historical and Literary Analysis	65
7.	Genre Analysis: Epistle	75
8.	Genre Analysis: Historical Narrative and Prophetic-Apocalyptic	107
9.	Grammar and Rhetorical Features	137
10.	Word Study: Focus the Meaning	169
11.	Word Study: Illumine the Meaning	183
12.	Theological Analysis	201
13.	Synthesis	215
14.	Interpretation and Application for Contemporary Culture	229
15.	Homiletical and Didactic Appropriation	247
16.	Periodic Preparation	279
	Appendix: Greek Grammar Guides	303
	Bibliography	337

FOREWORD

Dr. William Larkin has developed the material included in this volume for well over two decades, and as one who had Dr. Larkin as a teacher in the mid- to late 1980s I am grateful that at long last *Greek Is Great Gain* is available in published form. This is an all-business, no-nonsense manual for the serious exegesis of the Greek text. At the same time, Dr. Larkin is seeking to be practical in tailoring his exegetical method to the busy pastor, and for that he is to be commended.

As one who has dedicated his life to training and mentoring serious students of Scripture in the conviction that what counts for eternity is studying and teaching Scripture in the original languages by following proper principles of exegesis and hermeneutics, Dr. Larkin has produced what may be his most significant contribution to date. The chapter on interpreting the Epistles (Chapter 7 Genre Analysis: Epistle) alone is worth the price of the volume and provides an outstanding example of the meticulous research and analytical acumen that characterizes Dr. Larkin's work.

In his overall plan, Dr. Larkin moves swiftly from a discussion of using Greek in ministry to an exploration of Scripture with regard to history, literature, and theology. He is also keenly interested in matters related to contextualization as well as homiletical method. It is not necessary to follow Dr. Larkin's multi-faceted step-by-step approach in every detail to benefit from the wealth of information presented in this volume. Many will find this book an invaluable resource for their serious study of Scripture.

I have personally benefitted greatly from sitting under Dr. William Larkin's teaching, and I heartily commend *Greek Is Great Gain* to a new generation of students. Attaining mastery of Greek indeed is great gain, and this book, like very few, is able to assist serious students of Scripture in achieving their goal, in keeping with Paul's words to Timothy,

> "Do your best to present yourself to God as one approved, a workman who does not need to be ashamed and who correctly handles the word of truth" (2 Tim 2:15 NIV).

Andreas J. Köstenberger
Professor of New Testament and Director of Ph.D. Studies
Southeastern Baptist Theological Seminary

PREFACE

Introduction

What is the best way to instruct preachers and Bible teachers in exegesis? Shall we model before them good exegesis, give them a exegetical term paper to write, and consider our task accomplished? Or, shall we take the student step by step through the questions to ask, show them how to arrive at sound answers through direct interaction with the Greek text, and introduce them to supporting reference resources?

Greek is Great Gain: A Method for Exegesis and Exposition pursues this second apprentice approach. It has been written from the orientation of exegesis in the service of preaching and Bible teaching. It seeks to be comprehensive as it embraces various processes in a lifetime of ministry using the Greek New Testament. *Greek is Great Gain* provides guidance whether for maintaining Greek reading proficiency, doing weekly immediate preparation of sermons or lessons, planning for preaching and teaching, or pursuing periodic professional development through in-depth study in the Scriptures.

This text pursues integration by reaching back to a first year NT Greek grammar foundation, particularly as presented in John D. Harvey's *Greek is Good Grief*. And it reaches forward linking exegetical method to a homiletical method and lesson preparation scheme. In all, *Greek is Great Gain* seeks to be a practical manual. Employing Philippians as its primary biblical database, it presents the steps of a comprehensive exegetical method supported with explanation, resources, and examples.

How to Use this Book

Students

Students as apprentices can best benefit from this text as follows. They should seek to understand the purpose and content of each step of exegesis. They need to practice the steps repeatedly until they have gained such proficiency that they are able to use them efficiently in weekly sermon or lesson preparation.

Students should aim not only at comprehensiveness of approach, but also at developing discrimination, an ability to judge which aspects of each step will be most productive in studying a particular passage. Thus the method can become their toolbox from which they select the right items to use on any given passage.

Finally, students will want to customize the method as they make it their own. This may mean rearranging some of the steps, even using a number of analytical steps simultaneously, as they move in commentary fashion verse by verse. In this way they will progress from apprentice to master craftsman in their handling of the Word of God during a lifetime of ministry.

Pastors and Christian Workers

The pastor or Christian worker who has already received training in exegesis and exposition can use *Greek is Great Gain* as a refresher and strengthener. It can become a manual for giving his exegetical practice a diagnostic tune-up. After surveying the book he can select those steps, like grammatical analysis or word study, in which he would like to refresh himself. He may well find areas like genre analysis–historical narrative or parable with which he can strengthen his exegetical grip on a passage. He may want to use *Greek is Great Gain* to strategize about areas for in-depth study of the text he can pursue during his professional development study time. *Greek is Great Gain* is intended as a guide to mining the inexhaustible riches of God's truth present in the Greek New Testament.

Instructors

Instructors know that training in exegesis, particularly when approached from an apprentice model, is a very personal enterprise. Therefore, there are almost as many distinct approaches to how to teach exegesis, let alone how to do exegesis, as there are instructors. How can an instructor profitably use this work without feeling he is simply "putting on Saul's armor"?

The instructor should feel free to use as much or as little of the work as he sees will be helpful to him and his students, while still valuing the need for comprehensiveness in method. Certain steps, e.g., rhetorical features analysis or interpretation and application, may capture well for the instructor a particular area of exegesis. For others, he may substitute fruitful procedures which he has already developed. In other words, he should customize the book's content to meet his instructional needs. And, by all means, he should integrate his instruction in exegesis with what his own colleagues are doing in homiletical and lesson development instruction. Whether as a foundational framework or a supplementary resource, *Greek is Great Gain* can provide helpful support to instruction in exegesis of the Greek New Testament.

Further Resources

The reader has two further resources for exegesis related to this book. Throughout the text there are references to files posted at the author's faculty webpage at www.ciu.edu. These are additional charts and appendices in grammar, rhetorical features, textual criticism, word study, and genre studies, including historical criticism and Gospels analysis, in support of exegesis. There is also a file of templates for worksheets to use with the exegetical steps.

This method is taught and used in two courses available in distance education and online format from CIU Seminary and School of Missions. Look for GRE 6210 "Greek Three: From Exegesis to Exposition" and GRE 6307 "Greek Four: Exegesis and Exposition of Luke" under "Distance Learning" at www.ciu.edu.

Acknowledgments

Greek is Great Gain is the product of three decades of teaching exegesis at CIU Seminary and School of Missions. Thanks goes to my colleagues in New Testament studies, John D. Harvey, Don N. Howell, and Joel F. Williams, and in homiletics, Donald L. Hamilton, who have been constant and beneficial conversation partners about exegesis and exposition. Their particular contributions have been noted in endnotes throughout the work. I am grateful to Shirl Schiffman, educational ministries, for her stylistic improvements of this work in an earlier form.

Particular thanks goes to Junias Venugopal, dean, and the administration of CIU Seminary and School of Missions for the provision of study leave time in the 2007-08 academic year during which the manuscript was revised and edited. I am grateful to John Harvey for blazing the trail with *Greek is Good Grief* and his encouragement to submit this present work as a companion volume. I have greatly benefitted from the expert guidance of Jim Tedrick and his staff at Wipf and Stock.

I am grateful to my students over the years for their enthusiasm, encouragement, and insights as we have learned together the practice of exegesis and exposition. Luke Roberts, Anthony Rodriguez and Lashaundra Smith have been particularly helpful in the final stages of preparation.

I thank CIU staff members Joyce Hack, Daniel Janosik, and James Wilson for their invaluable technical assistance in preparing the manuscript in "camera ready" format.

Finally, special thanks goes to my wife, Edna, and my children, Thomas and Priscilla, for their continual encouragement during various phases in this decades long project.

May God be pleased to raise up in every spiritual generation those who preach and teach his Word with an accuracy and effectiveness born of Spirit filled exegetical interaction with the New Testament in the original Greek.

ABBREVIATIONS

ATLA	American Theological Library Association
BAGD	Walter Bauer, William F. Arndt, F. W. Gingrich, revised and augmented by F. W. Gingrich and Frederick W. Danker. *A Greek-English Lexicon of the New Testament and Other Early Christian Literature*. 2nd ed. Chicago: Univ. of Chicago Press, 1979.
BDAG	Walter Bauer, William F. Arndt, F. W. Gingrich, revised and edited by Frederick W. Danker. *A Greek-English Lexicon of the New Testament and Other Early Christian Literature*. 3rd ed. Chicago: Univ. of Chicago Press, 2000.
BDF	F. Blass, A. Debrunner, and R. W. Funk. *A Greek Grammar of the New Testament and Other Early Christian Literature*. Chicago: Univ. of Chicago Press, 1961.
BECNT	Baker Exegetical Commentary on the New Testament
BGU	Königliche Museen zu Berlin. *Aegyptische Urkunden aus den Königlichen Staatlichen Museen zu Berlin: Griechische Urkunden*. 9 vols. Berlin: Weidmann, 1895–1937.
BSac	*Bibliotheca Sacra*
BT	*The Bible Translator*
BTDB	Walter A. Elwell, ed. *Baker Theological Dictionary of the Bible*. Grand Rapids: Baker Academic, 2001.
CBQ	*Catholic Biblical Quarterly*
CC	Coordinating Conjunction
CIU	Columbia International University
CIU-SSM	Columbia International University Seminary and School of Missions
C-S-V-O	Conjunction-Subject-Verb-Object
CTM	*Concordia Theological Monthly*
CTJ	*Calvin Theological Journal*
DBI	Leland Ryken, James C. Wilhoit, and Tremper Longman III, eds. *Dictionary of Biblical Imagery*. Downers Grove, IL: InterVarsity Press, 1998.

DBW	Daniel B. Wallace. *Greek Grammar Beyond the Basics: An Exegetical Syntax of the New Testament*. Grand Rapids: Zondervan, 1996.
DJG	Joel B. Green and Scot McKnight, eds. *Dictionary of Jesus and the Gospels*. Downers Grove, IL: InterVarsity Press, 1992.
DLNT	Ralph P. Martin and Peter H. Davids, eds. *Dictionary of the Later New Testament and Its Developments*. Downers Grove, IL: InterVarsity Press, 1997.
DNTB	Craig A. Evans and Stanley E. Porter, eds. *Dictionary of New Testament Background*. Downers Grove, IL: InterVarsity Press, 2000.
DPL	Gerald F. Hawthorne and Ralph P. Martin, eds. *Dictionary of Paul and His Letters*. Downers Grove, IL: InterVarsity Press, 1993.
DTIB	Kevin J. Vanhoozer, ed. *Dictionary for Theological Interpretation of the Bible*. Grand Rapids: Baker Academic, 2005.
EBC	Expositor's Bible Commentary
EDNT	Horst Balz and Gerhard Schneider, eds. *Exegetical Dictionary of the New Testament*. 3 vols. Grand Rapids: Eerdmans, 1990-93.
EDT	Walter A. Elwell, ed. *Evangelical Dictionary of Theology*. Grand Rapids: Baker, 1984.
ESV	English Standard Version
ExpTim	*Expository Times*
GNT	Greek New Testament
HRCS	Edwin P. Hatch and Henry A Redpath. *A Concordance to the Septuagint*. 2nd ed. Grand Rapids: Baker, 1998.
IDB	George A. Buttrick, ed. *Interpreter's Dictionary of the Bible: An Illustrated Encyclopedia*. 4 vols. Nashville: Abingdon, 1962.
ICC	International Critical Commentary
Int	*Interpretation*
ISBE	Geoffrey W. Bromiley, ed. *The International Standard Bible Encyclopedia*. 4 vols. rev. ed. Grand Rapids: Eerdmans, 1979-88.
IVP	InterVarsity Press
IVPNTC	The IVP New Testament Commentary
JBL	*Journal of Biblical Literature*
JETS	*Journal of the Evangelical Theological Society*

K&D	Carl F. Keil and Franz Delitzsch. *Biblical Commentary on the Old Testament*. 10 vols. repr. Peabody, MA: Hendrickson, 1996.
KJV	King James Version
LCL	Loeb Classical Library. Cambridge, MA: Harvard Univ. Press.
LN	Johannes P. Louw and Eugene A. Nida, eds. *Greek-English Lexicon of the New Testament Based on Semantic Domains*. 2 vols. New York: United Bible Societies, 1988.
LSJ	Liddell, Henry, Robert Scott, Henry S. Jones, Roderick McKenzie, P. G. W. Glare. *A Greek-English Lexicon*, 9th ed. with *Revised Supplement*. Oxford: Clarendon Press, 1996.
LXX	Septuagint
M&G	I. Howard Marshall, ed. *Moulton and Geden Concordance of the Greek New Testament*. 6th ed. London: T & T Clark, 2002.
MLO	Mechanical Layout
MM	Moulton, James H. and George Milligan. *The Vocabulary of the Greek Testament: Illustrated from the Papyri and Other Non-literary Sources*. repr. Grand Rapids: Eerdmans, 1974.
MSJ	*Masters Seminary Journal*
MT	Masoretic Text
NAC	New American Commentary
NASB	New American Standard Bible
NAS95	New American Standard Bible, revised edition (1995)
NDT	Sinclair B. Ferguson, David F.Wright, and J. I. Packer, eds. *New Dictionary of Theology*. Downers Grove, IL: InterVarsity Press, 1988.
NDBT	T. Desmond Alexander and Brian S. Rosner, eds. *New Dictionary of Biblical Theology: Exploring the Unity and Diversity of Scripture*. Downers Grove, IL: InterVarsity Press, 2000.
NICNT	New International Commentary on the New Testament
NIDB	J. D. Douglas and Merrill C. Tenney, eds. *New International Dictionary of the Bible, Pictorial Edition*. Grand Rapids: Zondervan, 1987.
NIDNTT	Colin Brown, ed. *The New International Dictionary of New Testament Theology*. 3 vols. Grand Rapids: Zondervan, 1975-78.

NIDOTTE	Willem Van Gemeren, ed. *The New International Dictionary of Old Testament Theology & Exegesis.* 5 vols. Grand Rapids: Zondervan, 1997.
NIGTC	New International Greek Testament Commentary
NIV	New International Version
NIVAC	NIV Application Commentary
NKJV	New King James Version
NovT	*Novum Testamentum*
NRSV	New Revised Standard Version
NT	New Testament
NTA	*New Testament Abstracts*
NTS	*New Testament Studies*
OCD	Simon Hornblower and Antony Spaworth, eds. *The Oxford Classical Dictionary.* 3rd ed. Oxford: Oxford Univ. Press, 1996.
OT	Old Testament
OTP	James H. Charlesworth, ed. *The Old Testament Pseudepigrapha.* 2 vols. Garden City, NY: Doubleday, 1983-85.
Perseus	*Perseus Digital Library.* Somerville, MA: Tufts University. Accessed September 12, 2007. Online: http://www.perseus.tufts.edu/.
P.Flor.	Domenico Comparetti and Girolamo Vitelli. *Papiri Greco-Egizii.* 3 vols. Milano: U. Hoepli, 1905-15.
PGL	G. W. H. Lampe. *A Patristic Greek Lexicon.* Oxford: Clarendon Press, 1961.
P.Mich.	C. C. Edgar, ed. *Zenon Papyri in the University of Michigan Collection.* Ann Arbor, MI: Univ. of Michigan Press, 1931.
Presb	*Presbyterion*
Str-B	Hermann L. Strack and Paul Billerbeck. *Kommentar zum Neuen Testament aus Talmud und Midrasch.* 6 vols. 7th ed. Münich: C. H. Beck'sche, 1978.
TDNT	Gerhard Kittel and Gerhard Friedrich, eds. *Theological Dictionary of the New Testament.* 10 vols. Grand Rapids: Eerdmans, 1964-76.
TDOT	G. Johannes Botterweck, Helmer Ringgren, and Heinz-Josef Fabry, eds. *Theological Dictionary of the OldTestament.* 15 vols. Grand Rapids: Eerdmans, 1974–2006.
TJ	*Trinity Journal*

TLG	*Thesaurus Linguae Graecae (TLG®) CD-ROM.* Version E. Irvine, CA: Univ.of California, Irvine, 2000. Accessed September 12, 2007. Online (available by subscription): http://ptolemy.tlg.uci.edu.
UBS[4]	Barbara Aland, Kurt Aland, Johannes Karavidopoulos, Carlo M. Martini, Bruce M. Metzger, and Allen Wikgren, eds. *The Greek New Testament.* 4th rev. ed. Stuttgart: United Bible Societies, 1993.
WBC	Word Biblical Commentary
WJL	William J. Larkin
WJLFP	William J. Larkin faculty page; access at www.ciu.edu
WTJ	*Westminster Theological Journal*
ZPEB	Merrill C. Tenney, ed. *Zondervan Pictorial Encyclopedia of the Bible.* 5 vols. Grand Rapids: Zondervan, 1975-76.

Chapter 1
USING GREEK IN MINISTRY

In his merciful providence, the infinite God chose to communicate with us in human language. The Holy Spirit not only inspired human authors to write down God's message in Hebrew, Aramaic, and Greek, but made sure copies in the original languages survive to this day. Of course, only the person who knows these historical languages can read the text in the language in which it was given. Everyone else works from a translation that another individual or a committee made from original language manuscripts. Is it possible to understand and communicate truth working from a translation? Of course, but if one has a passion to communicate the Word, there is *great gain* in learning to study it in the original languages. This is true for pastors who will preach week in and week out, missionaries gathering people for a small group Bible study that will become the nucleus of a church plant, Bible teachers in churches, schools and universities, chaplains, and any Christian worker for whom preaching or Bible teaching is a central — and joyous — responsibility. The purpose of this book is to equip preachers and teachers to exegete the Greek New Testament with maximum precision and effectiveness so that they can confidently interpret and apply it to those to whom they minister.

A Question that Needs to be Asked

It's good to confront head-on the fact that many people question whether using Greek (or any biblical language) in sermon and lesson preparation is really worth the effort. With so many excellent translations and computer aids available, many fail to see an adequate payoff for years of difficult language study. John Stott has made clear his own opinion on this matter. "The higher our view of the Bible, the more painstaking and conscientious our study of it should be."[1]

Dr. Stott's opinion notwithstanding, the person, who purposes to make preaching or Bible teaching primary and views preparation in the original languages as essential, will stand against the tide of current opinion both within and without the church.[2] The culture at large no longer respects the intellectual leadership of the preacher.³ The prevailing anti-authoritarian relativistic mindset views as absurd a message which claims to contain God's absolute truth.⁴ The revolution in electronic communications media has challenged the effectiveness of preaching as a means of communication.⁵

Indeed, our late twentieth and early twenty-first century electronic environment has generated a postmodern disposition which favors "image" over "word." For Leonard Sweet this is one of the four main characteristics of the postmodern which he has captured in the acronym, EPIC.⁶ The postmodern has moved from a modern disposition in four ways: from rational to *E*xperiential; from representative to *P*articipatory; from word to *I*mage; and from individual to *C*ommunal. And preachers in their pursuit of effective communication are increasingly approaching preaching from within the "image" paradigm of Powerpoints and video clips. In the "zero-sum gain" of ministry preparation time, an unintended consequence of this approach could well be the temptation to foreshorten thorough preparation in the Word including setting aside the study of the text in the original languages.

With preachers, their message, and their medium, all under fire, students of the Word need to make a decision about the value of disciplined study in the New Testament in Greek.⁷ Each person needs to know that it is worth it. The following rationale will help the reader decide.

A Response

The Nature of Scripture

The fact that the very words of Scripture are inspired (2 Tim 3:16-17) means that being able to read and study Scripture in the original languages will help us know its precise and full meaning word for word. Keep in mind that revelation and inspiration encompass both form and content (1 Cor 2:6-16).⁸ New Testament Greek is the form whereby divine revelation in the New Testament communicates its content or meaning. Understanding the form is the path toward the clearest understanding of the content.

The Nature of Communicating God's Word

The essence of preaching and Bible teaching is the proclamation of the life-changing truth of God⁹ with authority and power. How do we prepare in such a way that we speak with authority and power?

Communicating with authority. How does a knowledge of the original languages promote communicating with authority? By enabling us to know the source—the Holy Scriptures, God's inerrant Word—as intimately as possible. Indeed, the source is our authority for what we are going to say (1 Cor 4:1-2; 1 Pet 1:23-25; 1 Thess 2:13). To preach or teach with authority requires having full confidence that we know as precisely as possible what the Bible says. We must be convinced that our sermons and Bible lessons are a faithful exposition and application of that message. Studying the New Testament text in the Greek creates the confidence for such preaching and teaching. Jay Adams asserts that preaching that flows from study of the passage in the original moves forward with "a more sure-footed stride." "A certain confidence derives from having examined the text for one's self."[10] For the one who does not know the original languages, James Barr wisely counsels that he recognize "that not knowing them places a limit on what you can claim you know about a text."[11]

Knowledge of the Greek also introduces communicators of the Word to the interpretational limits of the text. As Adams observes, ". . . knowing the exegetical difficulties in a preaching portion may deter one from rushing ahead when he ought to tread more cautiously."[12]

This does not mean that devout preachers cannot effectively preach knowing the Bible's content only in translation. But when the opportunity arises to know the truth of God for ourselves in the language in which it was given, is this not the "more excellent way"? At the very least such an approach will liberate us from complete dependence on secondary sources. We will no longer be confined to the conclusions of translators (remember that all translations involve interpretation) and commentators. Growing knowledge of the original languages gives us an independent vantage point from which to analyze and evaluate our handling of the text.

Communicating with power. How does knowledge of the original languages promote power, i.e., effectiveness, in preaching? Being able to read the original wording gives one immediate access to "the liveliness and vigor, the delicate turns of thought, and the subtle variations"[13] which are "troweled off" in any translation. Writers use various contrasts to describe the qualitative difference between reading Scripture in translation and in the original language. It's the difference between eating frozen or canned peaches and eating ones just picked from the tree.[14] It's the difference between watching a film on DVD compared to ordinary television.[15] But all analogies seem inadequate. How does one describe the joy of discovering that the perfect tense of the verb "to manifest" (πεφανέρωται) in Romans 3:21 indicates that in Christ's death, God graciously revealed his righteousness in such a way that it continues to be revealed down to today? How can one portray the impact experienced in the discovery that the phrase "spirit of fear" in 2 Tim 1:7 (δειλίας) really points to cowardice which, if it is a lifestyle, characterizes those who are excluded from eternal life (Rev 21:8, δειλοῖς)? How can one adequately convey the excitement that occurs when you discover that there are three different words for amazement in Acts 2:1-13, in tenses conveying both continuous and summary action (ἐθαύμαζον . . . ἐξίσταντο . . . διηπόρουν, Acts 2:7, 12)? With great vividness, these words describe the reaction of the crowd to the Pentecost signs and wonders. The crowd is not only "amazed," it "is beside itself" and "at a loss to explain" what is happening.

Power and effectiveness in preaching is promoted by a freshness born of the direct access to the text in the original language. R. E. O. White contends, "No mere translation can quicken the mind to all the overtones and undertones, the beauty and the sharpness, the nuances and the echoes, that kindle sympathy between the mind of the writer and the mind of the reader."[16] John Broadus concurs, ". . . even the slightest knowledge of the originals is of service in helping us to enter into intellectual sympathy with the sacred writers and to catch the vividness and flavor so often lost in translation."[17]

What can match the freshness of insight when we uncover the vibrancy of Paul's argument in triumphant defense of the elect in Rom 8:31-39? After laying down the challenge through a rhetorical question, "What, then, shall we say to these things?" Paul lays out his conclusion and provides a proof from past history. Through the repetition of the preposition "on behalf of" (ὑπέρ) he assures us that because God delivered his son "*on behalf of* us all" he is indeed "*for* us, i.e., will always act on behalf of us" (vv. 31-32). Then follows a series of rhetorical questions (vv. 33-37) placed in the future tense (τίς ἐγκαλέσει . . . τίς ὁ κατακρινῶν . . . τίς . . . χωρίσει). These potential obstacles to God's continued gracious care are answered by the present progressive action of a God who justifies (v. 33, θεὸς ὁ *δικαιῶν*) and a Christ who is presently interceding for us (v. 34, *ἐστιν* ἐν δεξιᾷ τοῦ θεοῦ, ὃς καὶ *ἐντυγχάνει*). We are right now "super conquerors" (v. 37, ὑπερνικῶμεν) through the one who loved us. Paul's strength of conviction comes through in every preposition and tense use, every cut and thrust of his question and response pattern. All builds to the perfect tense of a verb "to be convinced" (v. 38, πέπεισμαι) by which he confesses his settled conviction, something he has decided and continues to be convinced of, that no created thing has the potential to separate us from the love of God centered in Christ Jesus our Lord (vv. 38-39).

What can match reading the account in the original for understanding the tenderness and toughness, the full range of emotion present in Mark's recounting of Jesus's encounter with the father of the boy with an unclean spirit (Mark 9:21-24)? The father, discouraged by Jesus' disciples' lack of success but still desperate, begs Jesus for help. A conditional clause shows his doubt, "But if you should be able to do anything" (v. 22, εἴ τι δύνῃ). Then follows a command in the aorist tense, meaning "give us aid; do it at once" (v. 22, βοήθησον). Jesus' response seems sharp, but it is truly merciful. He picks up the man's doubt by repeating his words, "If you are able." Then he picks up the theme of the relation of power and faith. Jesus says, "All things are possible, can be done, to the one who keeps on believing or is characterized by faith"–present participle (v. 23, τῷ πιστεύοντι). Mark then graphically portrays the father's response. He lets out a cry (κράξας, a strong word, the same word used to describe the evil spirit's response to Jesus' rebuke, v. 26). Then Mark puts the main verb of speaking in the imperfect tense (v. 24, ἔλεγεν) which could indicate that he said the following repeatedly: "I am believing; be helping my unbelief." This fast paced encounter is told in Mark's simple but graphic style. It grabs one's attention, especially when read in the Greek.

Phillips Brooks says that preaching is basically "truth through personality." Powerful communication results when God's truth is spoken through a life which has encountered it directly. It is also true that exegetical study is the key to wedding the two (truth and personality) so that the result has a freshness and a vitality.[18] Study must involve an immersion in the Scriptures in which the text and the text alone acts on the preacher's mind and heart.[19] What better way for a deep, direct impression to be registered than when the we enter directly into the truth of the text by studying it in the original? When we apply ourselves to the text in extended, concentrated and intense study,[20] the text opens up to reveal all the riches conveyed by its original expression. Such freshness and vitality makes for interesting preaching and teaching that, by God's Spirit, will hold people's attention and change their lives.

The Nature of the Ministry

Ministering the Word. Pastors and others, whose primary calling is to minister the Word (1 Tim 4:13; 2 Tim 4:2; Eph 4:11, pastor-teacher), need to see the study of Scripture as "one of [their] foremost responsibilities."[21] They should willingly tackle the hard work of preparation for preaching and teaching, agreeing with Eugene Peterson:

> I need a drenching in Scripture; I require an immersion in biblical studies. I need reflective hours over the pages of Scripture as well as personal struggles with the meaning of Scripture.[22]

Pastors sometimes may need to reject even their church's role expectations, the desire that they be primarily counselors or administrators. They must instead choose to be the one thing no one else in society's helping professions or management ranks can be, "an expert on biblical revelation." As Leith Anderson contends,

> Modern churches include many educated persons who have not come to hear the pastor's lay views on current events; they have come to hear an expert on biblical revelation. The interesting sermon will maximize biblical exposition and minimize extraneous material.[23]

With the complexities of ministry in the twenty-first century, we may need to reevaluate our own priorities, as the apostles did in Acts 6:2-4. They concluded, "But we will devote ourselves to prayer, and to the ministry of the word" (6:4). Disciplining ourselves to study the New Testament in the Greek can help us be sure our time and energy is spent well. It forces us to slow down, to pause long enough over a passage to get the full benefit of its truth. In that way it insures in-depth study which penetrates beyond the obvious questions and insights about the text. By digging deeper, we can prove ourselves, by the Spirit's gracious illumination and our perspiration, experts on biblical revelation, true ministers of the Word.

Guarding against error. The multiplicity of translations and study aids today is sometimes cited as a reason for dispensing with Greek. On the other hand, the presence of differing translations (which involved differing interpretations) and interpretational study aids actually makes it imperative that Bible communicators have a platform from which to make an informed and independent judgment. Pastors in particular, as shepherds of local flocks, must be able to guard their congregation from error and misunderstanding and guide them into truth. With an understanding of the Greek they can explain how the differences in translation and interpretation have arisen. Take the example of δικαιοῦσθε in Gal 5:4:

KJV   Christ is become of no effect unto you, whosoever of you *are justified* by the law; ye are fallen from grace. (NKJV adds in italics, "attempt to be" before "justified")

NASB   You have been severed from Christ, you who are seeking (marg. Or *would be*) to be justified by law; you are fallen from grace.

NIV   You who are trying to be justified by law have been alienated from Christ; you have fallen from grace.

The simple present tense translation of the KJV could be taken to mean that Paul believed that it was possible to be justified by works. This, we know from the rest of Paul's writings, especially Galatians (cf. Gal 2:15-16), is not his understanding. The NASB and NIV try to avoid this misunderstanding by indicating that these people were "seeking," "wanting," or "trying" to be justified. But in doing so they have seemingly introduced the idea of a desire or attempt. Who is correct? Have the NASB, NIV, and NKJV simply added some wording to avoid a doctrinal difficulty? If their rendering is allowable why didn't the KJV translators word it this way?

With knowledge of the Greek, we can recognize that English translations have represented one word in Greek (δικαιοῦσθε) by a series of words in English: "are justified," "are seeking to be justified," "are trying to be justified." We can know this is necessary since English does not have the capability to represent nuances of meaning in verbs through prefixes and suffixes to the same extent as Greek does. The Greek verb is in the present tense indicating progressive action. One of the possible nuances of progressive action is that the action is progressive because the subject is desiring or attempting to do it. This is what the NASB and NIV translators and the NKJV revisers concluded about Paul's use of the present tense at Galatians 5:4.[24] The KJV did not reflect that nuance of the present tense and concentrated on placing the action in present time.

This example shows that translators have made choices. They have sought to convey the basic sense in as natural a way as possible. In doing so, they will ignore some aspects of meaning in the passage. Not all translators have ignored the same things. Not all have opted for the same interpretation of given words. Some have decided to make clear what the original writer intended to leave ambiguous or vice versa. To help their congregations cope with the resulting confusion, misunderstanding and potential error, pastor-teachers have an indispensable resource—the study of the New Testament text in the original Greek. By it and it alone, we should decide all matters of doctrine and life. As Archibald Hunter correctly assesses,

> Yet despite our wealth of good modern translations of the New Testament, a knowledge of Greek will undoubtedly make a man a better interpreter of gospel and epistle, as it will help him to decide which modern rendering best reproduces the original meaning of evangelist and apostle . . . but the man who can read 'the words which the Holy Spirit teaches' (1 Cor 2:13) in the original tongue will, other things being equal, be a better herald of the gospel than his Greekless brother.[25]

A Realistic Study Pattern Which Incorporates Greek

Understanding the Study Pattern

Comprehensive pattern. Convinced by now that it is well worth the time to learn New Testament Greek and incorporate the language into preparation for preaching and teaching, one may still have a few questions: Can I actually carve out time to maintain Greek proficiency, while preparing weekly sermons and lessons? There are only so many hours in the day! Also, isn't it common for people to forget their Greek after they leave seminary? True, yet while many people lose much of their Greek proficiency after leaving school, they never completely lose the concepts, principles, and methods useful for studying the text in the original language. Proficiency in a language is a skill and is never completely lost. There are ways to regain and grow in your proficiency in using the Greek.

You can devote enough time to sermon/lesson development and still have time in the week to keep your Greek fresh and alive. How? By following the three stage exegetical method presented in this book:

- *Life-long preparation:* maintaining Greek proficiency as a way of life (see chapter three)
- *Immediate preparation:* preparing during the week prior to delivering a sermon or lesson (see chapters four through fifteen)
- *Periodic preparation:* planning a year in advance for preaching/teaching and doing periodic in-depth study (see chapter sixteen).

Doable pattern. That Greek proficiency can be maintained with as little as fifteen minutes a day might come as a surprise, but fifteen minutes a day of practice for any language that is properly learned can make a huge difference in on-going fluency. As for "Immediate Preparation," the time estimates in this book are an average for a Sunday morning sermon based on the teaching and ministry experience of CIU Seminary and School of Missions New Testament, Homiletics, and Educational Ministries faculty, as well as, on a Spring 2001 survey of practicing preachers (see fig. 1.1).[26] You can budget less time for preparing Sunday or Wednesday evening sermons and Bible lessons.

The method described in this book is detailed and thorough, but repeated usage will make it second nature. The first time you use it on a passage, it will probably take you twice as long as the suggested time values

Figure 1.1. **Survey of Time Distribution in Sermon Preparation**

Survey of Preachers (Spring 2001)			
	Total Time (24 reporting)	Study of Biblical Text (23 reporting)	Sermon Development (23 reporting)
Range	2-6 hrs. = 4 (16.7%)	20 min.-4 hrs. = 11 (48%)	0-3 hrs. = 9 (39%)
	7-9 hrs. = 5 (21%)	5-9 hrs. = 7 (30%)	4-8 hrs. = 10 (43%)
	10-16 hrs. = 11 (46%)	10-15+ hrs. = 5 (22%)	9-12 hrs. = 4 (17%)
	17-25 hrs. = 4 (16.7%)		
Average	9.73 hrs.	6.21 hrs.	5.22 hrs.

Source: New Testament Study Group, CIU Seminary and School of Missions, Columbia, SC, Spring 2001.

in figure 1.2. A second time through, preparation normally takes one and one half times as long. By the third time through, you should be closer to the time estimates provided.

Making the Study Pattern Your Own

Customized use. Some areas in the method should be used selectively, i.e., expanded or contracted depending on the demands of the passage. For example, more sustained attention to grammatical features is called for in epistolary doctrinal passages like Romans 6. Ethical sections, especially lists of vices or virtues, need more time devoted to word study (e.g., Gal 5:22-23). In gospel narrative, cultural details and plot dynamics must be pursued. Part of mastering the method is to learn to be judicious in determining which part will expand and which will contract when dealing with a particular passage within the estimated time constraints (the minimum and maximum time suggested for a responsible handling of the passage).

Personalized use. As you gain experience with the method, one of your goals should be to understand and master each step. But don't stop there.

Figure 1.2. **Overview of Exegetical Method**

Overview: Exegetical Method			
	Lifelong Preparation: Maintaining Greek Proficiency 15 min per day, 5 days per week, 5 lines of the GNT per day		chap. 3
	Immediate Preparation of Sermon or Lesson Total: 14–16 hours		
2 hrs.	*Phase One: Preparing the Preacher/Teacher & the Text* 1. **Spiritual Preparation:** Prayer & Consecration 2. **Text Preparation:** Translation & Mechanical Layout		chap. 4

30 min.	*Phase Two: Studying the Text Exegetically*
	I. Survey
	  A. **Deal with Textual Critical Matters:** Validate the wording for the preaching/teaching passage.
	  B. **Raise Questions & Make Observations:** Brainstorm for questions, illustrations, ideas, & issues related to the passage that warrant further exploration.
			chap. 5

4 hrs.	II. Analysis
	  A. **Historical Analysis**
	    1. *Introductory Matters*: Determine how the passage relates to the particular historical situation in which and to which the book was written.
	    2.. *Historical-Cultural-Religious Details*: Gather details from the general historical situation.
	  B. **Literary Analysis**
	    1. *Context*
	      a. *General Context*: Determine how the passage fits within the total book outline.
	      b. *Immediate Context*: Determine how the passage relates to the immediately preceding and following paragraphs.
	    2. *Genre*: Analyze according to literary type.
	    3. *Syntax*
	      a. *Grammar:* Structure, Verbs, Cases, the Rest
	      b. *Rhetorical Features*: Word Absence, Word Order, Word Arrangement, Word Figures
			chap. 6
			
			chap. 6-11

Figure 1.2. (*continued*)

	4. *Word Study*
	       a. *Focus the Meaning*: Define key terms in context.
	       b. *Illumine the Meaning*: Illustrate key terms through background source or contemporary background study.
	  C. **Theological Analysis**
	      1. *Biblical Theology*: Identify background, parallel, or contrasting biblical passages.
	      2. *Systematic Theology*: Identify the passage's contribution to Christian doctrine.
	      3. *Remaining Theological and Interpretational Difficulties*: Identify and resolve potential conflicts with other biblical teaching; state and solve any remaining difficulties.
		chap. 12

45 min.	III. **Synthesis**
	  A. **Exegetical Outline**
	  B. **Biblical Coherence**
	      1. *Basic Message*: State the passage's message in one sentence.
	      2. *Promotion of Book's Purpose*: State how the passage promotes the book's purpose.
	      3. *Place in Salvation History and Biblical Thought*: Describe where the passage fits in the Progress of Redemption and Progress of Revelation.
		chap. 13

45 min.	IV. **Interpretation for and Application to Persons in Contemporary Culture**
	  A. **Communication**: Interpret the passage's message in equivalent contemporary terms.
	  B. **Correction**: Apply the passage's "bad news" for persons in the culture.
	  C. **Capturing the Significance**: Apply the passage's "good news" to the deep needs of the culture.
		chap. 14

	Phase Three: Homiletical/Didactic Appropriation	chap. 15
2 hrs. 2-3 hrs. 2-3 hrs.	1. **Framing the Sermon/Lesson** 2. **Developing Sermon/Lesson Outline** 3. **Sermon/Lesson Practice**	
	Periodic Preparation: Advanced Planning & In-depth Study 13 months prior, set up one year preaching/teaching program	chap. 16

You also need to personalize it. This means to come to the place where you tailor the method to your own study habits and thought processes. The more you do it, the less it will be a mechanical process. You may even find yourself doing a number of the steps simultaneously. Begin as one learns to do any complex operation, i.e., by consciously thinking through and practicing each aspect of the process. Your ultimate goal is to have all the elements of sound exegesis, interpretation and homiletical or didactic appropriation present, almost unconsciously, whenever you sit down to prepare a sermon or Bible lesson. This book is designed to help you move from the apprentice stage, when much is consciously mechanical, to the craftsman stage, when the elements of exegesis serve the art of effective preaching and teaching.

Conclusion

Men and women who will give themselves to the discipline of studying the Scriptures in the original language will be fulfilling their responsibility to "bring the Bread of Life to hungry souls with all its freshness and life-giving qualities."[27] Indeed, as David Alan Black rightly concludes,

> If our purpose as preachers is to understand and proclaim what God has said to his people for their spiritual growth, and if it pleased God to reveal himself in the Greek language, then a knowledge of New Testament Greek should not be regarded as a luxury, but as an imperative.[28]

The succeeding chapters explain the steps necessary for putting such knowledge to work through a method for exegesis and exposition.

Endnotes

1. Stott, *Between Two Worlds*, 182.

2. Hereafter we will focus on New Testament Greek. But the rationales given in this chapter are just as applicable to Hebrew.

3. Robinson, *Biblical Preaching*, 17-18; Anderson ("Excellence in Preaching," 54) observes, "Long gone are the days when the local parson was the best-educated person in the community and could speak with authority on every subject."

4. Stott, *Between Two Worlds*, 51-60.

5. Ibid., 64-76; cf. Robinson, *Biblical Preaching*, 18.

6. Sweet, *Post-Modern Pilgrims*.

7. This issue is not new. Compare, for example, Robertson, *Minister and Greek Testament*; Wuest, *Practical Use of Greek Testament*; Hunter, "Grammar and Godliness," 26; Adams, "Original Languages in Preaching," 29-31.

8. Kaiser, "Neglected Text in Bibliology Discussions," 301-19.

9. Cf. Stott, *Between Two Worlds*, 92-134; Robinson, *Biblical Preaching*, 19-21.

10. Adams, "Original Languages in Preaching," 30.

11. Quoted in Nichols, *Building the Word*, 29.

12. Adams, "Original Languages in Preaching," 30.

13. Malte, "Preaching from Greek Testament," 656; Peterson ("Foreword," 5) observes that those who know the original languages "acquire a taste for first-handedness, the resonating sounds and radiating meanings released into our lives by these ancient, but now new, texts."

14. Malte, "Preaching from Greek Testament," 656.

15. Robinson, *Biblical Preaching*, 61-62.

16. White, *Guide to Preaching*, 68.

17. Broadus, *Preparation of Sermons*, 29.

18. Stott, *Between Two Worlds*, 180.

19. Lenski, *The Sermon*, 46.

20. Peterson, "Unbusy Pastor," 72.

21. Stott, *Between Two Worlds*, 181.

22. Peterson, "Unbusy Pastor," 72.

23. Anderson, "Excellence in Preaching," 54.

24. Bruce (*Galatians*, 231) labels it a conative present.

25. Hunter, "Grammar and Godliness," 26. cf. Malte, "Preaching from Greek Testament," 656-57; Lenski, *The Sermon*, 47-48; Poovey, *Word Come Alive*, 19-25.

26. Harvey et al, "Faculty Discussion."

27. Malte,"Preaching from Greek Testament," 658.

28. Black, *Greek in Ministry*, 23.

Chapter 2
DEFINITIONS AND PRESUPPOSITIONS

To use an exegetical method properly you must first grasp some basic definitions and presuppositions concerning the text and yourself as the interpreter of God's Word. The definitions will help you identify your objectives. The presuppositions will shape your methods, determine the questions you ask of the text, and the criteria by which you judge your interpretational findings. Although much of this chapter emphasizes the preaching process, the content is important for all who would accurately interpret and explain the Word of God.

Basic Definitions: Preaching & Exegesis

Preaching

The basic method of sermon development this text follows is the "Keyword Approach," first conceived by Charles W. Koller, and popularized by Faris D. Whitesell of Northern Baptist Seminary and Lloyd M. Perry of Trinity Evangelical Divinity School.[1] Perry defines Christian preaching as

> . . . the declaration, interpretation and persuasive application of Christian truths. Preaching involves divine truth being channeled by the Holy Spirit through a God-chosen personality to meet human need.[2]

Three aspects of this definition of preaching deserve comment: its dynamic, its aim, and its content.

The Dynamic. When someone preaches or teaches the Bible, what actually happens is very different from when someone gives a lecture or speaks informally. The dynamic in preaching and Bible teaching is spiritual, indeed, supernatural. God the Holy Spirit is at work. Koller places this aspect at the center of his definition. "Preaching is that unique procedure by which God, through His chosen messenger, reaches down into the human family and brings persons face to face with Himself."[3] There are three elements in this dynamic.

- *God calls the preacher or Bible teacher.* Just as he did with his spokesmen in Bible times (Isaiah 6; Jer 1:4-19; Gal 1:15-16; Eph 4:11-13; 2 Tim 1:8-14), God calls his preachers and teachers today. God prepares preachers and teachers in godly character and in the grace and knowledge of the Lord Jesus Christ (1 Thess 2:1-6; 2 Cor 4:1-2). In the preparation of every sermon preached or lesson taught in the power of the Spirit, the Holy Spirit will first apply the message "to the personality and experience of the preacher, then through the preacher . . . to his hearers."[4]
- *God provides the message.* The primary and essential source for the content of a sermon or Bible lesson is the Bible, God's eternal and living Word (cf. Acts 13:16-41; 1 Thess 2:13).
- *God produces the results.* By God's power and his alone, listeners hear God's message, make a decision, and are supernaturally changed. They may experience the new birth, being transferred from the kingdom of Satan to the kingdom of God (1 Pet 1:23-25; 1 Cor 2:4-5; Acts 26:18; Col 1:13; Jas 1:18). Or, to those already in the kingdom, God grants grace in sanctification as they decide to change thinking and behavior patterns that have come under the scrutiny of the Word (Phil 1:9-11; Rom 12:1-2).

The Aim. The aim of preaching and Bible teaching is a decision which leads to changed beliefs, attitudes, and behavior. Daniel Baumann observes, " . . . a sermon has the explicit purpose of eliciting behavior change. That is to say that preaching worthy of the name calls persons to a decision, to a confrontation, which hopefully issues in modification of behavior."[5] A sermon might inform the mind or move the emotions. If it does not appeal to the will, however, it is not the type of preaching in which Jesus and the apostles engaged. And it is their pattern that we are called to follow (Mark 1:14-15; Acts 13:38-41; 17:30-31; 1 Tim 4:6-16; 2 Tim 4:2).

The Content. The basic content of a sermon or lesson is divine truth derived from the Bible. The Bible is the only source of divine truth that makes men and women "wise to salvation" and reveals to them what they are to believe, and how they are to act if they would please God (2 Tim 3:14-17). Expository preaching takes biblical content and communicates it in a form that does the most good for the most people over the longest period of time. Whitesell defines the product of such preaching this way:

DEFINITIONS AND PRESUPPOSITIONS

An expository sermon is based on a Bible passage, usually longer than a verse or two, the theme, the thesis and the major and minor divisions coming from the passage; the whole sermon being an honest attempt to unfold the true grammatical-historical-contextual meaning of the passage, making it relevant to life today by proper organization, argument, illustrations, application and appeal.[6]

Walter Liefeld describes well what preachers should be able to do:

The essential *nature* of expository preaching, then, is preaching that explains a passage in such a way as to lead the congregation to a true and practical application of that passage.[7]

Exegesis

Richard Soulen's general definition of exegesis states that it "is the process by which a text, as a concrete expression of a 'sender' to a 'receiver', is systematically explained."[8]

Historical and literary analysis. The Greek New Testament is a text in which human "senders" and "receivers" (writer and audience) are no longer directly accessible. Methods for explaining the "concrete expression" (the message the New Testament writers intended to communicate) will necessarily be confined to a historical and literary analysis of the text's features. These methods, however, are adequate for interpreting the text and identifying its meaning. In terms of historical elements, the biblical writer and audience shared a historical and cultural context, situation, and vocabulary stock, which was the environment in which and the medium by which they communicated. In terms of literary elements, the writers used grammatical syntax, rhetorical features, and literary genre to express their intended meaning. If we can analyze these features to identify the intended meaning, we have properly explained the text. In studying the text in this way we seek to bring "out of the text all that is contained of the thoughts, attitudes, assumptions, and so forth--in short, the whole expressed mind of the human writer."[9] We should also look for what the readers were expected to gather from the message.

Theological exegesis. Since the Bible is a closed canon of sacred Scripture, God's revelation of his will for mankind, our exegesis must involve more than a historical and literary identification of what the original human writers said to their original audiences. Any systematic explanation of the Bible must include theological analysis and expository exegesis. Theological analysis interprets any given passage with the conviction that this is God speaking.[10] It sees the truth of the passage within the context of the whole canon as "a theological context within which each document may be viewed and its contribution to the record of divine revelation and of human response to that revelation may be assessed."[11]

Expository exegesis. Expository means relating and applying a passage to the contemporary cultural context. If the Bible is God's revealed will for all mankind in every historical time and every cultural setting, then a systematic explanation of its content will include determining how Scripture's message relates to today's culture. It will identify Scripture's normative content, and propose ways in which those truths about doctrine and life should be implemented in the present historical cultural context. Indeed, you have neither understood nor explained the text's message according to the writer's intent unless you have applied it to yourself and your contemporaries whether in the church or the world (1 Cor 10:11; Rom 15:4; 2 Tim 3:14-17).

Preparation for expository preaching or teaching, then, requires a method of exegesis with two basic functions: "Analysis" (historical, literary, theological) and "Synthesis/Application." Karl C. Ellis has summarized well its aim and value.

> Careful exegesis enables the interpreter to get a clearer understanding of what the Scriptures meant to the original addressees, in their situation, at that particular historical time, so that the message can be expounded to the contemporary hearers to guide them, to enrich their spiritual lives, to enable them to carry out God's will more effectively.[12]

Presuppositions

What follows is a compact "short course" in hermeneutics, which you should take the time to digest and ponder. These assumptions[13] about the nature of the text, about you as the interpreter, and about appropriate methodology for studying the biblical text, are taken from the teaching of Scripture, the fully and finally authoritative Word of God.

Assumptions About the Basic Nature of Text and the Interpreter

The text. The text on which you will do exegesis and from which you will teach or preach is the Word of God. There are three important aspects of its unique nature. First, it is propositional revelation. God's revelation is his communication of a message to man in human language statements (e.g., "the Word of the Lord came to . . ." Isa 38:4; Jer 2:1; Ezek 1:3; Rom 16:25-27; 1 Pet 1:12; Luke 10:21-22).[14] God's revelation as acts in salvation history is always functionally subordinate to his revelation as verbal propositions, for the acts either fulfill or must be interpreted by the Word.

Second, the Bible as God's Word is fully inspired to the very words (2 Tim 3:16-17; 2 Pet 1:21). B. B. Warfield gives a classic description of inspiration as a mode of revelation that he labels "concursive operation."

> By 'concursive operation' may be meant that form of revelation illustrated in an inspired psalm or epistle or history, in which no human activity–not even the control of the will–is superseded, but the Holy Spirit works in, with, and through them all in such a manner as to communicate to the product qualities distinctly superhuman.[15]

Third, the Bible is divine truth. All its affirmations are absolute, objective, knowable truth (Ps 119:160; John 17:17; 1 John 2:27; Ps 119:43, 89-91, 150-52). The biblical view of truth embraces a correspondence theory of truth (Exod 20:16; Acts 12:9-11; Matt 22:16; 1 John 3:18; Gen 42:16; Deut 17:2-7; 18:22; 1 Kgs 8:26; Ps 119:163; Prov 14:25; Acts 24:8, 11; Eph 4:25). As Roger Nicole defines it, with reference to Old Testament evidence,

> Truth is that firm conformity to reality that proves to be wholly reliable, so that those who accept a statement may depend on it that it will not turn out to be false or deceitful.[16]

The interpreter. The nature of you as the interpreter must be understood in terms of negative and positive factors.[17] Negatively, all people since Adam operate with a mind corrupted by sin (Eph 2:3; 4:17). People as sinners are rebels against God (Rom 8:7; 10:2). The rebellion of the mind manifests itself as proud reason that asserts itself as the final arbiter of what can be known, believed, or obeyed. Such reason unenlightened by the Spirit is blind and futile with regard to knowledge of God, salvation, or his will for human conduct (2 Cor 3:14; 4:4; Eph 4:18; Rom 1:21, 28). When autonomous reason is used in the interpretation of Scripture, its conclusions are characterized by doubt (Heb 3:12; 4:2; cf. Luke 16:19-31), fragmentation (cf. Luke 24:25; 1 Tim 4:1-4, 6:4), and distortion (Gal 1:6-9; 2 Pet 3:16; 2 Tim 4:3-4).

All interpreters have a pre-understanding (a culture in their heads), a set of ideas, beliefs, and values, with which they approach the text. This, too, is corrupted by sin since it is the product of culture, the creation of generations of sinful human beings (Col 2:8; Rom 12:2). This negative factor must be guarded against if the exegetical process is to prove fruitful.

All interpreters have existential concerns (a culture in their hearts), which when corrupted by sin, can distort a passage's message by asking the wrong questions, and by finding the wrong answers.

Positively, all interpreters have the capacity of self-transcendence, to stand over and against their pre-understanding, evaluate it, and change it (Rom 12:2; Col 3:2). For unregenerate people, this capacity means they are not complete prisoners of their cultural pre-understanding. They can achieve valid insights about Scripture's meaning from which all can learn. Still, the unregenerate, when they are willing slaves to their sinful human natures, will be blind to or rebel against the truth of God in Scripture (cf. Acts 14:8-18, an account of blindness to the truth of God in nature).

For regenerate people, this capacity for self-transcendence is now at the service of a new spiritual nature, involving a spiritually transformed pre-understanding in those born again by the power of God the Holy Spirit. The Holy Spirit opens our eyes and makes us productive and obedient in matters of spiritual truth (1 Cor 2:12-16). We can interpret Scripture without doubt, fragmentation, or distortion. We implicitly trust Scripture's message. So, our pre-understanding increasingly is made up of a biblical set of ideas, beliefs, and values.

Regenerate people know that existential concerns are rightly addressed by Scripture when they see Scripture meeting their deepest needs, but only on Scripture's terms. A humble, repentant stance toward Scripture accomplishes this (e.g., Rom 11:11-36).

Having reviewed the presuppositions related to the text and the interpreter, we turn now to the presuppositions that undergird our practice of the exegetical method. Because the Bible is written by human writers, we must use methods of interpretation that apply to any other literature. However, any method or part of a method that leads to a conclusion that the Bible is not telling the truth is not appropriate for the study of inspired Scripture. Indeed, because the Bible is the inspired Word of God, we must also approach it differently from any other book.

Methodological Assumptions in Common with Other Literature

Textual basis for interpretation. The only proper basis for authoritative interpretation of the New Testament is the Greek text. Scripture's inspiration encompasses only the original autographs in Hebrew, Aramaic and Greek (2 Tim 3:14-17; 2 Pet 1:21). Any subsequent translation or interpretation does not share that inspiration. They are authoritative only to the degree that they faithfully reproduce the Hebrew or Greek text's message. Exegesis and interpretation in the final analysis must appeal to and work from the text in the original language.

We determine this textual basis by the exercise of "textual criticism" on the manuscripts so that at any given place, the probable wording of the original text has been determined. This book will follow a "modified eclectic approach" to establishing the wording of the Greek text.

Meaning sought. Any word, phrase, clause, or sentence of the Greek New Testament has a single, fixed, definite, referential meaning that is what the writer intended to say. Such a meaning is identifiable by studying the grammatical, literary, and historical features of the text.

Meaning is referential, i.e., any given word has a meaning or concept that refers to some aspect of reality, real or imagined. You have correctly understood the writer's message when you correctly identify the referent and the sense: what the writer is referring to and what he is saying about it.[18] This approach is necessitated by the biblical understanding of truth and language (cf. Gen 2:19-20).[19]

The Bible's meaning as definite or literal is contested by many who say that transcendent spiritual realities can only be spoken of in metaphorical or symbolic religious language.[20] But the fact that the Bible interprets much of its metaphorical material, putting the intended message into definite terms (cf. Jesus' approach to the parables, Luke 8:9-15), indicates that the basic meaning of the text, whether expressed in literal or figurative terms, is definite.[21]

The meaning of the Bible is single and fixed, according to the writer's intent (cf. 1 Pet 1:10-12). Yet, as Wayne Meeks notes,

> In our lifetimes a cacophonous chorus of philosophers, critical theorists, and practical critics have challenged the goal of finding some unchanging sense, whether residing in the intention of the author or somehow within the text itself.[22]

But, in line with biblical assumptions and affirmations, we contend that Scripture has one meaning that is fixed and can be identified with the writer's intent. This assumption runs throughout the New Testament interpretation of the Old.[23] Those, who believe such an original meaning is not recoverable, because only a multiplicity of potential meanings is characteristic of texts, at the least, set themselves up to be the final authority on what the text means. At the most, they would prevent anyone from exploring the text with the aim of uncovering what the author intended to say.

Truth status of biblical content. God's truth is absolute. It applies to persons in all times and places. The meaning of the statements that convey that truth are trans-cultural and trans-historical. Scripture assumes, even contends, this about its content (Matt 28:18-20; Ps 119:89-91). Scripture itself provides the key for distinguishing between Bible content which is universally normative and that which is culturally limited. God's truth is objective. Its meaning is to be found in the writer's intent.[24]

Role and rule of context. The role of historical and literary elements in the immediate context[25] should serve as a filter so that the precise referential meaning of any given word or phrase may be identified. Writers have chosen to set in juxtaposition various words and phrases as a means of communicating the exact part of the range of lexical meaning they intend for a given word or phrase. This same juxtaposition in context can also supply contextual meaning to a word by further nuancing it through its association with the other terms around it. A correct analysis of historical and literary features of the immediate context is essential for the identification of exact meaning.

The larger contexts of a writer's particular work, the corpus of his writings in Scripture, and the Scripture as a whole, provide ever-widening contexts through which the meaning of particular grammatical and rhetorical features and particular word usage may be traced. Such exploration will produce a pattern of usage at times diverse, but never contradictory. The proposed meaning in any given immediate context will be in agreement with the overall biblical pattern.

The extra-biblical historical and cultural context of ancient times provides the building blocks for meaning, whether it be the different types of significance for a grammatical feature, the meaning of a rhetorical feature, or the stock of potential meanings for given vocabulary words. Yet the appropriation of such materials must be circumscribed in several ways so that Scripture remains the final authority for its meaning, and so that, in the final analysis, God's message is not viewed as culture-bound.

The meaning of any given grammatical feature is determined by its use in its immediate context and its use elsewhere in Scripture. Extra-biblical cultural explanations of the meaning or function of a text's literary genre or rhetorical features should never set aside the authoritative declaration of Scripture which the grammar of the passage demands. Literary genres which by their very nature violate the biblical understanding of truth corresponding to reality are not employed in inerrant Scripture (e.g., pseudonymous writing, midrashic gospel narrative).

With respect to historical and cultural and word study matters, the uncovering of extra-biblical parallels to biblical thought should never be used to supplant the Scripture's claim that given meanings are of divine revelatory origin. God sovereignly chose the human words and meanings he employed to communicate his message.

Extra-biblical historical and cultural information may not be used to reduce or extend the authority of Scripture in a given passage by setting aside Scripture's single, fixed and definite meaning as determined by the syntactical and historical-lexical features of the immediate context.

Methodological Presuppositions Unique to Scripture

Purpose, authority and inerrancy. There are two purposes of Scripture. One is divine self-revelation which, as with any of God's means of self-disclosure, aims to evoke praise from man the creature (Psalm 119). The other purpose is the revelation of God's message concerning the way of salvation and the way of edification, what mankind is to believe and do (2 Tim 3:14-17). The writer's intended meaning in any given passage will in some way promote these purposes.

The authority of Scripture as God's inspired Word is full and final. The content of the Bible is the source and standard for all truth in all areas on which it touches. In understanding right doctrine in authoritative Scripture, never use extra-biblical information to set aside its plain sense, the single, fixed, definite meaning determined by historical and literary analysis of the immediate context.

Scripture's mandates on right conduct are normative unless Scripture itself limits the extent of the application. No extra-biblical historical or cultural information, ancient or contemporary, should be used to set aside the universal mandates of a fully and finally authoritative Scripture.[26]

Since the implications of inerrancy have been dealt with throughout this discussion, it is helpful at this point to provide a summary definition, using the International Council on Biblical Inerrancy's affirmations and denials.

> We affirm that Scripture in its entirety is inerrant, being free from all falsehood, fraud, or deceit . . . We deny that it is proper to evaluate Scripture according to standards of truth and error that are alien to its usage and purpose. We further deny that inerrancy is negated by Biblical phenomena such as a lack of modern technical precision, irregularities of grammar or spelling, observational descriptions of nature, the reporting of falsehoods, the use of hyperbole and round numbers, the topical arrangement of material, variant selections of material in parallel accounts, or the use of free citations.[27]

In relation to the last sentence above, note that a Scripture text should never be interpreted as fitting into one of the exception categories (hyperbole, round numbers, etc.) in a way that violates the principle of "correspondence to truth."

Unity and clarity. God is the one author, accomplishing his work through many inspired writers, of the sixty-six canonical books of the Bible.[28] The contents of the Scriptures form a unity (cf. the New Testament practice of quoting from various Old Testament passages to prove one point: Luke 24:25-27; Rom 3:10-18).[29] The meaning of one passage will not contradict another. Any interpretation of any passage must be congruent with the teaching of the whole of Scripture. There is progress in revelation. Later revelation can indicate the divinely intended limits of prior revelation and so set it aside (Mark 7:14-23). Yet, any interpretation that discerns diversity or progress must always be in harmony with Scripture's deep underlying theological unity.

In view of the unity, it is appropriate to use the "analogy of faith" rule of interpretation: the best interpreter of Scripture is other Scripture. Such a method must not violate the meaning of passages in their immediate historical and literary contexts. The passages used to interpret each other must be true parallels in meaning. The larger biblical context must not set aside the content of the immediate context and so create a "canon within the canon." The "analogy of faith" rule is best employed as a final check to make sure the interpretation is congruent with all of Scripture.[30]

The clarity[31] of Scripture means that the meaning is plain. It is recoverable by anyone through the use of historical and literary analysis.

Holy Spirit illumination.[32] God the Holy Spirit is a present guide to the regenerate interpreter. He does not reveal content beyond what is already present in inspired Scripture. He does not bring understanding in the sense of intelligibility. The basic meaning of Scripture can be understood by unregenerate and regenerate alike. Rather, the Spirit provides the interpreter with three things. First, a persuasion of the certain truth of what we are interpreting (1 Cor 2:4-5, 12-16; 1 Thess 1:5). Second, he manifests the nature and excellence of the things of God. He provides a fullness, clarity, and immediacy of knowledge that is only possible when he takes the Word he inspired and unveils its message to the mind and heart he has regenerated and renewed (Eph 1:17-19; cf. 1 Cor 2:6-10). Third, the Holy Spirit guides in application. He uses the Word to expose sin in the readers' life (Heb 4:12-13). He grants discernment so that believers may properly distinguish between good and evil and so walk in spiritual maturity (Col 1:9-12; Heb 5:14). No new revelatory content comes in this process, but there are insights for application.

Endnotes

1. Koller, *Expository Preaching*; Whitesell, *Expository Preaching*; Perry, *Manual for Biblical Preaching*; Hamilton, *Homiletical Handbook*. See chapter fifteen for steps of this method.

2. Perry, *Manual for Biblical Preaching*, 3.

3. Koller, *Expository Preaching*, 13.

4. Robinson, *Biblical Preaching*, 21.

5. Baumann, *Contemporary Preaching*, 205.

6. Whitesell, *Expository Preaching*, vi-vii.

7. Liefeld, *New Testament Exposition*, 6.

8. Soulen, *Handbook of Biblical Criticism*, 66.

9. Packer, "Infallible Scripture," 345; cf. Marshall, "Introduction," 11-18; Bock, "Opening Questions," 24.

10. Packer, "Infallible Scripture," 345.

11. Bruce, "Interpretation of the Bible," 566.

12. Ellis, "Nature of Exegesis," 153.

13. The Statements of two Chicago Summits on Biblical Inerrancy with their expositions give an excellent compendium of the essential assumptions which we are affirming, "Chicago Statement," 493-502; Geisler, "Explaining Hermeneutics," 889-904. For an exposition of the biblical evidence for many of these assumptions, see Larkin, *Culture and Biblical Hermeneutics*, 191-321.

14. Tenney, "Meaning of the Word," 11-27. Contrast the postmodern hermeneutical critique of this characterization of Scripture as modernist (Raschke, *Next Reformation*, 127-31). This critique, however, fails to take into account its own similarity to nineteenth century liberal approaches which led away from scriptural authority (Bolt, "Critique of Postmodern, Evangelical Church," 216). See Vanhoozer's ("Lost in Interpretation?" 127-29) proper call to participate in neither modern or postmodern philosophical captivity, but rather to diverge from each when necessary to preserve the integrity of witness to the gospel and the upholding of Scripture as the supreme rule for faith and life.

15. Warfield, "Revelation," 4:2577.

16. Nicole, "Truth," 288; cf. Köstenberger, gen. ed. *Whatever Happened to Truth?*

17. Larkin, *Culture and Biblical Hermeneutics*, 293-304.

18. Stein ("Author-Oriented Hermeneutics, 457, 461) labels "referent" as "subject matter" and "sense" as "meaning."

19. Feinberg, "Truth: Relationships," 3-50.

20. e.g., Ricoeur, "Biblical Hermeneutics," 29-148; ——. *Interpreting Theory*; cf. Paul, "Metaphor," 507-10.

21. Clark, "Special Divine Revelation," 39; cf. Noll, "Reading the Bible," 227-53.

22. Meeks, "Why Study New Testament?" 162; cf. Hayes and Holladay, *Biblical Exegesis*, 21-22; contrast Thomas, "Single Meaning," 33-47.

23. Kaiser, "Legitimate Hermeneutics," 133-38; Archer and Chirichigno, *Old Testament Quotations*.

24. Stein, "Author-Oriented Hermeneutics," 451-66.

25. Grassmick, *Greek Exegesis*, 11-13.

26. McQuilkin, "Problems of Normativeness," 217-40.

27. "Chicago Statement," 496. This statement has stood the test of time. A quarter century later, the Evangelical Theological Society appropriated the "Chicago Statement" to define what its members mean when they affirm inerrancy (Borland, "Fifty-eighth Annual Meeting," 215).

28. Frank Thielman, "New Testament Canon," 400-410.

29. Packer, "Unity of Scripture," 409-14; Carson, "Unity and Diversity," 65-95.

30. Thomas, "Hermeneutical Ambiguity," 45-53; cf. Kaiser, "Hermeneutics and Theological Task," 3-14.

31. Sandin, "Clarity of Scripture," 237-53; cf. Callahan, *Clarity of Scripture*.

32. Henry, *God, Revelation, and Authority*, 4:272-89.

Chapter 3
GREEK READING
AND
COMPUTER RESOURCES

As we begin our study of "A Method for Exegesis and Exposition," we find our first topic does not plunge us into the mechanics of translation and exegesis as part of sermon or lesson preparation. Rather, our Greek Reading topic acknowledges the importance of "Lifelong Preparation" and learning. Will you be a person who invests a lot of time and energy in learning Greek, but loses proficiency soon after completing your courses? Or will you be one who lays the foundation for lifelong Greek exegesis in your studies, and then continues to use the New Testament in Greek throughout your ministry? To a great extent the answer rests on decisions you make right now. In effect, you have two important objectives ahead of you. You need to learn New Testament Greek as thoroughly as you can, along with the exegetical tools that unlock the richness of the original text. Simultaneously, you need to learn to become a life-long learner of Greek, developing habits that are not driven simply by course assignments and deadlines. This chapter presents a manageable pattern for incorporating on-going study of the language into your schedule. Learning this pattern, practicing it throughout your formal language study, determining now—with God's help—to establish a lifelong discipline of study, these are the steps that will result in the greatest return on your investment in learning Greek.

Greek Reading: Principles

There are three keys to maintaining proficiency in reading and analyzing the Greek New Testament throughout your ministry. The first key is frequent (not sporadic) exposure to the text. The second key, essential to gaining comfort and efficiency in exegesis, is extensive exposure to the text through rapid reading of large portions. A final key is the on-going development of a fund of knowledge and insight for future preaching and teaching. The Greek Reading approach described in this chapter combines these three keys for success.

Read the Greek Text Often

Language knowledge is a skill, not a commodity. You won't forget what you have truly learned. On the other hand, any skill can become rusty through lack of use. If you don't intentionally keep up your skills, your ability to use New Testament Greek to inform and enrich your preaching or teaching can quickly begin to fade. But there is a simple solution: frequent use. Exposure to the Greek text for only *fifteen minutes a day, five days a week,* is more productive than reviewing for an hour and a half or even two hours once a week. There is no substitute for frequency and consistency in building and maintaining language proficiency.

Read the Greek Text Extensively

On-going proficiency in New Testament Greek involves being comfortable with both the "trees" and the "forest." You deal with individual trees every time you produce a finished translation based on an analysis of the important lexical, grammatical, and literary features of the text. On the other hand, you deal with the whole of the forest (as if in a helicopter) when you sight-read the Greek text with vocabulary and grammar helps, covering it extensively, even rapidly. The good news is that these areas reinforce each other. Analytical work on a text enhances your ability to sight-read. Likewise, rapid sight-reading, which gives you a bird's-eye view of the larger context of the words and phrases, is a great help with your analysis. Modern linguistic research demonstrates that making sense of an individual sentence is dependent upon the larger context of that sentence. In fact, linguists label the paragraph as the basic unit of thought in written and spoken discourse, noting that the *perikope* or paragraph is the "largest readily perceptible whole, but also the smallest sensible unit of discourse to be taken separately while still having some autonomy of its own and exhibiting its own peculiar structural pattern."[1] Greek Reading will help you strike a balance between grasping words and sentences and seeing those sentences in their more extensive context.

Read the Greek Text for Exegetical/Homiletical Payoff

One pastor[2] who believes strongly in maintaining original language skills contends that many of his colleagues abandon their Greek because they don't see an immediate payoff in their ministries. With many skills to develop and tasks to carry out, it is hard for many Christian workers to justify spending blocks of time reviewing textbooks and notes. The Greek Reading approach, however, can remedy these concerns. For one thing, daily sight-reading keeps your grammar and vocabulary fresh. However, the biggest payoff comes as you jot down exegetical and homiletical insights during your sight-reading. Do this for a year or two (not to mention five or ten) and you find to your delight that you have an incredibly valuable cache of exegetical insights, illustrations, and applications the next time you prepare to preach or teach on a passage you have covered in your Greek Reading. This is a considerable payoff for fifteen minutes a day, five days a week (perhaps undertaken as a part of your devotional time).

Greek Reading: As a Way of Life

Adopting the Discipline

If you see the benefits of the Greek Reading approach, the next question is how to begin making it an established part of your routine. The most important principle is to commit yourself to Greek Reading as a way of life. This means committing to sight-reading five lines in the Greek New Testament, spending fifteen minutes a day, five days a week. You will read any sentence in the context of its paragraph to gain familiarity with the text and to gain comfort in handling a verse in context. You will work your way through a book or passage by paragraphs. Faithful pursuit of such a discipline will enable you to sight-read the entire Greek New Testament in a little over fourteen years. See figures 3.1-2.[3]

If you miss a day, try, if possible, to make up the fifteen minutes. When important interruptions occur (and they will), take care of the family or ministry needs rather than carry out your Greek Reading. However, guard against allowing less important matters or a lack of personal discipline to become consistent excuses for not carrying out your Greek Reading. You should also guard against routinely spending more than fifteen minutes a day. Learn to use those fifteen minutes efficiently and effectively and to stop when they are gone.

Planning the Reading Program

How should you plan your Greek Reading program? Where should you start? You might select passages based on the order of the text (Matthew through Revelation); book length (shorter books to longer); increasing level of difficulty (figs. 3.1-2 arrange the books in this way); or according to your

Figure 3.1. **Pacing Greek Reading: Developing a Plan.** To maintain proficiency, the pace recommended for Greek Reading is five lines a day, five days a week (approx. fifteen minutes a day). This chart results from arranging the books of the NT in increasingly difficult Greek, and according to the number of lines in each book.

Book	Lines	Weeks	Months & Weeks
1. 1-3 John	303	12.12 wks	3 mos.
2. Gospel of John	1817	72.68 wks	18 mos.+ 1 wk
3. Revelation	1147	45.88 wks	11 mos.+ 2 wks
4. 1 Thessalonians	190	7.6 wks	2 mos.
2 Thessalonians	101	4.04 wks	1 mo.
5. Philippians	200	8 wks	2 mos.
6. Ephesians	303	12.12 wks	3 mos.
7. Colossians	201	8 wks	2 mos.
Philemon	41	1.64 wks	3 wks
8. Gospel of Mark	1365	54.6 wks	13 mos. + 3 wks
9. Gospel of Matthew	2215	88.6 wks	22 mos. + 1 wk
10. Titus	92	3.68 wks	1 mo.
11. 1 Corinthians	843	33.72 wks	8 mos. + 2 wks
12. Galatians	284	11.36 wks	2 mos. + 3 wks
13. Romans	857	34.28 wks	8 mos. + 2 wks
14. James	225	9 wks	2 mos. + 1 wk
15. Luke	2411	96.44 wks	24 mos.
16. 1 Timothy	220	8.8 wks	2 mos. + 1 wk
2 Timothy	163	6.52 wks	1 mo. + 3 wks
17. Jude	56	2.24 wks	2 wks
18. 2 Corinthians	565	22.6 wks	5 mos. + 3 wks
19. 1 Peter	223	8.92 wks	2 mos. + 1 wk
2 Peter	147	5.88 wks	1 mo. + 2 wks
20. Acts	2358	94.32 wks	23 mos. + 2 wks
21. Hebrews	644	25.76 wks	6 mos. + 2 wks

Source: William J. Larkin in collaboration with Don N. Howell, CIU Seminary and School of Missions, Columbia, SC.

Figure 3.2. **A Year by Year Reading Plan through the Greek New Testament Based on Thirteen "Four Week" Months per Year**

Year One			**Year Eight**	
1-3 John	3 mos.		Galatians	2 mos. + 2 wks
John	10 mos.		Romans	8 mos. + 2 wks
			James	2 mos.
Year Two			**Year Nine**	
John	8 mos. + 1 wk		James	1 wk
Revelation	5 mos.		Luke	12 mos. + 3 wks
Year Three			**Year Ten**	
Revelation	6 mos. + 2 wks		Luke	11 mos. + 1 wk
1-2 Thessalonians	3 mos.		1 Timothy	1 mo. + 3 wks
Philippians	2 mos.			
Ephesians	1 mo. + 2 wks			
Year Four			**Year Eleven**	
Ephesians	1 mo. + 2 wks		1-2 Timothy	1 mo. + 5 wks
Colossians	2 mos.		Jude	2 wks
Philemon	3 wks		2 Corinthians	5 mos. + 3 wks
Mark	8 mos. + 3 wks		1-2 Peter	3 mos. + 3 wks
			Acts	1 mo. + 1 wk
Year Five			**Year Twelve**	
Mark	5 mos.		Acts	13 mos.
Matthew	8 mos.			
Year Six			**Year Thirteen**	
Matthew	13 mos.		Acts	9 mos. + 1 wk
			Hebrews	3 mos. + 3 wks
Year Seven			**Year Fourteen**	
Matthew	2 mos. + 1 wk		Hebrews	2 mos. + 3 wks
Titus	1 mo.			
1 Corinthians	8 mos. + 2 wks			
Galatians	1 mo. + 1 wk			

preaching or teaching plan (see chapter sixteen). The latter choice is probably best if you are communicating the Word on a regular basis. Once you've picked the book, divide it into five portions per week, proceeding by sentences. See figure 3.3 for a Greek Reading plan for Philippians.

Proceeding with Sight-Reading

When sight-reading a passage for the first time, parse all verbal forms (cf. figs. 3.4-5), as well as any other unfamiliar forms, and identify any unfamiliar vocabulary with a handy aid like Sakae Kubo's *Reader's Greek-English Lexicon*. Record these parsings and unfamiliar word identifications in the right hand column of a page that will contain your finished translation (cf. fig. 3.6). Refer to this foundational resource page when doing a finished translation in preparation to preach or teach. It will also aid you when sight-reading the passage at another time.

To take full advantage of the sight and sound of the language as well as discourse context, before each daily sight-reading of five lines, you might want to read aloud the entire paragraph in which it is found. Reading through the whole paragraph every time you deal with a part of it will help you make better sense of both "the forest" and "the trees." Then, with the aid of your Parsing and Vocabulary list, sight-read the passage from Greek to English. Keep moving deliberately through the passage. Don't let yourself get stumped on the syntax. When you cannot understand the flow of

Figure 3.3. **Greek Reading Plan for Philippians**

WEEK #1	❏ 1:1-2	❏ 1:3-6	❏ 1:7	❏ 1:8-11	❏ 1:12-14
WEEK #2	❏ 1:15-17	❏ 1:18-20	❏ 1:21-24	❏ 1:25-26	❏ 1:27-28
WEEK #3	❏ 1:29-30	❏ 2:1-4	❏ 2:5-8	❏ 2:9-11	❏ 2:12-13
WEEK #4	❏ 2:14-16	❏ 2:17-18	❏ 2:19-22	❏ 2:23-26	❏ 2:27-28
WEEK #5	❏ 2:29-30	❏ 3:1-4	❏ 3:5-6	❏❏ 3:7-11 (2 days)	
WEEK #6	❏❏ 3:12-14		❏ 3:15-17	❏ 3:18-19	❏ 3:20-21
WEEK #7	❏ 4:1-3	❏ 4:4-6	❏ 4:7-8	❏ 4:9	❏ 4:10-11
WEEK #8	❏ 4:12-14	❏ 4:15-16	❏ 4:17-18	❏ 4:19-20	❏ 4:21-23

Figure 3.4. **Parsing Abbreviations**

TENSE			VOICE			MOOD		
P	=	Present	A	=	Active	I	=	Indicative
I	=	Imperfect	M	=	Middle	S	=	Subjunctive
F	=	Future	P	=	Passive	O	=	Optative
A	=	Aorist	D	=	Deponent	Imv	=	Imperative
Pf	=	Perfect				Inf	=	Infinitive
PlPf	=	Pluperfect				Ptc	=	Participle
PERSON /GENDER			CASE			NUMBER		
Person			N	=	Nominative	S	=	Singular
1	=	first	G	=	Genitive	P	=	Plural
2	=	second	D	=	Dative			
3	=	third	A	=	Accusative			
Gender								
M	=	Masculine						
F	=	Feminine						
N	=	Neuter						

Figure 3.5. **Parsing Format.** When parsing verbs, include these components in this order, using the abbreviations of figure 3.4.

Tense	Voice	Mood	Person		Number	1st Princ. Part	Transl. of Form Parsed
			Gender	Case			

thought, refer to a translation like NASB or ESV or NIV for help, and keep moving through your five lines.

Conserving Exegetical Questions and Insights

Finally, to achieve maximum benefit for preaching and teaching from this exercise, jot down on your "Greek Reading/Translation" or "Survey" worksheets exegetical and homiletical questions, observations, or insights from the passage. Then, when you begin immediate preparation of a sermon or lesson, return to these notes. One final idea is to print out your paragraphs for the week, and carry them with you for meditation and reflection during ministry rounds. The more frequent and extensive your exposure to

Figure 3.6. **Sample Greek Reading**

GREEK READING/TRANSLATION

Passage: Phil 1:3-5

	Translation	Vocabulary, Parsings, Exegetical Observations
1:3		εὐχαριστῶ=PAI1S εὐχαριστέω "I thank" ἡ μνεία= remembrance
1:4		ἡ δέησις = entreaty, prayer ποιούμενος = PMPtcMNS ποιέω "making"
1:5		ἡ κοινωνία = partnership, fellowship

God's Word in the original language, the more useful it will be to you in communicating his truth.

Greek Reading: Resources

Main Resources:

    Abbott-Smith, *Manual Greek Lexicon.*
    BDAG
    Bible Software, e.g., *Bibloi CD.*
    UBS[4]
    Kubo, *Reader's Greek-English Lexicon.*
    Newman, *Concise Greek-English Dictionary.*
    English Bible, e.g., NASB, ESV, NIV.

Other Aids:

    Culy, gen. ed. *Baylor Handbook on Greek Testament.*
    Friberg and Friberg, eds. *Analytical Greek Testament.*
    Han, *Parsing Guide.*
    Kohlenberger, *UBS[4] with NRSV and NIV.*
    Perschbacher, *Analytical Greek Lexicon.*
    Rogers and Rogers, *Linguistic Key to Greek Testament.*
    Zerwick and Grosvenor, *Grammatical Analysis of Greek Testament.*

GREEK READING AND COMPUTER RESOURCES

Greek Reading: Procedure

I. **Orientation to Parsing and Vocabulary:** On the "Greek Reading/Translation" worksheet, (see fig. 3.6; see WJLFP for worksheet templates) write down the parsing of all verbs, following the parsing format (figs. 3.4-5) in the Parsing (and vocabulary) column. Write down any words not immediately recognizable, even with the aid of Kubo. Define these with the aid of Abbott-Smith or Newman.

II. **Reading in Context:** As time permits, read aloud in Greek the paragraph that contains your reading portion. How does what comes before and after the reading portion contribute to your understanding of it?

III. **Sight-reading:** Sight-read the portion by looking at the Greek, referring to your "Greek Reading/Translation" worksheet as necessary, and saying the meaning of the text in intelligible English. Keep moving through your reading portion. When you get stumped, refer to an English translation like NASB or ESV or NIV. Use the following list (in this order) to make sense of the text. Also translate these features roughly in this order, but also taking into account word arrangement motivated by literary considerations.

- *Extent of the syntactic unit* – indicated by punctuation (clauses and subclauses)
- *Connective introducing a clause* – what does it tell about the relationship of that clause to the rest of the sentence(s)?
- *Verb of the clause*
- *Subject of verb and modifiers*
- *Object of verb and modifiers*
- *Modifiers of the verb* – adverbs and particles, prepositional phrases, participial and infinitive constructions, subordinate clauses
- *Word arrangement* – for purposes of emphasis

IV. **Exegetical/Homiletical Observations:** Record questions, observations, and insights to aid you in preparing to preach or teach the passage.

V. **Portable Exposure for Meditation and Reflection:** Copy or print the paragraph(s) with your reading portions for the week. Arrange them on a page, leaving space for recording your questions and insights. Take the text along, and when you have opportunity in the "hurry up and wait" pattern of ministry life, reflect on the passage and record your interactions.

Biblical Languages and Text Software

Commonly Used Programs

The following are commonly used software programs for Biblical Studies.

- *Bibloi CD* and *BibleWorks CD* offer both the ability to work and search in the original languages (GNT, LXX, MT) and English Bible versions, and the ability to view reference works. They are integrated programs that are sold in a single configuration for one price. Bible Works has a more extensive range of Bible versions and ancient Jewish works and offers add-on modules including BDAG. *Bibloi* can search the *Logos Bible Software Series* resources. For *Bibloi* see www.silvermnt.com. For *BibleWorks* see www.bibleworks.com.
- *Gramcord CD* is a *gram*matical con*cord*ance that can perform a virtually unlimited variety of lexical and grammatical searches in the original languages (GNT, LXX, MT). NAS95 is also available. See www.gramcord.org.
- *Logos Bible Software CD* is an electronic library providing a range of original language search capabilities. It has a large number of Bibles, reference works, and commentaries. It contains, for example, *The Essential IVP Reference Collection*, an electronic library of thirteen IVP dictionaries and reference works. See www.logos.com.
- Zondervan has bundled and stand-alone resources including *Expositor's Bible Commentary* and *NIDNTT*. See www.zondervan.com.

Such software provides Greek font, Greek text, and search capabilities. The Greek font of the software program (e.g., Sgreek for *Bibloi CD*) enables you to type in Greek lettering as you record parsings and other matters. With such Greek text software, you will be able to paste germane texts into documents, and manipulate them for study purposes. The search capabilities of such programs come in handy in grammar searches and word searches. The added features of Hebrew text and Septuagint (OT Greek text) make study of the Old and New Testaments in the original readily accessible.

Word Processing Software Customizing

Four steps can make word processing programs more serviceable for the study of the Greek New Testament.

- Copy a Greek font to the Fonts Directory of your operating system. For example, see figure 3.7 for the "Greek Keyboard Arrangement" of Sgreek of *Bibloi*. You can download it from the Internet for a nominal fee.
- Create a macro to toggle between Greek and Hebrew. For example, for your standard English font in Word Perfect/MS Word use *Ctrl-Sft-e* keystrokes for the macro. For a Greek font, use *Ctrl-Sft-g* keystrokes for the macro.
- Construct templates for the exegetical method worksheets using Headers and Tables.
- Use the Graphics or Draw function to prepare Mechanical Layouts.

Internet Sites

Mark Goodacre's "New Testament Gateway" (www.ntgateway.com) includes a wide range of topics such as the Greek New Testament, Historical Jesus, Textual Criticism, NT Books, Ancient World, with links to many other sites. The "Greek New Testament" portal includes such topics as a) Greek New Testament Texts; b) Learning NT Greek; c) Fonts; d) Grammars; e) Language; f) Lexica; g) Discussion; h) Computer Software; i) Bibliography; and j) Septuagint.

Endnotes

1. Louw, "Discourse Analysis" 103.

2. Paul Doriani, "Pastor's Advice," 105-6.

3. These figures involve arranging the books of the New Testament in order of increasing Greek difficulty. The number of lines for each book was determined by counting as a line any line of text in UBS[4] with two or more words. Two indented verse lines were counted as one line. Four weeks were treated as a month and thirteen "four week" months as one year.

Figure 3.7. **Greek Keyboard Arrangement (Sgreek Font for *Bibloi*)**

Greek	Letter	Key	Greek	Letter	Key
α	alpha	a	π	pi	p
ᾳ	alpha + iota subscript	#	ρ	rho	r
β	beta	b	σ	sigma	s
γ	gamma	g	ς	sigma final	j
δ	delta	d	τ	tau	t
ε	epsilon	e	υ	upsilon	u
ζ	zeta	z	φ	phi	f
η	eta	h	χ	chi	x
ῃ	eta + iota subscript	$	ψ	psi	y
θ	theta	q	ω	omega	w
ι	iota	i	ῳ	omega + iota subscript	%
κ	kappa	k	ӓ	diaeresis	a+
λ	lambda	l	ἀ	smooth breathing	a)
μ	mu	m	ἁ	rough breathing	a(
ν	nu	n	ά	acute accent	a/
ξ	ksi	c	ὰ	grave accent	a\
ο	omicron	o	ᾶ	circumflex accent	a=

Source: Character map of *Sgreek* font available at www.silvermnt.com.

Chapter 4
FINISHED TRANSLATION AND MECHANICAL LAYOUT

We now come to the section of the "A Method for Exegesis and Exposition" that begins the journey of our Immediate Preparation for preaching or teaching a biblical text. This might seem to be the time to roll up our sleeves, pull out our reference materials, and start analyzing the text. To do that now, however, would be akin to rushing to meet a ministry need without seeking God's guidance. We need to be sure our own hearts are pure before we try to help the heart problems of others.

Spiritual Preparation

Perspective

Any study of the Word of God is a spiritual exercise. Our best efforts, even the efforts of the "star" of the Greek class, are worthless unless illumined and empowered by the Holy Spirit. Prayer is an essential part of exegesis of God's Holy Word for it indicates our intentional reliance on the Holy Spirit for guidance in insight and application.

Your Immediate Preparation, then, must always begin with prayer, consciously placing yourself under Scripture's authority, and humbly asking for the Spirit's illumination. Then, continue your work in an attitude of prayer. Pray at points when you pick up your study after a break for other ministry duties. Pray whenever the Spirit prompts throughout the study. Prayer is the way to make exegesis a truly spiritual exercise, and to be confident God is guiding you to the truth he wants you to declare.

Procedure

To be properly prepared to "think God's thoughts after him" in exegesis, you must have a mindset–ideas, beliefs, and values–which are thoroughly biblical. Because, since the Fall, sinful human beings do not naturally think this way, even those who know Christ, you must be intentional in your approach to Scripture. You need to consciously adopt a biblical pre-understanding by praying for the Holy Spirit's illumination as you embrace these stances.

Faith. Thank God for the spiritual understanding that is yours as a result of your regenerate state, and affirm to him your implicit trust in the truth of his Word.

Humbly repentant stance toward self. Identify the concerns and questions out of your personal historical circumstances with which you approach the text. Declare your desire that the Holy Spirit lay bare your soul, helping you to repent of wrong thinking and acting spawned by your historical and cultural conditions.

Receptivity to revealed truth. Consciously embrace a biblical world view: biblically mandated ideas, beliefs, values, structures, and behavior patterns, confident that the Holy Spirit will illumine your mind to the nature and excellence of the things of God.

Finished Translation

Having prepared yourself spiritually, the next step is to prepare the text for your sermon or lesson by completing a finished translation and mechanical layout to guide your subsequent exegetical work. To get the most good out of Greek exegesis, you need as precise an understanding as possible of what the author is saying in the original. Only then can you accurately represent the text's message in English.

Understanding Translation

Translation is "an attempt to put the idea defined by the words and syntax of one language into the words and syntax of a second language that will define the same idea."[1] Put another way, the goal of a translator, stated as a question is, " . . . are they (translators) trying to express the meaning of the text in such a way that those who receive it can fully appreciate how the original text must have been understood by those who first read it or heard it read?"[2]

The surface structures of languages differ both lexically and grammatically. It may take a number of words in English to represent what can be expressed by one word in Greek (Gal 5:4, δικαιοῦσθε, "you are trying to be justified") or vice versa. One word in English does not necessarily represent the full range of potential meanings of a word in Greek (παρακαλέω means, " I comfort, exhort, appeal to"). This encourages idiomatic, though not dynamically equivalent, translation. Your ultimate goal is to produce a translation characterized by accuracy to the text and clarity to the reader.

What clues does a text give you about the meaning (message) it intends to convey? In any written text, writers communicate their meaning through two kinds of signals: *historical* and *literary*. In the case of Scripture there is a third, *theological*.

Historical Clues for Translation

In a text written in a different historical-cultural setting, it is not surprising to find terms that are self-evident and meaningful to the first audience, but that must be researched by those removed in time. Historical analysis pursues, among other things, the meanings of such historical-cultural-religious details in the passage.

Literary Clues for Translation

Since it is the Greek New Testament you are analyzing, part of literary analysis will be signals from the Greek grammar. Greek grammar provides certain types of clues that are true for any language system. A language communicates through four grammatical phenomena: the *morpheme*, the *function word*, *word order*, and *punctuation*.

Morpheme. "The minimal meaningful part of a word" (syllables, even letters, prefixes and endings), a morpheme indicates a particular grammatical feature or relationship. In English the addition of *-ed* to a verb shows that the verb's action took place before the time the speaker talks about it; e.g., "I *baked* a cake," vs. "I bake a cake." In Greek the declensions and conjugations learned as paradigms contain patterns of morphemes each of which indicates a grammatical relationship. For example, Philippians 1:3 begins with Εὐχαριστῶ, present active indicative, first person singular form, meaning "I thank." One letter ω–a morpheme–signals for the reader a number of grammatical relationships. The action of thanking is done by one person, the speaker (first person singular). He declares (indicative mood) that he, the subject, is doing so (active voice) and that his action is occurring at the same time as he is speaking and is probably continuous in nature (present tense). Morphemes are a vital key to getting at a text's meaning. They not only communicate a component of meaning for the word to which they are attached, but they may also point to the type of relationship the word has to other words in the sentence. The accusative case ending on ἔργον in Phil 1:6 shows it is the object of the verb's action.

Function word. The function word has a single or limited range of meaning and no morphemes. It serves to show the link between words or groups of words in a sentence. It can also provide emphasis. In English, conjunctions, prepositions, and particles, such as *and, but, in, out of, not, indeed*, are function words. The same is the case in Greek, where the equivalent terms are καί, δέ, ἐν, ἐκ, οὐ, γέ. In Phil 1:3 (ἐπί) as a preposition links its object, πάσῃ τῇ μνείᾳ ("every remembrance"), with the verb Εὐχαριστῶ ("I thank"). The whole prepositional phrase modifies the verb's action by showing the time for Paul's thankfulness: "I thank my God at every remembrance . . . "

Word order. Since English does not have as well developed a system of morphemes, especially for nouns, it depends more heavily on word order than does Greek. In English when you say, "Man bites dog," which is news and, "Dog bites man," which is not, you depend totally on word order to communicate the different meanings. Word order alone indicates in one sentence "man" is the subject of the verb's action, while in the other he is the object. In Greek it is the morphemes that would show this, the nominative and accusative case endings on the words. Though the same in word order, these two Greek sentences are equivalent of the English above: ὁ ἄνθρωπος δάκνει τὸν κύνα and τὸν ἄνθρωπον δάκνει ὁ κύων.

Word order does communicate meaning in Greek. Word order in conjunction with the presence of function words and morphemes creates certain boundaries and connections which again determine meaning. In Phil 1:3, the fact that ἡ μνεία in the dative case comes directly after a preposition that governs a dative case indicates that it is probably the object of the preposition, whereas the dative τῷ θεῷ, which occurs before it, is not.

Punctuation. Although the original authors did not supply punctuation, the editors have. This is an invaluable tool in translating. The placement of commas, raised dots, periods, paragraph and section indicators shows the degree of connection or separation the editors believe exists among words, phrases, sentences, paragraphs, and sections. UBS[4] has a very helpful punctuation apparatus that details editors' and translators' decisions.

Other types of literary clues are *genre* and *subgenre structure, rhetorical features* and *word study*. In finished translation grammar and semantics (word meanings) rightly receive the most attention.

Theological Perspective

Your translation and exegesis is foundational to a theological understanding of the passsage. Whether Biblical Theology (contribution of the "whole counsel of God"), Systematic Theology (a coherent exposition of biblical truth), or Apologetic Theology (an exploration of implications for contemporary culture), all will benefit from your close attention to the text. Of course, these are not the immediate concern of finished translation, though all translation practice seeks to avoid theological error. But finished translation is the "working document" on which exegesis is practiced. And exegesis is the source of theological conclusions.

Context in Translation

If the areas described above provide clues to meaning, the literary-linguistic context is the matrix in which all the clues operate. In other words, a person may have translated correctly individual words and still not understand what a sentence or paragraph is saying. The meaning of all words must be viewed, not only in terms of themselves (dictionary definition), but also in relation to each other in context, if the precise and full meaning is to be obtained.

Finished Translation: Resources

Main Resources:

Abbott-Smith, *Manual Greek Lexicon.*
BDAG
English Bible, e.g., ESV, NASB, or NIV.
UBS^4
Kubo, *Reader's Greek-English Lexicon.*
Newman, *Concise Greek-English Dictionary.*

Other Aids:

Bible Software, e.g., *Bibloi CD.*
Friberg and Friberg, eds. *Analytical Greek Testament.*
Han, *Parsing Guide.*
Kohlenberger, *UBS^4 with NRSV and NIV.*
Perschbacher, *Analytical Greek Lexicon.*
Rogers and Rogers, *Linguistic Key to Greek Testament.*
Zerwick and Grosvenor, *Grammatical Analysis of Greek Testament.*

Finished Translation: Procedure

With two hours allocated for your spiritual and text preparation, you may need to be selective about what you will render into a finished translation, especially which verses will be completed as a mechanical layout. Determine which verses of your preaching portion you will translate according to their centrality or difficulty. If you have already sight-read the passage as part of your Greek Reading, the parsing and vocabulary list on the right side of your "Greek Reading/Translation" worksheet will already be in hand (cf. fig. 3.6; see WJLFP for template). If so, you can now add your translation on the remainder of the page, spaced out to keep pace with your parsing and vocabulary notes (e.g., every other line).

The following section places in sequential steps the thought process involved in translation. Depending on your level of proficiency, many of these steps after the basic identification of vocabulary and parsings will take place simultaneously. Follow the analysis and synthesis steps to the extent they are helpful. Do not omit filling in the vocabulary/parsing portion of the worksheet, the practice of making scratch notes as you build the text, or the step of writing out a translation.

I. **Survey the Text**
   A. **Scope out the grammatical units of the passage.** Use punctuation (period, raised dot, question mark–in Greek a semi-colon) to identify the extent of each sentence. A sentence is often longer than one verse of Scripture. With the aid of the editor's commas and the identification of any subordinate conjunctions or relative pronouns, isolate any subordinate clauses within each sentence.
   B. **Identify words that need definition and parsing.** This is normally done as part of Greek Reading (see chapter three). Write down on the vocabulary/parsing portion of the "Greek Reading/Translation" worksheet those words whose meaning or parsing is not immediately recognizable. Also write down words, whose most frequently occurring meaning you know, but whose meaning does not seem to suit the immediate context. Define or parse with the aid of dictionary and as needed parsing aids.

II. **Build the Text Sentence by Sentence**
   A. **Translate the Main Clause.**
      1. *Coordinate conjunctions.* Identify and translate any coordinate conjunction(s) linking the main clause to what precedes it. Remember that some coordinate conjunctions are *post-positive*, meaning that in terms of word order they cannot stand first in a clause or sentence, though in meaning they belong first.
      2. *Main verbs.* Identify and translate the main verb(s). Note: the main verb is usually in the indicative or imperative mood. The main verb is usually *not* a participle or an infinitive.

Figure 4.1. Sample Translation

Passage __Phil 1:3-8__

TRANSLATION	VOCABULARY; PARSING
3,4 I am thanking my God at every remembrance of you, always in every prayer of mine on behalf of all of you, making entreaty with joy,	Εὐχαριστῶ PAI1s Εὐχαριστέω I thank + dative of person ἐπί + dat. -at ἡ μνεία - remembrance ἡ δέησις - entreaty ποιούμενος PMPtcMNS ποιέω making of oneself, middle voice emph.; function? "all . . . all"; is inclusiveness customary or does it point to a special relationship?
5 because of your fellowship in the gospel from the first day until now,	ἐπί + dat. cause εἰς + acc. in; nature of emphasis?
6 because I am confident of this very thing, that the one who began a good work in you will complete it until the day of Christ Jesus.	πεποιθώς PfAPtcMNS πείθω pft with pres. meaning: being confident; cause ἐναρξάμενος ADPtcMNS ἐνάρχομαι substantival "the one who began" ἐπιτελέσει FAI3s ἐπιτελέω will complete
7 In so far as it is right for me to think this about all of you, because I have you in my heart, because, both in my chains and in the defense and confirmation of the gospel, you all are fellow participants with me of grace.	καθώς - causal, since ἐστιν PAI3s εἰμί - is φρονεῖν PAInf φρονέω to think; significance pres. time? ὑπέρ + gen. concerning ἔχειν PAInf ἔχω have; significance of pres. tense? Does ἐν τε τοῖς δεσμοῖς . . . βεβαιώσει go with what precedes or follows? ἡ βεβαίωσις confirmation ὄντας PAPtcMAP εἰμί are
8 For God is my witness, that I am longing for you all with the compassion of Christ Jesus.	ὡς - that ἐπιποθῶ PAI1s ἐπιποθέω I long τὸ σπλάγχνον affection

Figure 4.1. *(continued)*

Passage __Phil 1:9-11__

TRANSLATION	VOCABULARY; PARSING
9 And this I am praying, that your love may be abounding yet more and more in knowledge and all insight,	προσεύχομαι PDI1s προσεύχομαι I pray περισσεύῃ PAS3s περισσεύω may be abounding ἐν - sphere ἡ αἴσθησις - insight
10 in order that you may be testing and proving the things that are excellent in order that you might be pure and blameless at the day of Christ,	εἰς τό - purpose δοκιμάζειν PAInf δοκιμάζω may be testing διαφέροντα PAPtcNAP διαφέρω things that are excellent ἵνα- in order that ἦτε PAS2p εἰμί might be εἰλικρινεῖς - unmixed ἀπρόσκοποι - blameless
11 having been filled with fruit of righteousness which is through Jesus unto the glory and praise of God.	πεπληρωμένοι PfPPtcMNP πληρόω having been filled; significance of perfect tense? Agent of the passive?

3. *Subject(s) and modifiers.* **Identify any expressed subject(s) and modifier(s).**
   a. *Subject(s).* The subject will usually be a noun or other substantive in the nominative case with the same number (singular or plural) as the main verb. Remember that neuter plural subjects take singular verbs.
   b. *Modifiers.* Modifiers will usually be nouns in the genitive case (following the subject) or adjectives in the nominative case. Another type of modifier is a prepositional phrase that is attached to the subject.
4. *Direct object(s) and modifiers* Identify any direct object(s) and modifier(s).
   a. *Direct object(s).* The direct object will usually be a noun or other substantive in the accusative case.

b. *Modifiers*. Modifiers will usually be nouns in the genitive case (following the direct object) or adjectives in the accusative case. Another type of modifier is a prepositional phrase that is attached to the object.
5. *Adverbial Modifiers*. Identify any adverbial modifier(s) of the main verb.
   a. *Adverbial-type forms*. Adverbial modifiers will usually be adverbs, adverbial participial phrases, adverbial infinitival phrases, or prepositional phrases.
   b. *Cases*. The genitive, dative, and accusative cases may also be used adverbially. (For example, the dative of indirect object acts adverbially to tell to/for whom the action is done.)

B. **Construct a translation for any subordinate clause(s) following the same steps as in II.A.1-5.**
C. **Connect subordinate clauses to the main clause(s) in a sequence that conveys the intended meaning.**

III. **Translation Synthesis: Build the Text**
   A. **Proceed to translate the text in order mentally.** Now that you have translated all the units and subunits, give a continuous translation of the text by reading it through with the aid of the vocabulary/parsing list and scratch notes. This will include deciding the relationship of the clauses and constructions to one another and to the whole so that you can render a coherent and accurate translation.
   B. **Note any variation in regular word order.** Regular word order consists of subject-verb-object; or verb-subject-object (Semitic style imitation); modifiers following their governing words: noun-adj; article-adj-noun; noun-genitive; verb-prepositional phrase; participles and infinitives are first in their subordinate constructions. Any variation may indicate that the writer is stressing the "out of place" word(s).
   C. **Write out a translation of the passage next to the vocabulary/parsing list.** This completed translation (see fig. 4.1) will be a valued aid to any future reading or analysis of the text.
   D. **Check your translation.** Compare your translation with NASB or ESV or NIV to see whether you have inaccurately represented the Greek at any point. Make necessary corrections.
   NOTE: Insights from a number of these steps may be preserved on the "Survey" worksheet (see fig. 5.1).

Mechanical Layout

A helpful way to study a passage and maintain the proper balance between a focus on individual grammatical features and on their relationships in context is to lay out the passage visually. It is like identifying which bones are connected to which other bones in a skeleton. Such a visual representation will enable you to distinguish between main and subordinate thoughts in a passage, as well as trace the flow of thought and note emphases. It will be invaluable as you outline the passage for preaching or teaching, and think over main and subpoints you will want to make.

Use the "Mechanical Layout" worksheet for this step (see fig. 4.2; see WJLFP for template). The mechanical layout will serve as a basic grid from which all other analysis may be read. As you grow in proficiency, you may want to combine the translation and mechanical layout processes.

Organizing Principles

The mechanical layout reads from left to right and from top to bottom. Treat each sentence as an individual unit. The word order of the Greek text is preserved at all times, except for post-positive conjunctions that are moved to the beginning of the unit they introduce.

Basic placement order. The basic order of the elements in any clause or verbal construction (e.g., participial or infinitival phrases) is presupposed to be *conjunction-subject-verb-object*. The "Mechanical Layout" worksheet identifies columns for Coordinate Conjunction, Subject, Verb, and Direct Object of main clauses. You should use these columns *only* for the basic elements of *main clauses*.

CC	S	V	O

Any subordinate clauses or other verbal constructions should be laid out according to the c-s-v-o schema (while preserving the word order of the original Greek) but *not* using the columns at the top of the worksheet. In fact, graphically, these subordinate constructions could be placed in brackets or boxes and their own c-s-v-o schema. Greek syntax is of such a nature that you might find a number of subordinate constructions modifying each other, which will result in "boxes within boxes" (see Phil. 1:9-11 in fig. 4.2).

FINISHED TRANSLATION AND MECHANICAL LAYOUT 49

Figure 4.2. **Sample Mechanical Layout**

Passage: __Phil. 1:3-7__

CC	S	V	O

```
1.3              Εὐχαριστῶ              τῷ θεῷ μου
                    ▲ ἐπί πάσῃ τῇ μνείᾳ ὑμῶν
1.4              πάντοτε
                 ἐν πάσῃ δεήσει μου
                       ▲ ὑπὲρ πάντων ὑμων,
                 ┌─────────────────────────────┐
                 │ μετὰ χαρᾶς       τὴν δέησιν │
                 │ ποιούμενος,                 │
                 └─────────────────────────────┘
1.5              ἐπί τῇ κοινωνίᾳ ὑμῶν
                    ▲ εἰς τὸ εὐαγγέλιον
                      ἀπὸ τῆς πρώτης ἡμέρας
                      ἄχρι τοῦ νῦν,

1.6              πεποιθώς    αὐτὸ τοῦτο, =

= ὅτι ὁ ἐναρξάμενος
       ▲ ἐν ὑμῖν        ἔργον ἀγαθὸν    ἐπιτελέσει
                                       ▲ ἄχρι ἡμέρας
                                          ▲ Χριστοῦ᾽ Ἰησοῦ·

1.7 καθὼς       ἐστιν                δίκαιον
                 ▲ ἐμοί              ▲     ┌──────────────────┐
                                           │     τοῦτο        │
                                           │ φρονεῖν          │
                                           │  ▲ ὑπὲρ πάντων ὑμῶν │
                                           └──────────────────┘

                διὰ τὸ     ἔχειν
                            ▲
                       με      ἐν τῇ καρδίᾳ ὑμᾶς,

                ┌──────────────────────────────────┐
                │ τε   ἐν τοῖς δεσμοῖς μου          │
                │ καὶ  ἐν   τῇ ἀπολογίᾳ             │
                │          καὶ βεβαιώσει            │
                │              ▲ τοῦ εὐαγγελίου    │
                │            συγκοινωνούς           │
                │              ▲ μου               │
                │                 τῆς χάριτος       │
                │  πάντας ὑμᾶς ▼ ὄντας.            │
                └──────────────────────────────────┘
```

Figure 4.2. *(continued)*

Passage: Phil 1:8-11

CC	S	V	O

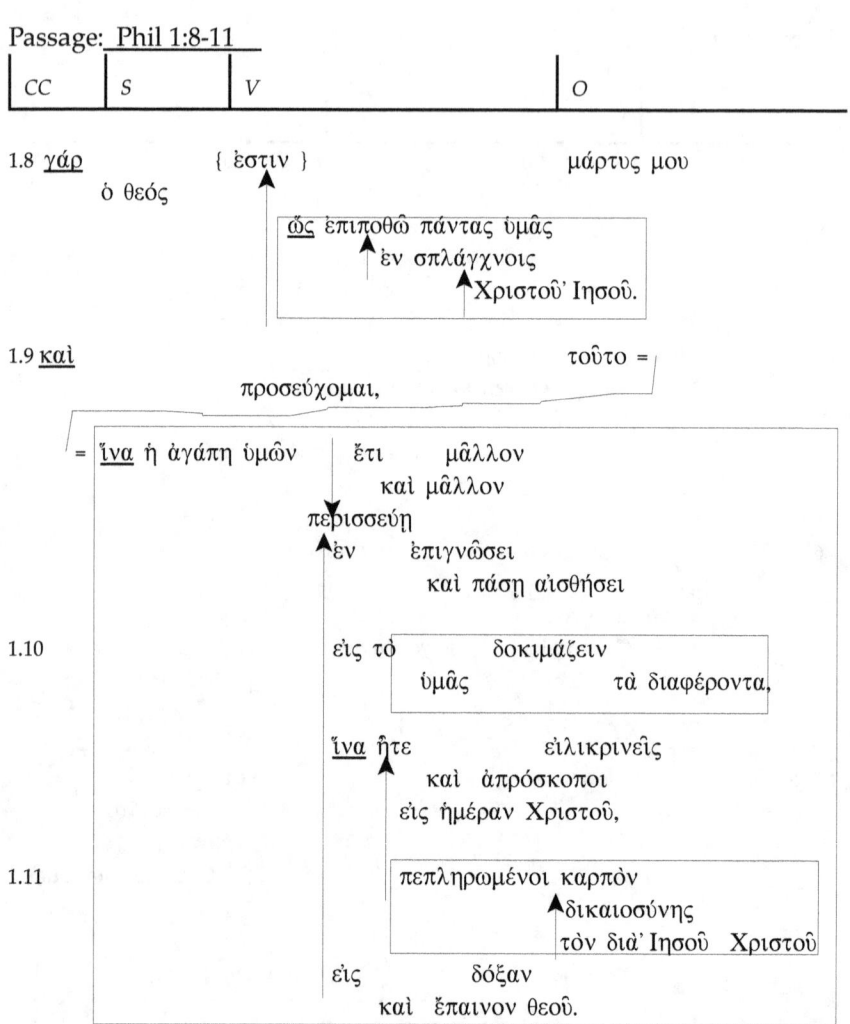

Observing the above principles may involve moving to the next line before a word can receive its proper placement. For example:

Εὐχαριστῶ τῷ θεῷ μου (I thank my God) is placed on one line.

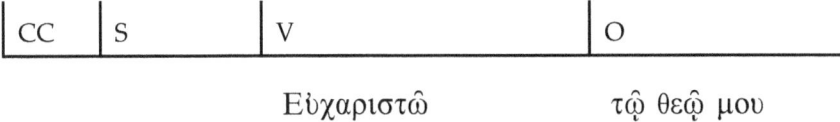

But μάρτυς γάρ μου ὁ θεός (God is my witness) must be placed on three lines.

CC	S	V	O
			μάρτυς μου
		{ἐστιν}	
	ὁ θεός		

The same principle is also true of subordinate clauses:

ἵνα ἡ ἀγάπη ὑμῶν ἔτι μᾶλλον καὶ μᾶλλον περισσεύῃ . . . ἵνα ἦτε εἰλικρινεῖς (that your love may abound more and more . . . in order that you may be sincere)

Main Clause

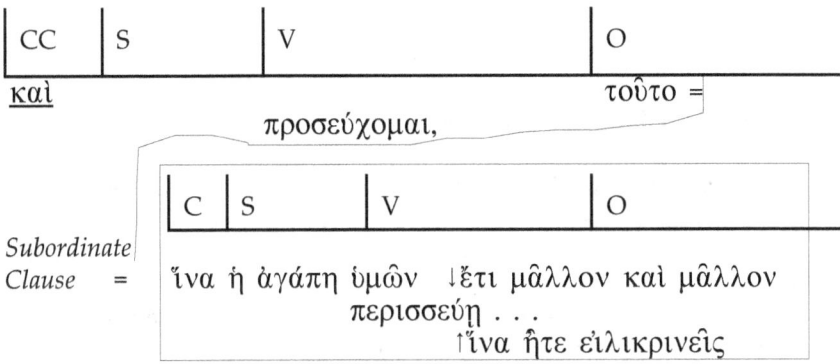

It is often easier to identify and place the main clause elements first—regardless of where they come in the sentence—and then relate other elements to them. Note: If you use this approach, be sure to plan spacing that will allow for the Greek word order.

Adjectival and adverbial placement; particles and vocatives. Modifiers which precede the word they modify are placed over it and indented. Those modifiers which follow the word modified are placed under it and indented. In a similar way, adverbial modifiers are placed over or under the verb modified. Normally place particles over the verb and indented; vocatives and intejections go above the line in the subject slot.

Treat all prepositional phrases as acting adverbially unless word order indicates they modify a substantive. Show them modifying the nearest verbal form (verb, participle, infinitive).

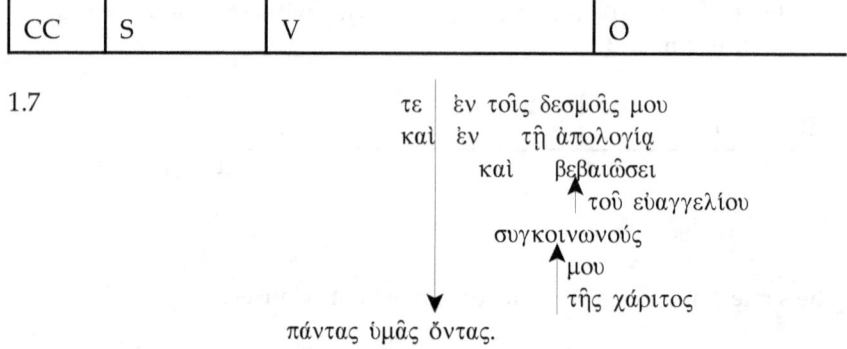

General placement principles:

- *Closer is better.* It is more likely that a modifier will be related to an element that is close at hand than to an element several words away.
- *Simpler is better.* A simple syntactical relationship is usually more likely than a complex one.

Computer Aided Mechanical Layout

Make a template. Consider creating a template like the one below for your Mechanical Layout sheet. Create a header to show the passage designation. Below it, using a table with top and outside right lines hidden, make the framework for main clauses. Set tabs at the starting point of each column and at each point of indentation. This will allow you to readily position connective, subject, verb, and object, as well as modifiers.

Passage:____

CC	S	V	O

FINISHED TRANSLATION AND MECHANICAL LAYOUT

Paste and manipulate the text. Paste in the text to be laid out from Greek New Testament text software. Segment the text using "HRt"s (hard returns) according to punctuation and clause or phrase clusters. For example, Philippians 1:3-4 may be initially segmented as follows:

Phil. 1:3-4
1.3   Εὐχαριστῶ τῷ θεῷ μου
      ἐπὶ πάσῃ τῇ μνείᾳ ὑμῶν
1.4   πάντοτε
      ἐν πάσῃ δεήσει μου
      ὑπὲρ πάντων ὑμῶν,
      μετὰ χαρᾶς τὴν δέησιν ποιούμενος,

Place text and add graphics. Place the words and phrases on the Mechanical Layout worksheet in such a way that their position reflects their function, and their relationship to other words, phrases, and clauses in their immediate context. Symbols and graphics can be used to introduce arrows and other relationship markers. (cf. complete example in fig. 4.2).

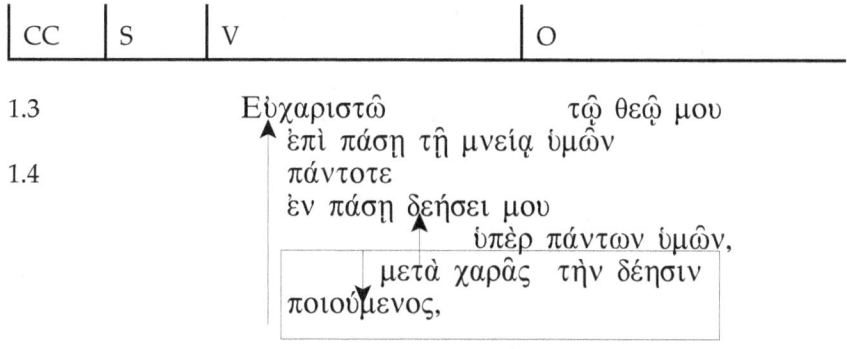

Mechanical Layout: Resources

Materials from Previous Study

"Greek Reading/Translation" worksheet

Greek is Great Gain

Chapter four
Chapter nine
Appendix

Reference tools

Bible Software, e.g., *Biblio CD*.
UBS⁴
DBW
Robertson, *Grammar of Greek Testament*.

Commentaries

Fee, *Philippians*.
Hawthorne, *Philippians*.
O'Brien, *Philippians*.
Silva, *Philippians*.

Mechanical Layout: Procedure

I. **Scope out Sentence and Clause Extent.** Proceed by sentences.
   A. **Sentences:** With the aid of punctuation (periods and raised periods), divide your passage into its basic units (sentences).
   B. **Clauses:** With the aid of punctuation (commas) subordinate conjunctions (adverbial, substantival and relative pronouns), and verbal constructions (infinitives and participles), identify the subclauses in each basic unit. Jot down the extent of each subunit, its beginning, and its ending term.

II. **Mechanical Layout Construction**
   A. **General Instructions**:
      1. *Follow text word order*. Follow the New Testament writer's word order except for post-positive conjunctions that should b placed in their proper first position.
      2. *Follow word order standard (c-s-v-o)*. Treat conjunction, subject, verb, object as the proper c-word order for the main elements in any clause or verbal construction.
      3. *Take account of variations*. If the New Testament writer varies, follow his word order by placing each item in its proper slot, and, if need be, moving down a line, and then correctly positioning the next item. This procedure holds for main clauses and subordinate constructions. For example, if the object comes before the verb in the text, position the object, then move down a line, and position the verb.
      3. *Place parallel items underneath each other*. Show parallelism, i.e., items connected by coordinate conjunctions, at whatever level

(clause, phrase, word), by placing them in the same position underneath each other and connected by the coordinating conjunction.

B. **Placing Main Clause Items** (see appendix).
 1. *Place main items.* When you come to main clause items, whether coordinating conjunction, subject, verb, or object, place them in the appropriate column on the sheet.
 2. *Take account of substantival constructions.* Sometimes a noun clause or verbal construction (substantival use of infinitive or participle) is functioning as a subject or object. Place the entire construction, with its own elements appropriately positioned, in the appropriate main clause slot and enclose in brackets or within a box.

C. **Placing Subordinate Items**.
 1. *Identify item modified.* When you come to a subordinate item—a word, phrase, or clause that modifies another word in the sentence—identify the item it modifies. To aid in identification, remember nouns are normally modified by adjectives; nouns in genitive and dative; relative clauses (introduced by relative pronouns); adjectival participles; or sometimes prepositional phrases. Verbs are normally modified by particles, adverbs; prepositional phrases; adverbial subordinate clauses; adverbial participles; or adverbial uses of the infinitive. Vocatives and other interjections go in the subject slot and above the line. This step often involves interpretational options (e.g., do the ἐν prepositional phrases in the middle of Philippians 1:7 modify what precedes or what follows?). Consult commentaries for options and their rationale and choose the one which makes the best sense of the passage's flow and meaning.
 2. *Place modifier in indented position.* Place the subordinate element in an indented position underneath, if it follows, or above, if it precedes, the word modified.
 3. *Organize subordinate clause elements.* If the subordinate element is a clause, arrange the elements within the clause, assuming the normal order: conjunction, subject, verb, object, and accounting for differences indicated by the writer's word order and enclose in brackets or within a box.
 4. *Arrange multiple modifiers.* Begin each subordinate element that modifies the same word at the same point of indentation, but on its own line. Once all the modifying elements related to a particular item have been identified and listed, draw a vertical line to the left of the list up to the word modified and cap it

with an arrow. This will help you link visually, in larger blocks, items and their modifiers (see Phil 1:3-5 in fig. 4.2).
5. *Keep brief modifiers on same line.* Some modifiers are so brief that they must be placed on the same line as the word modified (see Phil 1:3, 11 in fig. 4.2).

D. **Special Conventions:**
1. <u>Underline</u>. Underline all conjunctions introducing clauses for ease of identification (see Phil 1:6-7 in fig. 4.2).
2. *Equals sign* (=). Use an equals sign for items in apposition (see Phil 1:6 in fig. 4.2).
3. *Square Bracket or box* [ ] or ☐ .

   Enclose in square brackets [ ] or a box all word clusters which function as one item, e.g., as a subject, object, object of a preposition. In Greek, substantival participles, substantival infinitives, and noun clauses function this way. The same may be done with other subordinate clauses or verbal constructions like participle or infinitive phrases, which modify verbs.
4. *C-V-S-O template.* For ease of placement identification, you may want to use this within subordinate, bracketed or boxed constructions as well as with main clause constructions.
5. *Curved brackets* { }. Enclose in curved brackets items not present in the text, but which need to be supplied (e.g., a verb) in order to complete the clause or sentence's thought (see Phil 1:8 in fig. 4.2).
6. *Solid line.* Use a solid line to move items to the left when necessary (see Phil 1:6 in fig. 4.2).
7. *Arrow and dotted line.* Use a dotted line with an arrow to link relative pronoun with its antecedent.

Endnotes

1. LaSor, *Handbook*, 2: 7.

2. Nida, "Establishing Translation Principles," 209.

Chapter 5
SURVEY

With your finished translation, mechanical layout, and hopefully some in-depth study in hand (see chapter sixteen), you are ready to begin your six hours of studying the text exegetically as part of your Immediate Preparation. This involves an exegetical journey from "Survey" to "Analysis" to "Synthesis" and finally on to "Interpretation/Application." At each step along the way you'll gain insights that will enrich and enliven the message you will craft and deliver.

Perspectives on Survey

General Approach

Your first half hour in exegesis is spent in "Survey," or "brooding" over the passage. "Survey" is primarily a matter of raising questions and making observations based on your own knowledge and experience. The best mindset for this brooding is one of being a curious, discriminating, comprehensive, and creative learner.

Curious. Let your curiosity get the best of you as you come up with every question that you or your congregation/class could possibly wonder about. Since there is no pressure to answer all these questions at this point, this should be a relaxed enjoyable part of your process.

Discriminating. Look at the passage and try to discern the important historical, literary, and theological features which you will need to later probe in exegetical analysis. However, at this early stage in your immediate preparation, follow the principle of direct interaction with the text. Use no secondary works, e.g., commentaries. Fred Craddock's observations are to the point:

> Direct engagement with the text in a kind of critical naïveté precedes and is foundational for all other study. It is in the text that the interpreter listens for the Word; it is in the text that the interpreter and the congregation will meet.[1]

Commentaries can short circuit direct interaction. If introduced too early, "the commentary may obscure the centrality of the text, come between the interpreter and the text, abbreviate the time that should be spent living with the text, and therefore unduly influence the sermon" or lesson.[2]

Comprehensive. Be intentionally comprehensive by raising questions from various contexts, e.g., historical and literary analysis, biblical and systematic theology, contemporary culture, and application.

Creative. Finally, set your mind to work creatively. Let the text suggest to your mind, by free association, all the riches of God's truth and its application. Daniel Baumann counsels,

> . . . survey the passage . . . jot down ideas. This begins a creative process known to all artists, musicians and creative writers, a process that taps the mind for available resources. Jot down every idea via free association and exhaust *your own* thinking. Let other resources remain on the shelf. Do not turn too quickly to outside sources lest you quench the personal touch, that unique element that is yours as a preacher. Take from others only after you have gleaned all you can from the reservoirs of your own mind.[3]

"Survey," then, should be completed with as little outside help as possible. It is your questions and your congregation/class's questions you want to identify so that, in the course of your delivery, you can answer them (or at least the more important ones). It is your insights, illumined by the Holy Spirit, which are the vital starting points for your exegetical work. You must make the truth of God your own if you are to communicate it authentically and effectively.

In summary, your task is to plot out the exegetical and expositional territory of your text, plumb your own mind and heart for insights that the text evokes, and project a superstructure that will ultimately be the sermon or lesson. With the use of your "Survey" worksheet, you will address the following two areas (see fig. 5.1; see WJLFP for "Exegetical Worksheets" template).

Deal With Textual Critical Matters

The first step in "Survey" is to establish to your satisfaction the probable Greek wording of the original text for your preaching/teaching portion. With the aid of the UBS[4] textual apparatus, Metzger's *Textual Commentary*, and your knowledge of textual critical principles, you can fairly quickly decide these issues with a degree of independent judgment and record your results

Figure 5.1. **Sample Survey**

Passage Phil 1:3-8

Textual Critical	Exegetical Questions/Observations
	v. 3. Present tense consistently used throughout to describe Paul's activity - significance?
	v. 4. Note the use of πᾶς to describe the Philippians and his relation to them - emphasis on inclusion
	δέησις - type of prayer described?
	ποιούμενος - ptc function?
	"With joy"– a theme of Philippians (2:18; 3:1; 4:4). Other themes in this thanksgiving and prayer?
	v. 5. κοινωνία - nature of "fellowship in the gospel"?
	"From first day until now" - note Acts 16:11-40; 18:5; 20:1-3 and 2 Corinthians 7:5; 8:1 for founding and contact with Macedonian church
	v. 6. πεποιθώς - ptc function?
	How does this confident assertion relate to apostasy and backsliding?
	v. 7. Καθώς - function in starting a clause?
	φρονεῖν, ἔχειν - significance of present tense?
	διὰ τό + inf.=cause
	τῇ ἀπολογίᾳ καὶ βεβαιώσει - difference?
	"fellow participants of grace" - theological background and meaning?

Figure 5.1. (*continued*)

Passage Phil 1:9-11

Textual Critical	Exegetical Questions/Observations
v. 11. Textual Problem: καὶ ἔπαινον θεοῦ Alternate Readings: 1) and praise of God 2) and praise of Christ 3) and praise to me 4) of God and praise to me 5) and his praise 6) and praise Metzger (*Textual Commentary*, 544): *Reading #1* has widest attestation and is most in line with Paul's thought. *Readings ##2, 5, & 6* are probably related through scribal error or avoidance of redundancy. *Readings ##3 & 4* are unusual. Does Paul think the climax of their glorification is to bring him praise? Decision: Reading #1	v. 9. other similar prayer requests in Paul - Col 1:9-11; Eph 3:14-19 love abounding - 1 Thess 4:9-10; John 13:35 ἐν - instrumental or sphere? Contemporary background study for ἐπιγνώσει and αἰσθήσει and for εἰλικρινεῖς and ἀπρόσκοποι v. 10. εἰς τό = purpose or result? Discern the best - Phil 4:8-9; Heb 5:14; Rom 12:2 pure and blameless - cf. Eph 5:25-27 A mark of spiritual maturity is the ability to distinguish good and evil. In an age of relativism, how can Christians be taught to discern between good and evil? v. 11. πεπληρωμένοι - significance of perfect? identity of agent of passive?

for future reference (see WJLFP for "Methods and Aids for Textual Criticism").

Textual criticism is important for three situations which may or may not occur in a particular text. Conduct textual criticism when you need to (1) establish the passage's wording at points where important theological themes are being handled, (2) undergird your choice of wording when it differs from the "Pew Bible" (the version your audience normally uses), or (3) identify and settle issues raised through marginal notes in the "Pew Bible."

Obviously, any one of these areas represents an opportunity for confusion, or for you to be caught off guard by questions you are not prepared to answer. Your audience's trust in the reliability of Scripture and in your credibility as an interpreter are vital to expository preaching and teaching. Therefore, take seriously the task of clearly explaining any differences in wording from the "Pew Bible" stemming from different textual critical choices.

Raise Questions & Make Observations

This step is the heart of "Survey." As you pore over the Greek text, give yourself the freedom to raise questions and make observations as they come to mind. For example, jot down every ambiguity you wonder about (or think your audience would question), whether dealing with historical, literary, grammatical, rhetorical, or theological aspects of the text. Jot down every feature of the text that is strikingly important for its interpretation.

Although you do not want to limit your questions or observations at this stage, because of time it is helpful to develop the ability to distinguish between the more important and the less important exegetical features of the text while completing your "Survey" work. Here are two guidelines to help you focus in on the most important features.

Interpretation. Make use of the following interpretative questions in your "Survey" work to help you get at the heart of the passage's meaning:

1. *Reference:* What is being discussed in the passage?
2. *Sense:* What is being said about it?
3. *Purpose/Intent:* Why is the writer talking about this subject and saying what he does about it?

Three other supplementary questions that are helpful during Survey are: *How, When,* and *Where* will the passage's meaning (reference and sense) be realized? All observations about the passage should contribute to answering these six interpretive questions.

Meaning and significance. Your aim in brainstorming relevant questions and observations from the text is not simply to find a meaningful understanding of the truth of the passage. You should desire to grasp this truth's significance for the people of today's culture. What are the contemporary points of contact? How does this Scripture correct our culture? How is this passage *good news* for today? How will you encourage your hearers to apply this truth in their lives? What will preach from the passage, and how will it preach? What may be taught from the passage, and how could it be taught? Whenever ideas along these lines come to mind, jot them down on the "Survey" worksheet.

Survey: Resources

UBS[4]
Metzger, *Textual Commentary.*
"Pew Bible"
"Greek Reading/Translation" and "Mechanical Layout" worksheets

Survey: Procedure

As you work through the procedure outlined, use your "Mechanical Layout" and a "Survey" worksheet (available at WJLFP; cf. fig. 5.1) to raise the following types of questions or make the following observations. With practice, your goal is to complete this step in thirty minutes.

I. Survey
    A. **Deal with Textual Critical Matters** (see WJLFP for "Method and Aids for Textual Criticism"):
        1. *Identify textual problems.* Look at the marginal notes of the "Pew Bible," i.e., the translation(s) that the majority of your congregation uses. Do the notes identify any alternatives in wording for any verses in your passage? Record briefly the alternatives and identify which reading the "Pew Bible" follows. Check the textual critical apparatus of UBS[4] for any other text problems the editors deemed significant. Record the alternatives.
        2. *Read Metzger's Textual Commentary on the text problem.* It gives the reasoning of the committee that decided the wording for the UBS[4]. In brief, they judged based on these criteria (see UBS[4] Introduction for further explanation):
            a. *Manuscript evidence.* Identify the reading supported by the oldest, best, and most widely distributed texts (normally text families: Alexandrian-א, A, B plus Western-D, it).

b. *Scribal practices.* Copyists tended to lengthen texts and smooth out difficulties, so prefer the "shorter and more difficult reading."
  c. *Author's style and vocabulary.* The reading which best fits the immediate context and the writer's practice elsewhere is preferred.
 3. *Decide the probable original wording.* Using the criteria cited above, choose the most probable original reading and explain your choice. Your choice will more often than not agree with UBS⁴. In any case, it should be the reading which gives the criteria their due weight. Your choice should also enable you to explain the origin of the other readings. Record your reasoning and decision on the textual critical portion of the "Survey" worksheet.
B. **Raise Questions & Make Observations**: Be curious, discriminating, comprehensive, and creative in your approach to the passage. In a "free floating" manner, jot down things as they come to your mind. Always keep in mind your audience and anticipate the questions they will have. Address the five areas below to help you be appropriately comprehensive. The issues raised related to any of these areas, especially the questions, will be items you will study during the subsequent exegetical steps.
 1. *Historical.*
  a. *Introductory matters.* Read through the passage again and ask yourself what additional information about the author, his original audience, and the circumstances which occasioned the book would be helpful in interpreting your passage.
  b. *Historical-Cultural-Religious details.* Record any terms, ideas, or practices from ancient geography, history, culture, or religion you don't understand (see chapter six).
 2. *Literary.*
  a. *Literary genre.* Decide on the literary genre of your passage (see chapters six through eight): epistle; historical narrative or prophetic-apocalyptic. Identify any subgenre units present in the passage: forms of argumentation or ethical instruction such as deliberative speech or household codes; liturgical elements such as hymn or confession; use of the Old Testament in the New; teaching forms such as parable.
  b. *Syntax (grammar).* From your finished translation and mechanical layout, raise questions and make observations

about syntax (grammar matters; see chapter nine): Structure, Verbs, Cases, and the Rest.
   c. *Syntax (rhetorical features).* Identify rhetorical features (e.g., word absence, word order, word arrangement, word figure) which need to be analyzed (see chapter nine).
   d. *Word study.* Identify peculiar or distinctive or repeated terms, especially those of theological significance which would repay careful *word study* (see chapters ten and eleven).
3. *Theological* (See chapter twelve and thirteen).
   a. *Biblical theology.* To which parallel or contrasting themes/passages of Scripture does your passage relate?
   b. *Systematic theology.* To what central teaching of Scripture does your passage contribute?
   c. *Theological/Interpretational problems.* What theological or interpretational problems appear to be present in your passage?
   d. *Biblical Coherence.* What is your passage's place in salvation history and the progress of biblical thought?
4. *Contemporary Cultural Interpretation/Application.* Identify points of contact for communication and points of correction or need between your passage and the contemporary culture in which you preach or teach. Strategize on how your can capture the significance of the good news of the passage for the culture and how you can make application points (see chapter fourteen).
5. *Homiletical/Didactic.* Think about various ways to preach or teach this passage. Consult Hamilton, *Homiletical Handbook*, chapters seventeen through twenty-two to find those methods most appropriate to the genre and content of your passage (see fig. 15.1). Brainstorm about sermon method, subject, theme, proposition, (also interrogative, keyword, transitional sentence, if using Keyword method), main points, subpoints, and illustrations. Or brainstorm about lesson planning: logistics, audience, and objectives, and designing learning activities.

Endnotes

1. Craddock, "Commentaries," 386.

2. Ibid.

3. Baumann, *Contemporary Preaching*, 118.

Chapter 6
HISTORICAL AND LITERARY ANALYSIS

With our "Survey" questions and observations duly noted, and our curiosity about the passage primed, we begin the complex, but fascinating area of "Analysis." The multiple steps in "Analysis" could be practiced exhaustively on a passage—and to good effect. But since only four hours are allocated, your goal is to complete your "Analysis" work comprehensively (i.e., not leaving out any area), but judiciously.

Part of developing skill in "A Method for Exegesis and Exposition" is to learn to choose those features worthy of concentrated attention for a particular passage, and those which can be ignored or which need only cursory attention. For example, study of grammatical structure in order to understand the close reasoning of the doctrinal portion of Romans will yield many insights, while the same attention to connectives in a gospel narrative will not be as fruitful. In the latter material, your time is better spent concentrating on narrative plot structure in order to understand the gospel passage's storyline. Word study will not result in the same profit for all terms in a passage. Theological issues do not surface with the same rate of frequency throughout a passage, etc. Learn to train your eye to catch those challenging and significant features on which you should concentrate.

Exegesis, then, particularly in the area of "Analysis," is as much about what you won't study in a given passage as about what you will study. This is why we complete our "Finished Translation," "Mechanical Layout," and "Survey" first. For, our insights from these practices can be excellent guides for making right choices about what is important to analyze. When using "A Method for Exegesis and Exposition," your aim should always be to complete your study—not exhaustively—but comprehensively and judiciously, probing those areas which show the most promise for unlocking the meaning of the text.

Purpose of Analysis

To arrive at a clear, full and coherent meaning of a biblical passage, we must analyze it in three contexts: *historical, literary,* and *theological*.

Since Bible books were written in a particular historical setting, the more the we can understand about that setting through historical analysis, the better we will be able to comprehend the passage's message. This setting includes both the particular circumstances of the book's writing (introductory matters) and the general historical-cultural-religious background assumed by a given passage's content.

As a written document, the Greek New Testament naturally requires literary analysis to uncover the message the writer intended to convey. Our literary analysis work includes four areas of study: literary context, genre, syntax (including both grammar and rhetorical features), and word study.

Finally, since every Bible book has a divine author, we do theological analysis to uncover the message God inspired the human author to pen. Here we consider the contribution of the passage to the "whole counsel of God" (biblical theology), its contribution to Bible doctrine (systematic theology), and finally, we address any remaining theological or interpretational difficulties on which we need clarity.

Once a thorough analysis of a passage in its historical, literary, and theological context is done, we have an accurate, rich understanding of the writer's intended meaning. A preacher or teacher who diligently pursues "Analysis" will have more than enough to proclaim. This chapter will present the first steps in Analysis: Historical Analysis and Literary Analysis–Context and Genre.

Historical Analysis

Introductory Matters

The first task of "Historical Analysis" is to set your passage in its historical-cultural context (see fig. 6.1). This involves paying attention to any clues in the passage about the circumstances surrounding the writing of the book. Begin by reviewing the basic "Introductory Matters," developed during "Periodic Preparation" (see chapter sixteen and fig. 16.7). Who was the author of the book? Who was the audience? What was the occasion and purpose for the composition of the book? In the answers to these questions lies your ability to puzzle out how your passage spoke to specific needs of the first readers. For example in Phil 1:1-11, Paul refers to God completing the salvation work begun (Phil 1:6) and describes it as "the fruit of righteousness" (1:11). Are Paul's comments countering some "works-righteousness" thinking, which was creeping into the church?

Figure 6.1. **Sample Historical Analysis**

Text Phil 1:3-11

Introductory Matters

Author: Paul's heart is transparent–his great affection for them (Phil 1:7-8); he is in prison now (1:7); cut off from direct access to them.

Audience: The Philippians are strong witnesses for Christ and strong supporters of Paul (Phil 1:5)

Occasion and Purpose: His prayer may indicate some potentially weak areas: unity–he prays for love (Phil 1:9; cf. 2:1-18; 4:2-3); purity, holiness of life (1:10; cf. 3:17-21; 4:8) fruit of righteousness–are they pursuing the way of righteousness by faith or works (1:11; cf. 3:1-16)?

Clues to purpose from this passage–Thanksgiving (1:3-5) and possibly some correction in the areas of unity, purity, and righteousness by faith (1:9-11) may be Paul's purpose in writing.

Historical-Cultural-Religious Details

Caesar's household (Phil 4:22)

The term's range of meaning included two groups:

1) the immediate imperial household– Caesar's household "includes the whole of the imperial household, the meanest slaves as well as the most powerful courtiers" (Lightfoot, *Philippians*, 171).

2) the imperial civil service– "more commonly applied to imperial civil service, usually at Rome, but also throughout the empire, particularly in the imperial provinces" (ZPEB 1:683); Philo's comment (*In Flaccum* 35), "Even if Agrippa had not been a king, yet as a member of Caesar's household, did he not deserve to have some precedences and marks of honor?" is probably an instance of this usage.

Comment: Paul's witness has been fruitful even in the highest levels of Roman society. There are saints in Caesar's household.

Historical-Cultural-Religious Situation

Your second task in "Historical Analysis" is to understand as much as possible about the general historical situation as it relates to your passage (see fig. 6.1). Research any important geographical features, as well as important references to the political, socio-economic, cultural, intellectual, or religious life of ancient times. The writer and first readers held all of this cultural understanding in common, and as a result, it is sometimes assumed in the text. Cultural terms have a fairly limited range of meaning. They point to particular conditions, physical objects, institutions or practices of first century life. They refer to items or matters in the socio-economic and political as well as the intellectual and religious spheres, e.g., the phrase "Caesar's household" (Phil 4:22). The character, make-up, size, function and location of the socio-political grouping "Caesar's household" is not readily uncovered simply by concordance work.

Thus, begin by consulting secondary sources (dictionaries, encyclopedias, historical background reference works, commentaries) for basic definition of the items you want to study. A good secondary source will give primary source evidence: reference to ancient sources, antecedent or contemporaneous with the New Testament. For example, *ZPEB* (1:683) mentions first century Jewish philosopher Philo's use of "Caesar's household" in *In Flaccum* 35. As you are able, look at this use in the primary source.[1]

As you preach or teach through a book, make it a goal to grow in your understanding of "the life, events, tensions, emotion, personalities, issues, and other items that contribute to the background color of the New Testament."[2] As you see your historical-cultural understanding coming out in your sermons/lessons, you can be confident with Walter Liefeld that

> The more 'stage scenery' the preacher provides, the more easily the congregation can identify with the biblical circumstances. The more we understand the religious and intellectual currents of a situation, the better we can understand and apply the biblical message to our own day.[3]

Historical Analysis: Resources

Materials from Previous Study

"Greek Reading/Translation" worksheets for the passage
"Survey" worksheets

Texts

English Bible (NIV or ESV or NASB)
UBS[4]

Dictionaries and Specialized Reference Works

ISBE
ZPEB
NIDB
DJG
DPL
DLNT
DNTB
Carson and Moo, *Introduction to New Testament*
Finegan, *Archeology: Life of Jesus.*
Finegan, *Archeology: Christian Apostles.*
Beitzel, *Atlas of Bible Lands.*
Keener, *Bible Background Commentary.*

Commentaries

Fee, *Philippians.*
Hawthorne, *Philippians.*
Lightfoot, *Philippians.*
O'Brien, *Philippians.*
Silva, *Philippians.*

Historical Analysis: Procedure

I. Survey
II. Analysis
   A. **Historical Analysis**
      1. *Introductory Matters.* Review the basic introductory information (prepared during "Periodic Preparation," see chapter sixteen) concerning the author and audience's historical circumstances and the occasion and purpose for the work. Explain how your passage addresses specific needs in the readers' situation. Record your answer on the Introductory Matters portion of the "Historical Analysis" worksheet (See fig. 6.1 for an example and WJLFP for "Exegetical Worksheet" template).
      2. *Historical-Cultural-Religious Details.* For each detail you want to study, consult commentaries and/or background reference works (Bible dictionary, encyclopedia, reference work or Bible atlas) for a basic definitions of term(s); a description of the characteristics of the detail; and references to primary sources (ancient works) in which it is mentioned (for primary sources see Chapter 11 and WJLFP for additional materials at "In-Depth Word Study"). As you are able, consult the primary sources to see the term's usage in context. Record enough of the immediate context to give background. Comment on what knowledge of this detail contributes to your understanding of the passage's meaning. Note your finding on the Historical-Cultural-Religious Details portion of the "Historical Analysis" worksheet.

Literary Analysis (Context)

"Context is king" is a familiar principle in biblical hermeneutics. The writer's message does not come to us in isolated words, but in phrases, clauses, sentences, sentence clusters, paragraphs, and sections. In other words, the message is conveyed through words placed in context in relation to other words. In order to understand the parts (words, phrases, etc.) we must see them in relation to the whole. As we begin our literary analysis of a passage (see fig. 6.2), we will look at its *general context*. By consulting an outline of the book, we can see how our passage relates to the book as a whole. We will also focus on the passage's relation to its *immediate context*, the few paragraphs which precede and follow. The editor's punctuation helps us here. Haddon Robinson observes that there are often more clues to a passage's meaning in its immediate context than in the passage itself.[4]

Figure 6.2. **Sample Literary Analysis**

Passage **Phil 1:3-11**

Context
General Context: The passages at the beginning of the letter set the tone of joyful thanksgiving for the Philippians, as well as, signal its content through prayer concerns: love, holiness, fruitfulness (see comments and Scripture references under "Historical Analysis–Introductory Matters, fig. 6.1).

Immediate Context:
"Before" contains the standard beginning of a letter (1:1-2).

"After" the body of the letter begins with an introductory "disclosure" formula, "I want you to know." Paul informs the Philippians about his present circumstances in prison and how it has advanced the gospel (1:12-14).
Note: These "immediate context" comments were made with the aid of the epistolary genre information in chapter seven.

Genre	
New Testament Epistle _X_	Historical Narrative___
Salutation___	Narrative Analysis___
Thanksgiving _X_	
Body___	
Subgenre within Body	*Subgenre within Narrative*
Type of Argumentation	Parable Analysis___
_____	Prophetic-Apocalyptic___
Type of Ethical Instruction	Use of the OT in New ___
_____	
Formal Worship Element(s)	Prophecy ___
Intercessory prayer (1:9-11)	Prophetic-Apocalyptic ___
Use of the OT in New ___	Use of the OT in New ___
Apostolic Parousia ___	
Closing ___	

Literary Analysis (Genre)

One of the tools New Testament writers used to communicate their message was literary form and convention. In ancient times, as today, a culture would develop patterns of expression in its written communication. Cultural or literary custom determined the make-up and organization of the literary form as well as the function and meaning of its various parts. For example, today custom dictates that one begin a personal letter by noting the date and identifying the addressee, "Dear."One ends the letter by a "commitment" term, "Sincerely yours" or "Your friend," etc. and the signature of the sender. In ancient times one began a letter with the following formula: Sender's name to Addressee's name, "Greetings."

Genre analysis identifies a piece of writing's literary form or genre and its constituent elements, as well as subgenre the writer employs. It studies the purpose and function of those units and how writers use them to accomplish their own purposes.

The two main genre of the New Testament are *epistle* (Romans-Jude, 35% of the New Testament) and *historical narrative* (Matthew-Acts). The last book, Revelation, is unique combining "elements of prophecy, apocalypse, and letter."[5] The next two chapters of this book will discuss these three genre in more detail: chapter seven–epistles; chapter eight–historical narrative and prophetic/apocalyptic.

Within each of these main genre there are other subgenre, i.e., other literary conventions, which the writer may use. In epistles we find formal elements from first century worship, forms of ethical instruction, methods of argumentation and ways of appealing to authority to substantiate one's message. In the case of the New Testament, the authority quoted consistently is the Old Testament.

Within historical narrative in the Gospels and Acts, the writer will present discourse materials with their distinctive forms of argumentation including appeal to the Old Testament. And we will meet types of sayings, particularly parables. In prophetic-apocalyptic material we encounter imagery and symbols playing a large role, as well as quotes and allusions to the Old Testament.

Literary Analysis (Context & Genre): Resources

Materials from Previous Study

"Greek Reading/Translation" worksheets
"Survey" worksheets
Book outline, chart or sentence paragraph summaries and supporting notes from "Synthetic Analysis" of the book (see chapter sixteen).

HISTORICAL AND LITERARY ANALYSIS

Texts

EnglishBible (NIV or ESV or NASB)
UBS⁴

Commentaries

Fee, *Philippians*.
Hawthorne, *Philippians*.
O'Brien, *Philippians*.
Silva, *Philippians*.

Literary Analysis (Context & Genre): Procedure

I. Survey
II. Analysis
   A. Historical Analysis
   B. **Literary Analysis**
      1. *Context*
         a. *General Context*. Using a detailed outline from a commentary or one you developed during "Periodic Preparation" (see chapter sixteen), scan through the book familiarizing yourself again with its flow of thought. When you come to your passage, read it completely, then return to scanning. Note the place of your passage in the book's argument. Note down your observations on the General Context portion of the "Literary Analysis: Context/Genre" worksheet (see fig. 6.2 for an example and WJLFP for "Exegetical Worksheet" template).
         b. *Immediate Context*. Read the passage again, but this time note its connection with what immediately precedes and follows. Scan verses or paragraphs of the immediate context and answer the following questions: How does what immediately precedes prepare for your passage's content? How does your passage prepare for and relate to what follows? Note your answers on the Immediate Context portion of the "Literary Analysis: Context/Genre" worksheet.
      2. *Genre*
         a. *Identification*. Identify the main and subgenre items for genre analysis of your passage. Observations from the "Survey" worksheet, content from chapters seven and

eight, and insights from commentaries should aid you in your study. Note down on the Genre portion of your "Literary Analysis—Context and Genre" worksheet the results of your evaluation (see fig. 6.2 for an example and WJLFP for "Exegetical Worksheet" template).

b. *Analysis and evaluation.* Do genre and subgenre analysis of your passage using the appropriate procedures and worksheet as found in chapters seven and eight. See chapter seven, figures 7.6-7 for an example. You will find additional help in "Additional Genre and Literary Form Analysis Procedures" at WJLFP.

Endnotes

1. See chapter eleven and WJLFP "In-Depth Word Study" for bibliography to primary sources.

2. Liefeld, *New Testament Exposition*, 29.

3. Ibid., 31.

4. Robinson, *Biblical Preaching*, 60.

5. Carson and Moo, *Introduction to New Testament*, 716.

Chapter 7

GENRE ANALYSIS: EPISTLE

Twenty-one of the twenty-seven books in the New Testament are, to a greater or lesser extent, in the epistolary form (see figs. 7.1-2). Probably the apostle Paul was the formative influence in establishing "the letter as the primary means whereby a Christian leader communicated his authority to the Christian community."[1] The letter was a most appropriate medium to communicate the truth of God. It was viewed by the ancients as a means for friends to communicate, as a substitute for the physical presence of the sender, and as way to continue a conversation.[2] Paul and those after him took over the form and Christianized it, so that a letter's functions could promote both the acceptance of apostolic authority and the spiritual unity of apostle and church community.[3]

Ancient Letter Form

To understand the transformation of the ancient letter form into the NT letter form, we need to compare and contrast the two structures (see fig. 7.3). The ancient letter began with an opening formula[4] in which the sender and the addressee were identified and a greeting, normally χαίρειν, was expressed. The sender also stated his wish or prayers for the addressee's physical health and reported his own. The body of the letter[5] contained the message, the reason for writing it. The body began with an introductory formula: either of disclosure ("I want you to know"), request ("I request, ask") or other disposition[6] (e.g., counsel from the sender; scolding ironic rebuke—"I am amazed that"). Generally, this formula indicated to the recipient whether the sender was imparting/seeking information or requesting/ordering something. At the close of the letter there would be greetings[7] to others not named in the opening or elsewhere. Then the writer would repeat the health wish/prayer for the recipient and say goodbye.

Figure 7.1. **Epistolary Form of Pauline Letters**

	Rom	1 Cor	2 Cor	Gal	Eph
Opening	1:1-7	1:1-3	1:1-2	1:1-5	1:1-2
Thanksgiving	1:8-12	1:4-9	1:3-7 (Blessing)	1:6-10 (Rebuke)	1:3-23 (Blessing, 1:3-14)
Expression of Thanks	1:8	1:4-9	-----	-----	1:15-16
Prayer	1:9-10	-----	-----	-----	1:17-23
Body	1:13-15:33	1:10-16:12	1:8-13:10	1:11-6:10	2:1-6:22
Disclosure Formula	1:13	-----	1:8	1:11	-----
Request Formula	-----	1:10	-----	-----	-----
Other Formula	-----	-----	-----	-----	-----
Ethical Instruction	12:1-15:13	throughout	-----	5:13-6:10	4:1-6:20
Apostolic Parousia	15:14-33	4:14-21 16:5-12	13:1-10	-----	6:21-22
Closing	16:1-27	16:13-24	13:11-13	6:11-18	6:23-24
Greetings	16:3-16; 16:21-23	16:19-21	13:12	-----	-----
Benediction	16:25-27	16:23	13:13	6:18	6:24

Figure 7.1. (*continued*)

	Phil	Col	1 Thess	2 Thess
Opening	1:1-2	1:1-2	1:1	1:1-2
Thanksgiving	1:3-11	1:3-23	1:2-10	1:3-12
Expression of Thanks	1:3-6	1:3-8	1:2-5	1:3-10
Prayer	1:9-11	1:9-14	- - - - -	1:11-12
Body	1:12-4:20	1:24-4:9	2:1-5:24	2:1-3:16
Disclosure Formula	1:12	2:1	- - - - -	- - - - -
Request Formula	- - - - -	- - - - -	- - - - -	2:1-2
Other Formula	- - - - -	1:24 (Joy)	- - - - -	- - - - -
Ethical Instruction	1:27-2:18; 4:1-4:9	3:1-4:6	4:1-12; 5:12-22	3:6-15
Apostolic Parousia	2:19-30	4:7-9	2:17-3:13	3:16
Closing	4:21-23	4:10-18	5:25-28	3:17-18
Greetings	4:21-22	4:10-17	5:26	3:17
Benediction	4:23	4:18	5:28	3:18

Figure 7.1. (*continued*)

	1 Tim	2 Tim	Titus	Philemon
Opening	1:1-2	1:1-2	1:1-4	1-3
Thanksgiving	-----	1:3-5	-----	4-7
Expression of Thanks	-----	1:3-5	-----	4-5
Prayer	-----	-----	-----	6
Body	1:3-6:21a	1:6-4:18	1:5-3:14	8-22
Disclosure Formula	-----	-----	-----	-----
Request Formula	-----	-----	-----	8-10
Other Formula	1:3-4 (Compliance)	1:6 (Compliance)	1:5 (Compliance)	-----
Ethical Instruction	-----	-----	2:1-3:11	-----
Apostolic Parousia	-----	4:9-18	3:12-14	21-22
Closing	6:21b	4:19-22	3:15	23-25
Greetings	-----	4:19-21	3:15a	23-24
Benediction	6:21b	4:22	3:15b	25

Figure 7.2. **Epistolary Form of Non-Pauline Letters**

	Hebrews	James	1 Peter	2 Peter
Opening	- - - - -	1:1	1:1-2	1:1-2
Thanksgiving	- - - - -	- - - - -	1:3-9 (Blessing)	- - - - -
Body	1:1-13:17	1:2-5:20	1:10-5:11	1:3-3:16
Disclosure Formula	- - - - -	- - - - -	- - - - -	1:12
Request Formula	- - - - -	- - - - -	- - - - -	- - - - -
Other Formula	- - - - -	1:2 (Joy)	1:10	- - - - -
Ethical Instruction	throughout	throughout	throughout	chapter 2
Closing	13:18-25	- - - - -	5:12-14	3:17-18
Apostolic Parousia (equiv.)	13:18-23	- - - - -	5:12	- - - - -
Greetings	13:24	- - - - -	5:13-14a	- - - - -
Benediction	13:25	- - - - -	5:14b	3:18b

Figure 7.2. (*continued*)

	1 John	2 John	3 John	Jude
Opening	1:1-4 (Prologue)	1-3	1	1-2
Thanksgiving	-----	-----	2 (Health)	-----
Body	1:5-5:21	4-11	3-12	3-23
Disclosure Formula	-----	-----	-----	-----
Request Formula	-----	-----	-----	-----
Other Formula	1:5 (Proclamation)	4 (Joy)	3 (Joy)	3 (Writing)
Ethical Instruction	throughout	-----	-----	-----
Closing	-----	12-13	13-15	24-25
Apostolic Parousia (equiv.)	-----	12	13-15a	-----
Greetings	-----	13	15b	-----
Benediction	-----	-----	-----	24-25

Transformation via Spiritual Dimension & Apostolic Authority

Two factors unique to the early church context led to the transformation of the ancient letter form into the NT letter. First, there was the spiritual dimension of life in the Body of Christ. Christians gave verbal expression to this spiritual reality in corporate worship. And NT letters were read at church services. It is not surprising, then, that liturgical forms: benedictions, doxologies, thanksgiving and prayers, were one means by which the ancient letter was transformed into a written communication between joint heirs of the grace of God.

The second factor was apostolic authority. It stamped NT letters with a normativeness that extends beyond the original audience and occasion. The official yet familiar tone of the letters and the use of general doctrinal and ethical instruction (paraenesis) to undergird the specific occasional instructions indicate an intended scope of application wider than the original audience.

Admittedly, each New Testament letter is occasional. It was written in or in response to specific first century circumstances. Still, we need to recognize that the NT letter written by apostolic authority is normative throughout unless it explicitly limits the extent of application.

New Testament Epistle Form with Its Epistolary Genre Subunits

Opening

What, then, was the influence of these factors: spiritual dimension and normative apostolic intention, on the form of the ancient letter? See figure 7.3 for the comparison and contrast. Our discussion will use evidence from Paul's letter writing practice. The spiritual dimension is introduced at the very beginning. The apostolic writer designates himself and his readers with spiritual titles. The simple greeting is replaced by a benediction of "grace and peace" (Semitic greeting) which is further Christianized as the divine source receives explicit mention ("... from God our Father"; cf. Phil 1:2).

Thanksgiving

The apostolic writer replaces the pagan wish/prayer for physical health with a thanksgiving to God for the spiritual health of the recipients as manifested by their faithfulness in given religious (virtuous) activities. Often an intercessory prayer or prayer report is attached with the request that these virtues increase even more until Christ's return.

Figure 7.3. **A Comparison and Contrast of the Epistolary Form of the Ancient Letter and the New Testament Letter**

Ancient Letter[8]		New Testament Letter (Philippians)	
OPENING		OPENING	
Addressor	Irenaeus	Addressor	Paul & Timothy, servants of Christ Jesus (1:1)
Addressee	To Apollinarius his dearest brother	Addressee	To all the saints in Christ Jesus at Philippi (1:1)
Greetings	Many greetings (πολλὰ χαίρειν)	Greeting	Grace and peace to you from God our Father and the Lord Jesus Christ (1:2) (χάρις ὑμῖν καὶ εἰρήνη ἀπὸ θεοῦ.)
		THANKSGIVING	
Wish/Prayer	I pray continually for your health (διὰ παντὸς εὔχομαι) and I myself am well	Thanksgiving	I thank my God... always in every prayer of mine for you (1:3-6) (Εὐχαριστῶ τῷ θεῷ μου... πάντοτε ἐν πάσῃ δεήσει)
		Intercession	And this I pray, that your love may abound (1:9-11) (καὶ τοῦτο προσεύχομαι ἵνα ἡ ἀγάπη ὑμῶν... περισσεύῃ)

GENRE ANALYSIS: EPISTLE

Figure 7.3 *(continued)*

Ancient Letter[8]		New Testament Letter (Philippians)	
BODY		**BODY**	
Introductory Formula		Introductory Formula	
(Disclosure)	I wish you to know (γινώσκειν σε θέλω)	(Disclosure) Now I want you to know, brothers (1:12) (Γινώσκειν δὲ ὑμᾶς βούλομαι, ἀδελφοί,)	
		Paraenesis	Rejoice in the Lord... Do not be anxious... whatever is true... noble... think about such things (4:1-9)
		Apostolic Parousia	But I hope in the Lord to send Timothy (2:19-30)
CLOSING		**CLOSING**	
Greetings	Many salutations to your wife... (ἀσπάζομαι πολλὰ)	Greetings: Greet every saint in Christ Jesus. The brothers who are with me send greetings (4:21-22) (Ἀσπάσασθε πάντα ἅγιον ἐν Χριστῷ Ἰησοῦ. ἀσπάζονται ὑμᾶς οἱ σὺν ἐμοὶ ἀδελφοί)	
Phys. health wish/prayer	"Before all else I pray you may have health... unharmed by the evil eye"		
Farewell	Goodbye (ἔρρωσο)	Benediction	The grace of the Lord Jesus Christ be with your spirit (4:23)

Body

Body proper and ethical instruction. The body of most NT letters is quite lengthy and covers more than one topic. Introductory formulae (e.g., "disclosure" and "request") are used to introduce the body. They may also function within the body of the letter at various points to signal a transition from one topic to the next.[9] Also present are "confidence" formulae, (expressing the author's conviction that the readers will act in a certain way, Gal 5:10; Rom 15:14). We may also find "expressions of joy" as the basis for a request or commendation (Phil 4:10). We often find "compliance statements" referring to instructions already or not yet implemented (1 Tim 1:3; 2 Tim 1:6; Titus 1:5). One standard element in Paul's body is ethical instruction. When it is general ethical teaching (paraenesis), it may be taken from apostolic tradition. Paul uses it as a way "to bring the full weight of the Christian apostolic tradition to bear upon the more specific claims of the letter . . . ."[10] The section on "Other Subgenres" which follows notes the various forms paraenesis can take.

Apostolic parousia. The closing portion of the body of the NT letter, especially in Paul, has the same themes.[11] The writer repeats the occasion for writing and seeks to secure the compliance with any requests or commands he has given (often introduced by a verb of writing; e.g., Rom 15:15-33; 2 Cor 13:1-10; cf. Heb 13:18-23; 1 Pet 5:12; 1 John 5:13). He also lays the basis for future correspondence. Paul does this by stating his confidence that the readers will carry out his directives (Rom 15:14; Phlm 21). He will describe his or his emissary's plans to visit the readers (e.g., Rom 15:22-32; 1 Cor 16:5-12; 2 Cor 12:14-13:4; Eph 6:21-22; Phil 2:19-30; Col 4:7-9; cf. Heb 13:18-19; 2 John 12; 3 John 13-14). This announcement of his next visit indicates to the readers his intention that they treat the letter as a substitute for his apostolic presence.[12] The body concludes with a peace-wish.

Closing

The closing itself has some elements which deserve mention. There are *final notes* which might include such items as instructions, warnings, commendations, and requests for prayer. There are *personal greetings* which serve to maintain the author's relationship with the readers and/or to make explicit that relationship by identifying readers he knew (Phil 4:21-22). The command to greet with a holy kiss is often linked to a grace-benediction (e.g., Rom 16:16; 1 Cor 16:20b, 23; 2 Cor 13:12-13; 1 Thess 5:26, 28; 1 Pet 5:13-14). This may well reflect the communal worship setting in which the letter was read. Finally, in the letter's closing there are indications of the methods of composition (Rom 16:22; Gal 6:11) and, in Paul's writings, a validation of the letter's authenticity by signing it in his own hand (1 Cor 16:21; Gal 6:11; 2 Thess 3:17).[13] The closing ends with a *grace-benediction* ("Peace be with you . . . Grace be with you"; e.g., Phil 4:23).

It should be noted that the closing of the letter is also altered in line with the spiritual dimension of the epistle. The wish/prayer for physical health and a simple goodbye are replaced by a benediction, which prays God's grace for the recipients. Other liturgical elements such as the "holy kiss" command indicate the worship setting in which the writer intends the letter be heard.

These transformed elements also point again to the normative apostolic intention of the work, for an apostle calls down God's grace upon his people and intercedes for them, that they will be given strength to keep on doing what they ought to be doing.

Perspectives on Interpreting the Epistle as a Literary Form

When examining the standard epistolary formulae (elements which comprise the letter form, e.g., salutation, thanksgiving, body, apostolic parousia, closing), remember that these were primarily tools for the writer to communicate his relational disposition toward his readers (cf. fig. 7.4 for further information on form/function/background).[14] At their heart they are social gestures. For example, Mullins calls the greeting formula ("Greet . . . greet . . . etc.) an epistolary wave of the hand communicating emotion, but no intellectual content.[15] Mullins' point, that here the formal relationship of writer and reader is in the foreground, is well taken. But this assessment must not lead to two false interpretive conclusions. First, we need to avoid thinking that the New Testament writer, when using a common literary convention, really didn't mean what he was saying. For example, we should not conclude that, because Paul's statement that he thanks God every time he remembers the Philippians in prayer is part of a standard literary convention, a thanksgiving, that he did not mean it literally. Given the general tone and content of his letters, we can be confident that Paul was consistently and passionately praying for the churches.

Second, we need to avoid thinking that we can glean nothing from the epistolary formulae about the writer's purpose. Rather, the epistolary formulae give us information we may take at face value and which, especially in the case of the introductory thanksgiving, contribute to our understanding of the writer's purpose.

Figure 7.4. Form/Function/Background of Major Literary Units & Subunits for the New Testament Epistle

FORM	FUNCTION	BACKGROUND

OPENING
 Addressor:
   X with authoritative designation
 Addressee:
   Y with spiritual designation (e.g., saints, church, called, sanctified, beloved)
 Greeting:
   Wish (usually χάρις and εἰρήνη)
   Recipient
   Divine Source
	NT writer conveys his authority but also that both sender and recipient are spiritually united by means of God's grace.	Ancient Letter, but Christianized
		
		 Ancient Letter, but Christianized
		
		 LXX cf. Judg 19:20 Replaced Ancient Letter's greeting (χαίρειν)

THANKSGIVING
 Thanksgiving:
   εὐχαριστέω + Ptc + purpose clause
   or
   εὐχαριστέω + ὅτι causal + ὥστε subord. to ὅτι
   or
   variants on thanksgiving: ἐγὼ χάριν (constructions with χαρά words)
 	
 or
 	
 Blessing:
   εὐλογητός
   (or μακάριος)
	Fourfold:
	 1) Epistolary: introduces and presents the main themes of the letter.
	 2) Pastoral: evidences deep pastoral and apostolic concern
	 3) Didactic: recalls previous teaching
	 4) Paraenetic: expressly or implicitly indicates behavior desired for recipients
		Primitive Christian liturgical style related to the Jewish and OT *hodayot* and *beracha*.
		
		 The Thanksgiving replaces ancient letter's physical health wish/prayer and health report.

Figure 7.4. (*continued*)

FORM	FUNCTION	BACKGROUND
THANKSGIVING (*continued*) Intercession: prayer verb in indicative or participle (τοῦτο προσεύχομαι) (This is a wish prayer) content of prayer: purpose or object clause mention of one prayed for (optional: eschatological climax; closing)	Thanksgiving underscores recipient's welfare in its spiritual and Christian dimension. Then follows a prayer that they will abound more and more in Christian virtues. The prayer often previews the letter's message, announcing what Paul expects of his recipients. It often closes with a reference to Christ's second coming, the historical end point and goal of maturing in Christ.	Linking Thanksgiving and Prayer is probably Jewish liturgical practice based on OT (cf. Ps 9:1,13,19; 59:1, 16-17; 69:1, 20; 71:4, 22; 144:7, 10; 1 Chr 16:7-36). Since according to the canons of ancient letter style the reader is the only one addressed directly, all prayers in NT letters are either in the form of "wish-prayers." ("May God do__") or "prayer reports" (I pray that . ..)

Figure 7.4. (*continued*)

FORM	FUNCTION	BACKGROUND
BODY Introductory Formulas	Indicates writer's and reader's relationship to each other and to the letter's subject matter.	Ancient Letter
Disclosure: θέλω/βούλομαι + person addressed + noetic verb (inf. - οὐ ἀγνοεῖν; γινώσκειν) + ὅτι information clause	Indicates body's main or initial purpose is to impart information.	
Request: Background + petition verb (παρακαλέω; ἐρωτάω) + divine authority (prep. phrase) + desired action (ἵνα clause; infinitive; or imperative)	Indicates body's main or initial purpose is to request something. Background gives necessary evidence for assuring a favorable response to the request.	
Compliance: Intro. Conj. (Καθώς, ὡς, καθότι) + verb of instruction (ἐντέλλομαι) + object of instruction (περί) + statement about fulfillment of instruction or confidence in addressee	Indicates body's main or initial purpose is to remind, with apostolic authority, that instructions previously given still need to be carried out.	

Figure 7.4. (*continued*)

FORM	FUNCTION	BACKGROUND
BODY (cont.) Introductory Formulas		
Joy: Verb or noun (χαίρω, χαρά) + adv. of magnitude + statement about arrival of letter or hearing + object which was heard (ὅτι clause) + vocative	Expresses relief at addressees' welfare or significance of letter to sender.	apostolic relation to churches or subordinate co-workers
Rebuke: θαυμάζω + ὅτι clause	Indicates a scolding for undesirable behavior.	
Ethical Instruction (see description in text)	Provides guidance for behavior in general or specific areas	Authoritative apostolic role and responsibility
Apostolic Parousia (see description in text)	Sets out apostle's plans for next personal contact.	Ancient Letter
Peace Wish (see description in text)	Invokes God's peace upon the readers.	Ancient Letter

Figure 7.4. (*continued*)

FORM	FUNCTION	BACKGROUND
CLOSING	Final communication, reiterates letter's theme, brings to fore worship setting of letter's reception	Ancient Letter heavily influenced by Early Christian worship practices
Final Notes: instructions, warnings, commendations, and requests for prayer	Indicates apostle's final and sometimes strongest concerns.	Ancient Letter with Christianizing elaboration
Greetings Greeting verb (ἀσπάζεσθαι, sometimes noun ἀσπασμός) + person doing the greeting + person greeted (optional: πολλά with verb; personalizing κατ' ὄνομα; personal description of person greeted; identifying phrases attached to person doing greeting)	An epistolary gesture intended to maintain a bond of friendship.	
Benediction Wish Divine Source (sometimes omitted being assumed in the Christian meaning of χάρις) Recipients (sometimes a doxology substitutes for a benediction)	A wish-prayer requesting God's grace to be with the recipients.	LXX cf. Num 6:24-26 Replaces closing Wish/Prayer and Farewell (ἔρρωσο)

Other Subgenres Within Epistles

New Testament writers also used more specialized literary forms, subgenre, within the basic structure of the NT letter. For example, in doctrinal sections, they employed various devices from ancient rhetorical practices to strengthen and further their "Argumentation."[16] Their "Ethical Instruction" used various features common in philosophical treatises of ancient times. Since the letters were written to the church and read within a church worship context, it is quite natural to find "Formal Elements from First Century Worship" woven into the letters' contents. A sensitive study of these three important subgenre will bring into greater relief the writer's purposes and emphases, increasing our understanding of the communication process as it was practiced in that ancient setting.

Argumentation

General patterns of persuasion. The ancients, schooled in rhetoric, the art of persuasion, learned three speech forms, each with a particular purpose for a particular setting. The *judicial* speech court would make an accusation or a defense/apology in the law court. The *deliberative* speech sought to persuade or dissuade the assembly considering a future action. The *epideictic* speech praised or blamed someone before a gathering. *Judicial* and *deliberative* speeches have the same basic form:[17]

- *Proem* or *Exordium*–an introduction acknowledging the audience and the situation (e.g., 2 Cor 1:3-7 [judicial speech]).
- *Narration* and/or *Proposition*–a *narration* giving background and a *proposition* succinctly stating the thesis of the argument (1:8–2:13; *deliberative* speeches often lack *narration*).
- *Proof*–the part of the argument providing evidence and reasoning to support the thesis (3:1–7:1).
- *Refutatio* (in *judicial* speech)–the part of the argument anticipating and negating opposing points of view.
- *Epilogue*–summary and encouragement to embrace the thesis (7:2-16).

The *epideictic* speech is simpler in form. It contains a *proem* or *exordium* and an *epilogue*. In between there is a body made up of a series of colorful laudatory or blameworthy statements about the person or topic under discussion. Some examples of these types of persuasive argumentation in Paul's letters are *judicial* speech: 1 Corinthians 9; 2 Cor 1–7, 10–13; possibly

Galatians; *deliberative* speech: 1 Corinthians 1, 15; 2 Cor 8–9; possibly Galatians; and *epideictic* speech: Romans; 1 Corinthians 13.

Types of evidence to support a proposition. In ancient rhetoric, there were four main types of evidence appealed to as proof, the first two of which are used consistently in NT epistolary argumentation:

- *Paradeigma* proper–historical examples (e.g., 1 Cor 9:1-6).
- written authorities–mainly Scripture and apostolic tradition (e.g., 1 Cor 9:8-10).
- Analogy–invented examples taken from nature or normal social practice (types of people, normal events, regular natural processes; e.g., 1 Cor 9:7, 24-25).
- *Mythos* (fables)–examples from the imaginative world created by fiction.

Argumentation moves. In addition to the creative employment of rhetorical features (see chapter nine), the NT letter writer could pursue the following "moves" in argumentation to persuade his readers:

- Rhetorical questions–serving a variety of functions, such questions draw the read/hearer into the argument as the writer either takes a further step in the argument (Rom 8:31) or seeks to affirm or deny the assertion in the question (3:29; 6:1, 15).
- Arguing the "opposite"–showing the absurdity of the opposing point of view in order to establish ones thesis (1 Cor 15:12-19).
- Arguing from "the lesser to the greater"–showing that if something is true in an insignificant case, it must be true in a more significant case and vice versa (Rom 5:6-10).
- Making emotional appeals (Gal 4:12-20).[18]

Diatribe. Scholars have proposed that a special style of reasoning, the diatribe—derived from Cynic and Stoic pedagogical tradition—appears particularly in James and Romans.[19] It is a style which assumes a dialogical teaching process and the presence of wrong thinking and behavior which needs to be corrected. According to Stowers, those engaged in wrong thinking and behavior are not enemies of the writer or speaker, but actually his students. So in NT letters, the diatribe style "is designed for those who have already made the basic commitment and who need to be instructed in the implications of the gospel for their lives and in what it means to be God's people."[20] The NT writer uses three devices from diatribe.

Address to imaginary interlocutor. The imaginary interlocutor device is an address to a fictitious person (ὦ ἄνθρωπε) with an indicting question, statement or retort ("you are without excuse," Rom 2:1). A series of rhetorical questions follows, which uncovers the interlocutor's lack of perception, wrong opinions or erroneous logic ("and do you suppose this, O man, . . .," 2:3). Other instances of the imaginary interlocutor address in Romans include Rom 2:17-24 and 9:19-21. Although an imaginary person is addressed, he is real or true in the sense that he is a personification of actual wrong thinking or wrong behavior present among the readers. So in "diatribal address to the interlocutor there is a calculated duality or ambiguity by which the teacher could speak indirectly to his students and at the same time vigorously censure students whose vices corresponded to the imaginary interlocutor's."[21]

Interaction with objections or false conclusions. The second device involves interaction with the interlocutor's objections to, or false conclusions about, the writer's argument (e.g., Rom 6:1-2). After an "introductory formula": Τί οὖν, "What . . . then?" there follows the "objection" or "false conclusion," often in the form of a question (e.g., "Are we to continue in sin that grace might abound?"). Then, there is a response. This involves a "rejection formula" (μὴ γένοιτο [Optative Mood], "May it never be!") followed by the "reason" why the objection or conclusion is wrong ("How shall we who died to sin still live in it?"). Instances in Romans of objections and false conclusions presented and answered are Rom 3:1, 3, 5, 9, 27, 31; 4:1, 2; 6:1, 15; 7:7, 13; 9:14, 19; 11:1, 19. The function of this device is to allow for the expression of the addressee-respondent's half of the diatribe's dialogical element and to indict false thinking and behavior.

Dialogical exchange and objection with its exemplum. Examples of this third aspect of diatribe style are Rom 3:27–4:2 and 4:2-25. This aspect involves a series of questions and responses by which the writer (teacher) leads his readers (students) to the conclusion he envisions for the argument. ("Where then is boasting? It is excluded. By what kind of law? Of works? No, but through a law of faith . . . ," 3:27). Sometimes an objection to the writer's thesis or his interpretation of an authoritative example, *exemplum*, is answered by an exegesis of and appeal to that example:

"What then shall we say that Abraham, our forefather according to the flesh has found? For if Abraham was justified by works, he has become something to boast about; but not before God. For what does the Scripture say? . . . " (4:1-3a).

Ethical Instruction

New Testament letters appear to contain two types of ethical instruction. The first is "occasional," i.e., it addresses specific problems that have arisen in the Christian community to which the letter is sent (e.g., lawsuits among believers, 1 Cor 6:1-11; a warning against idleness, 2 Thess 3:6-15). The second is "general," labeled by scholars as paraenesis.[22] This type includes exhortations to depart from evil, seek good, pursue brotherly love, cultivate the higher virtues. These exhortations "do not appear to be immediately motivated by a question or specific problem of the community addressed. They appear instead to be directed to the church as a whole for the purpose of general edification."[23]

Scholars have identified five types of paraenesis for which there is some external evidence: moral maxims, vice and virtue lists, *topoi*, summary advice, and household codes.

Moral Maxims. Instructions quite unrelated to each other are often clustered together in no apparent pattern (1 Thess 5:14-22; cf. Proverbs),

Vice & Virtue Lists. Intertestamental Judaism[24] had its lists of vices and virtues, which commonly warned about three areas: idolatry, fornication, and greed (*T. Dan* 5:5-7; cf. D 4:17). Though not as consistently present, unbrotherly behavior, which plays a major role in Paul's lists, is also mentioned (Sir 28:10; 30:24; cf. Prov 27:4).

The form of the list has no distinctive features except that sometimes positive and negative lists are paired (Gal 5:19-21; 22-23); the list's word order may involves word play (e.g., Rom 1:29, μεστοὺς φθόνου φόνου; 1:31, ἀσυνέτους ἀσυνθέτους); and the list has an attached statement warning of God's judgment for those who practice such vices (Gal 5:21; Eph 5:5; cf. Wis 14:27-30; 1QS 4:9-14; *2 Enoch* 10).

The function of the *vice* lists is descriptive (in which case threats, or condemnation or a contrast with Christian believers is attached). In the case of a *virtues* list its function is paraenetic. A moral code of behavior is being preached. Doty's "list of lists of vices and virtues"[25] includes the following:

Vices: Rom 1:29-31; 13:13; 1 Cor 5:10-11; 6:9-10; 2 Cor 6:14; Gal 5:19-21; Col 3:5-8; Eph 4:31-32; 5:3-4; 1 Tim 1:9-10; 6:4; 2 Tim 3:2-4; 1 Pet 4:3 (cf. Rev 9:20-21; 21:8; 22:15; Mark 7:21-22).

Virtues: Gal 5:22-23; 2 Cor 6:6-7; Phil 4:8; Col 3:12-15; Eph.6:14-17; 1 Tim 3:2-3; 6:11; Titus 1:7-8; Jas 3:17; 2 Pet 1:5-8 (cf. Matt 5:3-12).

Topos. A *topos* is "a self contained unit in paraenetic style which treats a topic of proper thought or action, a virtue or vice . . . a moral essay in miniature."[26] The three essential elements in a *topos* paragraph (e.g., Rom 13:8-10) are:

- "injunction" ("Let no debt remain outstanding, except the continuing debt to love one another," 13:8a)
- "reason" ("*for* he who loves his fellow man has fulfilled the law," 13:8b)
- "discussion" (the commandments' content, 13:9-10).

Analogous situation and refutation are optional elements.[27]

The background of the *topos* form can be found both in Greek ethical thought (Isocrates, *To Demonicus* 22-23, 32, 41) and Jewish Intertestamental literature (Sir 31:25-30; *T. Jud.* 16).

Its function is, as Mullins proposes,

> What the Topos supplied was a set of conditions which measured the adequacy of the answers which the user made to common questions. Anyone using the Topos would give a clear indication of the behavior required, would give a reason why that behavior was required, and would indicate one or more consequences which might be expected from such behavior. Its function, therefore, was to assure the speaker or writer that he had given the kind of answer to the question which his audience would be most likely to accept as valid.[28]

Although the presence of identifiable *topoi* in the New Testament continues to be questioned,[29] scholars do suggest they may be found in James; 1 Peter; 1 John 4:1-6; Rom 13:1-5, 8-10, 11-14; 1 Thess 4:1-8, 9-12; 5:1-11; cf. Matt 5:43-47.

Summary Advice. The writer often brings together the themes of the letter as a whole and takes the form of a statement of encouragement (Phil 4:4-9).

Household Codes. In both ancient Greek (Aristotle, *Politics* 1253b, 1259b, 1278b; Xenophon, *Oeconomicus*), Stoic (Plutarch, *Liberal Education* 10B; 13D; cf. Seneca, *Epistle* 94; cf. Neopythagorian Callicratides, *On the Happiness of Households* 105-6) and Jewish (Philo, *Decalogue* 165) ethical discourse there are lists of duties which "free adult males" have within the household and society.[30] Scholars have labeled these "household codes" or "housetables." A similar form occurs in the New Testament at Eph 5:21–6:9; Col 3:18–4:1; 1 Tim 6:1-2; Titus 2:9-10;1 Pet 2:13–3:7 (cf. churchtables 1 Tim 2:8-15; 5:1-2; Titus 2:1-8). The New Testament passages give instructions on proper behavior for husbands and wives, parents and children, masters and slaves, church members and church leaders, citizens and political rulers.

The form[31] for the instruction includes three elements:

- "person addressed according to his role" ("Wives . . . ," Eph. 5:22)
- "command" ("be subordinate to your own husbands," 5:22)
- "motive"—reason, why the command should be obeyed ("as is fitting to the Lord, for the husband is the head of the wife . . . ," 5:22-23).

There are several distinctive characteristics of the New Testament housetables.[32] Whereas ancient Greek and Stoic housetables address only the "free adult male" with his duties, in the New Testament wives, children and slaves are addressed equally with husbands, fathers, and masters. Thus, NT housetables see both those in leadership and subordinate roles as ethically responsible. New Testament housetables often qualify their commands by "in the Lord" (Eph 6:1). The Christian rationale is not alignment with the cosmic order, as the Stoics would urge, but reference to the good will of God who protects the weak, the unimportant, the unfree. Indeed, living out one's responsibilities in these relationships, "as to the Lord/Christ" (5:22; 6:5) shows that love and service to God is the basis for all life's relationships. And the "in/as to the Lord" qualifier, also indicates that divine service goes on in all of life.

Formal Elements from First Century Worship

Though scholars have labored long and hard in exacting research to identify elements of early church worship (confessions, doxologies, hymns, prayers) embedded in the New Testament, the lack of contemporaneous, direct, external evidence makes it difficult to arrive at certainty in these matters.[33] As with each of these literary forms, subjectivity can take over too easily when there is no objective standard of comparison from extra-biblical sources. We present here only the most obvious clues for identifying the following liturgical formulae in the Epistles: confessions, doxologies, hymns, and intercessory prayers.

Confessions. Early church worship confessions "represented the agreement or consensus in which the Christian community was united, that core of essential conviction or belief to which Christians subscribed and openly testified."[34] The key words which introduce confessional material in the New Testament are ὁμολογέω and its cognates (Rom 10:9-10; Phil 2:11; 1 John 4:2-3, 15; 2 John 7) and its antonym ἀρνέομαι and its cognates (1 John 2:22; Jude 4).

Doxologies. Doxologies give praise to God either by declaring Him blessed (εὐλογητός, Rom 1:25; 9:5; 2 Cor 11:31; Eph 1:3) or by applying glory to him (δόξα, Rom 11:36; Gal. 1:5; Phil 4:20). Doxologies are often interjections attached to the name of God in the text according to traditional Jewish practice. The very thought of God the Father or Son awakens praise in the New Testament writer's heart which he immediately expresses (e.g., "... and worshipped and serve the creature rather than the Creator—who is blessed forever. Amen." Rom 1:25).

Hymns. This form is the most difficult to identify and analyze. Except in passages where there is an explicit introductory formula and/or the edited text identifies the hymn's lines (strophe; e.g., Eph 5:14; 1 Tim 3:16; 2 Tim 2:11-13), one is left with only internal criteria for hymn identification:

- opened by relative pronoun and continued by participles
- pronounced rhythmic quality
- conscious parallelism
- rare terms or elevated style
- concluding statements summarize point of hymn
- content extraneous to flow of thought.[35]

A brief listing of possible hymnic material in the New Testament, according to Doty,[36] includes the following:

Sacramental Hymns:	Eph 2:19-22 (14-18?); 5:14; Titus 3:1-7; Rom 6:1-11 (?); Col 2:9-15.
Initiatory Hymns:	Eph 2:4-10; Rom 3:23-25; Titus 2:11-14; 3:3-7; 2 Tim 1:9-10 (Eph 1:3-12; Col 1:12-20).
Confessional Hymns:	1 Tim 6:11-16; 2 Tim 2:11-13; Col 3:16; Eph 5:19; Heb 13:15.
Christological Hymns:	Heb 1:2-4; 5:5; 7:1-3; Col 1:15-20; Phil 2:6-11; 1 Pet 1:18-20; 2:21-24; 3:18-22; 1 Tim 3:16.
Hymnlike Meditations:	Eph 1:3-14; Rom 8:31-39; 1 Corinthians 13 (12:31–14:1?).
Scriptural Centos:	Rom 9:33; 1 Pet 2:6-7.

Hymns can be analyzed by identifying the literary structures which are present. Because New Testament poetry developed out of the tradition of the Old Testament, it must be remembered that lines or couplets rhyme not by sound, but by meaning.[37] Parallelism may be

- "synonymous," two lines or sets of lines say the same thing (2 Tim 2:11-12, verse eleven. "If we *die* with him, we will also *live with him*" and verse twelve a – "If we *endure*, we shall *reign with him*")
- "antithetical," two lines or sets of lines say opposite things (1 Tim 3:16: "was seen by *angels*. . . was preached among the *nations*")
- "synthetic," two or three lines build on one another, usually synonymously, to complete a thought or come to a climax (Eph 5:14, "Wake up, O sleeper/and rise from the dead/and Christ will shine on you").

Intercessory prayers. Such prayers are the most common in Paul's letters. They follow two basic forms: the "wish-prayer" ("May God do_") and the "prayer report" ("I pray that __"). These two oblique forms of praying result from the ancient letter convention that the only the readers should be addressed directly in correspondence.

The background for such prayers is the Old Testament, especially the Psalms (e.g., "wish-prayers," Ps 20:1-5; 1 Kgs 8:57-61; 2 Chr 30:18-19). Wiles notes that such prayers follow regular patterns.[38]

"Wish Prayers" include the following elements:
- God addressed and described by various attributes
- verb (one or more, usually in optative mood)
- noun or pronoun of the one benefited
- "additional benefit" in purpose (ἵνα, εἰς τό), or additional clause joined by καί, or adjectival or prepositional phrase.

"Prayer Reports" include the following elements:
- Verb of praying: ἐντυγχάνω, προσεύχομαι, εὔχομαι, δέομαι, συναγωνίζομαι, μνείαν ποιεῖν ἐπὶ τῶν προσευχῶν, μνημονεύειν, δεήσει ἐπιποθέω.
- prepositional phrase or pronoun to indicate one prayed for
- purpose (ἵνα) or object clause (ὅτι) to give the substance of the prayer.

Frequently found in epistolary greetings, thanksgivings and closing benedictions, intercessory prayers can also be found throughout the body of the letter (e.g., "wish prayer," Rom 15:5, 13; 1 Thess 5:23; cf. 2 Tim 1:16, 18; 2:25 (4:16b); Heb 13:20-21; "prayer report," Rom 9:3; 10:1; 2 Cor 9:14; 13:7, 9b; Eph 3:14-19; cf. prayer reports as part of an epistle's opening thanksgiving).

Genre Analysis: Epistle–Resources

Materials from Previous Study

"Mechanical Layout" worksheet
"Survey" worksheet
"Literary Analysis—Context/Genre" worksheet

Reference Works

Bailey and Vander Broek, *Literary Forms*.
DNTB
DPL or *DLNT*

Commentaries on Philippians

Fee, *Philippians*.
Hawthorne, *Philippians*.
O'Brien, *Philippians*.
Silva, *Philippians*.

Genre Analysis: Epistle–Procedure

I. Survey
II. Analysis
   A. Historical Analysis
   B Literary Analysis
      1. Context
      2. *Genre analysis: epistle*
         a. *Epistolary genre subunit and components.*
            1) *Identification.* Identify the "epistolary genre subunit" and components in your passage. Use the "Genre Analysis: Epistle" worksheet (see example on fig. 7.5; see WJLFP for "Exegetical Worksheets" template), charts and descriptions in this chapter (see figs. 7.1-2, 4), and

commentaries to aid in filling out the reference column of the section which applies to your passage.
2) *Analysis.* Analyze the "epistolary genre subunit" and components present in your passage. Using the Form/Function/Background Chart of Major Literary Units and Subunits of the New Testament Epistle (see fig. 7.4), observe how the expression of the subunit in your passage is similar or different from the basic model of the subunit.
3) *Evaluation.* Evaluate the writer's use of the subunit and components.
- What do these similarities or differences tell you about how the form is functioning?
- What do they tell you about the writer's emphases?
- How does his use of the form and his emphases further his overall purpose in writing and help you understand the message of the passage?

Note down your findings on the back of the "Genre Analysis: Epistle" worksheet (see fig. 7.7 for a sample).

c. *Other subgenre items within epistles.*
1) *Identification.* Identify any "other subgenre items" present in your passage. Do this with the aid of "Genre Analysis: Epistle" worksheet (see WJLFP "Exegetical Worksheets" for template), descriptions in this chapter, and commentaries. Fill out the reference column of the section which applies to your passage on the "Genre Analysis: Epistle" worksheet and/or use the back of the worksheet (see example on fig. 7.6).
2) *Analysis and evaluation.* Analyze and evaluate the writer's use of the "subgenre item."
- How is the form functioning in promoting the writer's purpose?
- What do they tell you about the writer's emphases?
- What do your findings contribute to your understanding of the passage?

Note down your findings on the back of the "Genre Analysis: Epistle" worksheet. (See Figure 7.8 for a sample.)

Fig. 7.5. **Sample Genre Analysis: Epistle**

Book and Passage: Phil 1:3-11			
Major Literary Unit	Ref.	Subunits	Ref.
Opening		Addressor	
		Addressees	
		Greeting	
Thanksgiving	1:3-11	Expression of Thanks	1:3-8
		Verb of Thanks	1:3a
		Time Reference	1:3b-4
		Object of Thanks	1:3b
		Cause of Thanks	1:5-8
		Prayer	1:9-11
		Prayer Verb	1:9a
		Purpose/Content	1:9b-10a
		Eschatological Climax	1:10b-11
Body		Introductory Formula	
		Ethical Instructions	
		Apostolic Parousia: writing/emissary/visit units through peace wish	
Closing		Final Notes	
		Personal Greetings	
		Grace-Benediction	

Fig. 7.6. **Sample Genre Analysis: Epistle–Other Subgenre**

Book and Passage: Phil 3:2-11			
Major Literary Unit	Ref.	Subunits	Ref.
Opening		Addressor	
		Addressees	
		Greeting	
Thanksgiving	1:3-11	Expression of Thanks	
		Verb of Thanks	
		Time Reference	
		Object of Thanks	
		Cause of Thanks	
		Prayer	
		Prayer Verb	
		Purpose/Content	
		Eschatological Climax	
Body		Introductory Formula Ethical Instructions a topos--"Injunction"-3:2; "Reason"-3:3; "Discussion"-3:4-11 Apostolic Parousia: writing/emissary/visit units through peace wish	3:2-11
Closing		Final Notes	
		Personal Greetings	
		Grace-Benediction	

Figure 7.7. **Sample Genre Analysis: Epistle–Evaluation of Epistolary Genre Subunits**

Phil 1:3-11

This section is a thanksgiving period and contains a thanksgiving (1:3-8) and an intercessory prayer (1:9-11).

The thanksgiving follows the form of εὐχαριστέω + participles. It lacks a purpose clause probably because Paul emphasizes his confidence in God and in them that they are going to persevere in their Christian lives. This implied paraenetic function is accompanied by an epistolary one. He is thankful for their "fellowship in the gospel," which points to the financial support he writes to recognize (Phil. 4:10-20). And there is a pastoral function. He expresses his affectionate and positive relationship with them.

The intercessory prayer (1:9-11) contains all the elements including the optional ones: eschatological climax (1:10b) and closing (1:11b). It announces important themes of the letter: growing in love (2:1-18), moral discernment (3:17-21; 4:8), and life of righteousness by faith (3:1-11).

Figure 7.8. **Genre Analysis: Epistle–Evaluation of Other Subgenre Items**

Phil 3:2-11

This section is a *topos* on the topic of the nature of true right standing before God. It begins with an "injunction," warning command, to watch out for false teachers, the Judaizers (3:2) who depend on the badges of ethnic identity and religious performance to give them right standing with God.

The topos then proceeds briefly to give the "reason" for the warning (3:3) by making the positive contention that those who "boast in Christ" already have the right standing. They are the true circumcision, since they bring their worship by the Spirit of God. They place no confidence in human effort or attainment.

Paul then makes a transition easily into a "discussion" of the nature of true right standing with God, by pointing to his personal history and testimony as a study in contrasts (3:4-11). He could claim all the badges of Jewish ethnic identity and performance and even outstrip the Judaizers (3:4-6). Yet, he has counted all these "loss" for the surpassing worth of knowing Christ Jesus his Lord, which is having a true right standing, not from the law based on performance, but from God based on faith (3:7-9). Knowing Christ in suffering and resurrection power is central to true right standing with God (3:10-11).

Endnotes

1. White, "Paul and Letter Tradition," 444.

2. Doty, *Letters in Primitive Christianity*, 11-12; Wilder (*Early Christian Rhetoric*, 39) notes that the ancients would cast compositions for general publication in epistolary form as a way of personalizing them.

3. White, "Paul and Letter Tradition," 437; Wilder, *Early Christian Rhetoric*, 42.

4. Doty, *Letters in Primitive Christianity*, 14.

5. White, *Body of Greek Letter*; cf. Weima, "Letters, Graeco-Roman," 642-43.

6. White, "Introductory Formulae," 91-97. For more information on such formulae see Sanders, " Transition from Opening to Body," 348-62; Mullins, "Disclosure as Literary Form," 44-50; Mullins, "Formulas in Epistles," 380-90; Mullins, "Petition as Literary Form," 46-54.

7. Mullins, "Greeting as Form," 418-26.

8. Barrett, *New Testament Background*, 29; Hunt and Edgar, *Select Papyri* 1:306-7; Closing: Physical Health Wish/Prayer from Barrett, *New Testament Background*, 28; Hunt and Edgar, *Select Papyri* 1:296-97.

9. Sanders, "Transition from Opening to Body," 349; cf. Mullins, "Petition as Literary Form," 46-54.

10. White, "Paul and Letter Tradition," 441.

11. Mullins ("Visit Talk," 350-58) correctly labels these features as themes and not literary formulae because they do not have consistently recurring formal elements. Robert W. Funk ("Apostolic Parousia," 249-68) and his student John Lee White (*Body of Greek Letter*, 160-62; "Paul and Letter Tradition," 440-41) see identifiable epistolary formulae for this portion of the ancient and New Testament letter's body.

12. cf. White, "Paul and Letter Tradition," 440.

13. Doty, *Letters in Primitive Christianity*, 39-42; cf. Weima, *Neglected Endings*.

14. Mullins, "Formulas in Letters," 388.

15. Mullins, "Greeting as Form," 418.

16. Bailey and Vander Broek, Literary Forms, 31-38.

17. Ibid., 34-35.

18. See ibid., 32-33, for types of evidence and argumentation moves.

19. Stowers (*Diatribe and Romans*, 84, 179) identifies diatribe elements elsewhere in Paul as follows: Imaginary interlocutor addressed: 1 Cor. 4:7; 7:2; 15:36; Objections and False Conclusions: 1 Cor. 15:35; Gal. 2:17, 3:21; possibly 1 Cor. 6:12, 13. Ropes (*James*, 10-16) notes diatribe features in James, e.g., the Imaginary interlocutor: Jas 1:18; 5:13.

20. Stowers, *Diatribe and Romans*, 183.

21. Stowers, *Diatribe and Romans*, 110.

22. Bradley, "*Topos* in Pauline Paraenesis," 239-40; Funk, *Language, Hermeneutic*, 254-55; cf. Thompson, "Teaching/Paraenesis," 922-23.

23. Bradley, "*Topos* in Pauline Parenesis," 240.

24. Schweizer, "Traditional Ethical Patterns, 195-97.

25. Doty, *Letters in Primitive Christianity*, 51.

26. Funk, *Language, Hermeneutic*, 255.

27. Mullins, "Topos as Form," 547.

28. Ibid., 546-47.

29. Brunt, "More on *Topos*," 495-500.

30. Schweizer, "Traditional Ethical Patterns," 201-2; Balch, *Let Wives Be Submissive*, 2-10; Lührmann, "Neutestamentliche Haustafeln," 83-97; Keener, "Family and Household," 353.

31. Lillie, "Pauline House-tables," 180.

32. Schweizer, "Traditional Ethical Patterns," 202-4.

33. Lampe ("Evidence for Early Creeds," 359) rightly concludes: "The direct evidence is almost wholly internal, and this fact warns the reader of the New Testament that this is a sphere in which there are very few fixed points of reference; what is known of first-century Jewish practice is a guide on one side, and the worship, creeds and catechetical homilies of the Church of the second century may serve to some extent to elucidate the apostolic literature in retrospect, but it is dangerous to rely too heavily on external evidence of this kind, partly because in parts (such as the *Didache*) it is notoriously difficult to date, partly because there is a temptation to assume too easily that the developed liturgical forms which we encounter in the latter part of the second and the early third century may safely be read back into the New Testament literature."

34. Neufeld, *Earliest Christian Confessions*, 20; cf. Porter, "Creeds and Hymns," 232.

35. Doty, *Letters in Primitive Christianity*, 61; cf. Sanders, *New Testament Christological Hymns*; Martin, *Carmen Christi*.

36. Doty, *Letters in Primitive Christianity*, 61-62; cf. W. Porter, "Creeds and Hymns," 231-36.

37. For example, Sanders' (*New Testament Christological Hymns*, 10) analysis of the structure of Phil 2:6-11; cf. "Poetry, Hebrew," 3:829-38.

38. Wiles, *Paul's Intercessory Prayers*, 29, 157.

Chapter 8

GENRE ANALYSIS: HISTORICAL NARRATIVE & PROPHETIC-APOCALYPTIC

Twenty-one New Testament books are letters (Romans–Jude), but the remaining six books comprise two thirds of its content. Five of those books, Matthew — Acts, are historical narrative, and one of them, Revelation, is prophetic-apocalyptic. Different literary genres call for different strategies in analysis. This chapter will set out those strategies.

Postmoderns have a fascination with "story" and picture, as well as subversive strategies in communication. Thus, it is especially important to understand how narrative and prophetic-apocalyptic, as well as, parable genre work, if the preacher or teacher is to effectively use them to communicate God's message to postmoderns.

Historical Narrative

Great stretches of Scripture are stories, true historically, but stories nonetheless. In the New Testament, the Gospels and Acts are primarily historical narrative. Because they are historical they should be studied with standard procedures of historical criticism to test for accuracy and authenticity (see "Additional Genre and Literary Form Analysis Procedures" at WJLFP). Because they are narrative we should also analyze them according to the standard categories of literary criticism. This chapter will address historical narrative analysis from the standpoint of literary criticism.

Historical narrative analysis can be applied to an entire gospel, Acts as a whole, or to portions of a book where a series of narratives have a unity (e.g., Mark 2:1--3:6; Acts 13-14). Most often, however, you will conduct this kind of analysis in relation to individual episodes that you plan to use for preaching or teaching (e.g., Mark 2:1-12; 2:23-28). The categories to investigate are parameters, plot, point of view, characters, and features (see Figure 8.1).[1]

Figure 8.1. **Genre Analysis: Historical Narrative–Overview**

1. *Parameters:* The boundaries of a particular episode or scene within an episode; it is indicated by a particular time and place designation.

2. *Plot:*
   a. *Progression*

   BEGINNING

   1) *Exposition:* "Lay it out," time, place, local color, participants.

   2) *Inciting Moment:* "Get something going," the planned and predictable is broken up.

   3) *Developing Conflict:* "Keep the heat on," situation intensifies or deteriorates depending on the point of view.

   MIDDLE

   4) *Climax:* "Knot it all up proper," everything comes to a head/bring in contradictions and add all sorts of tangles until confrontation is inevitable.

   5) *Denouement:* "Loosen it," a crucial event happens which makes resolution possible; one sees a way out.

   END

   6) *Final Suspense:* "Keep untangling," work out details of a resolution.

   7) *Conclusion:* "Wrap it up," bring story to some sort of decent or indecent end.

   b. *Pace:* The relation between length of time in telling narrative and length of time of actual events; retarding of pace indicates emphasis.

Figure 8.1. (*continued*)

3. *Point of View (Narration)*
   a. *Character*

	POINT OF VIEW	
NARRATOR	Internal Analysis of Events	Outside Observation of Events
As character in the story	1. Main character tells his own story	2. Minor character tells main character's story
Not as a character in the story	4. Analytic or omniscient author tells story	3. Author tells story as observer

   b. *Planes*
      1) *Spatial*–identifies with one character or jumps from scene to scene.
      2) *Temporal*–tells the story chronologically or freely interrupts with flashback or flash forward.
      3) *Psychological*–does or does not tell the thoughts and emotions in hearts and minds of the characters.
      4) *Ideological/Theological*–gives evaluations, estimates, analyses directly or indirectly from God's point of view (salvation historical perspective); *Implied Reader* (the ideal audience) provides the ideal response to the narrative.
4. *Characters*
   a. *Details*: normally spare; significant when present.
   b. *Number and Relationships*: usually two or three per scene with God (or Christ in the Gospels) as one; often contrasting pairs.
   c. *Types*: "agent," no personality, just moves the action along; "flat," one idea or quality, or "round," complex in temperament and motivation; less predictable, more real.
5. *Features*
   a. *Dialogue*: main message or point of view of passage often in speech of main character; when introduced, reveals character of speaker; differences in stylized repetition give clues to interpretation.
   b. *Stylistic Items*: plot twists, characters' ignorance or misunderstanding vs. reader's information, rhetorical features–repetition, omission, inclusion, chiasm, symbolism, irony– as clues to writer's intentions.

Parameters

The NT writer will use a particular time and/or place designation to indicate the boundaries of a particular episode or a scene within an episode. In Mark 2:23-28, the time and place markers are very general: "And it happened on one of the sabbaths, he was passing through grainfields" (2:23). Still they function to indicate the start of a distinct episode. Mark 3:1 with its place marker, "And he came again into the synagogue," shows one episode is over and another is beginning.

Plot

Progression. Plot is the heart of narrative. It is the ordered sequence of events and characters in their dialogue and action which forms a completed whole and achieves certain emotional or artistic effects.[2] Identifying the parts of a plot's movement and then observing how the writer frames them is one way we can discern his theological interpretation of the historical events he is reporting.

In the simplest of terms, a story has a beginning, middle, and end. Robert Longacre has studied story telling in a variety of cultures and arrived at a standard seven step plot sequence which can be placed within this general framework.[3]

- *Setting.* At the "Beginning," the narrator will take some time to give the story's "setting": its time, place, participants, local color. In Mark 2:23-28, the setting or exposition is brief, giving the time, place and participants: On the Sabbath Jesus and the disciples pass through grainfields (Mark 2:23a).
- *Inciting moment.* Stories capture and hold the hearer's interest by presenting a conflict which needs to be resolved. The next plot step is the initial presentation of the conflict, or the "inciting moment." The planned and predictable is broken up by words or deeds. In Mark 2:23-28 this is the moment the disciples break a Sabbath law by working—"harvesting and threshing" grain to eat it (2:23b).
- *Developing conflict.* From the "Beginning" to the "Middle" high point of the plot, the storyteller keeps the heat on. The situation intensifies. In Mark 2:23-28, the Pharisees' remonstrating with Jesus serves this function (2:24).
- *Climax.* The first of two central pivotal steps in the "Middle" of the plot, the "climax" is where everything comes to a head. All the tangles and contradictions that can be introduced are

present. The story is so knotted up that there seems no way forward. Confrontation is inevitable. In the confrontation between Jesus and the Pharisees, his response to them in which he cites the Davidic precedent of eating the consecrated shewbread is the climax (Mark 2:25-26). Old Testament precedent has been set over against Pharisaic application of Old Testament law.
- *Denouement.* The second pivotal step in the "Middle" is crucial, for it makes resolution possible. One can see a way out. In the Mark two interpretation and authority struggle, Jesus speaks a word which declares the Sabbath's purpose and the authority of the Son of Man over it (Mark 2:27-28). If one accepts Jesus' authoritative interpretation of the Sabbath's purpose ("made for man") and accepts his position in relation to the Sabbath ("Son of Man is Lord of the Sabbath"), there is a way out. The disciples' actions can be reconciled with Old Testament law. And the Pharisee's application of that law is seen to be not in keeping with the true purpose of the Sabbath.
- *Final Suspense.* The "End" of the story commences with the working out of the details of this resolution (e.g., in Mark 2:1-12, the paralytic's taking up of his mat and going out before the whole crowd, 1:12a).
- *Conclusion.* Normally, the "End" section brings the story to some sort of decent or indecent end (e.g., in Mark 2:1-12, "all are amazed and glorify God," 2:12b). Note that Mark 2:23-28 lacks the last two steps. The unresolved conflict of Jesus with the Pharisees will continue throughout the Gospel's larger plot.

Pace. A narrator can also use time to show the relative importance of various events by expanding or contracting the time devoted to them in the story. For example, for Mark as a whole, 36 percent is devoted to the last week—indeed the last hours—of Jesus' life. This shows the great importance of these events to the writer. The standard for judging the nature of narrative time in a given episode is whether the narrator takes less, more, or the same time to narrate the events as it took for the events to occur. This is the difference between *narrative time* and *historical time*. In Mark 2:23-28 the inciting moment and the development of conflict (vv. 23-24) are given less time than it took for them to occur, especially if the imperfect tense (ἔλεγον, Mark 2:24) indicates the continuous questioning by the Pharisees. Jesus' reply which comprises the rest of the narrative takes the same time it would have taken to occur.

Point of View (Narration)

Character of Narrator's Point of View. Every narrative is narrated by someone. He may be a character in the story, as is the case in the "we passages" in Acts 16:10-17; 20:5-15, 21:1-18, 27:1--28:16, although this is not the case for most New Testament writings. The degree to which the narrator provides an analysis of the events he describes indicates the character of his narrator's "point of view." Does he limit himself to outside observation of events? Or, does he provide internal analysis of the events, explaining the thoughts, feelings, and motives of the characters (his own or other characters), as if from an omniscient stance? The narrator in the Gospels is not a character in the story, but provides internal analysis of events. He tells the story as an omniscient, analytic narrator.

Planes of Point of View. The writer communicates his point of view and the type of response he desires from his audience through certain angles of vision we will call "planes of point of view."

- *Spatial.* The narrator will either identify with one character and tell the story from his position in the narrative. Or, he may choose to adopt the position of a different character from episode to episode. In the Gospels, Jesus is the character from whose position the story is consistently told. In Mark, though John the Baptist is the initial spatial focus (Mark 1:1-8), very quickly the spatial focus shifts to Jesus in each episode (1:9, 12-13, 14, 16, 21, 29, 35, 40).
- *Temporal.* The narrator may tell his story chronologically, in topical order, or with flashback or flash forward. Because of the nature of plot development, the assumption is that events are reported chronologically unless the author explicitly indicates otherwise. Order of presentation is probably more significant when dealing with a series of episodes than with an individual episode. For example, it is a common place in Gospels criticism to see Matthew's arrangement of perikopes or episodes as "demonstrably topical" in chapters eight and nine (a series of miracles), when compared with the Gospel of Mark. Any observation like this, however, needs to be tested continually by the explicit statements of the text. Acts 11:19, for example, through a brief flashback, picks up a strand of the narrative not told in Acts 8:1, 4. This shows a conscious awareness of some topical arrangement.
- *Psychological.* The narrator will either tell or not tell the thoughts and emotions in the minds and hearts of the characters. What

he does reveal, especially from an omniscient, analytical stance, will be a key to the purposes of his story. So, in Mark 2:6, 8, the objection to Jesus' declaration that a man's sins are forgiven is lodged in the hearts of the Pharisees.

- *Ideological/Theological Plane*. The narrator will give evaluations, estimates, analyses directly or indirectly from God's point of view. That is, he will bring a salvation historical perspective to bear on the events he presents. In Mark 2:23-28, the narrator will make an explicit evaluation of the Pharisees' accusations against the disciples through Jesus' response. In it Jesus sanctions the disciples' Sabbath practice–eating to satisfy hunger– in the light of Jesus' authority as Messiah, David's son, for he acts as his father did. Further he appeals to his authority as Son of Man and to the Sabbath's purpose: man's benefit (2:25-27).

This "plane of point of view" also involves the narrator's signaling to his readers the "ideal response" to what they are reading. He does this through his approval of certain reactions to the main characters in the story. Those who give the "ideal response" are the *implied readers*, the "ideal audience." There is no explicitly signaled implied reader response in the Mark 2:23-28 passage, but in the last verse of Mark 2:1-12, we see the author prompting the desired response to the healing of the paralytic by noting the crowd's reaction ("This amazed everyone and they praised God").

Characters

The description and development of characters is the fourth element in the literary analysis of narrative.

Details. Normally biblical narrative is pretty spare with regard to details describing characters. When they do occur, they are normally significant to the character's role. In Mark 2:23-28, the only detailed description of a character's action is Jesus' disciples' activity of "harvesting" and "threshing" grain with their hands, which Pharisees interpret as working on the Sabbath.

Number and Relationships. In any biblical episode or scene, the number of characters is usually limited to two or three, with God (or Christ in the Gospels) being one of them. Often the characters occur in contrasting pairs. So, in Mark 2:23-28, three characters appear: Jesus' disciples, the Pharisees, and Jesus. The contrasting pairs are two opposing interpreters of the Law: Jesus versus the Pharisees.

Types. Three types of characters populate biblical narrative. The "agent" is the most colorless. He has no personality, but simply moves the action along. The disciples in Mark 2:23-28 seem to fulfill this role. A "flat" character embodies one idea or quality. The Pharisees in their opposition to the disciples embody one idea: a casuistical interpretation and application of Sabbath keeping. "Round" characters are complex in temperament and motivation. They are less predictable and more real. Jesus, in his astonishing claims to authority over the Sabbath, is the most "rounded" in the narrative.

Features

Dialogue. Biblical narrative often progresses as much by conversation as it does by action. The *main message* or point of view of a passage is often in the speech of the main character. This is obvious from our Mark 2:23-28 sample. Jesus' response, which comprises the bulk of the narrative (2:25-28), gives the authoritative interpretation of the purpose of the Sabbath and the guiding principles for Sabbath practice. Dialogue often reveals the *character* of the speaker. So, the Pharisees put into words a judgmental, casuistical approach to Sabbath practice (2:24). *Stylized repetition* in discourse often gives clues to interpretation. For example, Jesus' encounter with the desperate, yet somewhat skeptical, father of an epileptic boy, underscores through repetition, both the issue of Jesus' authority and ability, and the necessity of faith: "If you are able" (twice in 9:22-23); "all things are possible to the one who believes . . . I believe, help my unbelief" (9:23-24).

Stylistic items. Through *plot twist*, through pitting the character's *misunderstanding* or *ignorance* against what the narrator has revealed to the reader, through rhetorical features, such as *repetition, omission, inclusion, chiasm, symbolism,* and *irony* (see chapter nine), the narrator will give further indication of his intentions.

A narrator will use misunderstanding as a way to judge an action. In the Mark 2:23-28, the author reports the Pharisee's misunderstanding of the disciples' action. This leads to Jesus' response and explanation which corrects the Pharisees' misunderstanding. In Luke 22:35-37, Jesus instructs his disciples to arm themselves in the future. They respond, "See, Lord, here are two swords." Jesus replies with an ironical statement: "That is enough" (22:38). In this way Luke indicates that the "sword" statement was not intended primarily as an instruction about defense but about the change in times when the Son of Man is absent and the world opposes the church. John consistently uses symbolism and imagery throughout his narrative and at points interprets it. For example, he uses the phrase "lifted up" to picture the crucifixion and its saving significance. "Just as Moses lifted up the snake in the desert, so the Son of Man must be lifted up, that everyone who believes in him may have eternal life" (John 3:14-15).

Parable: A Subgenre within Historical Narrative

Within the historical narrative of the Gospels, there is one subgenre that was so customary with Jesus that it deserves special attention. Whether a pithy epigram or an extended story, Jesus' parables are a distinctive and powerful characteristic of his teaching.

Definition and "Point(s) of Comparison" Paradigm

A parable is a figure of speech which communicates by comparison in order to overcome an obstacle in communication and evoke a decisive response (see fig. 8.2). The "point(s) of comparison" paradigm for understanding parables is

A	is like	B	because of	C
Spiritual Reality		Earthly Illustration		Common Quality

The main challenge in interpreting a parable is to try to correctly identify and accurately understand the intended significance of all the elements in this paradigm. The NT writer does not always explicitly explain all the elements. For example, what is the "common quality" salt and Christians share (Matt 5:13)? Preservative power? Flavoring function? What "spiritual reality" does Jesus point to when he warns: "Do not cast your pearls before swine" (Matt 7:6)?

Historical Setting

Another challenge is to identify the circumstances in which and to which the parable was spoken. What was the obstacle in communication Jesus was trying to overcome? What was the decision he desired? The NT writer often assumes, rather than explains, historical and cultural factors which are key to answering these questions. An exception that proves this rule is Mark's explanatory comments in Mark 7:3-4.

Figure 8.2. Subgenre Analysis: Parable–Overview

Definition: A parable is a figure of speech which communicates by comparison in order to overcome an obstacle in communication and evoke a decisive response.

"Point(s) of Comparison" Paradigm:

A	is like	B	because of	C
Spiritual Reality		*Earthly Illustration*		*Common Quality*

Types:
1. Proverb - a pithy saying, often enigmatic or ironic.
2. Metaphor - a saying which affirms that one thing is another and suppresses the common quality.
3. Simile - a saying which uses "like, as" and may or may not give the common quality.
4. Similitude - a typical situation or event used for comparison.
5. Parable - an interesting particular situation.
6. Illustration - an invented story used as an example.
7. Allegory - a story in which many elements stand for spiritual realities.

Parable Analysis

A. The "Jesus" Context
   1. Historical Setting: Since Jesus spoke the parables to specific people at specific times in his ministry, studying the original historical setting is essential.
      a. *When* in the course of his ministry, as well as in the course of immediate events, did Jesus speak it?
      b. *Where* did he present it? What is the relation of physical surroundings to elements in the parable?
      c. *To whom* did he say it? What attitude did the audience have to Jesus' ministry and the coming of the kingdom? Did they show in their attitudes or level of understanding an obstacle to communication?
      d. *Why* did he say it? What controversy gave rise to it?
      e. *What* parable details from *first century culture* need to be explained in order for them to be understandable? Give explanations using

Figure 8.2 (*continued*)

> > Bible background resources. Note: This step may have already been completed under "Historical Analysis: Historical-Cultural-Religious Details."
> > f. *So What*? What results issued from his statement of it?
> 2. The Parable's Function
>   a. *Classify* the parabolic saying according to *type*.
>   b. What are the *point(s) of comparison* which Jesus uses to drive home the truth? Use Jesus' *interpretation* of the parable to help you identify the elements of the point(s) of comparison in the figurative saying:
>   A=spiritual reality
>   B=earthly illustration
>   C=common quality.
>   c. How does the parable *persuasively communicate*? As appropriate, identify and comment on *plot development*: exposition, inciting moment, developing conflict, climax, denouement, final suspense, conclusion and/or *rhetorical devices*, such as, contrast, irony, hyperbole.
>   d. What kind of *application* does he make and what kind of *response* does he expect?
>   e. What *contribution* does the parable make to Jesus' teaching?

B. The Evangelist's Context: How did the gospel writer use the parable to further his own theological purposes? (see "Additional Genre and Literary Form Analysis Procedures" at WJLFP.)

C. The Contemporary Context: Since a parable is intended to evoke a decisive response, no analysis is complete without thinking about Application to today. This will usually take place during the "Interpretation/Application" stage of exegesis (see chapter fourteen) and may use the following questions:
> 1. What is the main point(s) of the parable? State in the form of principle(s).
> 2. What in the needs, aspirations, understandings, or circumstances of the contemporary church and world is similar to the situation to which the parable speaks?
> 3. How may the parable be applied to today? What form would the decisive response to Jesus' message take today?

Types of Parables

A parable may be a *proverb*, a short pithy saying, often enigmatic or ironic. For example, "For whoever has, to him it shall be given; and whoever does not have, even what he has shall be taken away from him" (Mark 4:25). It may be a *metaphor*, a saying which asserts that one thing is another and suppresses the common quality (Matt 5:14). A *simile* will use the word "like" in the assertion and may or may not explicitly name the common quality (1 Pet 5:8). A *similitude* is a typical situation or event used for comparison (Matt 13:33, "The kingdom of heaven is like . . . "). A *parable,* i.e., as a particular type of parabolic saying, is an interesting, particular situation relevant to the point of a teaching lesson (Luke 15:11-32). An *illustration* is an invented story used as an example (10:25-37). An *allegory* is a story in which many elements stand for spiritual realities (8:4-15).

Parable Analysis

When we seek to analyze a parable of any type, we must consider three different contexts, two ancient and one contemporary. We examine the " Jesus Context," i.e., what is the historical setting and function of the parable within our Lord's ministry and teaching activity? We can also examine the "Evangelist's Context," i.e., how did the Gospel writer/evangelist use the parable to further his own theological purposes? Finally, we can consider the "Contemporary Context," i.e., what is the main point of the parable and how does it apply to us today? (see fig. 8.2 for an overview of all three contexts.)

Because of its time extensive nature, researching the "Evangelist's Context" will not be a normal part of your immediate preparation. But it could be part of "Periodic Preparation–In depth Study" (see "Additional Genre and Literary Form Analysis Procedures" at WJLFP for more information on redaction criticism). Consideration of the "Contemporary Context" occurs at the "Interpretation/Application" phase of exegesis (see chapter fourteen). Hence, in the information below, we address only the "Jesus Context," particularly, "Historical Setting" and the "Parable's Function."

Historical setting. If parables are concerned with communicating truth to persons who are experiencing some obstacle in receiving the communication, then the more we can reconstruct the setting in which Jesus spoke the parable, the better we can understand the parable's function and message. To do this we must ask some basic historical questions:

- *When?* We need to identify "when" in the course of Jesus' ministry, including in the immediately surrounding events, Jesus told the parable. For example, Jesus was on the way to Jerusalem toward the end of his ministry when He told the parable of the Prodigal Son (Luke 15:11-32). Prior to giving this parable, he had repeatedly warned the Pharisees that God would shut out of the kingdom those who had been invited into it, but refused the invitation. But—by his grace—sinners would enter (13:22-30; 14:15-24). The story of the Prodigal was a dramatic follow-up designed to drive home the implications of that point.
- *Where?* It is also important to know "where" Jesus told a parable, especially if the surroundings reinforce the details of the story. Jesus tells the story of the parable of the Sower out of doors along the shore of the Sea of Galilee (Matt 13:1-2). Depending on the time of the year, an actual sower could have been in sight of Jesus' audience.
- *To whom?* We then need to study the person or group "to whom" Jesus addressed the parable. If we can identify the audience's view of Jesus' ministry and the coming of the kingdom, we may be able to detect the obstacle to communication which Jesus is confronting. In particular, we need to be alert to whether the obstacle is a *matter of attitude* (heart issue) or *level of understanding* (head issue). For example, in the introduction of the parables of Luke fifteen, Luke tells us plainly that Jesus is responding to a *matter of attitude*: the Pharisees' and scribes' grumbling at Jesus' welcoming of tax collectors and sinners (Luke 15:1-3).
- *Why?* Looking at the same factor from Jesus' perspective, we need to ask ourselves "why" he told a particular parable. What controversy gave rise to it? So, Jesus tells the parable of the Prodigal Son, to help the Pharisees see from God's perspective their brooding, unloving spirit in contrast to Jesus' joyous welcoming spirit toward those who come to him in repentance.
- *What?* Our understanding of the parables will be greatly enhanced the more we grasp the cultural setting in which they were spoken. Diligently investigate not only the "historical setting" of the parable, but also the "cultural background" of the individual details. It will help you present the parable's message clearly and forcefully in your preaching and teaching. For example, concerning the parable of the Prodigal Son, was it common for a son to ask for and receive an inheritance before

the father's death? Culturally, what was the extent of shame associated with caring for swine and eating their food? The robe, the ring, the fattened calf were all positive responses to the son's return, but what did they mean in that culture? Answers to questions like these will bring the message alive for twenty-first century listeners.
- *So what?* The results or "so what" of the parable are not always reported. We don't know how the Pharisees responded to Jesus' parables in Luke fifteen. But in Luke 20:19, Luke does tell us that as a result of the parable of the Wicked Tenants, the Jewish leaders determined to arrest him as soon as possible.

Parable's function. With the historical setting investigated, turn your attention to looking at the literary analysis of the parable itself.

- *Type.* Determine the "type" of parable, whether proverb, metaphor, simile, similitude, parable, illustration, or allegory.
- *Point(s) of comparison.* Now identify the "point(s) of comparison," the complex(es) of "spiritual reality" and "earthly illustration" and "common quality" which Jesus uses to drive home his point. One of the main areas of hermeneutical dispute in the last few centuries is whether a parable has one point of comparison or numerous points of comparison. Incorrect allegorical interpretation of parables in the ancient and medieval church has led many modern interpreters to assert that each parable has only one point of comparison, one message. While the proper starting point for interpretation should be looking for only one figurative complex (A=B because of C), we must let Jesus enlighten us concerning the number of points being made in any given instance.

  Another common mistake in parable interpretation is to so concentrate on the identification of the "spiritual reality" and the "earthly illustration," that you pay no attention to the "common quality" between them. It is the common quality—often an action— which is always Jesus' main point. For example, in the parable of the Prodigal Son, identifying the father as God, the prodigal son as the sinner, and the elder brother as the Pharisees is only the beginning of interpretation. It is the attitudes and actions of the three characters, as they interact with each other, in which Jesus and Luke are really interested. The humble repentance of the Prodigal, and the Father's gracious waiting and celebration of the Prodigal's return, as contrasted with the objections of the elder brother, are at the heart of Jesus' message. The similarity between the elder brother's attitude and the attitude of the Pharisees is what Jesus wanted his listeners to grasp.

- *Persuasive communication.* Next you want to trace out how the parable "persuasively communicates" its message. If the parable is in the form of a story, this is a good time to do "narrative analysis," particularly *plot progression* (setting, inciting moment, developing conflict, etc.; see fig. 8.1). For example, note the development of conflict in the parable of the Good Samaritan (Luke 10:30-32). Two persons from the religious establishment, whom one would expect to act in compassion "pass by on the other side." Jesus pushes the story to its climax and denouement when an ethnic enemy arrives. No one expects the Samaritan to help, but he does (10:33-34).

  With most types of parables, be on the look out for "subversive twists" to overcome attitudinal obstacles in communication, i.e., rhetorical devices such as contrast, irony, hyperbole. Jesus frequently makes his points strongly through contrast—invitees refusing to come to a banquet, while those not originally invited come when asked (Luke 14:15-24) and hyperbole—how easy is it for a camel to squeeze through a needle's eye? (18:25).

- *Application.* All of Jesus' parables were meant to prompt the audience to make a decision. Sometimes Jesus expressly indicates an "application," relating the kind of "response" he expects. The close of the parable of the Good Samaritan is an excellent example of this, given in the form of a question and an imperative.

"Which of these three do you think proved to be a neighbor to the man who fell into the robber's hands?" And he said, "The one who showed mercy toward him." And Jesus said to him, "Go and do the same" (Luke 10:36-37).

- *Contribution to Jesus' teaching.* As a final step, ask yourself what "contribution" this particular parable's message makes to Jesus' teaching as a whole. What would be missing from our understanding if it were absent?

Other Subgenre within Historical Narrative

Other subgenre in historical narrative, particularly in discourse portions, come to light when we use rhetorical criticism. For, it helps us assess the types of sayings materials and forms of argumentation in Jesus' teaching in the Synoptic Gospels, as well as the distinctive features of Jesus' discourse in John.[4] Comparing the speeches in Acts against synagogue preaching practices and Graeco-Roman rhetorical instruction can help the student see more clearly the persuasive "moves" the characters were using (e.g., Acts 2, 13, 24, and 26).[5]

"Use of the Old Testament in the New" is a subgenre used throughout the New Testament. This phenomenon repays careful study during times of "Periodic Preparation."[6] New Testament writers appeal to the Old Testament either as foundational in the progress of revelation or as authoritative divine revelation. They use it on four *levels*: quotation (Luke 22:37/Isa 53:12), allusion (Luke 22:20/LXXJer 38:31), idea (δόξα, Luke 24:26), imitated style (καὶ ἐγένετο, Luke 7:11; 8:1/LXX1 Kgdms 4:18; 5:4).

The quotation's *text form*, wording compared with LXX and MT, and *introductory formula*, give clues about the NT writer's view and appropriation of the OT. The *function* of the OT quotation may be to point to Christo-centric soteriological fulfillment, whether prophetic (Acts 2:17-21/Joel 2:28-32) or apologetic (Acts 2:25-28/Ps 16:8-11) or typological (1 Cor 10:6-7/Exod 32:6). Or it may function as an authority for theology (Acts 15:15-17/Amos 9:11-12) or practice (Jas 2:8/Lev 19:18).

Scholars differ on the NT writers' *interpretational method* for appropriating the Old Testament use in the New Testament. In particular, they debate where the NT writers found "the locus of meaning" with regard to the Old Testament text, a key to understanding how they made that appropriation. Is it in the OT writer ("full human intent")? Or, may there be a divine intent which goes beyond the OT writer's intent (*sensus plenior*)? Or, should we look to the NT writer's use of Jewish hermeneutical methods (midrash pesher) as part of the historical progress of revelation? Or, is the NT writer working according to a typological or analogical correspondence? In that case, the NT writer's interpretation, as part of canonical Scripture, should be given the priority in arriving at the OT text's meaning? The first and last of these understandings best accounts for the practice of writers of divinely authoritative Scripture.

Genre Analysis (Historical Narrative): Resources

Materials from Previous Study

"Survey" worksheet
"Literary Analysis–Context/Genre" worksheet

Greek is Great Gain

Historical Analysis
- Descriptions in chapter eight
- Figure 8.1

Parable
- Descriptions in chapter eight
- Figure 8.2

Gospels Study Resources

Aland, *Synopsis Quattuor Evangeliorum.*
Blomberg, *Jesus and Gospels.*
Thomas and Gundry, eds. *Harmony of the Gospels.*

Commentaries on Mark

France, *Mark.*
Guelich, *Mark 1–8:26.*
Evans, *Mark 8:27–16:20.*
Gundry, *Mark.*

Commentaries on Luke

Bock, *Luke 1:1–9:50, 9:51–24:53.*
Green, *Luke.*
Marshall, *Luke.*

Special Works on Parables and Jesus' Teaching

Bailey, *Poet and Peasant.*
Bailey and Vander Broeck, *Literary Forms.*
Blomberg, *Interpreting Parables.*
Stein, *Introduction to Parables.*
Stiller, *Preaching Parables to Postmoderns.*

Genre Analysis (Historical Narrative): Procedure

I. Survey
II. Analysis
   A. Historical Analysis
   B. Literary Analysis
      1. Context
      2. *Genre analysis: historical narrative*
         a. *Historical narrative genre*:
- Fill out the "Genre Analysis: Historical Narrative" worksheet giving information on parameters, plot, point of view, characters, and features (see fig. 8.1; sample, fig. 8.3; worksheet template at WJLFP).
- Note the contribution of each observation to your understanding of the meaning of the passage.

         b. *Parable Analysis* (as appropriate):
Fill out the "Genre Analysis: Parable" worksheets (template available at WJLFP) giving information for the "historical setting" and "parable function." Do this with the aid of figure 8.2, descriptions in this chapter, and commentaries and other aids (see example on fig. 8.4).
- Note the contribution of each observation to your understanding of the meaning of the passage.

Prophetic-Apocalyptic

While there are Old Testament antecedents (Isa 24-27, 56-66; Ezek 38-39; Daniel; Joel 2:28-3:21; Zech 1-6, 12-14), the prophetic-apocalyptic genre of literature arose in the Jewish environment between 200 BC and 200 AD. Once the authentic voice of prophecy fell silent with the closing of the Old Testament canon, the Jewish people were in what might be called spiritual limbo. Their future was uncertain in the face of a succession of Gentile national oppressors. They needed hope. They needed to make sense of their circumstances. Apocalyptic literature[7] addressed this perceived need. Writing in the name of an ancient, especially one who went to heaven without dying (e.g., Enoch), the apocalyptic writer traced Jewish history up to his own day. There might be visions and tours of heaven and the underworld. There is a reliance on symbolism and imagery to convey the realities of the present/future and heaven/earth dimensions of the genre's content. The overall tone is pessimistic with a prophetic promise of victory *only* when God ends history with judgment and reigns in the kingdom he establishes. How do the prophetic/apocalyptic passages of the New

Figure 8.3. **Sample Genre Analysis: Historical Narrative**

Passage (Parameters episode and scene[s]) __Mark 2:23-28__

Plot–progression: Identify verse(s) devoted to various stages of plot.

> *Beginning*
> _2:23a_ Exposition: "Lay it Out"
> _2:23b_ Inciting Moment: "Get something going"
> _2:24_ Developing Conflict: "Keep the heat on"
>
> *Middle*
> _2:25-26_ Climax: "Knot it all up proper"
> _2:27-28_ Denouement: "Loosen it"
>
> *End*
> _-----_ Final Suspense: "Keep Untangling"
> _-----_ Conclusion: "Wrap it up"

Plot–pace: Comment on emphases indicated, particularly by retarding pace.

> The inciting moment and developing conflict take less time than historical time. Jesus' words take the same amount of time and, by contrast receive the emphasis.

Point of View (Narration–Character): Check one
  ___ Main Character tells own story
  ___ Minor Character tells main character's story
  ___ Author tells story as observer
  _X_ Analytic or Omniscient Author tells story

Plane: Comment on what narration on the following "point of view" planes tells you about the writer's point of view and the type of response he desires.

> *Spatially,* Jesus is consistently the central character, even when his disciples' actions are the point of controversy (Mark 2:18, 23-24).
>
> *Temporally,* the story is told chronologically.
>
> *Psychologically,* there is nothing revealed of emotions, though what is on the Pharisees' and Jesus' minds is expressed (2:24-25).

Figure 8.3. *(continued)*

> *Theologically,* Jesus' response sanctions the disciples' Sabbath practice: eating to satisfy hunger. Jesus makes an implicit appeal to his authority as Messiah, David's son, for he acts as his father did (2:25-26). Further, he appeals to his authority as Son of Man and to the Sabbath's purpose: man's benefit (2:26-27).
>
> The *Implied Reader* is not explicitly given, but from the pronouncements at the end of the narrative, evidently the *implied reader* should follow Jesus and understand Sabbath practice as he did.

Characters: Give significant details; Identify relationships and God's or Christ's role as a character; Identify characters according to types: agent, flat, round.

> *Significant Details*: The only significant detail is that the disciples are "working" on the Sabbath by "harvesting" and "threshing grain" with their hands (Mark 2:23).
>
> *Characters, Numbers and Relationships:* Jesus is the central character, even though his disciples spark the controversy, for the Pharisees address their objection to him, not the disciples (2:24). The contrast is the disciples and Jesus versus the Pharisees.
>
> *Characters according to Types*: The disciples' seem to function as "agents" just to get something started (2:23). The Pharisees are "flat" embodying the one idea of a casuistical approach to Sabbath keeping (2:24). Jesus is the most "rounded" character in his retort to the Pharisees: "Have you never read?" (2:25) and his claim of authority over the Sabbath (2:28).

Features: **Comment on**

> *Dialogue* (main message/point of view communicated; introduction timing; stylized repetition function): Dialogue is what carries the narrative to its climax and denouement. As a pronouncement story, Jesus' verbal declaration at its end (without final suspense or conclusion) presents the main message: "Jesus had authority to interpret and apply Sabbath practice because he is 'Lord of the Sabbath'" (2:28).

Figure 8.3. (*continued*)

> *Stylistic Items* (repetition, omission, characters' ignorance or misunderstanding vs. reader, inclusion, plot twists, chiasm, symbolism, irony as clues to writer's intentions): In an ironic twist, Jesus uses the phrase in the Pharisees' accusation, "what is not lawful," as a counter proof in David's action, who acts authoritatively and for his men's good, by taking and giving to his hungry men "what is not lawful" (2:24, 26).

Testament line up with this sketch of the wider body of Jewish prophetic/apocalyptic literature?

Similarities

When we compare NT prophetic-apocalyptic material: Jesus' eschatological discourses (Matt 24; Mark 13; Luke 21), Paul's and Peter's teaching (1 Thess 4:13–5:11; 2 Thess 2:1-12; 2 Pet 3:1-13), and the Book of Revelation with Jewish apocalyptic literature we find many similarities. Using the Book of Revelation as a point of comparison, we find both deal in symbolism and often bizarre imagery (Rev 5:6; *1 En.* 90:9-12). Both use the vehicle of vision and an angelic mediator/guide to relate their heavenly content (Rev 1:10; 4:1; 22:1, 6-7; *1 En.* 27:1-5). Both emphasize the end of history and dawning of eternal life as a coming of the kingdom (reign) of God, the new Jerusalem, a new heaven and earth (Rev 11:15; 21:1, 9-11; *T. Dan* 5:12-13). Both see all existence as subject to the temporal dualism of this age and the age to come (Rev 21:1-8; *2 En.* 65:6-11).

Differences

The differences between Jewish apocalyptic literature and NT prophetic-apocalyptic material, particularly the Book of Revelation, are actually much more striking than the similarities. No Jewish or non-canonical Jewish Christian apocalyptic book claims to be a book of prophecy. Revelation does, and in so doing identifies its message as the Word of God (Rev 1:3; 22:7, 10, 18-19). Jewish apocalyptic literature uses "the literary form of prophecy to trace the course of history from ancient times down to their own day."[8] John, on the other hand, as did Old Testament prophets Jeremiah and Ezekiel, places himself in the contemporary world of his own day, the first century, and speaks of a future eschatological consummation (Rev 1:19; 4:1). Jewish apocalyptic literature is clearly pseudonymous (e.g., Enoch, Abraham, Ezra,

Figure 8.4 **Sample Genre Analysis: Parable**

Passage Lk 15:11-32

The Jesus Context (Historical Setting)

When?

in the course of *Jesus' ministry*–the latter part of his ministry. According to Thomas and Gundry (*Harmony of the Gospels*, 154) it was during ministry in and around Perea, Winter of A. D. 30, on his way to Jerusalem

in the course of *immediate events*–Jesus had several times warned the Pharisees that God would shut out of the kingdom Jews who refused his invitation, but that by his grace sinners would enter (Luke 13:22-30; 14:15-24).

Where?

Relation of *physical surroundings* to parable's details–There is nothing in the physical surroundings of the setting which relates directly to the parable's details.

To Whom?

Their *attitude* to Jesus' ministry and the coming of the kingdom–There is a mixed crowd around Jesus. The taxgatherers and sinners draw near to hear him (Luke 15:1). The Pharisees and scribes grumble that Jesus receives such (15:2). The parable is immediately addressed to the Pharisees and scribes with the rest listening in (15:3). Their attitude to Jesus is negative.

Obstacles in their attitude or level of understanding–It is an obstacle of attitude (Luke 15:2). They do not consider it "proper to eat with those excluded from the religious community. Besides such dangers as eating untithed food, intimate table fellowship connoted acceptance" (Keener, *Bible Background Commentary*, 231).

Why?

Controversy which gave rise to it–Jesus wants to interpret to the Pharisees the incorrectness in grumbling about his reception of taxgatherers and sinners and eating with them (Luke 15:1-3).

Figure 8.4. *(continued)*

What? *Cultural background* to parables—
- Son demanding and taking inheritance before father's death (Luke 15:13) indicates the son's rejection of the father. "Jewish law did permit a father to determine which assets (especially land) would go to which sons before he died, but they could take possession only on the father's death; the father was manager and received the land's profits until then. Thus this son could know what would be his but he could not legally sell his assets; he does it anyway" (Keener, *Bible Background Commentary*, 232; *m. B. Bat.* 9:7; *b. B. Bat.* 136a-b).
- Fattened calf (15:23) indicates extent of celebration. It is enough for a whole village. It was specially fed and prepared for that purpose. It would take time to prepare for the meal. The meal was special since meat was rarely consumed at meals in first century Palestine (Keener, *Bible Background Commentary*, 233; Bock, *Luke 9:51–24:53*, 1315; cf. 1 Sam 28:24-25).

So What?
Results–Luke does not tell us the results.

	The Jesus Context (Parable Function)	
Type	___ Proverb ___ Metaphor	___ Simile
	_X_ Parable ___ Illustration	___ Allegory

Points of Comparison/Interpretation
- The father in the parable (B) is God the Father or Christ (A); both express joy at the repentance of a sinner (C).
- The younger brother (Prodigal, B) is the sinner (cf. taxgatherers and sinners, A); both repent and turn to God (C).
- The elder brother (B) is the self-righteous person (cf. Pharisees and scribes, A); both grumble at the joy and acceptance that God/Jesus gives the sinner (C). There is no explicit interpretation, but the correlations are self-evident.

Persuasive Communication

Plot Progression--exposition, Luke 15:11; inciting moment, 15:12 (asking for the inheritance before the father's demise); developing conflict, 15:13-20a (leaves home with inheritance, wastes it, ends in

Figure 8.4 (*continued*)

> a deplorable condition, decides to return, repent, and request slave status); climax, 15:20b-21 (encounters father, makes confession); denouement, 15:22-24 (father accepts son, calls for signs of honor and feasting, declares recovery of son); final suspense, 15:25-30 (elder brother confronts father objecting to the celebration for the younger brother); conclusion, 15:31-32 (father gives proper perspective and rationale for joy for younger brother which elder brother should embrace).
>
> *Rhetorical Devices*: Contrast, Irony, Hyperbole--There is contrast throughout between the two brothers and their treatment of the father, and the father and elder brother in their treatment of the younger brother. There is the contrast between what the younger brother declares he deserves: slave status, and what he receives: son status. There is hyperbole in the actions of the father in the granting of the request in giving the inheritance.

Application/Expected Response
> Joy at the turn of sinners from death to life. It comes in the form of a command (Luke 15:23) and an explanation (15:32).

Contribution to Jesus' Teaching
> Though Jesus has taught on grace elsewhere (Matt 20:1-16), here the emphasis is on the response of joy to the coming of saving grace to others.

Baruch), but the writer of Revelation explicitly identifies himself (Rev 1:1,4, 9; contrast e.g., *1 En.* 1:1; *Apoc. Ab.* 1:1-2; *2 Bar.* 1:1). Many non-canonical apocalyptic works are *morally passive*. They place Israel in a privileged position, blaming the oppression they are experiencing on evil in the world, but not condemning the Jews for their unfaithfulness (*2 Bar.* 70-74). Revelation also sees the pervasive evil of this world system as the source of the church's persecution (Rev 17-18), but John does not hesitate to call Christians to repentance (Rev 2-3).

Additional differences include the fact that the Jewish apocalyptic perspective on present history is basically pessimistic. God's victory comes only beyond history. John sees victory as *already present* in Christ's death and resurrection (Rev 5). The final victory is but the consummation of what Christ has already begun on the cross and in the resurrection. While Jewish apocalyptic literature may provide analogous material, the true background to the content and symbolism of New Testament prophetic-apocalyptic material is the prophetic-apocalyptic material found in the Old Testament prophets, mainly Ezekiel, Daniel, and Zechariah.

Interpretive Schemes

New Testament prophecy consistently speaks of three time periods for future events (see fig. 8.5). First, there are "events before the end": events which fill the time between the first and second coming of Christ, commonly called "the last days" (2 Tim 3:1-9). "Wars and rumors of wars," natural catastrophes, persecution of the church, and heresy and apostasy could be present in any given generation (Matt 24:4-14). Second, there are "events at the end," immediately before and at the return of Christ: the Great Tribulation (Matt 24:15-28; Rev 6-16) and the Millennium (Rev 20:4-6). Third, there are the events, we simply label "the end": the general resurrection, last judgment, followed by new heavens and new earth (Matt. 24:29-31; Rev 19-22). The challenge in interpreting NT prophetic-apocalyptic, particularly Revelation, is to figure out into which time period the content of any given passage fits. This challenge is exacerbated by the fact that we are more than two thousand years removed from the time when Jesus taught and the NT writers wrote. For example, John wrote that he would speak of things present, things in the near future, and things future (Rev 1:1, 19; 4:1). But, what was future to him could be present and even past to us.

Naturally, then, interpreters differ in the way they relate the content of NT prophetic-apocalyptic material, particularly Revelation, to past, present, or future human history.[9] The "Preterist school" sees Revelation as an anti-government tract written for Christians in persecution at the end of the first century. The symbolism is code language to conceal its message from Rome (Rev 17:9-13; 13:18). There is no predictive prophecy present. The "Historicist School" sees the events of Western civilization chronicled consecutively throughout the book (e.g., Rev. 9:3 prophesies the invasion of barbarian hordes). The "Idealist school" says that the book is not intended to give details about future events, particularly "events at the end"–the Great Tribulation and the Millennium (Idealists are often Amillennialists). Rather, its imagery graphically pictures the ongoing struggle of good and evil and the victory in the later passages is intended to encourage Christians with the truth of God's final triumph. A variant on this approach is the "Partial Preterist" view, which sees Jesus' prophecies of a Great Tribulation (Matt 24:15-28) fulfilled in the AD 66-70 Jewish War, which climaxed in the fall of Jerusalem.[10]

Then there is the "Futurist school" which claims that NT prophetic-apocalyptic material gives details about future events surrounding the

Figure 8.5. **Sample Genre Analysis: Prophetic-Apocalyptic**

Passage Rev 22:1-5

Passage's Content

     _X_ Content of a Vision   ___ Message within a Vision

     ___ Interpretation of Vision   _X_ Prophetic Message

Comments: The passage begins with "He (that is the angel) showed me" and places the content of the verses clearly as a vision. How the vision, the symbolism, and the final reality of heaven relate to each other is the challenge of interpretation. Because it is a vision there cannot be absolute certainty about the relation of each detail to the final reality.

Time of Fulfillment

___ Events before the End

___ Events at the End (pre-millennial view--Great Tribulation, Millennium; a null category for preterist; moderate preterist, and idealist amillennial view)

_X_ The End

Comments: The passage comes at a point in Revelation after the last judgment (Rev 20) and when eternal life is being described (Rev 21-22).

Figure 8.5. (*continued*)

Symbolism			
Spiritual Reality	Symbol	Common Quality	Background
Eternal Life	River of the water of life	ever flowing, life giving	Ezek 47:1- 12; *1 En.* 17:4
Eternal Life	Tree of Life–12 fruits, healing leaves	consistent, abundant, restorative provision	Ezek 47:12; Gen 2:9; 3:22; *1 En.* 25:4-5
Eternal Relationship	Name on forehead	ownership, protection, possibly holiness, likeness	Rev 3:12; 7:3; 9:4; Exod 28:36-38

return of Christ. Of course there are differences in understanding among Futurists, particularly concerning "events at the end." What is the relation of Christ's return to the thousand years? A- and Pre- and Post-millennial views coalesce around the answers to these questions. If Christ returns before the thousand year reign, will there be a *rapture*, removal, of the church before, at the mid-point, before the wrath of the Lamb falls, or after the Great Tribulation? Answers to these questions result in pre- or mid-tribulational, pre-wrath rapture, or post-tribulational views of the number and timing of Christ's return. Of course, the Amillennialist, as an Idealist, would not affirm a distinct seven year Great Tribulation period. You can see from these many options the challenges in interpreting this genre!

Symbolism

The symbolism in Revelation and other NT prophetic-apocalyptic passages falls into three categories. First, some symbolism is explained in the book, e.g., the seven stars=the seven churches, Rev 1:20; the great dragon=the Devil, Satan (12:9). Second, some symbolism unexplained in the NT text is paralleled by Old Testament imagery, e.g., the tree of life, 2:7; 22:2/Gen 2:9; the four horsemen, Rev 6:1-8/Zech 6:1-8. Third, some unexplained NT symbols find parallels in extra-biblical sources, whether Jewish or pagan, e.g., the great white throne of Rev 20:11/*1 En.* 18:8; the seals on the book, Rev 6, part of the Roman practice of sealing a will was that the seal would be broken only by the rightful heir.[11]

When we interpret symbolism a slight adjustment to the "Point of Comparison" paradigm, used with parables, will make it serviceable for our analysis. Symbolism involves a "transcendent/spiritual" and/or "future reality" (A), i.e., characters and events that really exist or will really occur, though not in the literal manner indicated by the "concrete symbol."[12] A "concrete, literal symbol" (B) represents this reality, because the two share a "common quality" (C). In his vision in Rev 22:1, John sees a "river of the water of life," which is a concrete symbol. It points to the spiritual (now and in the future) reality of eternal life. The common quality is the gift of overflowing life to all that it touches. Just as the presence of water brings desert places alive so that vegetation flourishes, so eternal life from God "waters" and sustains those who participate in it.

It is well worth your time to recover any relevant background from the Old Testament, Jewish apocalyptic literature (which is usually dependent on the OT), pagan sources, or features of first century culture as you seek to understand and communicate the significance of biblical symbolism. For example, in Ezek 47:1-12, we see a river flowing out from under the threshold to the temple which brings refreshment to the land. This is probably a millennial picture, which also points ahead to the perfection in eternal life recorded in Rev 22:1-5.

Genre Analysis: Prophetic/Apocalyptic–Resources

Materials from Previous Study

"Survey" worksheet
"Literary Analysis--Context/Genre" worksheet

Greek is Great Gain

Descriptions in chapter eight
Figure 8.5

Commentaries on Revelation

Beale, *Revelation*.
Johnson, *Revelation*.
Tenney, *Interpreting Revelation*.
Thomas, *Revelation 1-7*.
———., *Revelation 8-22*.

Genre Analysis (Prophetic/Apocalyptic): Procedure

I. Survey
II. Analysis
   A. Historical Analysis
   B. Literary Analysis
      1. Context
      2. *Genre: Prophetic-Apocalyptic.* Fill out the "Genre Analysis: Prophet-Apocalyptic" worksheet for your passage with the aid of information in this chapter and commentaries. In the process address the following questions (see fig. 8.5 for an example and WJLFP for worksheet template):
         a. *Passage's content.*
            - Is the content of your passage, in the main, the content of a vision, the message given in a vision, interpretation of a vision, or a prophetic message?
            - Comment on how this contributes to your understanding of the passage.
         b. *Time of fulfillment.*
            - When will your passage be fulfilled?—during *Events before the End, Events at the End,* or *The End.*
            - Comment on how this placement in a time period in the future contributes to your understanding of the passage.
         c. *Symbolism.*
            - Identify details of the passage which are symbols.
            - Analyze the figurative complex—"A" the spiritual and/or future reality the symbol points to; "B" the symbol itself–the concrete, literal detail; and "C" the common quality between them.
            - Identify any Old Testament or extra-biblical background to the symbol. Look up the background text and note down reference and enough of the immediate context to make it useful in the future.
            - Comment on how the symbol contributes to the message of the passage.

Endnotes

1. Kaiser, "Narrative," 69-88.

2. Culpepper, *Anatomy of Fourth Gospel*, 80.

3. Longacre, *Grammar of Discourse*, 34-35.

4. Bailey and Vander Broek, *Literary Forms*, 129-36, 172-83.

5. See Larkin (*Acts*, relevant commentary sections) for literary analysis of speeches using rhetorical critical categories; cf. Bailey and Vander Broek, *Literary Forms*, 166-72.

6. See bibliography, discussion and procedures in "Additional Genre and Literary Form Analysis Procedures" at WJLFP; cf. Beale and Carson, *Commentary on NT Use of OT*.

7. *1 Enoch (Ethiopic Apocalypse); T. Levi* 2-5; *T. Ab.* 10-15; *Apocalypse of Abraham; 3 Baruch (Greek Apocalypse); Apocalypse of Zephaniah; 2 Enoch (Slavonic Apocalypse); Jub.* 23; *4 Ezra; 2 Baruch (Syriac Apocalypse);* cf. "Apocalypse, Genre of," 35-7; Allison, "Apocalyptic," 17-20.

8. Johnson, *Revelation*, 401.

9. For further orientation on interpretational schemes for NT prophetic-apocalyptic literature see Archer, *Three Views on Rapture*; Bock, ed., *Three Views on Millennium*; Pate, ed., *Four Views on Revelation*.

10. Sproul, *Last Days*.

11. Tenney, *Interpreting Revelation*, 191; cf. Keener, *Bible Background Commentary*, 777.

12. "Revelation, Book of," 715.

Chapter 9
GRAMMAR & RHETORICAL FEATURES

Literary Analysis has four steps. Thus far we have covered the first two: "Context" (chapter six) and "Genre" (chapters six through eight). We deal with the third step: "Syntax," in this chapter, and the last step: "Word Study," in chapters ten and eleven. At that point we will have a complete set of Literary Analysis tools for exegesis. Analyzing syntax sends us on a quest for clues to the meaning of a text through the *grammar* and the *rhetorical features* the author chose to use. We discuss grammatical analysis first, and later look to rhetorical features.

Grammar

Grammatical analysis is a process whereby the text's meaning can come alive in a most immediate sense. As we retrace the New Testament writer's thought patterns, deciding how he has used various grammatical features, we frequently have the sense of thinking his thoughts after him. Commentators and grammarians have traversed the territory before us and can serve as helpful guides. But armed with the right questions and a knowledge of the categories of possible correct answers, there is great benefit in interacting with the text directly and knowing the joy of discovery that direct encounter affords. Although you will only rarely mention a grammatical issue in a sermon or lesson, you nonetheless will be indebted to your grammatical analysis for the help it provides in developing the overall structure, main arguments, and subpoints of your message.

Principles for Grammatical Analysis

Basic building blocks. As we noted in our orientation to translation (chapter four) the basic building blocks of meaning in a Greek sentence, in addition to the lexical meanings of words, are these grammatical features: morphemes, function words, word order, and punctuation. These we will analyze during grammatical analysis in order to uncover what they contribute to the meaning of the passage. We will analyze these features within four large categories of grammar: *Structure, Verbs, Cases,* and *the Rest.* Much of this you met in first level NT Greek grammar as you learned vocabulary, paradigms, and basic syntax.

Under *Structure* we will study function words which connect words, phrases, clauses, sentences and paragraphs, i.e., coordinating conjunctions and subordinate conjunctions, including relative pronouns. *Verbs,* the very heart of a clause or sentence, will be investigated from a variety of angles: tense, voice, mood, mode (function of participle and infinitive), person, and number. We study nouns' and adjectives' *Cases*–nominative, accusative, genitive and dative–to tell us how they relate to other words in the sentence. Finally, for *the Rest* we probe the meaning conveyed by the use/non-use of the definite article, and the significance of particles, pronouns and prepositional phrases, adjectives, and adverbs.

Form and function. The basic dynamic to keep in mind when analyzing grammar is the relationship between grammatical form (a surface feature such as a morpheme like case ending) and grammatical function. Function refers to the contribution a grammatical feature (form) makes to the meaning of the passage.

In every language, one form may have multiple functions and one function may be implemented by many different forms. Figure 9.1 gives an overview of this phenomenon in NT Greek. Note how one form, the participle, may serve five functions. Within some categories there may even be a number of subfunctions. While the mechanical layout will enable us to visually represent the basic functions, grammatical analysis enables us to probe further and decide among subfunctions. For example, which of the eight uses of an adverbial participle is being employed in a given occurrence.

"Bones and Muscles." When we have completed a mechanical layout on a passage, you might say that we have constructed a skeleton. It shows us the arrangement of the basic grammatical relationships among the words and phrases, the individual "bones." When we begin to study the syntax of the passage, we go further in our understanding of those relationships. It is like looking at the muscles on the skeleton. As physical muscles direct how the bones will move, so syntactical analysis will tell us more precisely how words relate to each other.

For example, on your mechanical layout of Phil 1:4 you have already seen that the participle ποιούμενος modifies the verb εὐχαριστῶ adverbially. But you may not know yet the precise nature of that modification. Does "making prayer with joy" qualify "I thank my God" in terms of manner, means, time, cause, condition, concession, purpose, or attendant circumstance? See the Appendix for an explanation of these categories. Or, take the prepositional phrase ἐν ἐπιγνώσει καὶ πάσῃ αἰσθήσει in Phil 1:9. We know it modifies περισσεύῃ. But what is the nature of the

9.1. Form and Function in New Testament Greek

FORM	FUNCTION				
	Subject	Object	Verb	Noun Modifier	Verb Modifier
Subord. Conjunction+ Clause	Substantival (ὅτι, ἵνα)	Substantival (ὅτι, ἵνα)		Adjectival (Relative pronoun)	Adverbial (various conjunctions)
Prepositional Phrase	Def. Art.+ Prep. Phrase	Def. Art.+ Prep. Phrase		Adjectival Position	Adverbial Position
Participle	Def. Art.+ Participle	Def. Art.+ Participle	Complementary, Periphrastic, Imperative	Adjectival Position	Adverbial Position
Infinitive	Def. Art.+ Infinitive	Def. Art.+ Infinitive	Imperative (rare)	Adjectival Position	Adverbial Position (τοῦ + or various prep. + Inf)
Word(s)	Nominative	Accusative (Dative or Genitive)	Verb (Various Moods)	Adjective, Noun (genitive)	Adverb, Particle

relationship? Does ἐν indicate that "knowledge and all insight" is the "sphere" or "content" *in* which Paul prays their "love may abound"? Or is it the "means," the instrument, *by* which it is to abound? Perhaps you came to a conclusion about these two relationships when you made your finished translation, but now is the time to validate or refine that decision and reflect on all the meaning which grammatical features contribute to conveying the message of your passage.

Identifying the Most Important Grammatical Features

There will rarely be enough time in your immediate preparation to study *all* the grammatical features in your passage. Hence, it is very important to develop the skill of discerning what is important to analyze grammatically. Here are two tools you can use to make wise decisions. *Input from previous study*. The grammatical features which either give difficulty or appear to be key to the passage's flow of thought probably deserve your study. When it is time for grammatical analysis, refer to your finished translation and mechanical layout as well as your "Survey" worksheet. Your prior work on these aspects of the exegetical study should give you some ideas about key features to study. Also study any significant differences due to grammar between your finished translation and the *pew Bible* (English text of preference in the congregation).

Clues to grammatically significant items. When you start digging deeper with commentary, dictionary, and grammar to arrive at firm conclusions related to one or more of the four areas of grammar, what are some hints to help you focus in on potentially important details?

> *Structure.* All connectives are important, especially those which link sentences, main clauses and subclauses. Also important are connectives with a range of subfunctions, e.g., γάρ as a coordinate conjunction may be explanatory, inferential, or emphatic.
>
> *Verbs.* Look for patterns in the use of Tense/Voice/Mood, especially isolated uses which stand out. Always keep in mind the relationship of these features to lexical meaning. Sometimes a particular dictionary meaning is associated with a given use of Tense/Voice/Mood.
>
> - *Tense.* According to D. A. Black,[1] in terms of emphasis, the aorist is the "unmarked" "background" tense for "kind of action" and the others are "marked," stressed by the writer. The present and imperfect are "foreground" tenses, carrying more emphasis, while the perfect tenses receive the most as "frontground" tenses.
> - *Voice.* Black says the active voice is "unmarked" in NT Greek and middle and passive are "marked." Again, check occurrences against the dictionary, to uncover deponents or those with particular meanings in middle or passive.
> - *Mood.* The indicative is the "unmarked" mood and the

others are "marked." A rewarding part of grammatical analysis is studying the function of adverbial uses of the participle and infinitive.
- *Person and number.* The important items to note are changes in person and number within a passage (e.g., second person to first person), and what that says about how the passage's content relates to the readers, the author, and us.

Cases. Further analysis is required only in those instances when the function is not exhaustively indicated by their position on the MLO, e.g., adverbial uses, uses of the genitive, uses with a preposition.

The Rest: Definite Article, Particles, Pronouns, Prepositions, Adjectives, and Adverbs. These features should be pursued when neither the place on the MLO nor the dictionary definition has exhausted all that can be said about what they contribute to the passage. All prepositions are important, especially those used with a particular case which can have a number of functions, e.g. ἐν + dative, is it locative, "in," or instrumental, "by"?

One final thought, beginners tend to overanalyze, making more of a grammatical feature than the writer intended. Diligent, lifelong study will help you gain an ever more firm grasp of the New Testament's grammar and style. It will also help you gain efficiency in capturing all the benefits grammatical analysis can yield for your interpretation, preaching, and teaching.

Conducting Grammatical Analysis

Grammatical analysis involves two steps: "Classification" and "Comment." The first challenge for the interpreter is to properly classify the function of a given instance of a grammatical feature according to the categories and subcategories of use. A number of resources can help you, such as the descriptive outlines and the form and function charts in the Appendix and at WJLFP, intermediate and standard reference grammars like DBW and Robertson, and commentaries (see resources list). With the aid of these resources, your task is to determine the classifications and write down your decisions on the "Syntax: Grammar" worksheet (see fig. 9.2 ; template available at WJLFP). That is step one. You then need to comment on what that classification tells you about what that word and its grammatical

Figure 9.2. **Sample Grammatical Analysis: Phil 1:3-11**

v. Structure	Verbs	Cases	The Rest
3)	Εὐχαριστῶ, iterative, at intervals; "at every remembrance" he thanks God	τῇ μνείᾳ ὑμῶν, obj. Genitive–remembrance directed to them	ἐπὶ πάσῃ τῇ μνείᾳ, position–time; tells when he gives thanks
4)	ποιούμενος, temporal; Paul gives thanks when he makes prayers;		
5)	indirect middle; Paul makes prayer of himself		ἐπὶ τῇ κοινωνίᾳ ὑμῶν; causal; their participation in the gospel is the reason why he is thankful for them.
6)	πεποιθώς, attend. circum. or causal; a reason for Paul's thanks is his confidence in God's work in them	ἐμοι, dat. of reference; It is right *for* me to think this way.	
7) καθώς, compar. used as causal; his thanks God for them as feelings rightly due them			
	ὁ ἐναρξάμενος, ADPtc–ingressive; complements the main verb's meaning of completion	βεβαιώσει τοῦ εὐαγγελίου, obj. genitive; the gospel is what he confirms	εἰς τὸ εὐαγγέλιον, relation–goal; their participation was for the advance of the gospel
8) γάρ emphatic; calling on God as witness that his feelings are genuine			
	διὰ τὸ ἔχειν, causal; the fact he has them in his heart is the reason he is right in thinking thankfully about them. Note: Present tense is consistently used to describe Paul's actions (vv. 7-8); probably gnomics, indicating perpetually true conditions	συγκοινωνούς μου τῆς χάριτος, obj. genitive; grace is what he participates in	Use of definite article vv. 5, 7 indicate particular circumstance of sharing and imprisonment
ὡς compar. emphatic; stresses the strength of the truth about his affection			ἐν τῇ ἀπολογίᾳ καὶ βεβαιώσει, def. art. binds the two concepts together
			ἐν σπλάγχνοις, instrumental; with Christ's affections he longs for them

Figure 9.2. (continued)

v. Structure	Verbs	Cases	The Rest
9) καὶ transitional (resumptive) takes up the prayer report from v. 4 ἵνα substantival-gives content of prayer, "that their love would overflow more and more"		Possessive Genitive–eight times in passage (vv. 3, 4, 7-10); highlights personal involvement in subject matter	ἐν position, "in" marker of specification or substance, i.e., the content with a verb of filling, love overflows "in" knowledge
10) ἵνα –ultimate goal of his prayer that their love would overflow, is that they would be pure and blameless at Christ's coming 11)	εἰς τὸ δοκιμάζειν purpose-the goal of the prayer request is spiritual judgment PAI-customary action; their manner of life should be to test and approve what is excellent (11) πεπληρωμένοι causal; the reason for the blameless condition is "having been filled with fruit that comes from right standing with God" PfPPtc intensive; stresses existing results from God's work; note "divine passive"	(11) καρπὸν δικαιοσύνης genitive of source, Eadie: "fruit comes from right standing with God" ἔπαινον θεοῦ objective genitive; praise directed to God	εἰς position, "at"; eschatological time marker for ultimate purpose, "being blameless at the day of Christ" (11) διὰ Ἰησοῦ Χριστοῦ, means, "through": Jesus is the instrument for producing the fruit. εἰς δόξαν relation, "for"; final goal is God's glory and praise Non-use of Definite Article: quality, καρπὸν δικαιοσύνης, cf. v. 6, ἔργον ἀγαθόν

function contributes to the meaning of the passage. This will involve some paraphrasing of the particular word *and* those words and phrases in the immediate context to which it relates.

You can proceed with your grammatical analysis in one of two ways: either verse by verse (dealing with each selected grammatical feature as it is encountered in the text), or by following the standard grammatical analysis order, as follows (see Appendix for further explanation and some form/function charts; for some summary charts see "Grammar in Head" charts at WJLFP).[2]

Structure

Coordinate Conjunctions

Here we identify the nature of the relationship between items of equal value: words, phrases, clauses, sentences, paragraphs. We do so by classifying and commenting on the coordinate conjunctions, which create the equal connections, according to the major categories: *continuative, adversative, disjunctive, inferential, explanatory, transitional, emphatic, ascensive, correlative*. For example, the γάρ that introduces Phil 1:8 is emphatic and indicates that Paul is calling on God as witness as a way of stressing the genuineness of his feeling toward them (1:7). God is his witness that he indeed has this ongoing affection for them.

Sometimes coordinate conjunctions may be repeated at the same level throughout a passage, thus creating a pattern. You may want to note such a pattern and make a summary comment. The καί's in Phil 1:9-11 create a compounding effect so that one is impressed with the completeness of provision Paul is praying for: "love abounding more *and* more; knowledge *and* all insight; pure *and* blameless."

Subordinate Conjunctions

Here we identify the nature of the relationship between a subordinate clause and the verb or noun/pronoun which it modifies. We classify and comment on *adverbial* subordinate conjunctions according to the major categories: *comparative, temporal, purpose, result, cause, condition, concession local*. In the case of an *adjectival* clause we note the antecedent and the particular type of pronoun or connective used: relative pronouns-definite, indefinite, quantitative, qualitative, explanatory. In the case of *substantival* clauses, no further classification and comment is needed beyond what you have indicated by placement in the MLO. The two ἵνα subordinate conjunctions in Phil 1:9-10 may be classified as *substantival* and *purpose*. The former introduces the content of his prayer request: that their love may abound more and more. The latter gives a purpose of the request: that they may be blameless before Jesus at his coming.

Verbs

Tense

A verb's tense indicates the time and kind of action in the indicative mood, and primarily the kind of action in the other three moods and two modes. To determine the precise nuance of tense usage one must balance the tense employed with the lexical range of meaning and elements in the immediate context. Sometimes a particular tense expresses a distinctive part of the lexical range of meaning. For example, the perfect participle πεποιθώς in Phil 1:6 is translated "being confident" because the dictionary indicates the perfect tense of this verb takes a present meaning, "depend on, trust in, be convinced (that), be sure (that), (be) certain (that)" (BDAG, s.v. πείθω).

Take care neither to overanalyze the tense nor to miss the nuances intended. Begin with the basic categories for each tense and then move to specific nuances as the context or verb's lexical meaning requires. Identify and classify the time and kind of action of all verbs in your passage (except for those in the imperative mood) beginning with the following *general categories* (see Appendix for further explanation of categories):

Present:	Progressive Action in present time
Imperfect:	Progressive Action in past time
Aorist:	Summary Action in past (or present) time
Future:	Summary (or Progressive) Action in future time
Perfect:	Completed-Stative Action in present time
Pluperfect:	Completed-Stative Action in past time.

As context and lexical meaning converge to highlight a particular tense usage, identify and comment on that usage according to the following *subcategories*:

Present (Progressive):	instantaneous, iterative, customary, gnomic, historical, extending-from-past-to-present, futuristic, perfective, conative
Imperfect (Progressive):	ingressive, iterative, customary, instantaneous, pluperfective, conative
Aorist (Summary):	ingressive, consummative, gnomic, epistolary, dramatic, proleptic
Future (Summary):	imperative, deliberative, gnomic, progressive
Perfect and Pluperfect (Completed-Stative):	intensive, consummative, aoristic, gnomic, proleptic, perfect with present force, pluperfect with summary past force.

For example, the basic classification "progressive action" is sufficient for designating the participle's action in Phil 1:3, while we can be more precise with the main verb "I thank" since the prepositional phrase, "at every remembrance of you" indicates "iterative" progressive action. There are a cluster of present tense verbs at Phil 1:7-8 which, given their lexical meanings, probably point to gnomic, perpetually true conditions.

Voice

Since the mechanical layout permits us to identify the subject and object of active voice verbs, our concern here will be with middle and passive forms. Again the distinctive meaning for middle and passive voice of a verb form may be a separate part of its range of meaning and, therefore, dealt with in the lexica. You should identify, classify and comment on any true middle form occurrences according to the following categories: indirect, direct, permissive, reciprocal. For passives, comment on voice and the agent of action. For example, Phil 1:4, ποιούμενος is an indirect middle. Paul is making prayer of himself. Phil 1:11, πεπληρωμένοι, is a passive with no agent expressed except in prepositional phrase "through Christ Jesus." It is probably a "divine passive" with an emphasis on the supernatural nature of the righteousness produced.

Mood

A verb's mood is used in connection with particular conjunctions or particles to indicate whether the speaker views the action as actual (indicative) or in some way potential (volitionally—imperative; objectively probable—subjunctive; subjectively possible, but doubtful—optative). Note that some grammarians subsume participles and infinitives under the heading of *mode*, which they distinguish from mood. They define *mode* as a grammatical form which combines either the descriptive power of an adjective or the designative power of a noun with the action aspect of a verb. This work continues to subsume participles and infinitives under mood.

Indicative mood. The indicative expresses three types of actual statements: declaration, question, exclamation. Being alert to interrogative pronouns and punctuation (;), which indicate questions, and the presence of τί, πόσος, πῶς, ὡς, which can indicate exclamations, identify, classify and comment on any uses of the indicative that are questions or exclamations. For example, the ὡς of Phil 1:8 is a comparative emphatic which can be viewed as an exclamation. By it Paul stresses the strength of his affection for the Philippians.

Subjunctive mood. We have already analyzed the use of the subjunctive in subordinate clauses. The interpreter should identify, classify, and comment on its use in main clauses, as well, according to the following categories and functions: hortatory (1st plural)–command; deliberative–question; emphatic denial with οὐ μή–declaration; prohibitive (μή + 2nd person Aorist subjunctive)–negative command.

Optative mood. The optative occurs infrequently in the New Testament (less than seventy times), but when it does, it indicates a strong desire on the part of the speaker about an action viewed as possible, but doubtful. The interpreter should identify and comment on any optatives in the passage.

Imperative mood. NT writers use the imperative to convey positive and negative directives: commands and prohibitions. The tense used in each case indicates the nature of the action called for. Imperatives may be further classified as either request or permission, depending on the authority relationship of the parties and whether or not the imperative was originally the idea of the person giving it. You should identify, classify, and comment on all imperative mood forms in the passage taking into account, in each instance, whether it is a command or prohibition and what tense it is in. Also identify, classify, and comment an any entreaties or permissions.

Participle. You have already identified the basic usage of participles in your passage—substantival, adjectival, adverbial or verbal—and have indicated it by placement in the MLO. Now you need to specify more precisely the adverbial uses, i.e., how the participle modifies the verb's action. Do this using the following categories: *manner, means, time, cause, condition, concession, purpose, attendant circumstance*. For example, in Phil 1:6 "being confident" is probably causal, giving one reason Paul is thankful for them, namely, God is at work in them.

Infinitive. You have already identified the basic use of infinitives in your passage—*adjectival, substantival, verbal, adverbial*—and indicated it by placement in the MLO. Now you need to specify more precisely adverbial uses, i.e., in what particular way the infinitive modifies a verb. Do this using the following categories: *purpose, result, time, cause, means*. For example, Phil 1:7, διὰ τό + inf., shows *cause*, giving the reason why Paul is right to think this way about them, namely, he has this affection for them.

Person and Number

You have already given attention to person and number as you translated. Person tells you whether the speaker, audience, or a third party is doing the action. Number tells you how many are doing the verb's action. Now you need to look for patterns of usage throughout your passage. Also you should look for changes in person and number, as well as subject, which indicate a shift in focus. Include participles and infinitives in your analysis. You will preserve your findings by writing a summary statement about the pattern and any significant changes in person and number in your passage. For example, in Phil 1:3-11 the first person predominates. It highlights the personal relationship Paul has with the Philippians. There are shifts at points throughout his thanksgiving to focus on what God is doing in their lives (1:6, 11) and what the Philippians have done and are becoming by God's grace (1:7, 10).

Cases

Cases, or the morphemes that signal them, indicate a particular kind of relationship between the word marked by them and another word in the sentence. By placement in the MLO you have already identified the function of the nominative case as related to the verb, i.e., as subject or predicate noun/adjective. You have also noted the accusative case use signaling a direct object of the verb, and words in accusative, genitive, and dative cases that are objects of prepositions. You must now turn your attention to words in cases which modify nouns, adjectives or verbs. Your task is to identify, classify and comment on these uses of case using the following categories:

Nominative:	*Designation* (Nominative)
	Address (Vocative)
Genitive:	*Description*
	With action nouns: subjective or objective
	With non-action nouns: descriptive, possessive, partitive, attributive, apposition
	With verbs: price, place, means, agency, reference, association, time
	Separation (Ablative): comparison, separation, source
Dative:	*Personal interest* (Pure Dative): indirect object, interest, reference
	Position (Local Dative): sphere (spatial or logical), time
	Means (Instrumental Dative): association, means, cause
Accusative:	*Substantival*: direct object, double accusative, subject of infinitive
(Limitation/ Extension)	*Adverbial*: measure (extent of time or space), reference.

If there is a pattern of usage of one category, you may comment via a summary statement. An example of a summary statement for Phil 1:3-11 would be that possessive genitives occur consistently throughout the passage and show the personal involvement of Paul with his readers. The genitive θεοῦ in the phrase "unto the glory and praise of God" (εἰς δόξαν καὶ ἔπαινον θεοῦ, 1:11) may be particularly classified as an objective genitive. It modifies a noun of action: "praise." And "praise of God" is part of a prepositional phrase giving the purpose of the "love abounding in the Philippians" (1:9). These two contextual factors indicate that "God" in the genitive is the "object" of this activity.

The Rest

Aside from adjectives and adverbs, which we study lexically, all that remains for grammatical analysis in this category is the use or non-use of the definite article, and the use of particles, pronouns, and prepositional phrases. These we study under the general heading, *the Rest*.

Definite Article

The presence or absence of the definite article generally signals whether the writer is focusing on a particular instance of the noun or on its quality. Survey the use and non-use of the definite article in the passage, and then identify, classify and comment on any occurrences which are particularly significant for the passage's meaning. Since this may include patterns of use and non-use, summary statements may be in order. In Phil 1:7, Paul stresses the specific circumstances of his witness by use of the definite article in his description (ἐν τε *τοῖς* δεσμοῖς μου καὶ ἐν *τῇ* ἀπολογίᾳ καὶ βεβαιώσει τοῦ εὐαγγελίου). Note, the latter use is probably an example of the Granville Sharp rule: one definite article binding together two impersonal nouns connected by καί, here the former is a subset of the latter ("defense and confirmation of the gospel"). By contrast Paul in Phil 1:6, 11 seems to emphasize the quality of the life of righteousness, because the phrases "good work" and "fruit of righteousness" lack the definite article (ἔργον ἀγαθὸν . . . καρπὸν δικαιοσύνης).

Particles

Particles play an important role in communicating meaning. They may emphasize a verb's action (Phil 4:3) or negate it (3:12). They may add a sense of indefiniteness or potentiality to a construction (2:23). The interpreter should identify, classify and comment on any emphatic or negative or general sense particles. Interjections also fit into this category (1:12).

Pronouns

Pronouns can have a variety of functions and need to have their antecedents correctly identified so the flow of thought can be traced accurately. The interpreter should identify, classify and comment on any pronouns not already analyzed via placement in the MLO. Pay attention to the area of the pronoun's antecedent or postcedent and function: emphasis, reference, relation, question or general sense use. For example, in Phil 1:6, 9, the demonstrative τοῦτο is used in apposition to what follows, a substantival ὅτι or ἵνα clause which gives the content of what he is confident about and prays for.

Prepositional Phrases

Here we identify the relationship between the object of a preposition and the verb or noun/pronoun to which it is linked. We classify and comment on prepositional phrases (except infinitive constructions) according to the following categories of relationships: *direction, position, relation, agency, means, cause, association, purpose.* Clusters of prepositional phrase's related to the same word may be dealt with in summary fashion as long as each phrase's distinctive contribution to the passage's meaning is noted. For example, Phil 1:3 contains three prepositional phrases that modify the verb "I thank." They tell us position in terms of time, "*at* every remembrance of you," position in terms of manner, "*in* every prayer," and the cause of his giving thanks, "*because of* your fellowship in the gospel."

Literary Analysis: Grammar–Resources

Materials from Previous Study

"Greek Reading and Finished Translation" and "Mechanical Layout" worksheets for the passage
"Survey" worksheet

Greek is Great Gain

Descriptions in chapter nine
Figures in chapter nine
Appendix

Reference Tools

BDAG

Bibloi CD
DBW
Robertson, *Grammar of Greek Testament*.
Zerwick and Grosvenor, *Grammatical Analysis of Greek Testament*.

Commentaries on Philippians

Fee, *Philippians*.
Greenlee, *Exegetical Summary of Philippians*.
Hawthorne, *Philippians*.
Loh and Nida, *Handbook to Philippians*.
O'Brien, *Philippians*.
Silva, *Philippians*.

Literary Analysis: Grammar–Procedure

I. Survey
II. Analysis
   A. Historical Analysis
   B. Literary Analysis
      1. Context
      2. Genre
      3. *Syntax*
         a. *Grammar: Structure, Verbs, Cases,* and *the Rest*. With the use of the above resources, fill out the "Grammatical Analysis" worksheet as you follow these steps (worksheet template and "Grammar in Head" chart available at WJLFP).
            1) *Identify.* Identify significant or hard to understand occurrences of various grammatical features, instances of the sub-categories within Structure, Verbs, Cases, and the Rest.
            2) *Classify.* Classify as precisely as possible each chosen grammatical feature according to the function it is fulfilling (see fig. 9.2 for example).
            3) *Comment.* In each case, comment on what the word, functioning in this way, contributes to the meaning of the passage. This will involve some paraphrase of the passage's flow of thought.

Rhetorical Features

General Overview

You have gained helpful information from your grammatical analysis, but your passage can also be studied from the angle of the writer's literary art. You have looked at the "bricks and mortar" which are grammatical syntax. Now it is time to step back and see in what way the writer has created a "mosaic" through his literary artistry.

Sometimes writers exercise their art by leaving words out, i.e., *word absence*. You may find this confusing at first, but probing further, you'll come to see a reason for the missing words. For example, in didactic portions of the Gospels and paraenetic portions of the Epistles, conjunctions may be omitted so that the speaker or writer may pursue his instruction with rapidity or urgency (see Matt 5:3-17; Rom 12:9-15).

Writers sometimes also alter *word order* to create emphasis or to make something more clear. This nuancing is often lost in translations, especially those that do not follow the formal equivalence philosophy. For example, Phil 2:10 reads, ἐν τῷ ὀνόματι Ἰησοῦ πᾶν γόνυ κάμψῃ ἐπουρανίων καὶ ἐπιγείων καὶ καταχθονίων. Paul emphasizes by the word order that it is "at the name of Jesus" that every knee will bow, since normally the word order for a Greek sentence would have the prepositional phrase later, after the subject and the verb. The word order pattern of *chiasmus*, or reverse parallelism, is common in both the Old and the New Testaments (e.g., Col 3:11 ὅπου οὐκ ἔνι *Ἕλλην* καὶ **Ἰουδαῖος, περιτομὴ** καὶ *ἀκροβυστία*, the first and fourth and second and third members of this list go together in a chiastic construction, *a*-**b**-**b**-*a*).

The writer may engage in creative *word arrangement* in order to forward his argument. He might use *word play* with a word and its cognates or with similar sounding words which are unrelated in meaning. Paul's biting warning in Phil 3:2-3 plays with the circumcision/castration idea. βλέπετε τὴν *κατατομήν*. 3.3 ἡμεῖς γάρ ἐσμεν ἡ *περιτομή*. Whether by *parallelism* (similar or contrasting words or phrases) or *repetition* or *inclusions* (beginning and rounding off sections in a similar fashion), a writer can draw his audience along with him through the beautiful symmetry of his presentation. Again, unless one is dealing with a formal equivalence English translation, these rhetorical features are often hidden. But when read in the original we can appreciate Paul's turn of phrase. Note the interplay of κέρδη, ἡγέομαι, ζημία, ζημιόω, κερδαίνω in Phil. 3:7-8–[ἀλλὰ] ἅτινα ἦν μοι *κέρδη*, ταῦτα *ἥγημαι* διὰ τὸν Χριστὸν *ζημίαν*. ἀλλὰ μενοῦνγε καὶ *ἡγοῦμαι* πάντα *ζημίαν* εἶναι διὰ τὸ ὑπερέχον τῆς γνώσεως Χριστοῦ ᾽Ιησοῦ τοῦ κυρίου μου, δι᾽ ὃν τὰ πάντα *ἐζημιώθην*, καὶ *ἡγοῦμαι* σκύβαλα, ἵνα Χριστὸν *κερδήσω*.

Finally, the writer may employ *word figures*. A meaning other than the literal meaning may be used to create figures of speech which communicate by *comparison, association, personification, understatement, intensification* or *reversal of meaning*. By these means description, color, emphasis, and feeling are espressed in the text. At one point Paul will label false teachers "dogs," a metaphor, which is a figure of *comparison* (Phil 3:2). At another he will speak of opponents of the cross using a metonymy or figure of *association*, "whose God is their *belly*" (3:19).

Principles for Identifying Rhetorical Features

Because writers do not explicitly identify rhetorical features, this kind of analysis calls for a great deal of interpretive judgment. Still, when we find one of these features, based on solid reasoning from the context and the writer's stylistic practice, it enhances our understanding and appreciation of the writer's skill and adds to the richness of our sermon or lesson.

Word absence. Your mechanical layout will be a great help in looking for occurrences of absence of words. Since you are required to account for all the basic grammatical elements in a passage through graphical placement, when one is missing, you'll know it. The missing element will be represented by an "X" or by supplying a word in brackets. Thus, scanning the mechanical layout will bring to your eye any places where there are *ellipses,* or absent words (cf. Phil 1:8). The dashes and parentheses punctuation in the UBS[4] text are also clues. Be careful, however. Sometimes what is left out is omitted in the train of thought—*not* in the grammatical flow.

Word order. The placement of words on the mechanical layout assumes the normal word order (reading left to right and top to bottom): C-S-V-O and modifiers after the word modified. Whenever a word is shifted forward or backwards for emphasis, it catches your attention because it forces you to read right to left by dropping down a line. An example is Phil 1:8 where one must read the predicate nominative before the subject: *μάρτυς* γάρ μου ὁ θεός. The truthfulness of Paul's statement of affection is emphasized by the placement of God's role as witness first in the sentence.

Word arrangement. Your mechanical layout will also be helpful for studying the arrangement of words. For example, any *parallelisms* in the passage will be apparent in visual form, arranged one line under the other. It is important, however, also to look closely at the text itself, following the flow of thought not only in idea, but also in word choice and the way the words sound. The repetition of terms as themes, the presence of similar and contrasting vocabulary in parallelism, the word play of words with the same stem may be quite readily detectable. The most difficult to find is the word play of words with similar sounds but different meanings. For example, did Luke really intend as word play: λιμοὶ καὶ λοιμοὶ ἔσονται, (Luke 21:11)? Commentaries can often help in the identification process. Printing out the passage in Greek and marking it up, underlining or circling and then drawing lines between the same words and cognates is another way to grasp the writer's art.

Word figure. The figurative use of words is sometimes a matter of interpretational dispute. The dictionary will often distinguish figurative from literal meanings. The best rule of thumb for identification is to try the literal meaning in context and, if it does not seem to fit, see what figurative use the writer might be employing.

Pattern of Analysis

As you view the "mosaic" of the text from the angle of rhetorical features, use the following subcategories under our four major headings.[3]

I. **Word Absence**
   A. **Breaks in Thought**
      1. *Asyndeton*: omission of conjunctions
         a. Generally speaking, conjunctions are used to connect words (in a long list), clauses, sentences, and paragraphs (running style). Asyndeton ("not bound together") occurs when no conjunction is used where the reader would expect it.
         b. The use of asyndeton between clauses and sentences suggests rapidity of thought, urgency, or excitement (cf. 1 Cor 7:17-21).
         c. The use of asyndeton between paragraphs suggests that a new subject has been taken up (cf. Rom 9:1).
      2. *Parenthesis*: insertion of a clause in the middle of a sentence

without proper connection.

> τὴν δὲ αὐτὴν ἀντιμισθίαν, *ὡς τέκνοις λέγω*, πλατύνθητε καὶ ὑμεῖς. (2 Cor 6:13).
> "Now in the same response–I am speaking as to children–you open wide also."

3. *Anacoluthon*: failure to carry through a sentence as originally conceived. The change in direction might be accidental or intentional. It seems the more emotional an author is, the more likely he is to use an anacoluthon.

> Τούτου χάριν ἐγὼ Παῦλος ὁ δέσμιος τοῦ Χριστοῦ [Ἰησοῦ] ὑπὲρ ὑμῶν τῶν ἐθνῶν– 3.2 *εἴ γε* ἠκούσατε τὴν οἰκονομίαν τῆς χάριτος τοῦ θεοῦ τῆς δοθείσης μοι εἰς ὑμᾶς ... (Eph 3:1-2)
> "For this reason I, Paul the prisoner of Christ Jesus on behalf of you Gentiles–*if indeed* you heard the stewardship of the grace of God which was given to me for you," (The sentence begun in 3:1 is not resumed until 3:14).

B. **Omissions/Elipses** (An idea not fully expressed grammatically)

1. *Brachyology*: "the omission, for the sake of brevity, of an element which is not necessary for the grammatical structure but for the thought."[4]

> ... καὶ σχήματι εὑρεθεὶς ὡς ἄνθρωπος 2.8 ἐταπείνωσεν ἑαυτὸν ... (Phil 2:7-8)
> " ... and being found in form as a man (is found) he humbled himself ... "

2. *Zeugma*: a single verb which suits only one subject or object is used with two of them (i.e., a second verb must be supplied).

> γάλα ὑμᾶς ἐπότισα, οὐ βρῶμα. (1 Cor 3:2)
> "I gave you milk to drink, not food (to eat)."

3. *Aposiopesis*: a breaking off of speech due to strong emotion or to modesty.

> Τοῦτο ὑμᾶς σκανδαλίζει; 6.62 ἐὰν οὖν θεωρῆτε τὸν υἱὸν τοῦ ἀνθρώπου ἀναβαίνοντα ὅπου ἦν τὸ πρότερον; (John 6:61-62).
> "Does this scandalize you? If you were to behold the Son of Man ascending where he was before (would you then be scandalized)?"

II. Word Order
A. General
1. To a greater extent than in English, syntactical meaning in Greek depends on the *form* of words (their endings) rather than on word order. Therefore, the NT writers had greater freedom in arranging the words of a sentence. Words could be written more or less in the order in which they came into the writer's head.
2. What is normal word order might vary from NT author to NT author.[5] Nevertheless, it is still possible to make certain statements about "normal" word order.

B. "Normal" Word Order
1. *Conjunctions* usually begin clauses, sentences, and paragraphs.
2. *Main clauses* usually precede subordinate clauses (except for conditional subclauses).
3. The *most common word order* within a clause is
   a. Either: subject ... verb ... object
   b. Or: verb ... subject ... object (Semitic or LXX style imitation)
4. *Modifiers* generally follow the words which govern them:
   a. Noun ... adjective
   b. Article ... adjective ... noun
   c. Noun ... genitive
5. *Prepositional phrases* usually follow the verb.
6. *Participles* and *infinitives* usually occur first in their constructions.
7. *Temporal phrases* and *interrogative pronouns* tend to stand first in a sentence.
8. *Negative particles* usually stand before the word or phrase they negate.
9. *Adverbs* usually follow the verb they modify.
10. *Postpositive conjunctions* never stand first in a clause or sentence: γάρ, γέ, δέ, μέν, μέντοι, οὖν, τέ.

C. Changes in Word Order
1. Changes in word order, in all probability, meant that some word is made emphatic.
   a. J. W. Wenham: "When a writer wishes to emphasise a word, he will often either bring it forward to the beginning

of the sentence or leave it till the end of the sentence."⁶

τῇ γὰρ *χάριτί* ἐστε σεσῳσμένοι διὰ πίστεως . . . (Eph 2:8)
"For *by grace* you have been saved through faith . . ."
Ἑνὶ δὲ *ἑκάστῳ ἡμῶν* ἐδόθη ἡ χάρις . . . (Eph 4:7)
"Now *to each one of us* grace was given . . ."

    b. F. Blass: "Closely related elements in the sentence . . . are usually placed together in simple speech . . . a word, torn out of its natural context and made more independent, is emphatic even when placed at the end of the sentence."⁷

καὶ ἤμεθα τέκνα φύσει *ὀργῆς* (Eph 2:3)
"And we were children by nature *of wrath* . . ."
αὐτοῦ γάρ ἐσμεν ποίημα . . . (Eph 2:10)
"For *of Him (His)* we are a work . . ."

D. **Gradation of Emphasis**: There is also a gradation of emphasis in the placement of adjective with its noun.
    1. Noun+adjective (anarthrous)=focus on qualitative aspects.
    2. Article+adjective+noun=normal (no particular emphasis).
    3. Article+noun+article+adjective=more emphasis on the adjective.
    4. Article+noun+verb+adjective (predicative)=most emphasis on the adjective.

III. **Word Arrangement**
  A. **Repetition**
    1. *Anaphora*: the repetition of the same word(s) at the beginning of successive sentences.

Πάντα μοι ἔξεστιν ἀλλ᾽ οὐ πάντα συμφέρει· *πάντα μοι ἔξεστιν* ἀλλ᾽ οὐκ ἐγὼ ἐξουσιασθήσομαι ὑπό τινος. (1 Cor 6:12)
"*All things are lawful for me,* but all things are not profitable. *All things are lawful for me,* but I will not be mastered by any."

    2. *Antistrophe*: the repetition of the same word(s) at the end of successive sentences.

ὁ ἀδικῶν ἀδικησάτω *ἔτι* καὶ ὁ ῥυπαρὸς ῥυπανθήτω *ἔτι*, καὶ ὁ δίκαιος δικαιοσύνην ποιησάτω *ἔτι* καὶ ὁ ἅγιος ἁγιασθήτω *ἔτι*. (Rev 22:11)
"Let the one who does wrong, do wrong *still*; and let the

one who is filthy, be filthy *still*; and let the one who is righteous, do righteousness *still*; and let the one who is holy, keep himself holy *still*."
3. *Epanadiplosis*: the repetition of the same word(s) at the end of one phrase and the beginning of another.
Τοῦτο δέ, ὁ σπείρων *φειδομένως φειδομένως* καὶ θερίσει, καὶ ὁ σπείρων *ἐπ᾽ εὐλογίαις ἐπ᾽ εὐλογίαις* καὶ θερίσει. (2 Cor 9:6)
"The one who sows *sparingly, sparingly* also shall reap,
The one who sows *with blessings, with blessings* also will reap."
4. *Climax*: epanadiplosis repeated in successive sentences.
οὓς δὲ προώρισεν, τούτους καὶ *ἐκάλεσεν* καὶ οὓς *ἐκάλεσεν*, τούτους καὶ *ἐδικαίωσεν* οὓς δὲ *ἐδικαίωσεν*, τούτους καὶ ἐδόξασεν. (Rom 8:30)
"And whom he predestined, these he also *called*;
and whom he *called*, these he also *justified*;
and whom he *justified*, these he also glorified."
5. *Epizeuxis*: the repetition of the same word in the same sense.
Ἀμὴν ἀμὴν λέγω ὑμῖν ... (John 1:51)
"*Truly, truly*, I am saying to you ..."
οἱ δὲ ἐπεφώνουν λέγοντες, *Σταύρου σταύρου* αὐτόν. (Luke 23:21)
"But they kept on crying out, saying, 'Crucify, crucify Him'."
6. *Hendiadys*: the coordination of two ideas, the second of which is dependent on the first.
δι᾽ οὗ ἐλάβομεν *χάριν καὶ ἀποστολὴν* εἰς ὑπακοὴν πίστεως ... (Rom 1:5)
" through whom we received *grace and apostleship* (grace of apostleship) for obedience of faith ..."
7. *Pleonasm*: a redundant repetition out of habit with no literary or semantic significance.
καὶ ἐρεῖτε τῷ *οἰκοδεσπότῃ* τῆς *οἰκίας* (Luke 22:11)
"And you shall say to the *householder* of the *house*"

B. **Word Play**
1. *Paranomasia*: repetition of the same word or word stem in the immediate context.

καὶ ἐλέγξαι πᾶσαν ψυχὴν περὶ πάντων τῶν ἔργων *ἀσεβείας* αὐτῶν ὧν *ἠσέβησαν* καὶ περὶ πάντων τῶν σκληρῶν ὧν ἐλάλησαν κατ' αὐτοῦ ἁμαρτωλοὶ *ἀσεβεῖς*. (Jude 15)

"... and to convict every soul concerning all their *ungodly* deeds which they have *done in an ungodly way* and concerning all the harsh things which *ungodly* sinners spoke against him."

2. *Parechesis*: different words with similar sounding beginnings or endings.
   a. *Homoeoarcton*: similar sounding beginnings.
      *ἀσυ*νέτους *ἀσυ*νθέτους *ἀσ*τόργους *ἀ*νελεήμονας (Rom 1:31)
   b. *Homoeoteleuton*: similar sounding endings.
      καὶ οὐχ ὡς δι' ἑνὸς ἁμαρτήσαντος τὸ δώρη*μα*· τὸ μὲν γὰρ κρί*μα* ἐξ ἑνὸς εἰς κατάκρι*μα*, τὸ δὲ χάρισ*μα* ἐκ πολλῶν παραπτωμάτων εἰς δικαίω*μα*. (Rom 5:16)

C. **Parallelism**: similarities or contrasts in thought between successive sentences.
   1. In "synonomous" parallelism the second line reinforces the first.
      οὐδὲν γάρ ἐστιν *κεκαλυμμένον* ὃ οὐκ *ἀποκαλυφθήσεται*
      καὶ *κρυπτὸν* ὃ οὐ *γνωσθήσεται*. (Matt 10:26)
      "For nothing has been *hidden* which will not be *revealed*, or *hidden* which will not be made *known*."
   2. In "antithetical" parallelism the second line contrasts with the first.
      σπείρεται ἐν *ἀτιμίᾳ*,
      ἐγείρεται ἐν *δόξῃ* (1 Cor 15:43)
      "It is *sown* in *dishonor*
      It is *raised* in *glory*."

D. **Chiasmus**: the transposition of corresponding words or phrases at the sentence level.
   ἡ γὰρ *σὰρξ* ἐπιθυμεῖ κατὰ τοῦ *πνεύματος*,
   τὸ δὲ *πνεῦμα* κατὰ τῆς *σαρκός*, (Gal 5:17)
   "For the *flesh* lusts against the *spirit*,
   And the *spirit* against the *flesh*,"

E. **Inclusion**: the use of cognate words at the beginning and end of a discussion.

> Ἀναγκαῖον δὲ ἡγησάμην' Ἐπαφρόδιτον τὸν ἀδελφὸν καὶ συνεργὸν καὶ συστρατιώτην μου, ὑμῶν δὲ ἀπόστολον καὶ *λειτουργὸν* τῆς χρείας μου, πέμψαι πρὸς ὑμᾶς, . . . ὅτι διὰ τὸ ἔργον Χριστοῦ μέχρι θανάτου ἤγγισεν παραβολευσάμενος τῇ ψυχῇ, ἵνα ἀναπληρώσῃ τὸ ὑμῶν ὑστέρημα τῆς πρός με *λειτουργίας*.(Phil 2:25, 30)
> "I thought it necessary to send to you Epaphroditus, my brother and co-worker and fellow soldier, and your messenger and *servant* to my need . . . Because he came close to death, on account of the work of Christ, risking his life to complete what was lacking of your *service* to me.

F. **Ring Composition**: a correspondence in wording between sentences that frame a section.
   1. *Inclusive Ring-composition*: uses the similar sentences to begin and end the section to which they belong.
      > *Τὰ κατ' ἐμὲ πάντα γνωρίσει ὑμῖν* Τύχικος ὁ ἀγαπητὸς ἀδελφὸς καὶ πιστὸς διάκονος καὶ σύνδουλος ἐν κυρίῳ, 4.8 ὃν ἔπεμψα πρὸς ὑμᾶς εἰς αὐτὸ τοῦτο, ἵνα γνῶτε τὰ περὶ ἡμῶν καὶ παρακαλέσῃ τὰς καρδίας ὑμῶν, 4.9 σὺν Ὀνησίμῳ τῷ πιστῷ καὶ ἀγαπητῷ ἀδελφῷ, ὅς ἐστιν ἐξ ὑμῶν· *πάντα ὑμῖν γνωρίσουσιν τὰ ὧδε*. (Col 4:7–9)
      > "He will *make known to you all my circumstances* . . . They will *make known to you all the things* here."
   2. *Anaphoric Ring-composition*: stands outside the section and serves to resume a discussion interrupted by that section.
      > Τὸ λοιπόν, ἀδελφοί μου, χαίρετε ἐν κυρίῳ . . . Χαίρετε ἐν κυρίῳ πάντοτε· πάλιν ἐρῶ, χαίρετε. (Phil 3:1; 4:4)
      > "Finally, my brothers, *rejoice in the Lord* . . . *Rejoice in the Lord*, always; again, I say, rejoice."

IV. **Word Figures** (For an exhaustive list of figures with examples, see Bullinger, *Figures of Speech*)
   A. **Comparison**
      1. *Simile*: Using "like" or "as" to compare two objects which are different in nature, though sharing a common quality (1 Thess 2:7; 1 Pet 2:1).
      2. *Metaphor*: Making a forceful, implied comparison without the use of a comparative particle, i.e., "like" or "as" (John 6:35; 8:12; 10:9).
   B. **Association**
      1. *Metonymy*: Substituting one word for another which is naturally related to it.
         a. Cause for Effect (Luke 16:29).
         b. Effect for Cause (John 11:25).
         c. Container for thing contained (John 18:11).
      2. *Synecdoche*: Substituting one idea for another which is associated with it.
         a. A part for the whole (John 2:23; Rom 12:1).
         b. The whole for the part (John 12:19).
   C. **Humanization**
      1. *Anthropomorphism*: Attributing an element of human form to God (Matt 18:10; Jas 5:4; Luke 1:51).
      2. *Personification*: Attributing characteristics of life to inanimate objects, or characteristics of personality to impersonal objects (Luke 19:40; 1 Cor 12:15).
      3. *Apostrophe*: Turning aside from the real audience to address an imaginary one.
         a. To humans beings (Rom 2:1-8).
         b. To animals (Joel 2:22).
         c. To inanimate objects (Isa 1:2).
   D. **Illusion**
      1. *Hyperbole*: Exaggerating in order to make an impression (Mark 10:25).
      2. *Irony*: Stating something which is directly opposite to what is meant (2 Cor 12:13).
      3. *Paradox*: Making a strong statement, which at first seems to involve a contradiction, in order to communicate a truth (Mark 8:35).

E. **Understatement**
 1. *Meiosis*: Making a simple understatement to heighten the action described (Phlm 11).
 2. *Euphemism*: Using a less direct term to avoid a distasteful, offensive, or unnecessarily harsh term (Acts 1:25).
 3. *Litotes*: Making a positive statement in negative terms (Acts 1:5).

V. **Further Means of Emphasis**
 A. **Omission of Verbs**
 καὶ τοῦτο οὐκ ἐξ ὑμῶν, θεοῦ τὸ δῶρον (Eph 2:8)
 "And this not of yourselves, of God the gift"
 B. **Repetition of Terms or Cognate Forms**
 εἷς θεὸς καὶ πατὴρ *πάντων*, ὁ ἐπὶ *πάντων* καὶ διὰ *πάντων* καὶ ἐν *πᾶσιν*. (Eph 4:6)
 "One God and Father of *all*, the one who is over *all* and through *all* and in *all*."
 ἰδόντες δὲ τὸν ἀστέρα *ἐχάρησαν χαρὰν* μεγάλην σφόδρα. (Matt 2:10)
 "They *rejoiced* with exceeding great *joy*."
 C. **Repetition of the Definite Article**
 σπουδάζοντες τηρεῖν *τὴν* ἑνότητα *τοῦ* πνεύματος ἐν *τῷ* συνδέσμῳ *τῆς* εἰρήνης (Eph 4:3)
 "... being diligent to keep *the* unity of *the* Spirit in *the* bond of *the* peace."
 D. **Use of Strong Particles or Conjunctions**
 Τοιγαροῦν καὶ ἡμεῖς . . . τρέχωμεν τὸν προκείμενον ἡμῖν ἀγῶνα (Heb 12:1)
 "*Therefore also* we . . . let us run the race set before us"
 E. **Use of the Personal Pronoun**: when it is not necessary
 Αὐτός γάρ ἐστιν ἡ εἰρήνη ἡμῶν (Eph 2:14)
 "For he *himself* is our peace"
 F. **Use of the Possessive Adjective**: instead of the genitive form of the personal pronoun.
 . . . μὴ ἔχων *ἐμὴν* δικαιοσύνην (Phil 3:9)
 ". . . not having *my own* righteousness"
 G. **Use of ἴδιος**
 οὐδὲ δι᾽ αἵματος τράγων καὶ μόσχων διὰ δὲ τοῦ *ἰδίου* αἵματος εἰσῆλθεν ἐφάπαξ εἰς τὰ ἅγια . . . (Heb 9:12)
 "not through the blood of goats and bulls but through *his own*

blood ... "

Literary Analysis: Rhetorical Features–Resources

Materials from Previous Study

"Greek Reading and Finished Translation" and "Mechanical Layout" worksheets for the passage
"Survey" worksheet

Greek is Great Gain

Descriptions in chapter nine

Reference Tools

BDAG
BDF
Bullinger, *Figures of Speech*.
Larkin, "Rhetorical Features Chart."

Commentaries

Fee, *Philippians*.
Hawthorne, *Philippians*.
Loh and Nida, *Handbook to Philippians*.
O'Brien, *Philippians*.
Silva, *Philippians*.

Literary Analysis: Rhetorical Features–Procedure

I. Survey
II. Analysis
    A. Historical Analysis
    B. Literary Analysis
        1. Context
        2. Genre
        3. *Syntax*

a. Grammar
b. *Rhetorical Features: Word Absence, Word Order, Word Arrangement, Word Figure.* With the use of the above resources, fill out the "Rhetorical Features Analysis" Worksheet (template available at WJLFP) as you follow these steps (see fig. 9.3 for an example).
   1) *Identify.* Identify significant or hard to understand occurrences of various rhetorical features, instances of the sub-categories within Word Absence, Word Order, Word Arrangement, Word Figure.
   2) *Classify.* Classify as precisely as possible each chosen rhetorical feature according to the function it is fulfilling.
   3) *Comment.* In each case, comment on what the rhetorical feature contributes to the meaning of the passage. This will involve some paraphrase of the passage's flow of thought.

Figure 9.3. **Sample Literary Analysis: Rhetorical Features: Phil 1:3-11**

v. Word Absent	Word Order	Word Arrangement	Word Figure
3)		πάσῃ . . . πάντοτε . . . πάσῃ. . . πάντων, repetition; stresses his constancy of involvement in prayer for all of them	
5)		vv 5, 7 κοινωνίᾳ . . . συγκοινωνούς, word play (paranomasia); helps us understand the nature of the fellowship/participation	
6)		vv 6, 10 ἄχρι ἡμέρας Χριστοῦ Ἰησου . . . εἰς ἡμέραν Χριστοῦ, theme repetition; stresses eschatological endpoint of the "work" and helps us understand this is maturing sanctification, not perfection	

Figure 9.3. (continued)

v. Word Absent	Word Order	Word Arrangement	Word Figure
8) μάρτυς γάρ μου ὁ θεός, verb "to be" must be supplied, ellipsis; strengthens the emphasis on oath 9)	μάρτυς γάρ μου ὁ θεός, abnormal word order; "witness" is first to emphasize truthfulness of statement	vv. 9–11 ἐν ἐπιγνώσει καὶ πάσῃ αἰσθήσει . . . εἰλικρινεῖς καὶ ἀπρόσκοποι . . . δόξαν καὶ ἔπαινον, parallelism; three matched pairs creating a compounding effect to impress the readers with the completeness of provision and of the worship with issues from it	τοῖς δεσμοῖς μου, association –synedoche; the fetters stand for the whole condition of being in prison

Endnotes

1. Black, *Read New Testament Greek*, 179-81.

2. I am indebted to John D. Harvey, (*Greek Grammar Guides*) for the organization and much of the content of the Appendix. See also Harvey, *Greek is Good Grief*.

3. I am indebted to John D. Harvey (*Greek Grammar Guides*) for the organization and much of the content on Rhetorical Features. For a summary of this material in chart form see "Rhetorical Features Chart" at WJLFP.

4. BDF, 255.

5. For further discussion, see Turner, *Style*.

6. Wenham, *Elements*, 31.

7. BDF, 249.

Chapter 10
WORD STUDY: FOCUS THE MEANING

Whenever you communicate the Word of God, you stand between two worlds. One is the world of a biblical revelation spoken by God into the historical/cultural context of ancient times. The other is the world of contemporary twenty-first century culture. A strong hermeneutical bridge must be built to span these two worlds so that the original writer's intended meaning can be understood as the Bible's meaning today, though the outworking of the meaning's significance in application may be different than in ancient times.

Your task as interpreter (and later communicator) is to enter, as much as possible, into the ancient context of the Bible's writers and first readers. Understanding what the first century writer meant and how it was significant to the original audience is essential to your ability to present the text accurately, vividly, and in a way that prompts today's audience to make a full-hearted application. "Word Study," the last step in Literary Analysis, is an important and interesting tool that helps us uncover a first century frame of reference by putting significant words under the microscope of our analysis. Not only can "Word Study" yield valuable content, but it also guards against anachronistic interpretations and applications that can result if we read into the text our own cultural beliefs, values, and concerns. "Word Study" ensures that the biblical text is free to speak accurately, on its own terms.

When you encounter a significant or a difficult to understand term, it is time to do a "Word Study." There are two parts to the process: "Focus the Meaning" (covered in this chapter) and "Illumine the Meaning" (covered in chapter eleven). When you "Focus the Meaning" of a word, you seek for its most accurate definition in order to better understand its theological or spiritual importance. You arrive at such a definition by comparing and contrasting how the word is used in your passage with how it is used elsewhere in the same Bible book, in other books by the same writer, and—as needed—in the rest of the New Testament. Once you are confident of the definition, you can move on to "Illumine the Meaning." Here you will investigate biblical and/or extra-biblical background that sheds light on the ancient usage of the word and will aid in communicating it in a fresh way to today's audience.

"Focus the Meaning" has value in several ways.[1] First, it is a way of discovering directly for yourself the meaning of words. And this you do more or less independently of dictionaries' judgments. You are able to broaden and deepen your understanding of biblical thought through the inductive process of direct meditation on the text using only a print concordance or Bible software. Once you have completed your own inductive word study on the "kingdom of God" in Matthew or "salvation" in Luke, or "righteousness" in Paul, for example, your hard-won results will stay with you more firmly and much longer, than had you simply read a dictionary definition or article. "Word study" results in confident growth in your grounding in biblical thought.

Second, word studies provide data for the third and last step in Analysis: "Theological Analysis." There you must state with authority what God's message is in your passage. What better way to arrive at God's message than by comparing Scripture with Scripture through word study!

Third, one of the main ingredients of a thoroughly biblically based expository sermon or lesson is the provision of parallel and contrasting Scripture references which illuminate the truth of the preaching/teaching passage. You will discover these references during your "Focus the Meaning" study. For example, the theological significance of the phrase "fruit of righteousness" (Phil 1:11) as the content of Paul's prayer comes into clearer focus when we note that the one other positive occurrence of the term "righteousness" is Phil 3:9, in which salvation is characterized as "being found in Christ," having right standing with God which is from God and received by faith. This is contrasted with works-righteousness—a standing with God which one tries to achieve by obedience to the law (Phil 3:6, 9).

Principles Related to Word Study: "How Words Mean"

Words and Communication

The act of verbal communication among human beings involves four elements: the speaker or writer, the listener or reader, the thing referred to

Figure 10.1. **Semantic Taxonomy**

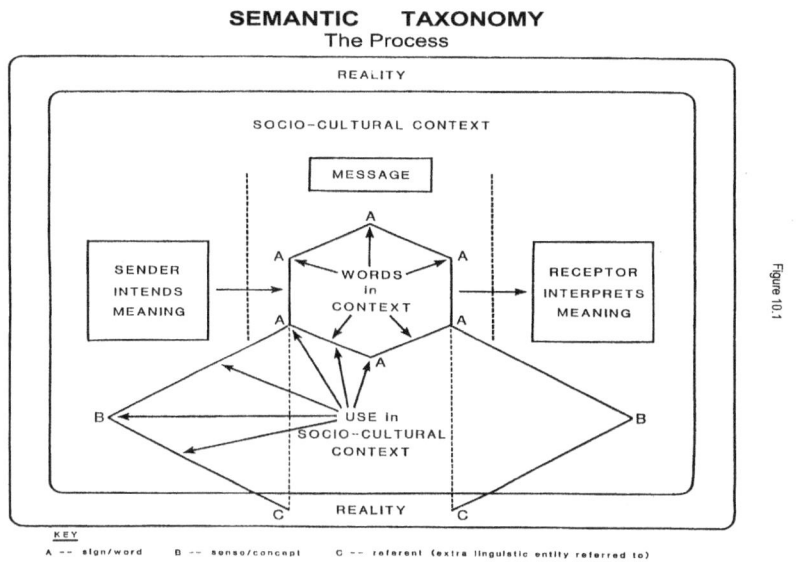

Source: Larkin, *Culture and Biblical Hermeneutics*, 73.

(referent) and linguistic materials (words; see fig. 10.1).[2] The speaker expresses himself in order to point his listener to a referent and say something about it (sense). The speaker/writer selects linguistic materials (words) from the vocabulary stock of his and his listeners'/readers' sociocultural context. He places them in a grammatical-literary context of his own formulation in order to communicate the meaning which he intends.

Words and Range of Meaning.

Some words have the same referent every time they are used, i.e., proper names,' Ἰησοῦς, and to a large extent technical theological terms like ἄγγελος, "angel." Yet many words, though they have a core meaning,[3] have the potential of pointing to a number of different referents. For example, πνεῦμα may refer to the third person of the Trinity or to a spirit being and be translated "Spirit" or "ghost." It may refer to a psychological, physical or physiological event and be translated "inner-self, wind or breath."[4] One word may also have the potential of giving a number of different characteristics (senses) to a given referent. For example, κοινωνία describes the state, the motivating attitude, the action or the sign of fellowship/participation and can be translated "association, generosity, sharing, or contribution"[5] its various senses. As you think about the range of meaning of words, keep in mind that the meaning of any given occurrence of a word comes from two sources: the vocabulary stock of the culture (its "lexical meaning") and the immediate grammatical/literary context (its "contextual meaning").

New Testament Greek dictionaries helpfully systematize these ranges of meaning for given words. This is the fruit of collecting and examining examples of the word's usage in works antecedent to and contemporaneous with the New Testament. But we must be very careful not to treat the dictionary description of the full range of potential meanings as giving the actual meaning of the word in one of its particular uses. This is the fallacy of "illegitimate totality transfer" of meaning.[6]

For example, the phrase "fellowship in the gospel" in Phil 1:5 should not be understood according to a comprehensive dictionary definition of "a close relationship, a generosity, a contribution, and a sharing in the gospel," though it could mean any of these. Rather, unless the writer is being ambiguous, he probably means only one aspect of the range. BDAG proposes "close relationship" as that part of the range of meaning employed at this verse. Paul, as his use in this particular grammatical-literary context indicates, has in his mind only one part of the range of meaning of κοινωνία as he composes his expression of thanksgiving (Phil 1:5). Paul's intention is that the reader identify one referent and sense of the word as he hears or reads it in context.

Words and Change of Meaning

Communication occurs in a dynamic environment of change. Historically and culturally, both the speaker's and listener's environment is in a constant state of change. The speaker as sub-creator, with a mind made in the image of God, sometimes adapts familiar language to accommodate change or formulates new ideas by expressing new words or new uses of old words. He may apply old words to a different referent. He may focus on a different characteristic of the referent, thus using the old word to carry a new sense. For example, space technology and the invention of a re-usable space ship added to the range of meaning for the word "shuttle" as it was applied to a new referent in the phrase "space shuttle."

Words, then, have the capacity for undergoing changes in their range of meaning over time. Sometimes a word's meaning narrows to a single referent so that it becomes a technical term tied to a specialized usage. For example, though there are a few examples of ἐκκλησία with a non-spiritual meaning of "a political assembly" (Acts 19:39) or, more generally, to "a gathering of people" (Acts 19:32, 40), the predominant use in the New Testament has as its referent the Christian church. Alternatively, sometimes a word's meaning is broadened or altered. Under the influence of LXX translation practice, δόξα ("reputation," Diodorus Siculus, *Works* 15.61.5) also came to mean "brightness, radiance, splendor" (Acts 22:11; cf. LXXExod 24:16-17).[7]

Either way, words change from one meaning to another for one of several reasons. Historical events may introduce or change referents or their characteristics so that the vocabulary stock must be adapted to account for these changes. Or, the speaker's knowledge of or attitude toward the referents about which he wants to communicate may change. When this happens he must express this change through new words or new uses of old words. There also appears to be a dynamic in language which moves it over time to abbreviation and less precision. Further, through ellipsis, one word can come to stand for other words which would normally accompany it. For example, αἱ γραφαί ("the writings") without the qualifier ἱεραί ("holy") can mean the Scriptures (Luke 24:27). Note the opposite phenomenon: word omitted and qualifier retained–οἱ δώδεκα ("the twelve"), the adjective alone as substantival means "the twelve disciples" (8:1).[8]

Words and Their History

Tracing the history of a word's usage can be valuable for helping us learn the origin of different parts of the range of meaning and giving us a comprehensive view of the range of potential meanings. But take note of two cautions about applying this kind of information to your passage.

First, a word's etymology: its root or original meaning or the literal meaning of its basic components, does not necessarily tell you what the word means in your passage. The term μετάνοια ("repentance") is not best understood by parsing its basic components: μετά ("complete change") + νοια (from νοῦς, "mind"), because the biblical understanding is much more comprehensive ("turning about, conversion")[9] than a change of mind. Now, if the word's spelling is transparent, which means that it is clearly related to its meaning either by sound (onomatopoeia, e.g. "splash," "clank"), form (e.g. "dreamer"); or semantic motivation (a figure, e.g. "foot of the hill"), etymological study can be helpful. But the majority of words are what linguists call "opaque." Their spelling gives little indication of their sense and referent.

Gordon Fee rightly concludes, "To know the etymology, or root, of a word, however interesting it may be, almost *never* tells us anything about its meaning in a given context."[10] The bottom line is to guard against representing meaning by what you glean from etymology or simply from translation equivalents (words in the receptor language which are used to translate words from the source language). The meaning of a word is best represented by a definition: a set of semantic features, which describes what it contributes to the passage.

A second caution is to avoid "parallelomania." To locate in the history of a word a prior parallel usage does not mean that you have discovered the source of the NT use. Priority in determining a NT meaning and its source should be given to factors in the NT writer's background, particularly prior divine revelation (i.e., the Old Testament).

Words and Context

Although it is correct to see words in themselves as having *lexical* (socio-culturally grounded) meaning, which they bring to a particular grammatical/literary context, we also need to note that words also pick up and carry *contextual* (grammatical/literary) meaning too. Take for example the use of the word "ball" in these two sentences.

> His daughter danced the night away at the governor's *ball*.
> John picked up the rubber *ball*.

The use of the verb "danced," placing the word in a prepositional phrase introduced by "at" and adding the modifier "governor's," all indicate that in this sentence "ball" refers to an event. In the second sentence, the verb "picked up" and the modifier "rubber" indicates "ball" refers to a physical object. The writer's choice of verb determines for us the particular part of the range of the lexical meaning of the word "ball" he has in mind. But the context also helps us grasp the meaning of the term "ball:" The word "governor's" informs us that this is a celebratory occasion in the political or governmental arena as opposed to a "harvest ball" or a "debutante ball." "Rubber" lets us know that the ball is probably a toy object.

Viewed comprehensively, three contexts provide the angles of vision for discerning word meaning: *grammatical/literary*, *authorial*, and *socio-cultural*. In addition to taking into account *grammatical/literary* context's role in identifying intended meaning, noting the impact of genre, subgenre, and rhetorical features on word usage, can help you decide whether the writer intends a literal or figurative meaning. As already noted, the larger *authorial* context, whether of the NT writer or of the entire New Testament, is helpful in delineating a term's range of meaning. Authorial context can also set parameters by which we can test whether the meaning we think we have found in our passage is probable. If it is congruent with the rest of the author's thought, we are probably on target. Finally, word usage is always grounded in the writer's and audience's *socio-cultural context*. Extra-biblical literature from ancient times supply us with potential lexical and contextual meanings with which the original audience would have been familiar.

Identifying Vocabulary for Word Study

Challenge of Frequency of Occurrence

Because our time is limited, we must be very judicious in our choice of terms to study. Important words sometimes occur frequently, e.g., πίστις ("faith"), which occurs 138 times in Paul's writings (eighteen in Prison Epistles) and δικαιωσύνη ("righteousness") fifty-six times in Paul (seven in Prison Epistles). Words like these would seem to be prime candidates for study. However, sometimes a word we want to understand only occurs a few times in a writer's works. ᾽Εξανάστασις (a particular form of the word meaning "resurrection"), for example, only occurs at Phil 3:11 in the whole New Testament.

Selection Criteria

The two basic criteria for selecting terms for word study are difficulty in understanding and significance for the flow of thought of the passage. Use your MLO again to identify the terms which are key to the passage's message. Look for repeated themes and placement on the MLO (e.g., in Phil 1:3-11, repetition–κοινωνία and συγκοινωνός, 1:5, 7; placement-θεός,

1:3, 8, 11). You can also use your "Survey" worksheet to remind yourself of key theological terms, as well as, those you found difficult to understand because they did not seem to point to a familiar part of the range of meaning. Also be alert to the occurrence of pairs of synonyms (e.g., ἐπιγνώσει καὶ . . . αἰσθήσει, εἰλικρινεῖς καὶ ἀπρόσκοποι, 1:9-10). Once you have identified possible candidates, decide which ones seem most likely to yield important insights for your work. You will probably have time to "Focus the Meaning" for two to three words for one sermon or lesson. For the others, turn to commentaries and dictionaries.

"Focus the Meaning" Analysis

The basic steps of "Focus the Meaning" are similar to grammatical and rhetorical features analysis: *identify, classify,* and *comment*.

Identification

Identify the words you want to study (probably two to three words) based upon the criteria just described: difficulty in understanding and significance for the flow of thought.

Classification

With the aid of a concordance or Bible software, collect all the instances of the word in the book in which your preaching/teaching passage is found. If the book is brief, like Philippians, and the instances few, you may want to broaden your database to a natural cluster of works by the same author, i.e., works written around the same time.

Book clusters and circles of context. Thinking in terms of book clusters can make word study more manageable when dealing with a major author in the New Testament like Paul. Here are some natural clusterings of Paul's letters: early Epistles (Galatians, 1-2 Thessalonians); Corinthian Correspondence (1-2 Corinthians plus Romans); Prison Epistles (Philemon, Colossians, Ephesians, Philippians); the Pastoral Epistles (1 Timothy, Titus, 2 Timothy). You can cluster John's writing into three units: the Gospel; 1-3 John; or Revelation.

When possible and appropriate work within the parameters of book clusters. However, in some cases, for clarity and validation you may need to reach out to the NT writer's works as a whole, to other NT writers, and/or to the entire NT. Each increasing circle of context will bring more light and more richness to your understanding.

Classification in range of meaning. Once you have all the instances, classify them according to the range of possible meanings. Although dictionaries are a great help and should be consulted for basic components of the range of lexical meaning, commit yourself to the inductive pursuit of the main and sub-categories of meaning.

The main categories are the equivalent to what a dictionary provides and may be found by comparing and contrasting uses in a number of passages. Sub-categories come from contextual meanings. To identify sub-categories from contextual meanings for a verb, study the subjects and objects used with it. For a noun, look at the verbs and modifiers used with it.

With such investigation, even without the help of a dictionary you will be able to arrive at the components which make up a profile of the writer's use of the term. For example, the LN dictionary, in essence, provides only one category of meaning for κύριος in Philippians, since Jesus is its consistent referent in the letter. They note that when "Lord" refers to Jesus, it is a title and means "one who exercises supernatural authority over mankind–Lord, Ruler, One who commands."[11] But there is so much more to understand about the title, when used of Jesus in this letter (see fig. 10.2). As we take a look at κύριος in particular contexts, we can identify a number of subcategories. Jesus is declared "Lord" (admittedly, often as a proper name) as the source of grace and peace (Phil 1:2; 4:23); at Christian conversion (3:8); and in descriptions of his future return and reign (2:11; 3:20; 4:5). We also note that there are a number of occurrences of the term in the stylized phrase, "in the Lord." Here the Christ's Lordship relates to actions in the Christian life ("stand" 4:1; "rejoice"3:1; 4:4, 10); relations (brethren, 1:14; "welcome," 2:29; "mind the same thing," 4:2); and planning (hope, 2:19; confident, 2:24). This is a much richer understanding than would have been possible based on dictionary study alone.

Recording the evidence. As you develop the categories and subcategories of your profile of the word's usage, record each occurrence and write down enough of the immediate context for each reference so that you can identify the term's meaning at that place. In time to come you will be able to review your work on the word study without having to look up every passage. For example, when classifying Phil. 2:11 under the main category of *Jesus=Lord*

Figure 10.2. **Sample Literary Analysis: Word Study (Focus the Meaning) for κύριος**

Phil 2:11–κύριος

Classification:

A. Jesus= Lord as ruler and God
   1. Source of Grace and Peace 1:2; 4:23
   2. Christian Conversion
      3:8 surpassing worth of knowing Christ Jesus my Lord
   3. The Future
      a. 2:11 every tongue will confess "Jesus is Lord"
      b. 3:20 await the Savior, the Lord
      c. 4:5 the Lord is near

B. Christian Life "in the Lord"
   1. Posture
      a. Stand, 4:1
      b. Rejoice, 3:1; 4:4, 10
   2. Relations
      a. Brethren, 1:14
      b. Welcome, 2:29
      c. Mind the same thing, 4:2
   3. Planning
      a. Hope to send, 2:19
      b. Confident will come, 2:24

Comment:

Summary profile. The Christian who has entered into a personal relationship that knows Jesus as "my Lord," lives his whole life "in the Lord" (main emphasis). From that perspective and with that accountability, he is to be steadfast and find his joy in his relationship with Jesus. He is to relate to other Christians as brothers, in harmony and graciousness "in the Lord." He is to humbly, but confidently, plan his future activities "in the Lord." He knows grace and peace from this Lord. He looks forward to a day when the Lord will come as Savior and Judge (another emphasis resulting in self controlled living now), a day when *every one* will confess, "Jesus is Lord."

Focus the Meaning. Jesus is supreme Lord, God, and will be recognized as such at the last day. The purpose clause and the universal homage referenced points to an eschatological fulfillment.

as ruler and God and the subcategory of *The Future*, write the Phil 2:11 reference and the phrase, "every tongue will confess, 'Jesus Christ is Lord'."

Comment

Summary profile. When your classification is complete, write a comprehensive summary of how the New Testament writer uses the word. Include comments on those parts of the range of meaning that the writer emphasizes (see fig. 10.2 for example).

Focus the meaning. The second task in commenting gets us to where we wanted to be all along. It is finally time to "Focus the Meaning" for your particular passage. What does the word mean in this verse in this chapter? From the range of meaning you have developed in your study, select the one that best fits the usage in your passage (see fig. 10.2). To be as thorough as possible, go one more step and substantiate your choice with reasons based on evidence from contextual considerations.

Word Study (Focus the Meaning): Resources

Materials from Previous Study

"Greek Reading/Translation" and "Mechanical Layout" worksheets
"Survey" worksheet

Greek is Great Gain

Descriptions in chapter ten
Figures in chapter ten

Reference Tools

Biblioi CD.
M&G
Wigram. *Englishman's Greek Concordance.*
BDAG
LN
EDNT

NIDNTT
TDNT

Commentaries

Eadie, *Philippians*.
Fee, *Philippians*.
Hawthorne, *Philippians*.
O'Brien, *Philippians*.
Silva, *Philippians*.

Word Study (Focus the Meaning): Procedure

I. Survey
II. Analysis
    A. Historical Analysis
    B. Literary Analysis
        1. Context
        2. Genre
        3. Syntax
        4. *Word Study*
            a. *Focus the Meaning.* With the use of the above resources, fill out the "Focus the Meaning" worksheet (see WJLFP for template) as you follow these steps (see example, figs. 10.2-3).
                1) *Identify.* Identify theologically significant or hard to understand words.
                2) *Classify.* Collect with the aid of print concordances or Bible software occurrences of the word in the writer's book(s). Classify all occurrences according to an inductively developed range of meaning (categories from a Greek Dictionary, subcategories from context). As you record each reference, include enough of the immediate context so the note is understandable and prompts the memory.

Figure 10.3. **Sample Literary Analysis: Word Study (Focus the Meaning) for δικαιοσύνη**

Passage and term Phil. 1:11, δικαιωσύνη (Prison Epistles database)

Classification: (main categories from BDAG, s.v. δικαιοσύνη)

2. Quality or state of juridical correctness with focus on redemptive action, "righteousness," right standing with God
   a. Faith the instrument–"through faith of Christ . . . based on faith," Phil 3:9
   b. God the source–"from God," Phil 3:9
   c. Source of uprightness, moral rectitude, Phil. 1:11
3. Quality or Characteristic of upright behavior, "uprightness"
   a. Uprightness which meets God's standards, "law-righteousness," a performance way of relating to God
      1) Paul's Pre-Christian life–"righteousness in the law, blameless," Phil 3:6; "my own righteousness, from law," Phil 3:9–salvation impossible this way
   b. Uprightness in general, particularly of the Christian
      1) General mark of Christian, who is called to put on "the new man created in righteousness," Eph 4:24; who as children of light have a fruit which is righteousness, Eph 5:9; Phil 1:11; and who in spiritual warfare have donned the "breastplate of righteousness," Eph 6:14

Comment:

Summary profile. Paul understands righteousness both as right standing with God and upright behavior. He contrasts the truly salvific right standing provided by God, received by faith (an emphasis), and which is the Christian's hope, with a performance way of relating to God through upright behavior according to the law. The latter Paul had practiced, but became convinced was loss (an emphasis), even rubbish, in comparison to knowing Christ and his saving work, for it was mutually exclusive of the saving effect of Christ's death, and involved following a law which could not make alive. Paul, however, did understand upright behavior as essentially marking the Christian (an emphasis), who must put on the "new man created in righteousness"; must as children of light produce the "fruit of righteousness"; and in spiritual warfare put on the "breastplate of righteousness."

Focus the Meaning. It is possible to see the word "righteousness" as a genitive of apposition and only referring to uprightness, "rectitude"

Figure 10.3 *(continued)*

> (Hawthorne, *Philippians*, 29). Yet the presence of Paul's emphasis elsewhere in the letter on "right standing" (Phil 3:6-9) whose theme Phil 1:11 serves to introduce, leads us to conclude that, though the fruit of righteousness is indeed moral rectitude, upright living, such righteousness is grounded first and foremost in "right standing with God."
>
> 3) Comment.
> - *Summary profile.* Comment on the word's meaning through a summary profile of the word's use, together with emphases.
> - *Focus the meaning.* Determine the word's meaning in the passage for your sermon or lesson. Substantiate your decision by reasoning from features in the immediate context.

Endnotes

1. Toussaint, "New Testament Word Study," 35-41; Bock, "Lexical Analysis," 135-53; Robinson, *Biblical Preaching*, 61-66.

2. Gardiner, *Theory of Speech*, 7.

3. Nida, *Componential Analysis*, 11.

4. Louw, "Greek Testament Workbook," 110-11.

5. BDAG, 552-53.

6. Silva, *Biblical Words*, 25.

7. BDAG, 256-58.

8. Silva, *Biblical Words*, 82-83.

9. BDAG, 640.

10. Fee, *New Testament Exegesis*, 79.

11. LN 1:139.

Chapter 11

WORD STUDY: ILLUMINE THE MEANING

You have "Focused the Meaning" of some key words so that you have clear, well supported definitions. Now it's time to investigate their ancient context. Finding background source references or instances of contemporary background usage for key words in your passage will enhance your understanding and provide illustrative color and vitality to your delivery. This is what is meant by "Illumine the Meaning." Whether by comparison or contrast, locating Old Testament or extra-biblical examples of word usage in the context of ancient life is time well spent.

As an example, a little research into the background of ἀρραβών, descriptive of the Holy Spirit in the New Testament (Eph 1:14, 2 Cor 1:22), tells us that this is a legal and commercial technical term for a "payment of part of a purchase price in advance . . . which secures the legal claim to the article in question, or makes a contract valid, . . . (it) is a payment that obligates the contracting party to make further payments."[1] This information certainly illumines our understanding of Paul's declaration that the Holy Spirit is God's ἀρραβών τῆς κληρονομίας ἡμῶν –"down payment, earnest money of our inheritance" (Eph 1:14). It helps us communicate more effectively the lengths to which God has gone to assure us that he indeed will give us our inheritance of eternal life.

As you tackle this second step in "Word Study," you will be hard at work comparing and contrasting within the biblical text, as well as, between the biblical text (Old and the New Testaments) and extra-biblical literature. In preparation for learning that procedure, let's take a few minutes to gain some perspective. What is the nature of biblical revelation as compared to all other literature?

The Nature of the Biblical Text

We know that Scripture is unique among all literature because it is fully divine and fully human. This uniqueness circumscribes the significance we will attach to even the best of the ancient parallels. Scripture will always be the ultimate authority. At the same time, the vocabulary of Scripture shares a commonality with the everyday speech of the time in which it was written. It is for this reason we should consider Scripture "the revelation of God . . . in the common language of the New Testament Era" (see fig. 11.1).

The Revelation of God . . .

Recovering meaning. The New Testament gives us God's message of salvation and his will for right doctrine and practice (2 Tim 3:14-17). Stop for a moment and remind yourself how important it is to correctly interpret such eternally significant content. God revealed his message in human language, but it was the language of the era in which the text was written. Because of the passage of time and translation practice, the meanings we attribute to biblical vocabulary today (sense and/or referents) may or may not be the same as the meaning attributed to the words in the ancient era. Your job is to identify when this is the case and do the work necessary to gain a correct understanding of what key words in your passage meant then and how that same meaning can be expressed now in twenty-first century context.

Understanding uniqueness. Much of the language in the NT text mirrors the spoken and written Greek of the day. However, the coming of Jesus—the watershed event of all history—should have a dramatic influence on our investigation. So significant was the impact of these climatic salvation events and the divine revelatory process used to express them in Greek, that some scholars have concluded that a distinct dialect—Christian Greek—was the result.[2] Others[3] are more cautious. Still, they note that the religious-theological vocabulary of NT Greek rejects, represses or excludes part or all of the range of meaning for Hellenistic Greek words as it creates religious-theological technical terms. New Testament Greek also deepens or adds new meanings by adding or shifting referents and senses. It even creates new words.

Using background. So how do we discern the meaning of this uniquely Christian New Testament Greek vocabulary? We turn to the Old Testament via the Septuagint. The Hebrew text is the first part of our authoritative biblical revelation and the Greek Septuagint serves as a bridge between OT Hebrew and NT Greek meanings (see fig. 11.1). It is here that we find the background and often the source of meaning for NT Greek words, especially religious-theological vocabulary. Meanings from Classical and Hellenistic Greek, both Jewish and non-Jewish, provide helpful background. But they should be used mainly as contrasting background against which to view the uniqueness of the New Testament meaning.

WORD STUDY: ILLUMINE THE MEANING   185

Figure 11.1. **Language and Thought Contexts for the Greek New Testament**

B.C.	435	330	200	100	0	A.D. 100	200	330
Divine Revelation	❷ OT MT*		❶ OT Greek LXX 3rd–2nd C. B.C.			GNT A.D. 40s-90s		
in the Language of the Time		❻ Classical Greek 900 B.C.–330 B.C.	❸ Jewish Intertestamental Literature 200 B.C.–A.D. 200					
			❹ Hellenistic Non-Literary Greek 330 B.C.– A.D. 330					
			❺ Hellenistic Literary Greek 330 B.C.– A.D. 330					

*Circled numbers indicate the relative nearness or remoteness to the New Testament of a given thought context. Divine revelation provides background source material. Literature in the language of the time provides contemporary background.

. . . In the Common Language of the New Testament Era

While recognizing the creative uniqueness of New Testament Greek as the language of divine revelation, we also need to note the continuities which exist between it and the Greek of NT times. This is especially true when considering Koine Greek, the common language of the day. For it is by these continuities that "the Christian communicated with his contemporary, with the large base of common vocabulary, syntax and accidence."[4] The three basic sources for examples of Greek usage in NT times are Hellenistic literature (e.g., Epictetus, Diodorous Siculus, Plutarch, Strabo); non-literary documents and evidence (papyri and inscriptions; 50,000 documents have been published); and Jewish intertestamental literature, (OT Apocrypha, OT Pseudepigrapha, Philo, Josephus, non-Greek Jewish sources: Dead Sea Scrolls, Mishnah, Talmud, Tosefta, Midrash, Targum).

Hellenistic literature and non-literary documents and evidence (papyri and inscriptions). The elevated style and religio-philosophical vocabulary and discussion found in some Hellenistic literature provides valuable background for NT study. But just as valuable are the non-literary documents (private letters, bills contracts, evidence for Koine Greek) because of

> their unconscious and ephemeral character. Herein they differ markedly from inscriptions, which were designed for public view and for posterity, and whose candor is not always above suspicion. The figures in the papyri, on the other hand, are as a rule off their guard; they are to be seen following their ordinary daily pursuits with a refreshing absence of prose and advertisement. They neither make nor possess any claim to fame, and therein lies their interest.[5]

Because of their nature as works not intended for publication, non-literary papyri also differ markedly from Hellenistic Literature, and they "throw the most vivid light on New Testament language and New Testament times."[6]

Jewish intertestamental literature. Jewish intertestamental literature is helpful in giving the most chronologically immediate extra-biblical background for the thought of the NT writers. In this literature, written after the Old Testament and into New Testament times, "the society, customs, issues and world views assumed by Biblical writers are illustrated and clarified."[7] Not only does the interpreter meet the language, verbal images, and literary genre with which the New Testament writers express themselves, he also meets "first-hand the interests, concerns, desires and frustrations of the NT world."[8] In sum, intertestamental literature introduces us to the broad but complex society in which Christianity had its origin. Through it

> new and clarifying insights may be gained into the cultural institutions, world views, tensions and aspirations of those groups that were parts of the milieu of Jesus and the early Christians.[9]

It is thus an indispensable tool for understanding the first century milieu of NT thought.

Types of "Illumine the Meaning" Study

There are two types of "Illumine the Meaning" study you may want to undertake during immediate preparation: *background source* and *contemporary background* studies. *Background source* study investigates background for key theological terms and their antecedent source. *Contemporary background* studies locate contemporary illustrations of words, often their concrete use. In the light of these examples we can better understand their theological or spiritual use in biblical passages.

Background Source Study

Since the Greek New Testament is divine revelation, the proper background source for key theological terms is Scripture itself as it records antecedent divine revelatory acts and their interpretation. Early church preaching (in Acts) and Jesus' teaching (the Gospels) are the Epistles' proper background. The Old Testament, particularly the Hebrew text, is the background source for the whole New Testament. For example, if you want to find the source of Paul's thought in the phrase "the fruit of righteousness" (Phil 1:11), the Old Testament is the best place to look. If you think you have found an extra-biblical background source for a particular biblical thought, be sure you can demonstrate how this background is congruent with the rest of biblical revelation.

Contemporary Background Study

Sometimes a New Testament word can be better understood when it is set against the background of its usage in everyday conversation. Knowing how the original audience would have understood a word's meaning enables you to see what is and is not new and different in the New Testament writer's usage. The two best direct sources for contemporary background for theological terms are Jewish intertestamental literature and Hellenistic philosophical and ethical writings. Contemporary background study may also involve illustrating a spiritual or figurative use of a term in the New Testament by giving an example from a literal/secular use from Hellenistic nonliterary documents: the papyri. For example, Paul seems to have appropriated κοινωνία from the world of commerce in which it signified close, economic partnership (BGU 2:586[11], a law contract of partnership in commerce), when he uses it to refer to the collection for the saints (Rom 15:26).

"Illumine the Meaning" Analysis

The five steps of "Illumine the Meaning" (for both types of study) are: *identify, choose, locate, record,* and *comment.*

Identification of Terms and Type of Study

The first questions to ask are "What terms will repay careful study? What type of background investigation will prove most fruitful with each?" Here are two questions together with suggestions for investigation that will help you identify such words and the appropriate type of study.

- *Is the word a key theological concept?* Investigating the *background source* context can help you understand the term's core meaning as well as the particular meaning in the passage (e.g., see fig. 11.4 for δικαιοσύνη study).
- *Is the word used in a theological or spiritual/figurative way which seems to compare or contrast with its religious-philosophical or secular/literal usage in the contemporary milieu?* A study of the *contemporary background* will help you understand how the writer used a word over against how the audience would have normally understood it (e.g., see fig. 11.5 for κοινωνία study).

Selection of Background Thought Context and/or Ancient Literature

Having identified the term and proposed type of study, we next must ask: "What thought context and/or ancient literature area would be beneficial for such a study (see fig. 11.2)?"

Clusters of thought contexts. Think about the thought contexts of ancient times as clustered into three: *biblical revelation, Jewish intertestamental thought,* and *Greek thought.* The ancient literature which supports these three areas is as follows.

- *biblical revelation:* New Testament; Old Testament (LXX and MT).
- *Jewish intertestamental thought:* Old Testament Apocrypha and Pseudepigrapha; Philo and Josephus; and non-Greek Jewish writings.
- *Greek Thought:* Classical (900–330 B.C.); Hellenistic Literary (330 B.C.–330 A.D.); and Hellenistic non-literary (papyri and inscriptions) material.

Figure 11.2. **Illumine the Meaning: Basic Matrix**

TYPE OF BACKGROUND	TYPE OF TERM	THOUGHT CONTEXT	LITERATURE
Background Source	Theological	Biblical Revelation	Jesus'/Early Church's Teaching Old Testament (MT–LXX)
Contemporary Background	Religious-Philosophical	Jewish Intertestamental Thought	OT Apocrypha & Pseudepigrapha; Non-Greek Jewish Sources; Philo; Hellenistic Literary–philosophers
	Spiritual/ Figurative	and/or Greek Thought	Josephus; Hellenistic Literary–historians; Hellenistic Non-Literary; (OT/NT Narrative)

Correlation of type of study with thought context (see fig. 11.2). If you need a *background source* study, choose the *biblical revelation* thought context. As you look for how a writer may have semantically borrowed from the Old Testament, be careful not to commit the fallacy of totality transfer, i.e., seeing all the possible meanings of the OT Hebrew term as present in a given occurrence of the Greek term. Be sure to test your analysis against the New Testament context.

If you need a *contemporary background* study, select a thought context, whether *Jewish intertestamental* or *Greek thought* depending on the word's meaning and its relation to ancient cultural usage. For a theological or ethical term, which could be illumined by ancient religious-philosophical thought, see Jewish intertestamental literature and Hellenistic Literary-philosophers. For a secular/literal example of a spiritual or figurative use see Josephus,

Hellenistic Literary-historians and Hellenistic non-literary documents. In either case, your goal is to compare or contrast the use of the biblical term with the other thought context with an eye toward understanding and illustration.

Clues in secondary literature (commentaries and dictionaries). If the thought context is clear, you should turn to pursuing evidence for the term's meaning in ancient literature by looking for ancient references in secondary sources. For example, if you need the background source for δικαιωσύνη, you know you are dealing with biblical revelation (with antecedent teaching in the New Testament and the Old Testament). Using a commentary or a theological dictionary, you can quickly find appropriate biblical references.

Inductive study via print concordance or computer. Another strategy is to pursue your own inductive study via print concordance or computer (e.g., *Bibloi* CD; *Perseus*; TLG). Though there are some print and computer concordances to extra-biblical literature, concordance work without access to a theological library is often hard to pursue. You'll need to rely on dictionaries to indicate whether the thought context desired will yield fruitful results. For example, if you think evidence from the papyri will help you with a contemporary background study, but BDAG and especially MM yield no such evidence, this is probably an indication that you should choose another type of literature or thought context. The listing of Classical, Hellenistic, and intertestamental Literature in the abbreviation lists in "In-depth Word Study: Introduction & Aids" (available at WJLFP) keys them for their content and should help you in this search.

Location of Ancient Source Reference & Example

"Illumine the Meaning" analysis will be the most exciting and rewarding when you can actually look up one or more ancient sources and see in context some examples of how your term was used in the literature of the times. A big challenge here is getting access to those ancient sources (see fig. 11.3). Hopefully, you have a Hebrew Bible, the appropriate concordance, and a copy of the Septuagint in your personal library either in hard copy or electronic form. It is less likely that you have a hard copy of Josephus, Philo, the Old Testament Pseudepigrapha, or Greek writers like Plutarch. An increasing number of ancient texts is available, however, as computer software or on the Internet.[10] Still, the challenge of easy access to many of these works remains and often requires a trip to a good theological library.

Methods of referencing. Once you accept the challenge of locating ancient sources, you'll find they are referenced three different ways:

- *By author and particular work.* For example, the reference of Josephus, *Ant.* 16:475 sends you to Josephus, *Antiquities of the Jewish People*, Book 16, Section 475. Scholarly secondary sources like dictionaries often use abbreviations to save space. A list of the abbreviations is available at the front of the secondary source and in "In-depth Word Study: Introduction & Aids" (available at WJLFP). Become familiar with the standard abbreviations as you carry out your exegetical work.
- *By author only.* For example, Polybius or Herodotus. When it comes to non-literary works (papyri and inscriptions), the reference is to a particular papyrus or a collection of papyri (e.g., P.Mich.=Michigan Papyri; P.Flor.=Papiri Fiorentini). C. A. Evans[11] is a handy guide to the editions in which many works may be found. A library card catalog will normally list ancient works by author.
- *By title of work only.* If only a title is available, the work is usually part of a collection of writings. Check the abbreviation tables in "In-depth Word Study: Introduction & Aids" (available at WJLFP) to find with what group of writings the work is normally combined. For example, *1 Enoch* is part of the OT Pseudepigrapha and will be found in the Charlesworth collection (see below listed under "Resources").

Sorting out numbers. The numbers associated with ancient works can be confusing. Remember that the most important numbering system is the standard one used by editors of various editions of an ancient writer's works (in the same way a standard chapter and verse scheme is used by all Bible translations). Disregard any volume numbers which are idiosyncratic to a particular edition. Look for those numbers which attach most directly to the text. For example, the spine of one of the volumes in the Loeb Classical Library edition of Josephus (ten volumes) has the following marking: "Josephus Antiquities Books XV-XVII VIII." The "VIII" refers to the Loeb volume and should be disregarded except as an entry point for finding, say, Book XVI (the reference noted above).

Record the Ancient Reference and Example

Once you've found your reference, read it to make sure it contains an example that will further your understanding and ability to develop a helpful illustration. For example, in the BAGD article on βέλος ("arrow," Eph 6:16) two references are made to Josephus (*War* 4:424; and *Ant.* 13:95).[12]

Figure 11.3. **Illumine the Meaning: Resources for Studying Thought Contexts**

Thought Context	Literature	Secondary Sources (Consistently consult BDAG, *TDNT*, *NIDNTT* for ancient literature evidence)
Biblical Revelation	New Testament	Concordances: M&G; Wigram, *Englishman's Greek Concordance* Dictionaries: *EDNT*; see above
	Old Testament	Concordance: HRCS; Wigram, *Englishman's Hebrew Concordance* Dictionaries: Lust, Eynikel, Hauspie, *Greek English Lexicon of Septuagint*; *NIDOTTE*
Jewish Intertestamental Literature	Apocrypha & Pseudepigrapha	Concordances: HRCS; *OTP* index
	Philo & Josephus	Concordances: Rengstorf, *Concordance to Josephus*; Mayer, *Index Philoneus*
	Non-Greek Sources	Str-B; Giannotti, *New Testament and Mishnah*; Kuhn, *Konkordanz zum Qumrantexten*
Greek Thought	Hellenistic Non-Literary	MM
	Hellenistic Literary	LSJ
	Classical	LSJ

The first refers to arrows in battle, but the combat described does not relate directly to Paul's directive, "Take the shield of faith, by which you will be able to quench all the flaming arrows βέλη) of the evil one." On the other hand, the *Ant.* 13:95 reference gives a great deal more help for it describes combat during the time of the Maccabees in which Jonathan

Figure 11.3. (*continued*)

Thought Context	Literature	Ancient Text Editions	Computer
Biblical Revelation	New Testament	UBS[4]	*Bibloi* CD; *BibleWorks* CD; *Logos Bible Software* CD
	Old Testament	Rahlfs, ed. *Septuagint*; Benton, *Septuagint with English Translation*	
Jewish Intertestamental Literature	Apocrypha & Pseudepigrapha	see above LXX; OTP	*Bibloi* CD; *Logos Bible Software* CD
	Philo & Josephus	LCL	*BibleWorks* CD; *Logos Bible Software* CD; *Perseus*; *TLG*
	Non-Greek Sources	Bibliographies: Chapman and Köstenberger, "Intertestamental and Rabbinic Literature"; Evans, *Ancient Texts*	Tov, ed. *DSS* CD; *Soncino Classics* CD
Greek Thought	Hellenistic Non-Literary	LCL	*Perseus*
	Hellenistic Literary	LCL	*Perseus*; *TLG*
	Classical		

ordered his own men to make a fence of their shields, and so receive the javelins thrown by the horsemen. Accordingly, they did as they were commanded, while the enemy's horsemen hurled javelins at them *until they had no more left* . . . the missiles did not reach their bodies, but glanced off the shields that were joined in a fence and compactly united, and so they were easily turned aside and fell back harmless.

This illustration from battle brings out vividly what Paul is contending in the spiritual realm. Our shield of faith is stronger than Satan's attacks and can outlast them. When an apropos illustration like this is found, do two things: Record the reference, in this case, Jos. *Ant.* 13:95. Then record enough of the immediate context so you can remember it and possibly quote it in your sermon or lesson. In this case, write or type the above sentences from Josephus. Always record both. The only thing more aggravating than having to look up a source again is not having the reference ready to hand.

Comment on Contribution to Understanding the Passage

The final step in *Illumine the Meaning* research is to thoughtfully apply what you have found to the content of your passage. In the Ephesians 6:16 example concerning βέλος, underneath your recording of the reference and the context, your comment might be:

This illustration from battle brings out vividly what Paul is contending in the spiritual realm. Our shield of faith is stronger than Satan's attacks and can outlast them.

Word Study (Illumine the Meaning): Resources

Materials from Previous Study

"Greek Reading/Translation" and "Mechanical Layout" worksheets for the passage
"Survey" worksheet

Greek is Great Gain

Descriptions in chapter eleven
Figures in chapter eleven

Reference Tools

BDAG
NIDNTT
TDNT

Specialized Tools

Evans, *Ancient Texts*.
DNTB

Old Testament
Rahlfs, ed. *Septuaginta*.
Brenton. *Septuagint with English Translation*.
HRCS
Kohlenberger, *NIV InterlinearOld Testament*.
Lust, Eynikel, Hauspie. *Greek-English Lexicon of Septuagint*.
Thomas, ed. *NASB Concordance*.
Wigram. *Englishman's Hebrew Concordance*.
NIDOTTE
TDOT

Jewish Intertestamental Literature
Chapman and Köstenberger, "Intertestamental and Rabbinic Literature," 577-618.
NRSV
OTP
Martínez, *Dead Sea Scrolls*.
Kuhn, *Konkordanz zu Qumrantexten*.
Herbert Danby, trans., *Mishnah*.
Gianotti, *New Testament and Mishnah*.
Montefiore and Loewe, *A Rabbinic Anthology*.
Str-B
Josephus, *Works*.
Rengstorf, ed. *Concordance to Josephus*.
Philo, *Works*.
Mayer, *Index Philoneus*.

Classical, Hellenistic, Koinē Literature
LSJ
PGL
LCL

OCD
MM

Computer Databases
Bibloi CD.
BibleWorks CD.
Logos CD.
Perseus.
TLG

Commentaries
Fee, *Philippians.*
Hawthorne, *Philippians.*
O'Brien, *Philippians.*
Silva, *Philippians.*

Word Study (Illumine the Meaning): Procedure

I. Survey
II. Analysis
    A. Historical Analysis
    B. Literary Analysis
        1. Context
        2. Genre
        3. Syntax
        4. Word Study
            a. *Focus the Meaning.*
            b. *Illumine the Meaning.* With the use of the above resources fill out the "Illumine the Meaning" worksheet as you follow these steps (see example, figs. 11.4-5).
                1) *Identify.* Identify theologically significant terms, hard to understand words, and words which because of their basic meaning or spiritual/figurative use could profit from an illumination from biblical and extra-biblical sources. For each term determine whether the investigation will be *background source* or *contemporary background.*
                2) *Choose.* Based on the meaning and use of the word, choose the *Thought Context/Ancient Litera-*

Figure 11.4. **Sample Literary Analysis: Word Study (Illumine the Meaning)**

Passage and term Phil. 1:11 δικαιωσύνη

Identify Term, Type of Study, and Thought Context/Ancient Literature:

δικαιοσύνη ("righteousness") in the phrase "the fruit of righteousness" (Phil 1:11); a theological term, therefore a *background source* study and the *thought context* of biblical revelation (Old Testament) is appropriate.

Record Ancient Source in Context:

Deuteronomy 6:20-25 (especially vv. 24-25): "'The Lord commanded us to do all these statutes, to fear the Lord our God, for our good always . . . And it will be *righteousness* for us, if we are careful to do all this commandment before the Lord our God as he has commanded us'" (ESV; cf. Deut. 24:13).

In the Old Testament, "righteousness" is a term of relationships, denoting that kind of conduct which serves to maintain the established ties in the covenant (*NIDNTT* 3:357). God establishes the covenant stipulations and promises blessings to those who obey them.

Because of sin, man cannot maintain that righteous conduct and, hence, the covenant relationship–right standing with God. In fact, when Amos indicts Israel for injustice he says, "But you have turned justice into poison and the *fruit of righteousness* into wormwood"(Amos 6:12 ESV). Only God can be the source of "righteousness," both right standing and right living. So God frames the promised restoration after the punishment of the exile this way: "Listen to me, you stubborn of heart, you who are far from *righteousness*: I bring near my *righteousness*; it is not far off, and my salvation will not delay . . ."(Isa 46:12-13 ESV; cf. Deut. 30:6; Jer. 31:31-34).

Comment:

The core meaning of righteousness in OT biblical revelation is right relationship in covenant with God and the kind of conduct, obedience to covenant stipulations, which shows one is truly in that relationship. This Old Testament understanding of righteousness takes into account the character of the covenant partners. Man is the inevitable covenant breaker, but God is the faithful covenant keeper and restorer.

This helps me understand why Paul stresses God as the source of the right standing and the righteous living, when he describes the Philippians in his prayer as "having been filled with the fruit of righteousness through

Figure 11.4 *(continued)*

Jesus Christ" (Phil 1:11). Note the divine passive of "having been filled" along with the prepositional phrase which presents Jesus Christ as the instrument–"through Jesus Christ." At the last day, this, God's work will be fully manifest.

       ture Area in which you think the study will be most fruitful.
3) *Locate.* Identify an ancient source reference to look up. Locate that reference in the ancient work and assess whether it is a suitable example for *Illumine the Meaning.* If it is not suitable, keep looking until you locate one.
4) *Record.* Record the ancient reference and enough of the immediate context that the content of the ancient source passage may be remembered.
5) *Comment.* Evaluate what this example contributes to your understanding of the term's use in your passage and think about its usefulness in communicating the truth of the passage. Write down your observations.
   - For a *Background Source* study, explain how would you use the reference to explain the theological significance of your word.
   - For *Contemporary Background*, explain how you could use your example as an illustration in a sermon or lesson.

Figure 11.5. Sample Literary Analysis: Word Study (Illumine the Meaning)

Passage and term Phil 1:5- κοινωνία

Identify Term, Type of Study, and Thought Context/Ancient Literature:

κοινωνία ("fellowship") in the phrase "fellowship in the gospel" (Phil 1:5) is a secular term used in a spiritual way. So, *contemporary background* study with the *Thought Context* of Greek Thought present in Hellenistic non-literary documents is probably the most fruitful to pursue.

Record Ancient Source in Context:

BGU 2:586[11] (*TDNT* 3:798) describes a law contract of partnership in commerce.

BGU 4:1051 (MM, 351) "Lucaina and Hierax have come together for a partnership of life" (πρὸς βίου κοινωνίαν). This is a marriage contract, which describes the closest, most intimate of personal relationships. Two aspects of association, then, are connoted by this term: its closeness and the sharing, which flows from the intimacy. This sharing is not just social or psychological, but also economic.

NIDNTT 1:643– Paul never used κοινωνία in a secular sense always in a religious sense. For him it is not companionship or community. It does not correspond to the Jewish haburah (fellowship, union). It is not as in the Stoa, a group of individuals united by a common idea. Κοινωνία is to be sharply distinguished from Greek ideas and Judaism.

Comment:

For Paul, the center which binds Christians together in fellowship is not human but divine: a person's relationship with Jesus Christ. Paul thus deepens or heightens the word's meaning by transferring it into the spiritual realm. The fellowship is all the more intimate, complete and lasting for it is centered in one's regenerated spiritual nature (1 Cor 1:9; 2 Cor 13:13; Phil 2:1). But, by centering fellowship in Christ, Paul does not eliminate the physical or economic aspect. An intimate sharing in Christian love will necessarily extend to meeting the needs of the whole person. So the collections for the poor among the saints in Jerusalem are called a κοινωνία (Rom 15:26; 2 Cor 8:4).

At Phil 1:5 the phrase "fellowship in the gospel" can mean either the spiritual relationship both Paul and the Philippians have to Christ by believing the gospel; *or* evangelistic work by the Philippians *or* the financial

Figure 11.5 (*continued*)

support from the Philippians to Paul which enables him to do his evangelistic work. The financial support is probably foremost in Paul's mind (Phil. 4:10ff). Yet this support is of a spiritual partnership (Phil 1:7; 2:1).

Endnotes

1. BDAG, 134.

2. Turner, *Christian Words*, viii-xiv.

3. Hemer, "New Moulton and Milligan," 97-123; S. Porter, "Greek of the New Testament," 430-31; BDAG, xvi-xxii.

4. Hemer, "New Moulton and Milligan," 118.

5. Hunt and Edgar, *Select Papyri*, I:xii.

6. Barclay, "New Testament and Papyri," 59.

7. Scott, "Value of Intertestamental Literature," 317.

8. Ibid., 318.

9. Ibid., 323.

10. Some ancient texts are available on *Bibloi CD; BibleWorks CD; Logos CD*; Tov, ed., *DSS CD; Soncino Classics CD*; and at *Perseus* and *TLG* websites; see Durusau, *High Places in Cyberspace*.

11. Evans, *Ancient Texts*.

12. BAGD, 139.

Chapter 12

THEOLOGICAL ANALYSIS

Theological Analysis is the third and final step in Analysis. We have sought the passage's meaning by probing its historical context. We have looked for further clues by investigating its literary context, genre, and syntax. We have conducted word studies on key terms. Now we ask and answer the question: What abiding message from God does this biblical passage contain?

Because this is the last stop before we synthesize our material and begin crafting our sermon or lesson, Theological Analysis is an important check on all our previous exegetical work. In it we will analyze our passage through two lenses: "Biblical Theology" and "Systematic Theology." Looking through the lens of "Biblical Theology" means peering into what the rest of Scripture has to say on the great themes of our passage. Our commitment to the unity of Scripture demands placing our passage in the overall context of divine revelation. Looking through the lens of "Systematic Theology" means locating the message of our passage within a systematic framework of theological thought. When this is completed, our final act is to deal with any "Remaining Theological & Interpretational Difficulties" so that we can declare with clarity and effectiveness, "Thus says the Lord."

Biblical Theology

Goal

All sixty-six books of the canonical Scriptures come from one author, God the Holy Spirit. He authored it to enable men to be saved and to believe and live as God intends (2 Tim 3:15-17). In the "Biblical Theology" analysis process we seek to understand the normative content, the doctrine and ethics of the Bible, and to place the themes of our passage within that context. This also helps us validate the understanding we have derived from studying the passage in its particular historical and literary context.

Studying "Biblical Theology" is less complex than some of the previous steps in Analysis. It is simply the process of comparing Scripture with Scripture and interpreting Scripture by Scripture. The goal is to arrive at a coherent understanding of how the biblical teaching in our passage fits with the whole of divine revelation. Occasionally, the diversity within the unity of Scripture makes certain passages look like they contradict each other. In such cases, our job is to wrestle through until Scripture's harmony is uncovered.

Advance over Word Study

During "Word Study" you probably have looked at the scriptural background for some key theological terms in your passage. Still there is more to be gleaned by considering the passage in relation to the totality of biblical thought. Studying parallel and contrasting Scripture references, as well as, key background Scripture portions lays the ground work for rounding out your understanding of where your passage fits in the Progress of Redemption and Progress of Revelation (see chapter thirteen). Cross reference editions of the Greek New Testament and English Bible, commentaries, dictionaries of biblical theology, and New Testament theologies (use their Scriptural reference indices), all can help you quickly identify key references for study. Use these resources judiciously, of course, looking for the most helpful references. Just because an editor sees a particular Scripture verse as an appropriate parallel does not mean it is. You will need to read these parallel passages in context in order to determine what light they might shed on your passage.

Procedure

The actual procedure for "Biblical Theology" is similar to that for "Illumine the Meaning"–*background source* study (chapter twelve). Your first step is to find an appropriate reference. If it is helpful, then jot it down with enough of the immediate context so you can remember its content. Finally, comment on what the parallel or contrasting reference contributes to your understanding of your passage. In particular, note how the parallel or contrasting passage can help you develop a helpful illustration for your sermon or lesson. Comparing Scripture with Scripture and interpreting Scripture by Scripture during a sermon or lesson often brings the most illumination and impact to your audience (see fig. 12.1 for examples).

Fig. 12.1. **Sample Theological Analysis**

Passage: Phil 1:3-11

v.	Biblical Theology	Systematic Theology
3) consistency in prayer - Ps 5:3 NIV "in the morning I lay my requests before you"; cf. Dan 6:10; Paul pursues biblical piety practices.		
6) "complete good work" - Phil 2:12-13 "God is at work in you"; background of God's work - God's creative activity (Gen 1-2).		
"day of Christ" - background is "Day of the Lord" which is a time of final accounting, judgment; Amos 5:20; Joel 2:2.	Phil 1:6, 9-11 speak of *Soteriology*, particularly salvation in its application with a focus on its continuation - sanctification.	
9) cf. other prayer reports - Col 1:9-11; Eph 3:14-19; "love abound" - 1 Thess 4:9-10; John 13:35, common Christian characteristic.	There is a focus on the conneciton between the beginning in divine regeneration and its continuation in sanctification (1:6). The verses also highlight the necessary link between present continuation and final completion (also 1:6). This latter connection, as it describes God's certain completion of what he has begun to do, undergirds the doctrine of "perseverance of the saints."	
10) "discern the best:" - Phil 4:8-9; Heb 5:14; Rom. 12:2; "pure and blameless" - Eph 5:25-27, church as spotless bride; moral excellence is the goal of the Christian.		
11) "fruit" - John 15:8 "In this is my father glorified that you bear much fruit"; Jesus says fruitfulness brings praise to God.	Paul's prayer (1:9-11) also speaks of the completion of sanctification letting us know that our glorification at the end will indeed be the culmination of the present moral and spiritual perfecting process.	

Systematic Theology

Relation of Exegesis and Theology

Comparing our passage against the backdrop of systematic theology gives us another way to see how the one divine author of the Bible speaks a unified truth. It also helps us ground our preaching and teaching within our understanding of Christian theology. There is definitely a synergy between a preacher or teacher's theology and his or her exegesis. For example, over the two decades that John Calvin perfected his *Institutes*, he wrote commentaries on Scripture. Moises Silva states that "Calvin's theological thought guided his exegesis, while his exegesis kept contributing to his theology."[1] The same author contends, "My theological system should tell me how to exegete."[2]

A Qualified Case for a Theologically Guided Hermeneutic

But how much should systematics—of human construction—guide our exegesis? Could the synergy between theology and exegesis lead to distorted exegesis? To investigate this issue, let's examine Silva's three-fold rationale for a "theological system controlled exegesis." Let's be on the look out for benefits, as well as potential dangers.

Same goal. Silva claims that systematic theology is essentially an "attempt to reformulate the teaching of Scripture in ways that are meaningful and understandable to us in our present context."[3] Since biblical exegesis has the same goal, Silva sees the value of systematics in immediate preparation. This is certainly true. Yet, we must be aware of a potential danger to which systematics is not immuned: syncretism, the mixing of Biblical truth with the culture's beliefs and values. At its best, systematic theology helps us judge the soundness of our exegesis. Still, we must always take care lest any cultural influences distort scriptural truth (e.g., contemporary challenges to Scripture's absolute truthfulness).[4]

Same "database." Silva further contends that systematic theology gives us a coherent and comprehensive pattern of biblical truth which helps us analyze a particular passage against the "whole counsel of God."[5] Although this is a proper role for systematics, the danger during this process is eisegesis: reading something into the text which distorts the passage's meaning. If that happens, our exposition of the text serves only as an apologetic for our theological system. For example, finding positive or negative evidence for infant baptism in Acts 16:15, 33, often wrings too much out of the meager evidence.[6] Instead, we need to continue first to understand the meaning of the passage on its own terms, in its immediate context. Once that is established we can beneficially relate that meaning to the "whole counsel of God" as represented in systematic theology.

Same presuppositions. Finally, Silva points out that "all of us read the text as interpreted by our theological presuppositions."[7] Because of this, he feels it is better to prosecute exegesis with one's chosen theological system consciously in mind than to think our exegesis is absolutely objective, while all the while, being unconsciously influenced by our theological system. In fact, awareness of theological presuppositions during exegesis is very important, and it should give us greater sensitivity to any aspects of our passage that disturb the overall interpretive framework of our systematics (e.g., Calvinists' handling the Hebrews "warning" passages, Heb 6:1-12; 10:26-31, and Arminians the Johannine "eternal security" passages, John 6:37; 10:27-30).[8] Wrestling with disturbing passages enables us to validate and refine our systematics framework in our lifelong efforts to bring it more and more in line with all of Scripture. Indeed, when Scripture is the final authority, the interpreter's presuppositions are always open to scrutiny by the biblical text.

Remaining Theological & Interpretational Difficulties

It is likely that throughout your Historical, Literary, and Theological Analysis theological and interpretational questions have arisen that you have not yet resolved. Your last task, then, is to find answers to them within Scripture before you begin pulling your material together to communicate the Word of God.

Theological Difficulties

Aspects of a passage may appear on the surface to be at variance with other teaching in Scripture. In Phil 3:11, Paul seems to express uncertainty about attaining to the resurrection from the dead, a hope he is certain about in 1 Corinthians 15. Or, Jesus says a person's righteousness must surpass that of the scribes and Pharisees, if he hopes to enter the kingdom of heaven, while Paul says it is not his righteousness by the law, but the righteousness from God by faith, which means eternal life (Matt 5:20; Phil 3:9). Solving such theological difficulties is an important part of your exegesis.

Interpretational Difficulties

Sometimes the text does not appear to answer clearly one or another of the standard interpretational or exegetical questions. Is the participial phrase ὃς ἐν μορφῇ θεοῦ ὑπάρχων concessive ("Although he was in the form of God") or causal ("Because he was in the form of God," Phil 2:6)? What does the "rock" refer to in Matt 16:18?

Perspectives on Certainty & Uncertainty in Interpretation

Solving any remaining theological or interpretational difficulties sometimes introduces a disconcerting (and usually unwelcome) aspect of exegesis: uncertainty. We all want to feel confident that we have arrived at a Scripturally valid interpretation. But wrestling with difficult content in Scripture may result in only a particular level of uncertainty. Let's look at some principles to help us navigate this aspect of the exegetical process.

The Meaning You Seek

The text's meaning is what the writer intends to say. The interpreter's task is to reconstruct that meaning from the clues the author provides in the text. The interpreter seeks to uncover what the author is talking about (referent) and what he is saying about it (sense). This seems straightforward enough. We just need to find the clues that tell us the referents, which will give us the sense, and then we'll have the meaning. Right?

Unfortunately, the clues in a given passage do not always point to that one meaning with the same degree of clarity. And this introduces the level of uncertainty. Also, the more the interpreter's culture differs from the beliefs and values reflected in the passage, the more likely it is that he or she will experience uncertainty about some of the possibilities in interpretation.

The Text's Meaning is not the Same as Your Interpretation

It gets worse. The text's message, or meaning, and the exegete's interpretation are not the same thing. Alas, they can be moderately or fundamentally different. Valid interpretation, however, can always be shown to say the same thing that the text says. This means that the interpreter's responsibility is to make choices among possible reconstructions of meaning (interpretations) and adopt the one he believes most accurately says what the text says. He or she does this through a reasoning, which assesses the interaction of meaning bearing elements in the immediate and larger context, based on sound hermeneutical principles.

Levels of Certainty

The result can be one of four conclusions:

- *Certain.* The interpreter can take as certain an interpretation which best accounts for all the evidence and whose rivals are significantly flawed.
- *Probable.* The interpreter can take as probable an interpretation which best accounts for the evidence though it has weaknesses and its rivals are not without their positive points.
- *Uncertain.* The interpreter can take as uncertain an interpretation which is one of several possible interpretations, which have almost equal amounts of cogency, though it is the least objectionable.
- *"I don't know."* A text in which all interpretations are of equal persuasiveness leave the interpreter saying, "I don't know."

Attitudes to Avoid

Not "salad bar." As you practice your exegetical skills, avoid two extremes: a "salad bar" and a "dogmatic" attitude toward interpretation. A "salad bar" attitude says, "All interpretations are equally valid, that it doesn't matter which one I choose." This extreme, in essence, abandons the goal of finding the writer's intended meaning. With such an attitude you cannot properly fulfill the preacher or Bible teacher's solemn responsibility to shepherd and teach the flock God's truth accurately (1 Tim 4:12-16; 2 Tim 2:15; Titus 1:9).

Not "dogmatic." A "dogmatic" attitude says, "My interpretation equals God's truth." It does not recognize the possibility of uncertainty in interpretation. It so identifies the exegete's interpretation with the content of Scripture that there is no openness to correction. Humility and love are left on the sidelines. Unity can be broken (1 Tim 6:3-5; 2 Tim 2:16-18; Titus 1:14-16).

Attitudes to Embrace

Love. If we avoid these extremes, what kind of attitude should we have? Pursue instead interpretation based on careful exegesis of the kind promoted in this book. Always be mindful you interpret Scripture in and for the church. And within the body of Christ, one man's "certain" interpretation on a particular aspect of a passage is another man's "probable" or "uncertain," or even, "I don't know" interpretation. Except where there is manifest error, error striking at the vitals of the faith, it is best to practice a mutual forbearance. We can learn from each other, if each one speaks the truth in love (Eph 4:15).

Your basic stance as an interpreter, then, should be to work for the peace, purity, and unity of the church. Work for a growing understanding of the meaning of the text in your own mind and that of your hearers. Receive with respect brothers and sisters with whom you differ (Rom 15:7).

Humility. Clearly, we must approach the task of exegesis and interpretation with humility. This does not mean, however, that we cannot preach and teach the Word with authority. View the truth of the Word as a unified whole, but also as having concentric circles of certainty. The core of Christianity—Christology and soteriology—is certain, and you should seek for clear and certain interpretations of passages undergirding these subjects. You can and must preach this core with conviction (Rom 1:16-17; 2 Tim 4:2).

As to the "whole counsel of God," start from these central convictions and move outward. As you pursue your exegesis, determine what level of certainty you can place on your interpretation of particulars of a given passage. If you are a beginner in exegesis, recognize that all interpretational options for a given problem may seem to have the same persuasive strength. Even when you are initially unsure, keep working with the text until one option, based on evidence and arguments from the text, emerges as most likely the correct interpretation.

And recognize this process is dynamic, not static throughout your ministry life. Your personal growth in spiritual maturity, as well as your growth in exegetical competence, is a factor. As you spend your life increasing in your understanding of the Word, in time, "I don't know" or "uncertain" interpretations can become, under the guidance of the Holy Spirit, "probable." And much of the "probable" can become "certain." This is one way Peter's encouragement will be true in your life and ministry: "Be growing in grace and in the knowledge of our Lord and Savior Jesus Christ" (2 Pet 3:18).

Theological Analysis: Resources

Materials from Previous Study

"Greek Reading and Finished Translation and Mechanical Layout" worksheets
"Survey" worksheet

Greek is Great Gain

> Descriptions in chapter twelve
> Figures in chapters twelve and thirteen

Cross-Reference Tools

> UBS[4]
> *NIV Reformation Study Bible.*
> *NIV Study Bible.*

Dictionaries of Biblical Theology

> *BTDB*
> *NDBT*
> *NIDNTT*
> *NIDOTTE*
> *TDOT*
> *TDNT*

New Testament & Old Testament Theologies

> Guthrie, *New Testament Theology.*
> Ladd, *Theology of New Testament.*
> Marshall, *New Testament Theology.*
> House, *Old Testament Theology.*
> Kaiser, *Old Testament Theology.*
> Sailhamer, *Old Testament Theology.*

Systematic Theologies (consult Scripture Reference Index for your passage)

> Erickson, *Christian Theology.*
> *NDT*
> Forlines, *Quest for Truth.*
> Grudem, *Systematic Theology.*
> Reymond, *New Systematic Theology.*

Commentaries
> Fee, *Philippians.*
> Hawthorne, *Philippians.*
> O'Brien, *Philippians.*

Silva, *Philippians*.

Essays and Periodical Articles
Indices: ATLA; *NTA*

Theological Analysis: Procedure

I. Survey
II. Analysis
   A. Historical Analysis
   B. Literary Analysis
      1. Context
      2. Genre
      3. Syntax
      4. Word Study
   C. Theological Analysis
      1. *Biblical Theology.* With the use of the above resources, fill out the "Biblical Theology" portion of the Theological Analysis Worksheet (template available at WJLFP) as you follow these steps (see example, fig. 12.1):
         a. *Identify.* Find theologically significant cross-references: parallel, contrasting, background passages.
         b. *Locate.* Look up the Scripture verses. If it is not suitable, keep looking until you locate one which is.
         c. *Record.* Write down the Scripture reference and enough of the immediate context that the Bible text may be remembered.
         d. *Comment.* Reflect on how this reference contributes to your understanding of the passage and think about its usefulness in communicating the truth of the passage. Write down your comments.
      2. *Systematic Theology.* Using the resources listed, especially the taxonomy of figure 12.2:
         a. *Identify.* With the aid of systematic theology reference works (see their scripture reference indices), decide the primary doctrinal area to which your passage relates (e.g., bibliology, Christology, soteriology) and note it down on the "Systematic Theology" portion of the Theological Analysis worksheet.

Figure 12.2. **Departments of Christian Theology**

DEPARTMENTS OF CHRISTIAN THEOLOGY	

Revelation
   General Revelation
   Special Revelation
 	
Bibliology: The Bible as Divine Revelation, Characteristics, Inspiration
 	
Theology Proper: God
   Nature of God: Essence and Attributes
   Nature of God: Unity and Trinity
   Decrees: in Material/Physical/Moral/Scriptural/Social/Political Realms (Law)
   Works: Creation, Providence
Angelology: Angels, Satan, Demons
   Origin and Nature
   Fall
   Work and Destiny
	Anthropology: Man
	   Origin and Original Character
	   Unity and Constitution
	   Fall
	      Origin in Adam's Act
	      Immediate Results
	      Imputation and Consequences for Mankind
	      Nature and Character of Sin and Fall
	      Final Results
	   Law of God
	
	Soteriology: Salvation
	   Provision
	      Purpose, Plan, Method of God
	      Covenant of Grace
	   Person of Christ
	      Christological Titles
	      Pre-Incarnate State
	      Humiliation: Incarnation; Virgin Birth
	   Two Natures and Character of Christ;
	      Sinlessness
	   Work of Christ
	      Teaching the Kingdom
	      Miraculous Life
	      Death: Nature and Extent of Atonement
	      Resurrection and Ascension

Figure 12.2. (*continued*)

DEPARTMENTS OF CHRISTIAN THEOLOGY	

Application
  at its Beginning
    Election and Calling
    Regeneration
    Conversion: Repentance and Faith
    Justification
    Union with Christ: Adoption
  in its Continuation: Sanctification
 	
Ecclesiology: Church
  Definition and Founding
  Foundation and Organization
  Sacraments: Baptism, Lord's Supper
  Mission, Character of Common Life
  Destiny
	Eschatology: The Future
	  Death and Intermediate State (after-life)
	  Prophecy
	  Second Coming of Christ
	  Resurrections
	  Millennium (Vision of Kingdom)
	  Judgment
	  Final State: Hell, Heaven
	
	Pneumatology: Holy Spirit
	  Person
	    Deity
	    Personality
	    Coming
	  Work
	    In the Believer
	    In the Church
	    In the World

Source: Dyrness, *Old Testament Theology*; Guthrie, *New Testament Theology*; Thiessen, *Systematic Theology*.

      b. *Explain*. Comment on the worksheet what your passage contributes to the biblical teaching on that doctrine (see example on fig. 12.1).
  3. *Remaining Theological and Interpretational Difficulties*.
      a. *Identify a theological or interpretational difficulty*. Under the "Problem" section of the "Remaining Theological and Interpertational Difficulties" worksheet note down the problem (see fig. 12.3; template available at WJLFP).
      b. *Identify the solutions*. With the help of commentaries and articles (use ATLA and *NTA* databases), identify the standard solutions to the problem. List each solution with supporting arguments and evidence.
      c. *Decide and express your preferred solution*. State both your conclusion and give the reasons why you have chosen it.

d. *Rate the degree of certainty.* Decide the degree of certainty with which you hold your solution. Circle either "certain," "probable," "uncertain," or "I don't know" and give reasons for your choice.

Figure 12.3. **Sample Theological Analysis**

Passage: __Phil 1:5__

Remaining Theological/Interpretational Problems

THE PROBLEM:
"from the first day until now" What action does this phrase describe?

THE SOLUTIONS *(State arguments with evidence)*:

1. "with joy making prayers . . . from the first day until now" (1:3)–this fits nicely with Paul's emphasis on intensity in prayer; it is smoother syntax; if the phrase modified "fellowship" (1:5) you would expect a repetition of the definite article creating an attributive, although its absence is not unusual.

2. "from the first day until now, being confident of this very thing" (1:6)–Paul's confidence is then emphasized, but this shifts the focus of the passage away from the Philippians' conduct to Paul's disposition.

3. "your fellowship in the gospel from the first day until now" (1:5)– it is the closest grammatical unit for receiving modification; this solution respects the shift from a focus on the fact of prayer to a motive for prayers; by highlighting the Philippians' constancy in support it supplies a motive for his thanksgiving and a ground for his confidence in the future.

MY PREFERRED SOLUTION *(with reasons)*:

#3 (1:5) Paul is describing their constancy in the fellowship of the gospel. All the positive reasons listed above, plus the negative reasons noted for #1 and #2 provide the rationale.

Figure 12.3. *(continued)*

RATE THE SOLUTION *(circle one and give reasons)*:

(Certain)   Probable   Uncertain   I don't know

See reasons above. The most telling cumulative arguments are:

a. There is a discreet change of thought between 1:4 and 1:5, from the fact of prayer to its motive. The phrase should not be jumped across that boundary.
b. There is a distinct shift away from the focus on Philippians' conduct to Paul's praying if the phrase is seen as introducing 1:6. This goes against the focus of the passage.
c. Therefore, the phrase should be seen as modifying what immediately precedes.

Endnotes

1. Silva, "Case for Calvinistic Hermeneutics," 251. The present writer standing in the reformed tradition, uses Silva, also reformed, as a conversation partner.

2. Ibid., 261.

3. Ibid.

4. cf. Grenz'(*Theology*, 401-2) interpretation of 2 Tim 3:16 in support of limited inerrancy.

5. Silva, "Case for Calvinistic Hermeneutics," 262.

6. cf. Polhill, *Acts*, 350, 356 and Reymond, *New Systematic Theology*, 942.

7. Silva, "Case for Calvinistic Hermeneutics," 263; also see above chapter two.

8. See Bateman, ed., *Four Views on Warning Passages* and Basinger and Basinger, eds., *Predestination: Four Views*.

Chapter 13

SYNTHESIS

The entire hermeneutical enterprise has been likened to an hour glass.[1] It moves from first viewing the passage as a whole: "Survey," to a detailed study of its individual parts:"Analysis"–Historical, Literary, Theological– and finally back to a gathering of those parts into a coherent whole: "Synthesis." "Synthesis" views the passage's content within three, ever-widening contexts: the passage, the book, and the Scriptures. This prepares the way for relating the passage to a final context: the contemporary cultural context of the interpreter's audience.

If possible, let a day pass between completing the steps of "Analysis" and starting your work on "Synthesis." This gives time for the various ideas you have garnered during "Analysis" to jell in your mind. When you start in on "Synthesis," some background information on human learning will help you understand the importance of this step in a "Method for Exegesis and Exposition."

Processes of Human Cognition: Analytical & Intuitive

Learning and the Brain

Psychological studies suggest that the two basic ways of learning appear to be associated, predominantly though not exclusively, with one brain hemisphere or the other.[2] Analytical, logical thought processes occur in left hemisphere cognition. Right hemisphere cognition controls intuitive, "globalizing" thought processes, which help us experience our world in terms of a pattern. Although one or other thought process may predominate for some individuals, neither can stand on its own. Both analytical and intuitive thinking is necessary for information to be correctly understood. Likewise for exegesis and exposition, both analytical and intuitive thinking are necessary for us to clearly and effectively communicate the message of a biblical passage. The individual parts of the passage, i.e., words, phrases, clauses, sentences, paragraphs—however correctly analyzed—can only be fully understood when seen in relation to their interconnections with the whole of the passage and the wider context of Scripture.

Communicators of the Word of God, then, demonstrate their understanding of a passage not only by their "Analysis" of each individual part, but also by "Synthesis." They need to be able to explain the passage's main thrust, its flow of argument, and its place in context, including how the passage fits into the message of the whole of biblical revelation. When we have done all of that under the guidance of the Holy Spirit, using both sides of the brain God has given us, we can preach or teach the message of our passage with confidence, clarity, and power.

Two Step Synthesis

Your work in the area of Synthesis will be two-fold. First, with all that you learned during "Analysis" in mind, you will develop an *exegetical outline* of the passage's flow of thought. This will be a graphical representation of the major and minor points in the passage and their interconnection. Second, you will establish *biblical coherence*. You will test your understanding of the passage, by stating in one sentence its main thrust, and noting how the passage fits within the immediate and overall context of divine revelation.

Exegetical Outline

Value and Distinctiveness

This is the beginning of your homiletical or didactic appropriation work. Once you have an *exegetical outline* you have the main points and sub-points of the passage nailed down in preparation for actually developing your sermon or lesson with all the interpretative and illustrative work that entails. Have you ever attended a presentation where the parts didn't seem to add up to the whole, or where the message seemed only marginally related to the biblical text? This is your opportunity to avoid those kinds of problems, and develop a well-crafted, biblically grounded sermon/lesson which springs from the passage, coherently develops its message, and moves to a climax.

Exegetical outlines have a lot in common with *mechanical layouts*. Both help you identify major thought units in your passage which, in turn, may serve as main points for the sermon or lesson.[3] Whereas the grammar of the passage is the starting point for a mechanical layout, the passage's flow of thought, aided by taking note of the grammar, is the starting point for the outline. Developing an *exegetical outline* helps you represent the coherent development of the passage's message according to the biblical writer's pattern of presentation. Here are three steps for creating your exegetical outline: *identify thought units, name the thought units,* and *organize the thought units into headings in outline form.*

Procedure

Identify thought units. Develop your passage's *exegetical outline* as an integral part of the outline of the book of which it is a part. For example, if you were working with Philippians 1:3-11, you would develop your outline under the heading I.B. "Thanksgiving and Prayer" (see fig. 13.1; cf. fig. 16.5).

- *Levels of content.* Once anchoring it in the overall flow of the book, you can represent your passage's content on five levels: sections, paragraphs, sentence clusters, sentences, and clauses/sub-clauses. You may or may not include all of these levels, and the length of passage will often dictate how detailed your outline needs to be.

  Sometimes you may need to be even more detailed than the five basic thought units, e.g., representing the content of prepositional phrases or other clause components when they contain material essential to the main flow of thought. Highly detailed exegetical outlines like this are beneficial when dealing with the closely reasoned argumentation of the Epistles. On the other hand, gospel narrative passages usually can be represented adequately with only sections, paragraphs, and sentences as components of narrative plot.

  As we noted, the length of your passage also has a bearing on the degree of detail in the exegetical outline. The amount of material you can cover in the normal preaching or teaching time frame does as well. Obviously, outlines for passages covering more than eight to ten verses can become too detailed to be covered during a standard sermon or lesson. You would need to divide it into multiple sermons or lessons in a series.

- *Identification keys.* Usually, sections, paragraphs, sentences, and clauses are easily identifiable within the text. Clauses/subclauses are introduced by subordinate conjunctions or in the form of an adverbial infinitives or participles.

  Sentence clusters (a group of sentences which develop the same thought) may be the hardest to isolate. Keys for uncovering them are coordinating conjunctions, repetition of words or phrases, and genre/subgenre analysis. Does a conjunction

Figure 13.1. **Sample Synthesis: Exegetical Outline**

Passage <u>Phil 1:1-11</u>

v.	Exegetical Outline
1:1-11	1. Opening
1:1-2	A. Salutation
1:3-11	B. Thanksgiving and Prayer
1:3-8	1. Thanksgiving
1:3-6	a. Thanks to God for Philippians
1:3-4	1) Temporal: In Prayer
1:5	2) Cause: Their fellowship in Gospel
1:6	3) Cause: Confident in God's Work in Them to Completion
1:7-8	b. Affectionate Attitude toward Them
1:7	1) His Attitude
1:7	a) Cause: Close Relationship
1:7	b) Cause: Joint Participation in His Gospel Activity
1:8	2) His Affectionate Longing for Them
1:9-11	2. Prayer
1:9	a. Request: Love to Abound in Moral Discernment
1:10	1) Purpose: Correct Moral Judgment
1:10	2) Purpose: Blameless Life at Christ's Coming
1:11	a) Cause: Filling with Fruit of Righteousness
1:11	3) Purpose: God's Worship

closely bind its sentence with what precedes, making it part of a sentence cluster with that sentence? Or does it signal a break, indicating that the thought is heading in a new direction, starting a new cluster? Does the repetition of words or phrases bind sentences together into a cluster?

- *Examples from Phil 1:3-11.* Here is an example of the various levels of thought unit from Phil 1:3-11:

  1) Phil 1:3-11 is one paragraph in the UBS[4]. According to genre analysis this is a subgenre unit: a thanksgiving.
  2) Phil 1:3-6, according to genre analysis, is a subgenre unit component: an expression of thanks. Phil 1:9-11 is a prayer.

3) Phil 1:7-8 are closely linked in thought, both speaking of Paul's affection for the Philippians. These verses may be treated as a sentence cluster.
4) According to UBS⁴, Phil 1:3-6 is one sentence as is Phil 1:9-11.
5) Clauses/subclauses in Phil 1:9-11 include object (ἵνα); purpose (εἰς τό + infinitive); purpose (ἵνα) and causal (πεπληρωμένοι).
6) Prepositional phrases: ἐπὶ τῇ κοινωνίᾳ ὑμῶν εἰς τὸ εὐαγγέλιον (Phil 1:5) and εἰς δόξαν καὶ ἔπαινον θεοῦ, (1:11) may also figure in the outline.

Name the thought units. Once your thought units are identified, give each a name by writing a heading which reflects its content and, as appropriate, its syntactical function in context. Indicate syntactical function by an introductory label (often just one word), and the content by a title, not a full sentence.⁴ For example, the ἵνα clause in Phil 1:10 may be designated as: "Purpose: Blameless Life at Christ's Coming.

Organize thought units as headings in outline form. Finally, arrange the headings for each thought unit in outline form and include the Scripture references for each at the left hand margin. When done, your outline should show at a glance the passage's thought flow, with main ideas and sub-points clearly delineated. It should show coherence, order, and a depth of differentiation extending at least to the level of subordinate clauses (see fig. 13:1). Let the text be your guide, not outlining conventions. For example, exegetical outlines are not bound by the customary rule that requires two items for any given level of an outline.

Relation to homiletical/didactic appropriation. One final point. Your exegetical outline is just that: an outline of the exegesis of the text. It is your blueprint of the structure of the passage. In "Homiletical/Didactic Appropriation," the last phase of a "Method for Exegesis and Exposition," you will develop a preaching or teaching outline. It will certainly reflect, but, for the purposes of effective communication, may well be different from your exegetical outline.

Biblical Coherence

Your second task in "Synthesis" is to establish *biblical coherence* (see example at fig. 13.2). As you did in "Survey," you will move out of and up above the "trees" of individual thought units so you can look again at the "forest" of the entire passage. In this task, apply three tests to validate your exegetical work: What is the passage's *basic message*? How does that basic message promote the *book's purpose*? and What *place* does this passage have in *salvation history* and *biblical thought*?

Basic Message

The first test seems simple, but it is a great way to be sure you "keep the main thing the main thing." Review your exegetical outline and then seek to summarize the main thrust of your passage in one sentence. Your goal is to succinctly and unambiguously state the subject and theme for your message.[5] If your first attempt ends up with a rambling confusing sentence, try again. Try a third or fourth time if you need to. Try it out on your spouse or co-worker.

A good statement of a passage's basic message should be clear enough for someone else to understand. This exercise insures that you are preaching or teaching a truly biblical message, that your subject is Scripture's subject. Having the main thrust crystal clear in your own mind can also make your delivery truly memorable. Your audience is far more likely to carry away one basic impression of what the Scriptures are saying and what God wants them to do, if the main thrust is clear to you.[6]

Promotion of the Book's Purpose

The next test in validating your understanding of the passage's central thrust is to reflect on the way it promotes the New Testament writer's purpose in writing the book. Refer back to your work in Periodic Preparation: Selected In-depth Study–Introductory Matters (fig. 16.7) and "Analysis," particularly to *historical analysis–introductory questions*. Why was the Bible book written? To whom and for what occasion? With all the time you have spent on your passage, can you now see clearly why the writer included this particular section in his book and how it contributes to his overall purpose? If there is not an evident congruence between the book's purpose and what you see as your passage's basic message, you'll need to rethink your analysis of one or both, until they are rightly related. When there is congruence, write a statement which explains how your passage promotes the book's purpose.

Place in Salvation History and Biblical Thought

Place in salvation history (the progress of redemption). The good news on this last task is that you already have a head start on the work. During "Word Study: Illumine the Meaning," you may have done some *background source* studies to probe key theological terms. During "Theological Analysis:

Figure 13.2. **Sample Synthesis: Biblical Coherence**

Passage: Phil 1:3-11

Biblical Coherence

Passage's Basic Message:

Paul expresses affectionate, grateful confidence with regard to the Philippians, partners in the gospel, and their spiritual life, that they will persevere and abound, by God's grace, in their love, moral discernment and righteous living until Christ comes, all of which he prays for them.

Promotion of Book's Purpose:

Phil 1:3-11 and 1:27-30 are key passages for explicitly expressing all the main themes of the letter. Thus the passage's *basic message* and the book's *purpose* are almost identical. One element in Phil 1:3-11, however, which can be said to contribute to the book's achieving its purpose of encouraging the Philippians in their Christian lives is the emphasis on God's role in producing spiritual fruit (Phil 1:6, 9-11).

Place in Salvation History and in Biblical Thought:

Philippians is written during the fulfillment stage of Salvation History when the Salvation Promise is being lived out by the New Testament Church: God's Chosen People in Christ. This passage speaks of the positive model of life of faith which lives out the promised salvation blessings. It presents the qualities of that life: unity, moral discernment, and righteous living.

This passage is *developmental*. It shows how in the Philippians' lives the salvation blessings poured out at Pentecost (Acts 2:42-47), as well as the covenant mandates (e.g., love, Lev 19:18; John 13:34-35) were being actualized. One traces these theological themes mainly through theological terms and concepts: love, fellowship, righteousness, holiness, moral discernment.

Biblical Theology," you've already thought about your passage's relationship to the rest of Scripture by finding parallel and contrasting passages. The only thing left in this area is to examine your passage in light of the entire scope of divine revelation and redemption. This is easily done by studying the "Biblical Theology" charts for the Old and New Testaments (fig. 13.3). Ask yourself this question: Where does my passage fit in the flow of God's *salvation history*? Since NT passages occur in the fulfillment stage of salvation history, it is often enlightening to read the charts "backwards," tracing your passage's theological themes back to their promise stage.

Place in biblical thought (the progress of revelation). A second way to understand your passage in the context of Scripture as a whole is to find its place in the flow of biblical thought as it developed—*the progress of revelation*. This is the ultimate guard against proof texting, against preaching or teaching out of biblical context. It is the ultimate reminder of the dynamic unity of divine revelation throughout a Scripture which has many human writers and many types of literature. Just a little time spent here can help you make clear how your passage furthers God's saving purposes and how portions of biblical revelation prepared for and build on your passage.

Developmental and/or foundational. One last decision to make to pinpoint the significance of your passage in the overall biblical context is to identify whether it is a foundational passage or a developmental passage. A foundational passage deals with a key aspect of salvation history for the first time. Examples would be the Passover/Exodus (Exodus 12-13), the cross (Mark 15), key biblical commands such as the Great Commission (Matt 28:18-20), or key biblical promises such as the coming of the Holy Spirit (John 14-16). A developmental passage builds upon the teaching in the foundational passage, further illuminating its basic turth. For example, Luke 22:15-20 expands on the OT teaching on the Passover. Romans 10:9-17 builds upon the Great Commission. Acts 2 shows the fulfillment of the promise of the Holy Spirit.

Here are four clues[7] that your passage is developmental:

- *Technical theological terms.* Can you trace the occurrence of technical theological terms in the passage back to previous teaching in salvation history? For example, in Phil 1:3-11, the terms love, righteousness, glory, etc. have earlier precedent in Scripture.
- *Direct or indirect reference to a previous salvation history event.* To which previous event in salvation history does the passage contain a direct or indirect reference? For example, in Phil 1:6, God beginning a "good work" may allude to the creation accounts of Genesis 1-2.

Figure 13.3. Biblical Theology: Old and New Testaments

		Salvation History	Biblical Thought (OT Witness)
Cent. B.C.	I.	The Foundation: God the Creator and Covenant Promise Giver	Pentateuch
		A. Pre-Patriarchal Era *Proto-evangel*	Gen 1-11 Gen 3:15
20th-16th		B. Patriarchal Era: *Abrahamic Promise;* At end of era: Slavery in Egypt	Gen 12-50 *Gen 12:1-3; 15:1-20; 17:1-14; 22:15-18*
15th	II.	Mosaic Era: Exodus and Wilderness Period	Exodus-Deuteronomy
		A great nation constituted by Divine Deliverance (Exodus) and Covenant Law (Exodus and Deuteronomy) as a royal priesthood (Leviticus) and a holy people (Numbers)	cf. Exod 20:2 with Gen 15:7, 13-14; Exod 6:2-8; 19:3-6 with Gen 12:1-3
14th-11th	III.	Pre-monarchial Era: Settlement Period	Deuteronomy-Ruth
		A. The Land Promise	Deuteronomy
		B. Conquest of Land	Joshua
		C. Land without order	Judges, Ruth
10th-6th	IV.	Monarchial Period	1 Samuel–2 Chronicles Wis. Lit.; Pre-Exile Prophets
		A. National History: How is the Kingdom? Davidic Era *Davidic Promise*	1 & 2 Samuel; 1 & 2 Kings; 1 & 2 Chronicles 1 Samuel 16–1 Kings 2 Davidic Psalms *2 Samuel 7*

Figure 13.3. (continued)

Cent. B.C.			Salvation History	Biblical Thought (OT Witness)
		B.	Inspired Reflection: What is life?	Job, Psalms, Proverbs, Ecclesiastes, Song of Solomon
		C.	God's Call: Who is the King?	Pre-exilic Prophets
9th				Obadiah, Joel
8th				Amos, Hosea, Jonah, Micah, Isaiah
			Book of Emmanuel;	Isa 7–11
			Servant Songs	Isa 42:1-4; 49:1-6; 50:4-9; 52:13-53:12
722 B.C.			Northern Kingdom Falls	
7th				Nahum, Zephaniah, Habakkuk, Jeremiah
586 B.C.			Fall of Jerusalem; Southern Kingdom to exile	
6th-5th	V.		Exile and Restoration Period: God's Judgment and Mercy	Exilic and Post-Exilic Prophets
		A.	A Broken People of Promise	Jeremiah, Lamentations, Ezekiel, Daniel
			New Covenant	Jer. 31:31-34
538 B.C.			The Return	
		B.	A People Restored in Hope	Haggai, Zechariah, Malachi, 1 & 2 Chronicles (indirect witness), Ezra, Nehemiah, Esther

Source: cf. Kaiser, *Old Testament Theology*, Table of Contents; Luc, "Old Testament Theology"; Guthrie, *New Testament Theology*, Table of Contents; Ladd, *Theology of New Testament*, Table of Contents.

Figure 13.3 *(continued)*

Salvation History	Biblical Thought (NT Witness)
I. The Promise Fulfilled: the seed of Abraham, the Lord Jesus Christ (A.D. 1-30)	Synoptic Gospels: Matthew, Mark, and Luke; John
A. His Message: The Kingdom	
B. His Mission: The Messianic Mediation of a Better Covenant through an Atoning Death and Resurrection	
C. His Person: Incarnate Son of God; Son of David	
II. The Promise Lived Out by the NT Church: God's Chosen People in Christ	
A. Witness to the Promise: The Primitive Church (A.D. 30-62)	Acts
B. Living out the Promise among the Gentiles	Paul (in order written)
1. Establishing Gentile Churches by a Gospel of Faith (Galatians) and Hope in Christ's Return (1 & 2 Thessalonians; A.D. late forties to early 50's)	Early Letters: Galatians, 1-2 Thessalonians
2. Strengthening the Church by Apostolic Authority (2 Cor) which faces Immorality and Discord (1 Cor; Rom; A.D. mid-50's)	Major Letters: 1-2 Corinthians, Romans
3. Encouraging the Church in True Knowledge (Col) and Unity (Phlm, Eph, Phil; A.D. early 60's)	Prison Epistles: Philemon, Colossians, Ephesians, Philippians
4. Preparing the Next Generation of Church Leaders (A.D. mid 60's)	Pastoral Epistles: 1 Timothy, Titus, 2 Timothy
C. Establishing Jewish Christians and others in the Faith (A.D. mid-late 60's)	
1. The Better Way	Hebrews
2. Wisdom	James
3. Handling Suffering and False Teaching	1-2 Peter, Jude
4. True Faith and Love (A.D. 90's)	1-3 John
III. The Promise's Final Consummation (A.D. 90's–)	Revelation

- *Direct or indirect Old Testament quotations.* Which direct or indirect citations of the Old Testament does the passage contain? For example, see how Eph 6:2-3 cites Exod 20:12.
- *Reference to covenants or foundational promise passages.* What references to the covenants or foundational promise passages (e.g., Gen 3:15; 12:1-3; Exodus 20; 2 Samuel 7): their contents or manner of expression (formulae), are present? For example, note the Ps 132:11 and 2 Sam 7:12-13 phraseology in Acts 2:30.

Note that NT passages may often direct your attention both backwards and forwards. A single passage may be developmental of the Old Testament and foundational for later NT passages. This is particularly true of the Gospels, Acts, and Paul's early letters. So, in Luke 22:15-20, Jesus develops the redemptive pattern of Passover (Exodus 12-13) applying it to his saving work on the cross. At the same time, the Last Supper exposition is foundational, for Paul draws out its saving, particularly sanctifying, significance for the church in 1 Cor 5:6-8.

Synthesis: Resources

Materials from Previous Study

"Mechanical Layout" worksheets for the passage
"Literary Analysis: Genre, Syntax--Grammatical and Rhetorical Features" worksheets
"Advanced Planning: Synthetic Study–Book Outline"
"Selected In-Depth Study: Introductory Matters"

Greek is Great Gain

Descriptions in chapter thirteen
Figures in chapter thirteen
UBS^4 punctuation apparatus

Biblical Theology

Kaiser, *Old Testament Theology*.
Marshall, *New Testament Theology*.
Van Gemeren, *Progress of Redemption*.
Wright, *Mission of God*.

Commentaries

Fee, *Philippians*.
Hawthorne, *Philippians*.
O'Brien, *Philippians*.
Silva, *Philippians*.

Synthesis: Procedure

I. Survey
II. Analysis
III. **Synthesis**
   A. **Exegetical Outline.** Using "Synthetic Book Study" outline (see fig. 16.5), mechanical layout, and observations from literary analysis: genre and syntax, together with the other resources listed above, compose an exegetical outline for your preaching portion; fill out the "Synthesis: Exegetical Outline" worksheet by following these steps (see fig. 13.1 for example; template available at WJLFP):
   1. *Identify thought units.* Isolate levels of content (including their extent–the number of verses they cover): sections, paragraphs, sentence clusters, sentences, clauses/subclauses–introduced by subordinate conjunction or in the form of an adverbial infinitive or participle.
   2. *Name the thought units.* Write a heading for each thought unit which reflects its syntactical function and content. Indicate syntactical function by an introductory label and the content by a title, not a full sentence.
   3. *Organize the thought units as headings in outline form.* Take each thought unit with its identified extent, level and heading, and arrange it in outline form. Include at the left margin Scripture references for each heading. The outline should represent the thought flow and will not necessarily have the customary two items for every level of the outline. Use your "Synthetic Study–Book Outline" as a skeleton and fill in the details of an *exegetical outline* at the appropriate place.
   B. **Biblical Coherence.** Using the resources cited above, develop a coherent summary of the passage which relates the passage's basic message to the overall teaching of Scripture. Do this by filling out the "Synthesis: Biblical Coherence" worksheet according to the following these steps (see fig. 13.2 for example; template available at WJLFP):

1. *State the passage's basic message.* State comprehensively, yet concisely in one sentence, the passage's content. Don't worry about the sentence length. Include an identifiable subject, what is being talked about; an identifiable theme (complement), what is being said about it; and appropriate qualifiers: how, when, where the subject and theme's (complement's) meaning is accomplished.[8]
2. *Express how the basic message promotes the book's purpose.* With the aid of introductory matters (see fig. 16.7), explain how your passage contributes to the author's overall purpose(s) in addressing the reader's situation. Note down your answer.
3. *Identify the passage's place in salvation history and in biblical thought.* Ask and note down the answer to this question: "What is this passage's place in salvation history and in biblical thought?"

    Particularly note whether the passage is foundational for subsequent NT texts or developmental of preceding OT and Jesus' life and teaching texts (See fig. 13.3 for "Biblical Theology: Old and New Testaments" chart). Note down your answer with reasons. Be aware that Gospels and Acts passages, as well as ones in Paul's early letters may be both developmental and foundational.

Endnotes

1. Robinson, *Biblical Preaching*, 66.

2. Johnson, *Psychology of Biblical Interpretation*, 61-64.

3. cf. Perry, *Manual of Biblical Preaching*, 10.

4. Smith ("Sentence Diagramming . . . Exegetical Outlining," 105) sees value in "full sentence" heading outlines.

5. Robinson, *Biblical Preaching*, 66.

6. Liefeld, *New Testament Exposition*, 90.

7. Kaiser, *Toward Exegetical Theology*, 137.

8. Robinson, *Biblical Preaching*, 66-70.

Chapter 14
INTERPRETATION & APPLICATION FOR CONTEMPORARY CULTURE

The Need

Connecting with the Audience

You've completed "Survey," "Analysis," and "Synthesis." You have a solid exegetical foundation for your passage. You've taken it apart and put it back together. You know where it fits in divine revelation and you know what God is saying through this particular section of his Word. It seems like the perfect time to start designing your sermon outline or lesson plan, doesn't it? It might be, but there is one more step that can make the difference between a biblically and theologically sound message, that gives the audience information for the head, and a biblically and theologically sound message that connects with their hearts. The missing step is "Interpretation & Application." Trying to communicate without careful attention to this area may not result in much actual communication. Why do corporations and political parties spend so much time studying their audience and the mood of the times before developing expensive media advertising? Why do education schools require courses in child growth and development and adult learning theory, in addition to those on curriculum design and lesson planning? Why do missionaries labor to learn the language and culture of the people they want to reach? Because skillful communicators are those who know their audience and the culture of their audience, as well as they know their message. The lack of such knowledge all too frequently leads to what is sometimes called *bypassing*: the failure to meaningfully connect with the hearts and minds of one's listeners.

Communicating God's Truth with Cultural Relevance

This step in "A Method for Exegesis and Exposition" will challenge you to exegete the culture of your congregation or class in the light of your passage so you know how to communicate God's truth in a culturally relevant way. With such cultural exegesis, you can identify specific ways in which your passage addresses your contemporaries. You will also uncover the congruities and discrepancies between the way the Bible and the contemporary context see faith and life. This kind of reflection allows the authoritative Word of God to do what it was intended to do: present the *whole* truth of God to people of any age, so that they can see life *whole*.[1] In this chapter we consider "Interpretation" as the general process of relating biblical truth to a culture and "Application" as the more specific process of identifying ways of implementing thought and behavior change which that truth calls for.

Interpretation

Culture and Scripture

Our primary task in "Interpretation" is to understand our culture so we can relate the truth of Scripture to people within the culture. A basic definition will get us started (see fig. 14.1):

> Culture is that integrated pattern of socially acquired knowledge, particularly ideas, beliefs, and values (ideology) mediated through language, which a people uses to interpret experience and generate patterns of behavior–technological, economic, social, political, religious, and artistic–so that it can survive by adapting to relentlessly changing circumstances.[2]

"Interpretation" involves understanding three relationships between Scripture and culture. First, we need to understand how verbal communication is influenced by culture so we can communicate Scripture's truth in a relevant way. Second, we need to understand where Scripture stands in judgment of the culture and is a correction to wrong thinking and behavior. Third, we need to understand the deep needs and longings of our culture so we can capture the significance of the "good news" of Scripture which can speak to those needs and longings.

Communication

Culture's way of speaking. Culture exerts a great deal of influence on our communication of scriptural truth. As noted earlier in our look at "Word Study," culture provides the basic vocabulary stock by which we communicate. If you want to communicate the Word clearly, you need to understand your culture's way of speaking. Then, you can find just the right words and

Figure 14.1. **Cultural Taxonomy**

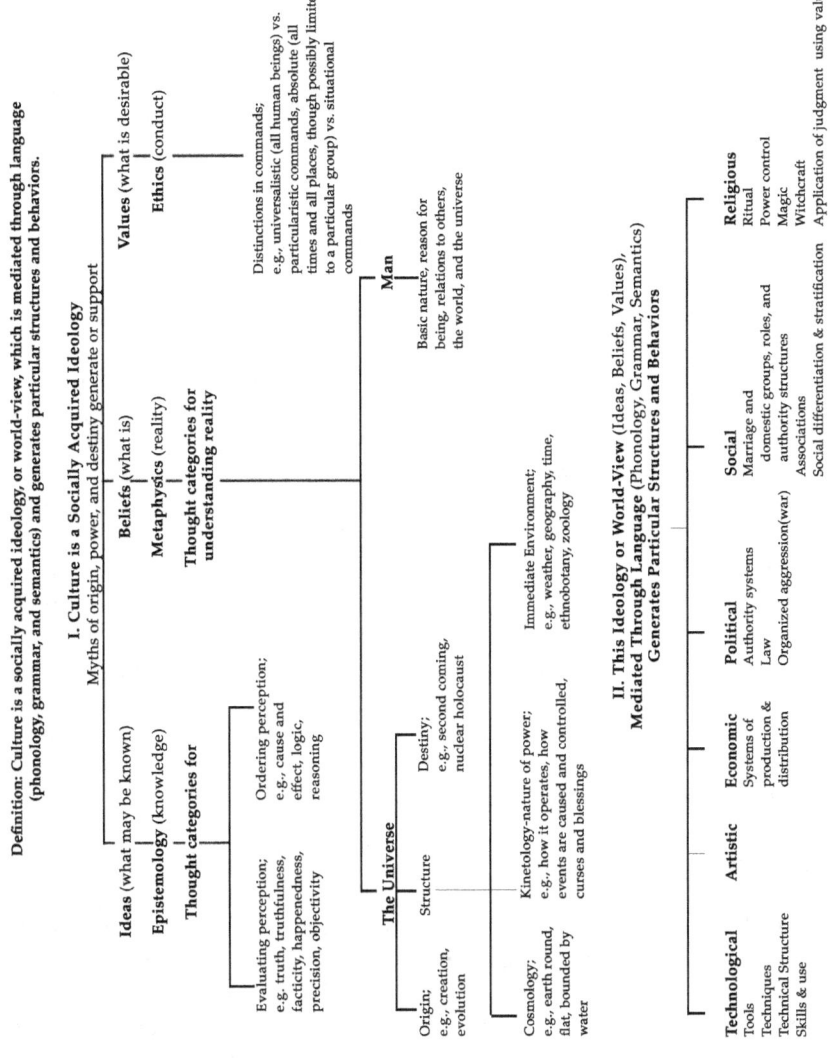

Source: Larkin, *Culture and Biblical Hermeneutics*, 194.

illustrations by which to convey the thought of your passage. This, of course, must be pursued with integrity, without falling into either anachronism or inappropriate forms of contemporary language, which might lead to syncretism.

Points of contact. A beginning step in communication is to look for places where the content of your passage is particularly congruent with aspects of contemporary culture. Make a note of the key points of contact between the culture and your passage. Then determine how you can best address these points in the language of your culture, using vocabulary stock, imagery, and illustrations from contemporary thought and life. What words, images and illustrations can you use to present the passage's content in a culturally relevant way?

For example, in relation to the salvation of the Philippian church, Paul makes the statement that God will complete what he has started (Phil 1:6). In many cultures, following through on a job is valued. Think of the public recognition which comes to a senior citizen, who in his younger years stopped out of college but returns many years later to complete the degree. Think of the police investigator who picks up a "cold case" and does not give up until the criminal is identified and apprehended, even if it takes years. These are examples from culture which become points of contact for illustrating, albeit by contrast, the much greater perseverance of an almighty and always faithful God. Spend time carefully and prayerfully seeking for illustrations like these that can improve your communication of the Word.

A pocket sized spiral notepad or three by five cards or electronic device are useful aids for jotting down "points of contact" phraseology or illustrations whenever they strike you. The preacher, with his preaching portion in mind, often responds to his everyday experiences with the question: "Will it preach?"

Correction

Culture's challenge to God's truth. The "anti-one true God" bent of the ideology or worldview of any human culture generates thoughts about truth, reality, and ethics that are at odds with God's revelation. Everyone, even evangelical preachers and teachers, are cultural beings and think with their cultural worldview, the product of generations of fallen human beings. So, it is most natural to embrace unconsciously the unbiblical perspectives and values of ones worldview. Indeed, if we pursue exegesis without consciously considering our cultural presuppositions, it is possible to find ourselves skeptical of, fragmenting, or distorting the truth of a passage in order to make it congruent with the beliefs of our culture.

Scripture's critique of culture. Instead, the interpreter must exegete the culture with a critical eye, asking this question: What in the contemporary culture (ideas, beliefs, values, structures and behavior patterns, cf. fig. 14.1) runs counter to my passage's content? Your answers to that question will give you points where Scripture has a corrective role to play as judge of culture. At these points you will be showing how the passage's content is "bad news" to contemporary culture. When Scripture comes as "bad news," it judges, but it also corrects. Be sure to articulate not only the reason for judgment, but also to explain how a correction may be accomplished.

For example, there is a distinct contrast between the Christian's goal of being "pure and blameless at the day of Christ" (Phil 1:10) and the approved lifestyles of many in North America, whether celebrities or ordinary citizens. Cheating at all levels of education seems the norm; virginity of the unmarried is the exception and not the rule. And Scripture passages, such as Phil 1:10, judge and correct this immorality, by showing a better way. But Phil 1:10 does not do it in a judgmental fashion, for Paul in the immediate context emphasizes that it is God's work, not ours, which enables us to demonstrate the "fruit of righteousness" (1:6, 11). Indeed, this goal will be part of an answer to prayer that Paul is offering to God on their behalf. So, the corrective is close at hand: dependence on God's strength to enable us to adopt a lifestyle which pleases him. How quickly the "bad news" is turned into the "good news" of the possibility of a lifestyle which is not only for God's glory but also for our good!

Capturing the Significance

Opportunity. In its rebellion against God, every culture tries desperately to meet felt needs in the wrong way or in an inadequate way. Or it may have no answer at all to a basic need in life. As you continue to reflect on contemporary culture in the light of your passage—and reflect on your passage in the light of the culture—you should pursue a third line of inquiry. Ask this question: How is this passage's message "good news" to my culture? Finding ways in which the passage is "good news" to the real, as well as, the perceived needs of your audience is an important and joyful part of fulfilling your calling as a communicator of the Word. When you bring "good news" you bring the "living bread" and "living water" to a people starved for both, though often unaware of the true nature of their hunger and thirst.

Points of need. Your task again is to exegete the culture, this time looking for areas of felt need and indications of real needs which may not be felt. Articulate these "points of need" as you think of them. Then, as you consider your passage's content in relation to them, ask yourself how the message of your passage is "good news"? That is, how does it capture for the culture the significance of a particular aspect of the "good news" of God's saving truth? How does the passage introduce thought forms and behavior patterns which meet human needs, but in God's way, for his glory and man's good? Once identified, explain how you would tell this "good news" as you communicate the passage's content.

For example, if we exegete North American culture in the light of Phil 3:7-11, we immediately see a contrast between what Paul values (the gift of salvation received by faith) and what society values (performance). No matter how highly we prize performance and achievement, whether in sports, business, entertainment, politics, or education, finding our sense of worth in these endeavors brings limited and fading satisfaction. There is always another competitor, another race, another more difficult challenge. There is always someone smarter than we, someone more attractive, someone stronger. The good news of Phil 3:7-11 is that God's grace—not our human performance—is what counts in attaining the greatest of all goals: *right standing with God*. This is more than good news. This is incredible news for a restless culture, full of longing for peace and fulfillment.

Having studied the culture in relation to these three areas, your final task is to make your insights and observations as personal and practical as possible by developing clear and appropriate "Application" for your audience in the areas of "Correction" and "Capture the Significance."

Application

The Need for Application

Essential for exegesis and exposition. Whether viewed from the standpoint of biblical exegesis or expository preaching and teaching, the "Application" step is essential if either process is to reach its intended goal. Robert Traina, champion of the inductive Bible study method, asserts, "The applicatory step is that for which all else exists. It represents the final purpose of Bible Study."[3] Homileticians consistently point out that a sermon without application is no sermon at all. They often reiterate Charles H. Spurgeon's observation, "Where the application begins, there the sermon begins."[4] If a message or, for that matter, an exegesis is not to "fall stillborn on baffled ears and hearts,"[5] there must be application.

Essential for hermeneutical bridge building. To change the metaphor, the preacher or Bible teacher is a bridge builder[6] over what people in the twenty-first century perceive of as a chasm between the world of the Bible and their world. Think of your role as a guide, taking your listeners across the "Application" bridge. In crossing they see the relevance of Scripture's eternal truth on one side, and the deeply personal responses required by that truth on the other. "Application" enables the hearer to carry biblical truth fully into his or her own world. In "Application," we take the point of the passage as we have exegeted it and make that point a *living word* for the twenty-first century audience.[7]

Not to be shortchanged. Far too many sermons and Bible lessons fail right here. How many have you heard that were devoid of application until the last sixty seconds? A hasty "Well, what does this mean for us today?" question substitutes for thoughtful application throughout the presentation. There are a number of reasons why "Application" tends to get shortchanged. One is running out of time in preparation. If you don't plan carefully, you may exhaust your available study time on the analytical aspects of exegesis and wind up with little or no time to work on "Interpretation" and "Application." As we noted, you can also run out of time during delivery. This is particularly problematic if the only application in your outline is toward the end of the sermon or lesson. Another reason is that coming up with good examples and illustrations to serve as personal applications is not always easy. It takes careful and prayerful thought, and time for research. "Application" is best thought of as something you consider throughout the exegetical process, from "Survey" on, and even during your "Greek Reading." The information which follows will give you more background on this very important area of "A Method for Exegesis and Exposition."

The Nature of Application: Meaning & Significance

Meaning. When literary critics and philosophers of language analyze the communication properties of a literary work they distinguish between a text's meaning and its significance.[8] A text's meaning is the message the writer intended to convey in his grammatical-literary construction of the text for an audience in his historical-cultural context. Meaning is what we have been uncovering through our exegesis to this point. The text's meaning is fixed, always the same since its source is the writer's intention. What it meant in the past, what it means in the present, and what it will mean in the future, are all three, the same thing.

Significance. A text's significance, however, "denotes a relationship *between* (note well, it must be linked) that meaning and another person, time, situation, or idea."[9] The significance of a text will vary depending on the nature of the relationship. For example, in the 1980's, the significance of the declarations in the Monroe Doctrine was different for the United States and for Nicaragua. One country viewed it positively, as giving legitimacy to active involvement in Central America to combat communism. The other country viewed it negatively, as the illegitimate pretext for United States imperialism. Of course, had a pro-Western regime been in place in Managua at the time, the significance of the Monroe Doctrine to them would probably have been positive. Thus we see that a text's significance can and does change from person-to-person, group-to-group, time-to-time, and situation-to-situation.

Potential confusion. There has been some confusion in hermeneutical thinking over the distinction between the meaning and the significance of a text. Consider that fact that we use the verb "to mean" in relation to both concepts:

> What does John 3:16 mean? (Meaning)
> What does John 3:16 mean for me? (Significance)

Given the two very different goals of these questions, any answer introduced by "this is what John 3:16 means" will be highly ambiguous. Further, under the influence of the historical-critical method with its framework of soft or hard historical relativism, many preachers have been taught to distinguish between two types of meaning in Scripture: what the text *meant* (when it was originally written) and what the text *means* today. It is no wonder, then, that the people in the pew, under a similar influence of the relativistic spirit of the age, also think in this dichotomy. The chasm is made only greater when they hear intellectual leaders in academia and the media ask, "How can an ancient book have the same meaning today?"

Avoiding the confusion. But, there are those of us who see a text's meaning as determined by the writer's intention and believe that such meaning can be intelligible across history and culture. For us, asking the distinct question: What does the text mean today? is actually not to inquire about meaning at all. Rather, it is to ask about significance.

It is vital that we maintain the distinction between meaning and significance, if we are to properly uncover the meaning of texts. A text's meaning, especially that of authoritative Scripture, must be read out of the text by exegesis which aims to uncover the writer's intended meaning. And we must make sure that any significance perceived for the text is always based on and controlled by a clear understanding of that meaning.[10] So, through a two step process we arrive at a full understanding of a passage. Step one does exegesis and interprets the meaning. Step two looks for the culturally relevant significance of that meaning. This latter step is the process of developing application.

Looking More Closely at Scriptural Application

Intended relevance. Any piece of literature from any time period can have significance to a modern reader simply because its author is another human being and its subject matter is life or imitation of life. The Bible is no different. But more importantly, the Bible explicitly claims a continuing relevance or significance for itself because of its intended audience and its purpose. The Scripture's originally-intended audience extends beyond the writer's immediate audience to either all humans or all the redeemed.[11] As the New Testament testifies about the Old (Rom 15:4; 1 Cor 9:9-10; 10:6-11) and the canonization process attests for all of Scripture, the Bible was intended to transcend the immediate situation in which it was written. And it has demonstrated its capacity to do so for millennia. It can and does directly address persons of other times and places. Further, the Scriptures carry their own relevance because their purpose is to speak the truth of God's saving solution to humans' most basic spiritual needs (2 Tim 3:14-17). As John Stott contends, we preach the "contemporary Christ who once lived and died, and now lives to meet human need in all its variety today. To encounter Christ is to touch reality and experience transcendence."[12]

Functional authority. Since the Bible is the Word of God, its significance for twenty-first century persons is to be the functional authority for faith and life. This means its content should control and direct the interests, concerns, and understandings of the contemporary interpreter and listener. There may be, however, more in a passage which is truly significant or relevant for the hearers than they want to perceive. Sinful human nature frequently blinds people, even Christian people, to some aspects of the biblical message. We have stressed from the beginning the need to be sure this is not true for the interpreter. To do justice to Scripture as the fully and finally authoritative Word of God, the best stance for the preacher/teacher and the audience is to treat all of its content as normative, unless Scripture itself indicates that it intends its application at a given place to be limited.

Listeners' needs. A word of caution, though. Just because the Scriptures are authoritatively relevant does not mean that expository sermons and Bible lessons are automatically meaningful for their audience. We need to know our audience's contemporary situation as much as possible so we can address their interests and concerns, i.e., "scratch where they itch." Beyond that, we want to know the individual members of the group as much as possible, or at least the general characteristics of the group. Walter Liefeld, writing in the mid-eighties of the last century, catalogued the potential needs of a congregation in a white middle class North American context like this:

- Personal needs (anxiety, loneliness, grief, depression, spiritual dryness, need for guidance, etc.).
- Corporate moods (economic concerns, discouragement, conflict, lack of enthusiasm in the church, shock over a recent death in the congregation, apprehension over a planned building program, etc.).
- Current social and ethical situations (among Christians or in the community).
- Public crises (elections, assassination attempts, international problems, accident in the community, etc.).
- Spiritual milestones in life of the church.
- Spiritual state of special groups (new believers, elderly, youth, those in mid-life crisis, singles, married, divorced, etc.)
- Ongoing needs for edification and instruction.[13]

How would you edit this list to reflect life in our post 9/11, increasingly postmodern, globalized, post-Christendom world?

Uncovering needs. Who is your audience? How can you learn more about them? Preachers find out the needs of their congregations through pastoral ministry. They take time to be with people even as they make time for study of the Word. Bible teachers look for opportunities to get to know the people in their classes. Missionaries spend time visiting and receiving people in their homes. Youth pastors keep up with the trends that affect today's teenagers. All communicators of the Word should be keen observers of their socio-cultural setting and the way it is impacting their target audience's behavior, beliefs, and values. High on the list of important ministry skills is learning to ask the right questions and learning to be a good listener. Isn't it interesting that good listeners are better able to be the good speakers, for they have discovered how to relate to those who listen to them?

Bringing the Word to life. With insights from your audience analysis, it is time to identify the principles of God's eternal truth in your passage, which will be particularly significant to your listeners. Here you run into the need to keep several potentially competing priorities in mind at the same time.

First, balance the concern for relevance and application with the commitment to preach the whole counsel of God whether all of it appears to be particularly meaningful at the moment or not. Second, make your applications relevant, personal, and challenging, but express them in such a way that the original intention and thrust of the passage is not distorted.[14]

In short, your goal in "Application" is to develop from "the simple interpretation of the passage the meaning (actually, the significance) for the congregation today in the context of their modern life situations."[15] So how do you do that? Follow this three step pattern: "principlize biblical truth"; "identify the contemporary context"; "call for implementation." Note that the first step is not to cast about for any kind of illustration or potential areas of application from your or your audience's context. True, you may introduce your presentation with material from contemporary life, intended to build rapport with the audience. But, "Application" is strictly for determining how to bring your listeners to a personal decision point in relation to the biblical passage. Therefore, when developing applications, always start with the text of Scripture.

A Pattern for Developing Applications

Principlize biblical truths. Frame the significant truths from your passage into principle form. The significant truths are the passage's commands, promises, statements of truth, or principles derived from examples in historical narrative. For an average length passage, there should not be too many. Kaiser defines the process of framing a principle as "to state the author's propositions, arguments, narrations, and illustrations in timeless abiding truths . . . "[16] Expressing biblical truth in a timeless, universal form makes it possible to apply that truth to the contemporary situation in such a way that a culturally meaningful implementation can be pursued.

Some have proposed that the only normative content in Scripture is what is already stated in the form of principles.[17] Yoder sums up this approach via the axiom,

> Because of the relativity of cultures on the one hand, and the fact of language being addressed to a specific context on the other, in order to apply Scripture appropriately to our context today, we need to be guided by principles which are applied by analogy.[18]

Although scripturally framed principles are, indeed, normative, there are places in Scripture where the writer clearly intends both the command and the principle behind it to be followed. Stated in anthropological terms, both the behavioral form and the meaning are normative (e.g., in Matt 28:18-20 command: "Baptize. . ."=form; principle: incorporation into the church= meaning) . And, as we study Scripture, there do appear to be passages in which scriptural mandates are limited by the writer and the principle is all that is normative. For example, the command in Gen 12:1-3 to "Leave your land . . . " is limited, but the principle of trusting God is normative. How can we know whether we should apply a biblical mandate or promise directly? Let Scripture settle the matter. Treat all Scripture as directly applicable unless Scripture indicates otherwise according to the following criteria:

- *Intended recipient.* Sometimes the immediate context limits the teaching by the intended recipient, e.g., the command to the rich young ruler in Matt 19:21.
- *Cultural conditions.* Sometimes the cultural conditions necessary for fulfillment limit the teaching, e.g., the command in 1 Pet 2:17 to "Honor the king."
- *Cultural rationale.* Sometimes there is a limited cultural rationale, e.g., the matter of hair length in 1 Cor 11:14-16.
- *Subsequent revelation.* Sometimes the broader context of Scripture limits application, as when subsequent revelation sets aside previous teaching, e.g., the rescinding of dietary restrictions in Acts 10:13-15.

In all of these cases of indirect application, the teaching is best applied on the principle level and implemented by behavior appropriate to ones own culture.

In sum, Scripture's normative content addresses the culture in two ways and results in two kinds of application: direct and indirect. When we encounter biblical mandates and the principles behind them, which are both normative for the contemporary context, we will draw direct applications (Matt 28:18-20). Other times, when only the biblical principle is normative, we make indirect application (Gen 12:1-3). In either case, we begin by stating as a timeless principle the meaning behind the form.

Identify the contemporary situation. Next, we look at the timeless principles from our passage in the light of our contemporary cultural context. We know that the contemporary situation should never be the final determiner of what mandates or principles are normative to ones situation. Nevertheless, the contemporary situation is a definite aid in determining which mandates and principles are particularly appropriate for this moment.

In identifying the exact contemporary situation to which the biblical mandates and principles apply, Liefeld[19] helpfully suggests that we study the historical context in which they were first given. Find out

- the circumstances and needs addressed.
- the purpose of the passage, including its contextual function.
- the immediate results the biblical writer sought.

Then look for similar circumstances and needs in your contemporary situation and apply the normative biblical content there. For example, studying the historical situation of Phil 4:19 ("My God shall supply all your need . . . ") shows that this promise cannot be applied appropriately to any Christian, but only to those involved in the Christian dynamic of sacrificial giving to further the Christian cause. These were the circumstances of the Philippians to whom the promise was originally given.

At the end of this step, you should have matched together one or more of the timeless principles included in your passage with relevant aspects of your audience's contemporary situation. You show people the timeless principle and show them how it relates to their personal lives. But don't stop there.

Call for implementation.[20] Every good sermon or lesson will call for a decision to change beliefs, attitudes and/or behaviors. And every good application should include practical *how to's* for actually changing attitudes and/or behaviors. Don't assume people will take this step on their own. Spiritual blindness or rebellion may make them resist seeing the actions they should take in relation to the truth they have heard. While it is ultimately the work of the Holy Spirit to lead people to repentance, your work as an expositor of the Word includes making God's truth as deeply personal as possible.

It takes prayerful and creative thinking to develop appropriate suggestions for implementation. With some direct applications based on biblical commands, implementation is mandated by Scripture itself, e.g., the prohibition of adultery in Exod 20:14. Indirect applications based on a biblical principles may require us to think harder to devise appropriate suggestions for change. Obviously, with either type of application, unless the implementation comes directly from Scripture, any examples suggested by the preacher or teacher are not binding, although obedience to the principle is binding. For example, for the command on a principle level in Phil 2:3 ("in humility consider others better than yourselves"), you might suggest implementation that involves praising someone in a thank you note, promoting someone else for role in the church you might like to have yourself, or more selfless behavior toward one's husband or wife. You should not present these suggestions—however excellent—as biblical mandates from the passage. It is the mandate for humility and other-centeredness, which the passage makes binding on all who hear the Word.

Don't relegate applications only to the end of your presentation. They should support the main points and subpoints of the content, encouraging the audience to consistently apply the Word to their lives. As you work in this important area always keep the passage's intended meaning in mind. Then seek to apply its significance imaginatively to the contemporary situation. Finally, prayerfully depend on the Holy Spirit's convicting and convincing work in your own life and the lives of those to whom you minister. This is the key to confidence that the "living and abiding Word of God" will do its work in transforming lives.

Interpretation & Application: Resources

Materials from Previous Study

    "Survey" worksheet

Greek is Great Gain

    Descriptions in chapter fourteen
    Figures in chapter fourteen

Commentaries

    Fee, *Philippians*.
    Hawthorne, *Philippians*.
    Melick, *Philippians, Colossians, Philemon*.
    Swindoll, *Laugh Again*.
    Thielman, *Philippians*.

Interpretation/Application: Procedure

I. Survey
II. Analysis
III. Synthesis
IV. **Interpretation & Application.** Using the resources cited above, determine how the truth(s) of your passage can be communicated to and "lived out" by men and women who hear its message. Do this by filling out the "Interpretation & Application" worksheet according to the following these steps (see fig. 14.2 for example; for template see WJLFP):
    A. **Interpretation**
        1. *Communication*
            a. *Identify* ideas (vocabulary and illustrations) from the contemporary culture which easily relate to the message of your passage.
            b. *Explain* how these contemporary ideas will help you communicate the content of your passage.
        2. **Correction:** Identify way(s) in which your passage is "bad news" to the culture in that it judges contemporary beliefs,

Figure 14.2. **Sample Interpretation & Application**

Passage: Phil 1:3-11

Communication:
1:3 Paul models constant thankfulness which should be the mark of every Christian
North American Culture: Young children are taught the common courtesy of responding to the receiving of a gift with "Thank you." The parent trains through question: "What do you say?"
A simple sermon illustration to point to how we in our society value it. So much the more should Christians value it.

Mandate or Principle	Contemporary Situation	Implementation
Correction: 1:10 the Christian's goal of being "pure and blameless at the day of Christ"	By contrast, in North America today, there is a lack of honesty or sexual purity. Cheating at all levels of education seems the norm; virginity of the unmarried is the exception and not the rule.	Turn from such a lifestyle to following a holy God and with his help. This goal is part of a prayer that God fill them with truth love as he has given them the "fruit of righteousness."

Figure 14.2. (*continued*)

Passage: Phil 1:3-11

Mandate or Principle	Contemporary Situation	Implementation
Capture the Significance: 1:6 God takes personal responsibility for the progress and completion of our salvation.	Persons in cultures impacted by a fatalistic world view of Islam or Hinduism are tempted to despair of life	Believe and rejoice in the "good news" of this passage that in the most important enterprise of life–our spiritual relationship with God–God himself guarantees that it will come out well. In fact, he takes personal responsibility for it.

        attitudes, or behaviors. You will frame these as principles during "Application."
    3. **Capture the Significance**: Identify way(s) in which your passage is "good news" to the culture in that it addresses basic needs in contemporary society. You will frame these as principles during "Application."
  B. **Application**: Once you have identified ways your passage is "bad news" or "good news" to the culture, develop appropriate applications related to these points following this procedure:
    1. *Principlize biblical truths* which are "bad news" and "good news" to the culture.
      a. *Mandates directly applied*. What "bad news" or "good news" to the culture does your passage express as directly applicable commands or promises? Assume that all commands or promises in Scripture are normative, i.e. directly applicable, unless Scripture indicates otherwise according to the criteria listed above (see p. 240).

b. *Principles indirectly applied.* What "bad news" and "good news" to the culture does your passage express as content which you should apply indirectly? (see p. 240 for criteria)
- Identify and frame the underlying principle for a command or promise which Scripture does not intend to apply directly?
- Do the same for statements of truth or narrative examples in your passage.

2. *Identify the Contemporary Situation.* To which contemporary situation does the "bad news" and "good news" speak?
   a. Study the circumstances/needs of the text's original audience, the writer's purposes for the teaching, and the results he expected from its application.
   b. Identify today's exact contemporary situation which matches the ancient context.
   c. Then reflect on your audience's present circumstances, needs, interests and concerns from the "bad news" and "good news" perspectives.
   d. Describe the situation to which you need to apply the "Correction" of "bad news" and "Capture the Significance" of the "good news."

3. *Call for implementation.*
   a. Determine the change(s) in attitude and/or behavior which must take place as a result of applying the passage's "bad news" or "good news" mandate(s) and principle(s) to the contemporary situation.
   b. Identify specific steps, practical "how tos" which your audience should take to implement those changes of "Correction" or "Capture the Significance."

Endnotes

1. Traina, *Methodical Bible Study*, 226.

2. Larkin, *Culture and Biblical Hermeneutics*, 192.

3. Traina, *Methodical Bible Study*, 217; cf. Grassmick's (*Greek Exegesis*, 183) comment on the necessity of application: "revelation demands response."

4. Baumann, *Contemporary Preaching*, 243; Whitesell, *Expository Preaching*. 91.

5. Kaiser, *Toward Exegetical Theology*, 162.

6. Stott, *Between Two Worlds*, 137.

7. Fee, *New Testament Exegesis*, 37-38.

8. cf. Kaiser's (*Toward Exegetical Theology*, 29-34) discussion of the issue.

9. Ibid., 32.

10. Liefeld, *New Testament Exposition*, 95.

11. Adams, *Preaching with Purpose*, 131-37.

12. Stott, *Between Two Worlds*, 154.

13. Liefeld, *New Testament Exposition*, 105.

14. Ibid., 107.

15. Adams, "Apply To You?" 77.

16. Kaiser, *Toward Exegetical Theology*, 152.

17. Ramm, *Protestant Biblical Interpretation*, 186-87; Longenecker, *New Testament Social Ethics*, 11-12; contrast Doriani (*Truth to Work*, 126) who sees Scripture mandating both precept and principle. See Webb ("Redemptive-Movement Hermeneutic," 331-49) for bibliography and discussion of the current range of options among evangelicals concerning application.

18. Yoder, *From Word to Life*, 224.

19. Liefeld, *New Testament Exposition*, 96-98.

20. Adams, *Preaching with Purpose*, 138-45.

Chapter 15

HOMILETICAL & DIDACTIC APPROPRIATION

You now have eight hours of exegetical work behind you and the results of those eight hours—exegetical insights, theological interpretations, contemporary applications—in front of you. How will you convert the fruit of your labor into a single sermon or Bible lesson with a clear focus and a specific aim?[1] While the chapters related to exegesis were appropriate for either preaching or teaching, at this point we will divide the material, addressing "Homiletical Appropriation" for sermon development first, followed by "Didactic Appropriation" for lesson development

Homiletical Appropriation

While there are a number of sermon preparation methods to choose from,[2] this chapter will present the Keyword and Analytical approaches as the most serviceable for the great bulk of the Bible's content.[3] It enables the preacher to identify from the Scripture passage the single subject and theme for a sermon. The Keyword Method facilitates identifying and formulating main points, which will develop and substantiate the sermon's subject and theme. The Analytical Method is useful for preaching portions, often narrative, which are longer than a paragraph and which do not contain parallel ideas which may serve as main points in answer to a *key word*.

Developing a sermon requires creative integration. If possible, let a day intervene between the conclusion of your exegetical work and the beginning of homiletical appropriation. This gives your subconscious an opportunity to work on all the exegetical insights and applications you have discovered.

Then, enter your time of "Framing the Sermon" and "Developing the Outline," prayerfully, asking God to apply the truths of the text first to your own life and to help you identify what in the text is especially applicable to the congregation as exhortation or encouragement. Although the work ahead demands a great deal of thought, this stage is also the most satisfying, as you watch a sermon being born before your eyes. You hear for the first time its central heartbeat, and see the basic outline of its features. Your hard won exegetical insights make the process run smoothly, providing not only background material, but also clues to how the sermon is best framed and outlined. You already have a wealth of illustrative and subpoint content at your fingertips.

With your homiletical work comes the joy of apprehending what God's Word is for his people at this time. And this brings a sense of anticipation about communicating the message. You'll find you can't wait to work out the sermon's details, internalize it, and stand and deliver it before God and your people.

But before that day comes, you have three more assignments. First, you will "Frame the Sermon." That is, you will select an appropriate method for the sermon and lay out its major theme and structure. Second, you will "Develop the Sermon Outline," identifying major points, supporting subpoints, illustrations, introduction, conclusion, and title. Third and finally, you will "Practice the Sermon" enough so your delivery is confident and powerful.

Framing the Sermon

Choose the sermon method. One of the greatest challenges preachers face is to choose a homiletical method of presentation whose logic properly expounds the flow of thought of their passage. The New Testament writer employs the formative influence of genre and the defining effect of syntax, both grammatical and rhetorical, to dig the channels of his flow of thought. The more closely the logic of the sermon method approximates these channels, the more truly expository the sermon will be. For, it will be more true to the writer's intent and manner of expression.

For example, when preaching historical narrative, you will use the Keyword Method less than the Analytical Method because narratives present their content according to plot movement, not in the parallel point fashion of discourse. Since parables are figurative sayings which communicate by comparison, the Comparative Method of sermon preparation will come into more frequent use. If the purpose of a given miracle is to prove something, the Syllogistic Method is a natural one to use. See figure 15.1 for a summary of Donald Hamilton's recommendations concerning which sermon methods to use with which genre.

In choosing a homiletical method for your passage, review some of the observations you made during your "Survey" of the passage. There may be some clues there to help your selection. Of all the possibilities, the two "workhorse" methods are the Keyword and Analytical. The description

Figure 15.1. **Matching Genre and Sermon Method**

GENRE		SERMON METHOD	HAMILTON CHAPTER
Epistle		All*	22
Historical Narrative			
	N T History	Analytical; Keyword; Textual–Implicational; Problem solving	18
	Miracles	Analytical, Keyword Syllogistic, Narrative	20
Teaching of Jesus		All*	19
	Parable	Analytical, Implicational, Comparative, Narrative	21
Apocalyptic		Analytical, Keyword	17

*Keyword; Analytical; Textual–Implicational, Telescopic, Illustrational; Problem Solving; Comparative; Syllogistic; Inductive; Narrative.

Source: Hamilton, *Homiletical Handbook*, Table of Contents.

which follows deals with the Keyword method. For Analytical, there is a sample in figure 15.2. For additional instructions on the Analytical Method, refer to Hamilton, *Homiletical Handbook*, chapter five.

Isolate the subject and determine the theme. Remember the one sentence *basic message* of the passage you wrote during "Synthesis"? Have that in hand as you re-read the preaching portion. From the partial list of subjects (fig. 15.3) or from your own devising, select one word that broadly describes the subject area of the passage, i.e., what the passage is talking about (referent). This now becomes the *subject* of your sermon.

Referring to your one sentence *basic message* statement and your one word *subject*, decide what particular aspect of the subject is being dealt with in the passage. This aspect will be the *theme* or complement (sense) of

Figure 15.2. Sample Analytical Method

Passage <u>Phil 3:7-11</u>

FRAME THE SERMON

Sermon Pattern: Analytical

Subject: Scripture's Evaluation of Reliance on Human Effort for being Right with God in Phil 3:7-11.

Theme: An Analysis of Scripture's Evaluation of Reliance on Human Effort for being Right with God in Phil 3:7-11.

Proposition: An Analysis of Scripture's Evaluation of Reliance on Human Effort for being Right with God in Phil 3:7-11 will persuade us to make "Knowing Christ" our goal.

Introduction: "Don't just stand there, do something!" How do we break such a habit in our attempts to relate to God? An analysis of Scripture's evaluation of reliance on human effort for being right with God in Phil 3:7-11 will persuade us to make "Knowing Christ" our goal. When we realize that "reliance on human effort" is a dead loss, disgusting rubbish, and disappears before the splendor of knowing Christ, then we will be persuaded to make knowing Christ our goal.

SERMON OUTLINE
---

vv. 7-8a	A. Reliance on Human Effort is a Dead Loss–How does Paul know that?
	1. His Conversion–"having reckoned"
	2. His Present Experience–"am reckoning"
vv. 8b-9	B. Reliance on Human Effort is Disgusting Rubbish–How do we know that? A Contrast of Two Ways to be Right with God
	1. Source: law or God
	2. Stance: prideful effort or humble faith
	3. Means/Goal: Me or Christ
vv. 10-11	C. Reliance on Human Effort Disappears before the Splendor of Knowing Christ: Why?
	1. Power–Greatest for the Worst
	2. Identity–Becoming like Him
	3. Destiny–"Out-resurrection"

Figure 15.3. **Partial List of Subjects**

Advent	Cross	Gospel	Legalism	Resurrection
Affliction	Cults	Government	Life	Righteousness
Agnosticism	Death	Grace	Loneliness	Salvation
Alcohol	Discipleship	Gratitude	Love	Sanctification
Angels	Discouragem't	Happiness	Man	Satan
Anxiety	Divorce	Healing	Marriage	Second Coming
Apologetics	Doubt	Heaven	Materialism	Sin
Atonement	Education	Hell	Ministry	Stewardship
Baptism	Encouragem't	History	Missions	Temptation
Bible	Eternity	Holy Spirit	Obedience	Thanksgiving
Brotherhood	Ethics	Hope	Patience	Time
Christ	Evangelism	Hospitality	Peace	Tongue
Christmas	Faith	Humility	Power	Unity
Church	Family	Idolatry	Praise	War
Communion	Fear	Joy	Prayer	Witnessing
Compromise	Fellowship	Judgment	Pride	Women
Conscience	Forgiveness	Justification	Prophecy	Work
Conversion	God	Kindness	Redemption	Worship
Courage	God's Will	Law	Repentance	

Source: Hamilton, *Homiletical Handbook*, 40–41.

your sermon's subject. The sermon's theme is what you are going to say about the sermon's subject. State it as a phrase. Often, the phrase will consist of theme linked to subject by the word "of." For example, some possible themes on the subject of the Holy Spirit are: The Person of the Holy Spirit; The Work of the Holy Spirit; The Gifts of the Spirit (Spiritual Gifts); Grieving the Holy Spirit; Blasphemy against the Holy Spirit.

Write a proposition. Think of the *proposition* as your contract with the congregation for the sermon. In a concise (eight words or less), simple sentence, accurately, clearly, and comprehensively describe the sermon's content. The proposition may draw from your *basic message* statement, but it has a different purpose. It tells the congregation what you will try to persuade them of. By stating it in the form of a timeless truth, you help the congregation to see that your sermon's subject matter is, indeed, worth their time.

A *proposition* consists of three elements: "personal reference," "helping verb," and "persuasion goal." The "personal reference" identifies those who are to respond to the sermon. The nature of the passage's audience will guide you here. For example, for Romans 12:3-8, the proposition could be "*Every Christian* should use his spiritual gift."

The "helping" verb indicates the type of response you are looking for. Review your "Mechanical Layout" and "Exegetical Outline" to identify the possible main points which will be used to develop and establish the proposition. These are normally the main clauses or, in the case of a larger portion, the main content of sentence clusters or paragraphs. Note what connectives introduce them. Do they answer the question Why? (causal, purpose, result) or How? (manner, comparative). Then decide, based on this information, as well as your congregation's needs, which type of persuasion goal you will adopt for the sermon. The following options (with examples) will help you select the helping verb or phrase:

Figure 15.4. **Proposition Helping Verb(s) or Phrases**

Type	Helping Verb(s) or Phrase	Question(s) Answered	Example
Obligation	Should; Must	Why?	Every person *should* pray daily
Ability	Can	How?	Every person *can* pray daily
Value	It is better	Why?	*It is better* to pray daily than to shoulder the load alone

Source: Hamilton, *Homiletical Handbook*, 43.

Since Rom 12:3-8 involves implied commands to pursue use of spiritual gifts, a helping verb of obligation is most appropriate for the proposition (e.g., "Every Christian *should* use his spiritual gift").

The third element, the "persuasion goal," picks up the sermon's theme and represents it by a main verb and object. The persuasion goal's main verb will indicate the type of attitude or behavior change which the congregation should decide for as they respond to the message. Since you preach for a decision, your proposition will normally seek to persuade your audience to adopt and act on new insights, attitudes or skills, though embracing new knowledge is also a possibility (see fig. 15.5 on the next page for a partial list of "persuasion goals"). By adopting one of these terms and adding it to the "helping verb or phrase," you will be clearly stating the persuasion goal within the proposition. For Rom 12:3-8, which speaks of the practice of spiritual gifts, it seems best to combine a main verb from the skills category with a previously selected "obligation" helping verb. The theme "spiritual gifts" can then provide the object and complete the persuasion goal. ("Every Christian should *use* his *spiritual gifts*").

As you frame your proposition, you will also be laying the foundation for both your sermon development, applications, and the conclusion. For, based on your proposition you will be able to delineate measurable goals in implementation. These will enable the congregation to live out during the week what they have decided for during the sermon.

Compose a propositional interrogative. Reread your proposition and identify again, this time from the following lists (fig. 15.6), what potential questions you are answering.

Figure 15.6 **Propositional Interrogatives**

Obligation	Ability	Value
"should"	"can"	"it is better"
*Why? When? Where? What?	*How? When? Where? What?	*Why? When? Where?

*the primary question of each category

Source: Hamilton, *Homiletical Handbook*, 44.

Look again at the "Mechanical Layout" and "Exegetical Outline" and identify those main clauses or paragraphs that are likely to be your main points. Note again the connectives which introduce them. Decide either from

Figure 15.5. **Partial List of "Persuasion Goal" Main Verbs**

IF THE PERSUASION GOAL IS . . .
    THEN THE MAIN VERB WILL BE . . .

Knowledge		Insight	
list	delineate	discriminate between	separate
state	become aware of	differentiate between	evaluate
enumerate	become familiar with		examine
recite			comprehend
recall	become cognizant of	compare	reflect on
write		contrast	think through
identify	define	classify	discern
memorize	describe	select	understand
know	recognize	choose	discover
trace			

Attitude	Skill
determine to	interpret
develop	apply
have confidence in	internalize
appreciate	produce
be convinced of	use
be sensitive to	practice
commit yourself to	study
be enthusiastic about	solve
desire to	experience
sympathize with	explain
view	communicate
plan	assist in
feel satisfied about	pray about

Source: Robinson, *Biblical Preaching*, 110.

the connectives (e.g., causal and inferential answer question: "Why?"; temporal answers "When?"; local, "Where?"; comparative, "How?") or the passage's content which one interrogative would best answer *all* the potential main points.

Preface the proposition with an interrogative and turn the proposition into an interrogative sentence, the propositional interrogative. This interrogative sentence gives the one question which all the main points answer as they seek to persuade the congregation to decide for the proposition. For example, from the proposition on Rom 12:3-8 comes the interrogative sentence: "Why should every Christian use his spiritual gift?"

Choose a keyword and formulate a transitional sentence. Look again at your "Mechanical Layout" and "Exegetical Outline." Isolate the two to five main points you will need to make in order to establish your proposition. Using the list of keywords in figure 15.7, decide which one is the category which best describes all the main points. Choose a *keyword* which is both broad enough to characterize all the main points, yet specific enough to precisely communicate the passage's content.

Next, place the keyword into a phrase or clause which is a direct response to the interrogative sentence.

- If you asked: "Why?", the response should be, "It is because of the___s (keyword in plural) ... "
- If you said: "How?", the response is, "It is by___ing the___s (keyword in plural) ... "
- If you said, "Where?", the answer is "It is in/at the__s (keyword in plural) ... "
- If you asked: "When?", you will say "It is in (or some time-related word) the___s (keyword in plural) ... "
- If you asked "What?", you should say, "It is___ (keyword in plural) about which ... "

The choice of the right keyword is vital to the construction of a unified sermon outline which moves effectively to its goal. It indicates the common way each main point answers the interrogative sentence and so establishes the proposition.

In formulating a *transitional sentence* you answer the interrogative sentence by adding a direct response phrase or clause to the proposition. See figure 15.8 for an example a propositional interrogative for a sermon based on Rom 12:3-8. Place the transitional sentence after the proposition at the conclusion of the introduction. It forms a logical bridge to the body (main points) of the sermon.

Develop the main points. Complete the framing of your sermon by identifying the substance of the main points (normally two to five) and the

Figure 15.7. **A Short List of Sample Keywords**

abuses	gains	methods	prescriptions
actions	gifts	ministries	principles
admonitions	guarantees	mistakes	privileges
affairs	guidelines	models	problems
affirmations	habits	motives	proofs
alternatives	hopes	movements	prospects
answers	hurts	names	purposes
arguments	ideals	natures	qualities
attitudes	ideas	necessities	quests
attributes	idols	needs	questions
beliefs	ills	norms	reactions
benefits	impacts	objectives	reasons
blessings	impediments	objects	results
blunders	imperfections	obligations	rewards
burdens	imperatives	observances	rules
causes	implications	observations	sayings
certainties	improvements	obstacles	secrets
charges	incentives	occasions	services
circumstances	incidents	offenses	situations
commands	invitations	options	skills
corrections	issues	paradoxes	solutions
dangers	items	parallels	sources
decisions	joys	particulars	talents
declarations	judgments	parts	tasks
deeds	keys	paths	teachings
details	kinds	patterns	tests
doctrines	laws	penalties	times
duties	lessons	perceptions	truths
effects	levels	perils	uses
elements	liabilities	periods	values
examples	liberties	petitions	virtues
exclamations	limits	phases	visions
facts	losses	pictures	vocations
factors	loyalties	plans	warnings
failures	manifestations	pledges	ways

Source: Hamilton, *Homiletical Handbook*, 45-46.

Figure 15.8. **Framing Keyword Method Sermon**

Proposition	"Every Christian should use his spiritual gift."
Propositional Interrogative	"Why should every Christian use his spiritual gift?"
Keyword	Affirmations
Transitional Sentence:	"Because of the affirmations Paul makes about spiritual gifts to the Romans, every Christian should determine to use his spiritual gift."

verse(s) in the passage from which they are taken. Make sure the points taken together cover the passage's essential content. Check that each point is relatively proportional with the others, i.e., covering more or less the same amount of biblical content. Each main point will be an instance of the keyword.

Next, express each main point as one sentence that is concise, complete and memorable. In form the points should be parallel: the same length, the same grammatical construction, and the same word order.

Finally, place the main points as roman numeral headings to form the skeleton of a sermon outline. Though their order may vary from Scripture in order to enhance a sermon's progression to a climax, it is best to begin structuring an outline by understanding the dynamic flow of thought which the Scripture passage exhibits and seeing if that flow may not best suit the sermon presentation.[4]

Developing the Outline

You have the main points of your outline already determined. Your remaining tasks are: formulating the sub-points, coming up with illustrations and applications, writing a good introduction, working on the manuscript, preparing a conclusion, and picking a title. You are on the home stretch.

Formulate the subpoints. With the basic framework of your sermon in place, you now need to fill it out by developing the subpoints. Sub-points are important because they are the means of establishing the main points you want to get across. Subpoints can fulfill this function either by explanation or argumentation. Using your "Mechanical Layout," "Exegetical Outline," and the rest of your exegetical insights, identify which of the following methods of development seems most suited to your passage.[5]

Explanation. If you develop a sermon by way of explanation, you will proceed with one of three styles: "Exposition," "Interrogation," or "Thought Categorization." Explaining by "Exposition" involves making the main point of your sermon clear by explaining its constituent parts and the significant features of the undergirding Scripture (e.g., material from "Historical Analysis," "Literary Analysis," particularly the line of argument from genre and subgenre analysis, grammar, or "Synthesis"). Explaining by "Interrogation" means that each subpoint of your sermon will be designed to answer one of the following questions about the main point: Who? What? When? Where? Why? and How?

Finally, explaining by "Thought Categorization" means that each of your subpoints provides information within a cluster of like ideas. If the sermon theme is biographical (e.g., on Peter or Paul), your subpoints may describe their name, roots, personality, achievements, successes and failures, relation to God, etc. If the sermon theme is an event, the subpoints may address time, place, causes, effects. If the sermon theme relates to time, sub-points on the past, present, or future may be engaged. Other sermon themes susceptible to "Thought Categorization" are relationships, parables, miracles, speeches, and doctrines.

Argumentation. Some sermons are better developed to advance the main points by way of argumentation. Here your subpoints can substantiate your main points either by formal reasoning, using deductive (syllogisms) or inductive thinking, or by persuasion, using emotional materials and logic.

Whether in the form of *Explanation* or *Argumentation*, you should aim for two to five subpoints for each main point. Each subpoint should be concise, complete, memorable, and parallel in form. Be sure to exhaust the preaching portion before looking elsewhere in Scripture. Develop at least one subpoint for application for each main point.

Illustrate the message. Illustrations bring attractiveness, clarity, and power to the sermon. They make the sermon interesting to listen to by attracting attention and providing variation in pace. They give needed psychological breaks, and in that way prolong the audiences' attention span. They also make repetition possible without weariness. Illustrations bring clarity by making an abstract truth concrete and visual. Illustrations bring power to a preacher's points by impressing the truth on the mind and heart of the hearer. They are a form of inductive reasoning and have a great ability to persuade. Visual media, such as video clips and Powerpoint, are technological extensions of the illustration function.

Make it a lifetime quest to collect illustrations that are true, plausible, in good taste, and powerful for supporting biblical teaching. As you get to this point in your sermon development, turn to your personal reservoir of illustrations, as well as other resources. Look at those reflections in answer to the question: "Will it preach?" you have salted away in your files. Your investigations in "Historical Analysis," "Literary Analysis: Word Study," and "Interpretation: Communication" will also be of aid in prompting good illustrations. Pray for guidance in selecting illustrations that will really drive your major points home. Place them at strategic points in your sermon, whether it be to illumine main points, subpoints, applications or to strengthen introductions and conclusions.

Devise an introduction. A sermon introduction should be no longer than 10-15 percent of the total speaking time. An introduction has three basic purposes.

- *Arouse interest.* The preacher awakens the listener's interest by communicating the relevance and value of the sermon subject.
- *Inform about subject.* You introduce the audience to the subject and how you plan to pursue it.
- *Promote respect.* The introduction also promotes the congregation's respect for the preacher.

Your very first sentence should include a reference to the sermon's general subject. The introduction can then progress from the general subject to the specific theme, to the biblical context, and finally to the proposition. But you are also free to begin with a reference to the congregations's situation, to the biblical context, to a recent world event, or any other rhetorical device that will set the stage for the sermon. However it begins, an introduction should always conclude with the proposition, for this is what launches you into the main body of the message.

Here are a few things to avoid in an introduction: Big words and long sentences; any material not related to the sermon subject; apologies for yourself or your subject; and hesitations (hem-hawing) due to lack of preparation.

Develop the sermon body (manuscript). Homileticians have differing opinions on the value of consistently preparing a written sermon manuscript. Some promote the use of only a homiletical outline. Some see preaching without notes as the goal. Eventually, you will find what is best for you.

Whatever technique you adopt, there is value in periodically writing out a complete manuscript of what you plan to say. This becomes a good exercise in self-evaluation, as you monitor yourself in a number of areas of sermonizing. Are you using too many cliches? Does your expression of main points, subpoints, and transitions show that the sermon has a coherence? Have you properly proportioned each part of your sermon? Watch out for a first point that take twenty-five minutes. A rule of thumb for developing a manuscript is that you can probably produce two pages per hour. Thus, in three to four hours you will have written a manuscript (six to eight pages) which will take twenty to twenty-five minutes to deliver.

Prepare the conclusion. A brief (5 percent of total sermon time), positive conclusion fulfills three functions.

- *Remind of important ideas.* In the conclusion, the preacher reviews for his audience the most important ideas in the message.
- *Reinforce major concepts.* The preacher reinforces the major concepts of his sermon, particularly where biblical truth bears on the will of the audience.
- *Encourage radical application.* Finally, a conclusion encourages change in either the belief, attitude or behavior of each listener.

The conclusion begins with a "purpose sentence" that is actually the sermon's proposition altered by adding the prefix, "Therefore" or "So you see," etc., and uses the helping verb "should." No matter the type of persuasion goal of a given proposition, every "purpose sentence" will be in "obligation" form. Therefore, the "purpose sentence" for a "value" persuasion goal, such as "It is better to pray daily than shoulder the load alone," would be "Therefore, every person should pray daily and not shoulder the load alone."

The purpose sentence in the conclusion unifies the sermon. After it will follow a very brief review of the truth content in the sermon; a challenge motivating the listener to act; a suggested course of action to take; and a climactic closing sentence.

A few things to avoid in a conclusion are: multiple conclusions; irrelevance, including new material; humor; abruptness; apologies; indecisiveness; and lack of preparation.

Choose a title. When everything else is done, devise a title for your sermon. It should both spark interest and indicate the sermon's content. A good sermon title is creative, but not sensational; contemporary, but not faddish; brief, but not vague; arousing interest or curiosity, but also delivering the goods

Practicing the Sermon

You've worked hard on your exegesis, and just as hard on the homiletical appropriation necessary to craft your biblical research into a well structured, well illustrated, persuasive sermon. Your work is done except for one thing: Practice. Very few communicators are skillful enough to move directly from a written manuscript or outline to delivery without rehearsal. Practicing your sermon can be a final check on your research and development. Don't be surprised if you make some changes along the way. Practice also helps you gain confidence in delivery and develop good pacing and tone of voice. It is helpful to speak the sermon out loud a number of times.

Homiletical Appropriation: Resources

Materials from Previous Study

    All worksheets

Greek is Great Gain

    Descriptions in chapter fifteen
    Figures in chapter fifteen

Commentaries

    Fee, *Philippians*.
    Hawthorne, *Philippians*.
    Melick, *Philippians, Colossians, Philemon*.
    Swindoll, *Laugh Again*.
    Thielman, *Philippians*.

Homiletical Appropriation: Procedure

I. Survey
II. Analysis
III. Synthesis
IV. Interpretation/Application
V. **Homiletical Appropriation**
    A. **Frame the Sermon:** Using the resources noted, frame the sermon and place the results at the appropriate places on the "Homiletical Appropriation" worksheet (See figs. 15.2, 9 for examples and WJLFP for template).

Figure 15.9. **Sample Framing and Outlining the Sermon (Keyword Method)**

Phil 1:3-11

#1 *Subject*: The Church

#2 *Theme*: Interpersonal Relationships within the Church

#3 *Proposition*: Every church *can experience* spiritually healthy interpersonal relationships

#4 *Propositional Interrogative Sentence*: How can every church experience spiritually healthy interpersonal relationships?

#5 *Keyword*: "Practices" *Direct Response Phrase*: "By following Paul's practices with the Philippians . . .

#6 *Transitional Sentence*: By following Paul's practices with the Philippians as presented in Phil 1:3-11, every church can experience spiritually healthy interpersonal relationships.

#7 *Main Points*

    I. Paul thanks God for the Philippians' spiritual life and tells them about it. Scriptural undergirding: Phil 1:3-8
    II. Paul prays for the Philippians' sanctification and tells them about it. Scriptural undergirding: Phil 1:9-11

#8 *Sub-points* and #9 *Illustrations* added to *Main Points*.

I. Paul thanks God for the Philippians' spiritual life and tells them about it. Phil 1:3-8
    Historical and *Literary Context* of the Portion.
    A. Because of their "fellowship in the gospel" (Phil 1:3-5)

Support: koinonia–contemporary background (*TDNT* 3:798; MM, 351) and Paul's usage indicates that the meaning includes financial support in the context of a spiritual partnership (Phil 4:10-16; 1:7; 2:1).

Figure 15.9 *(continued)*

> *Illustration*: Contemporary missionary/supporter relationship as evidenced by prayer letters.

> B. Because of his affection for them (Phil 1:7-8)
>
> *Support:* strength of the affection: in heart–2 Cor 7:3; 1 Thess 2:17; longing–Ps 42:1; 1 Pet 2:2.
>
> *Illustration*: cf. Jesus' messianic compassion–Mark 1:41; Luke 7:13.
>
> C. Because of his confidence in God's work in them (Phil 1:6)
>
> *Support:* the dynamic–Phil 2:12-13; OT background for assurance–God the creator and sovereign worker, Gen 1-2; Ps 139:13-16.
>
> D. Application: We can promote spiritually healthy interpersonal relationships if you will find someone in the congregation whose spiritual life has been an encouragement to you because of its vitality and contribution to the fellowship. Thank God in your prayers for that person. Tell him or her that this is what you are doing.

II. Paul Prays for the Philippians' Sanctification and tells them about it. Phil 1:9-11.
  A. What Kind of Sanctification is He Praying for?–Love abounding in Moral Discernment (Phil 1:9)

  > *Support:* "Christian self-giving love is to grow in knowledge of God's truth and depth of insight"–the capacity to apply knowledge to ethical situations so that the proper exercise of love takes place. cf. Heb 5:14; Prov 12:1; 19:25.
  >
  > *Illustration*: Difference between morally discerning love and non-discerning love in approaching a current social and ethical issue like economic justice for the disadvantaged.

  B. What Outcome is He Praying for?—Correct Moral Judgment; Blameless Life at Christ's Coming (Phil 1:10)

Figure 15.9 (*continued*)

> *Support:*
>
> 1. Correct judgment–illustrated by other passages, Rom 12:2; Phil 4:8.
> 2. Blameless Life: Contemporary background from papyri pointing to integrity (MM, 184).
>
> C. What Divine Resources is He Depending on?—Fruit of Righteousness through Jesus Christ
>
> *Illustration*: Vietnam Veteran who stood firm for a sexually pure life in the midst of mockery.
>
> *Support:* "fruit of righteousness"–"fruit," God is the source of the sanctified life; "righteousness"–"upright conduct" that maintains covenant ties grounded in "right standing" with God, granted by a covenant keeping God (Deut 30:6-8; Jer 31:31-34).
>
> D. Application: We can promote spiritually healthy interpersonal relationships in the church if we will choose a fellow Christian and consistently pray for his sanctification, i.e., that his life will be characterized by a love abounding in moral discernment which makes correct moral judgments.

#10 *Introduction*: Though superficial interpersonal relationships still characterize many quarters in the contemporary American church, there is a new hunger in the emerging generations for community. They want to be the church not just go to church. But in a world more comfortable with the electronic connectedness of text messaging and "Facebook," how can we learn to truly communicate in face-to-face community? If we return to the first century model as seen in Paul's relations with the Philippians we will see the dynamics of spiritually healthy interpersonal relationships. And we will see the practices that sustained them. Though separated by years and miles from a face-to-face encounter, Paul opens his letter to the Philippians with a tone that manifests fellowship at its best.

A study of Phil 1:3-11 leads me to the conviction that every church can experience spiritually healthy interpersonal relationships. How? By following Paul's practices with the Philippians as presented in Phil

Figure 15.9 *(continued)*

1:3-11, every church can indeed experience spiritually healthy interpersonal relationships.

#11 *Conclusion*: Therefore, every church should be experiencing spiritually healthy interpersonal relationships. A church can do this when its members thank God for each other. This they will do because of the spiritual and practical ministry, the strong affection, and the settled confidence in God's work, each has toward the other. A church can do this by praying for one another's sanctification: that each would have a love which abounds in moral discernment and thus is able to make correct moral judgments, but all by God's grace.

Do you long for such vital interpersonal relationships within our church? They can be ours if we will in obedience follow Paul's example. Today, this week, identify someone you want to thank God for. Do it and tell him or her you did it. Also, pray for that person's or another's sanctification. Covenant to pray once a week for a month for them. Check in with them for prayer requests. It may turn into a long term "prayer partner" relationship.

Let us pursue genuine face-to-face community. Let us be the body of Christ.

#12 *Title*: "A Body Needs to Communicate"

1. *Step #1: Isolate the subject.* Identify the one word which best broadly describes the subject area of the passage (see list at fig. 15.3).
2. *Step #2: Determine the theme.* Identify the one narrow aspect of the subject which is being dealt with in the passage. State it as a phrase, normally with the theme linked to subject by "of".
3. *Step #3: Write a proposition.* Compose a proposition which includes principlized theme, personal reference, helping verb, and persuasion goal (see figs. 15.4-5).
4. *Step #4: Compose a propositional interrogative* (Keyword Method Only). A Propositional Interrogative is the proposition in question form. Depending on the proposition's "helping verb" its propositional interrogative will be a "Why? How? or When, Where, What?" question (see fig. 15.6).
5. *Step #5: Choose one keyword* (Keyword Method Only). This is a category word which best describes all of the main points (see fig. 15.7 for sample keywords). Place your "keyword" (in the

plural) into a phrase or clause which is a direct response to the propositional interrogative.
   6. *Step #6: Formulate a transitional sentence* (Keyword Method Only). Answer the propositional interrogative by adding to the proposition the direct response phrase or clause, developed in Step #5, (see fig. 15.8 for a sample).
   7. *Step #7 Develop the main points.* Identify two to five main points which proportionally cover the content of the passage. Express them as parallel thoughts, in the case of keyword method, as instances of the keyword. Arrange the main points as a skeleton outline.
B. **Develop the Sermon Outline & Content**. Using the resources noted and the "Homiletical Appropriation" worksheet fill out the sermon outline and content (See fig. 15.2, 9 for examples).
   1. *Step #8: Formulate the subpoints.* Identify the type of explanation or argumentation method which is most suited to developing the main points from your passage. Frame appropriate subpoints, which are concise, complete, memorable, and parallel in form. Provide an application subpoint for each main point.
   2. *Step #9: Include illustrations.* Collect illustrations, which are true, plausible, in good taste, and–most importantly–supportive of a point made in the sermon. Place them strategically throughout the sermon.
   3. *Step #10: Devise an introduction.* Write an engaging introduction which has the sermon's subject in the very first sentence; moves from contemporary audience to text or vice versa; and concludes with the proposition.
   4. *Step #10a: Write the body of the sermon* (optional). Manuscript preparation in spoken style at the pace of two pages an hour (three hours for a six page manuscript to be delivered in twenty minutes).
   5. *Step #11: Prepare the conclusion.* Start with the proposition as a "purpose sentence." Briefly review the truth content of the sermon. Include a challenge for the listener to act and a suggestion for implementation. End with a climactic closing sentence.
   6. *Step #12: Write a title.* Compose a sermon title which is, at once, intriguing, concise, and captures the sermon's main thrust.

DIDACTIC APPROPRIATION

Differences Between Sermons & Lessons

Purpose. As mentioned at the beginning of this chapter, your exegetical work can be the foundation for either a sermon to preach or a lesson to teach.[6] How are these two forms of communication different and how are they alike? One difference is purpose. Sermons are primarily *applicational*. Preachers impart Biblical knowledge in their sermons (e.g., a brief summary of introductory matters; background on key words or historical setting, etc.), but the main purpose is to appeal to the will, to preach for a decision in response to biblical truth.

Bible teaching frequently combines two purposes: an *informational* purpose aimed at strengthening the biblical and theological knowledge of the people of God and an *applicational* purpose directing students toward the significance of what they learn for their lives. Book studies, topical studies, Bible overviews, and theological investigations are some types of study that can be profitably designed and taught with these two purposes in mind.

Presentation. Most preachers stand before congregations and present a sermon without interruption. They may make use of rhetorical questions to prompt mental interaction. They may use Powerpoint slides or sermon outlines with blanks to fill in to encourage retention. Some churches schedule forums to discuss the Sunday sermon. The sermon, however, is fundamentally a monological proclamation of the Word presented from a dialogical perspective. The preacher's goal is to persuade and draw a response (actually an on-going response) from each member of the congregation. People may respond verbally, e.g., the call and response style of some African American churches. Some may respond quietly in their hearts as they are led toward conviction and repentance. Decisions might be made that call for walking forward for prayer, salvation, rededication, or commitment to mission service. Responses will vary, but preachers should intentionally seek to keep their listeners mentally and emotionally engaged and direct them toward personal response to the biblical truth they hear.

Bible teachers have a wider palette of instructional methods to choose from. These methods can promote student-to-teacher and student-to-student interaction. They can engage students in more physical involvement than is possible during a sermon. While some Bible teaching may be monological in nature, it is best to think of Bible teaching as complementary to, but not the equivalent of preaching. Using a variety of interactive learning experiences in the classroom expands and enriches the teaching ministry of the church. Such experiences can also contribute to building community and helping students develop exegetical and ministry skills.

Audience age. Preachers normally aim their sermons at an adult audience, although children and youth are frequently in attendance. The wise preacher will be aware of different age levels in a congregation and seek to bring relevance to all, but the primary target audience is usually adults. Teaching, of course, is often age-segregated so that lessons can be tailored to the characteristics of the class.

Length of preparation. Exegetical preparation for Bible teaching normally requires less than the eight hours suggested for preachers. Many Bible teachers have limited time for lesson presentation with the remaining time allocated for prayer and other fellowship activities. Also, teachers using interactive instructional methods must limit the amount of content covered to allow time for discussion and other activities. Thus, the Bible teacher must pray for wisdom to address the *most* essential elements within each step presented in this text, particularly within Analysis.

Despite these differences, sermons and lessons both require *prayerful, diligent, Spirit-led exegetical preparation* so that the deep truth of the chosen passage forms the anchoring foundation for any homiletical or didactic appropriation. We now turn our attention to the latter.

Educational Philosophy for Bible Teaching

Outcomes oriented. The goal of all teaching—including Bible teaching—should be *learning*. Why teach if students do not learn? The next question is, how can we know someone has learned? A classic definition provides illumination: *Learning is a change in behavior that is persistent over time.* Learning is not a purely mental activity. It should result in a new capability. The students could not state Psalm 100 from memory before; now they can. They could not give a basic explanation of the Trinity before; now they can. They could not interpret the Bible with any confidence, but after learning some hermeneutical principles and Bible study skills in Sunday School, they can. They were apt to be self-focused before; now, after a rich study of Philippians, they share in discussion groups that they are growing to think of others more highly than themselves (Phil 2:3). This is the kind of observable change teachers should pray for as they design their lessons: learning that results in Christlike behavior, that persists beyond the classroom, and that results in not only personal spiritual growth but also growth in oneness and spiritual focus in the church.

Learning focused. Teachers who aim for these kinds of outcomes know that teaching is *a means to the end of learning*, not an end in itself. They understand teaching to be more than the teacher's exegetical study, lesson design, and presentation. They see teaching as the process of *arranging the instructional conditions in the classroom so that students are most likely to learn*. They use of a wide variety of instructional methods to promote deep engagement with the biblical passage.

Spirit dependent. Bible teachers praying for life change understand the spiritual battle waged for the minds of their students. The enemy actively seeks to disrupt any attention paid to God's Word. Boredom, confusion, a perceived lack of relevance, information overload, lessons perceived as too challenging or too simplistic, an unfriendly classroom environment—all of these, and many other factors, are potential hazards the enemy can exploit. Knowing this, "transformational Bible teachers" do two things. First, they prepare and teach in utter dependence on the Holy Spirit. Second, they learn as much as they can about learning principles so that their instructional planning aligns as closely as possible with how God created the human brain to learn (encode) information, attitudes, and skills.

Learning Principles for Bible Teaching

Few areas of behavior have been studied as extensively as human learning. In particular, today's "brain-based" research provides a great deal of insight into the learning process. This section will highlight a selection of learning principles of particular significance for Bible teachers.

The importance of gaining and maintaining attention. Human beings' mental process of *attention* has limits. Confronted with a never-ending stream of stimuli from the environment, they constantly make conscious or subconscious decisions on how to direct their attention. Stimuli perceived as interesting, unusual, intriguing, or amusing frequently grab a person's attention. The single most powerful "attentional magnet," however, is the perceived *relevance* of the stimuli. Simply put, people are most likely to pay attention to information they perceive to be of genuine personal value. Bible lessons are most engaging when the practical relevance of the teaching passage is made abundantly clear. This learning principle undergirds the emphasis in this text on the importance of determining the significance of biblical passages for contemporary culture (see chapter fourteen in particular).

The cumulative nature of learning. Children and adults sometimes learn completely new sets of data, e.g., a toddler first learning to read; an English speaking adult first learning Hebrew, Greek, or Arabic, etc. But learning is normally an additive process whereby new information is encoded with similar knowledge already encoded in a person's long-term memory. This principle cautions us about teaching "over the heads" of students who do not have the necessary prerequisite background. Of equal or greater concern is the importance of designing lessons with an appropriate level of challenge for students who have spent years or even decades in Bible classes. These people often have a great deal of biblical literacy. The question is, how can the teacher encourage them to build upon their current knowledge and take one or more steps toward greater maturity and fruitfulness? This principle reminds us that becoming more like Jesus and less like ourselves is a cumulative process with no end in sight until heaven. A single lesson may not bring significant life change (although the Spirit sometimes makes that happen). Still, one of the adventures of Bible teaching is to guide our students and ourselves toward on-going transformation into the image of Christ "from glory to glory" (2 Cor 3:18).

The importance of visuals and illustrations. God created the human brain in such a way that *all* people encode visual images more easily than abstract, theoretical information. A simple test is the way we are far less likely to forget faces than names. God created a very visual world. Unless impairment interferes, infants begin learning the countless visual images before them.

Teachers who understand this aspect of neurological functioning learn to skillfully incorporate visuals to help students encode the most important points in a lesson. Charts can clarify the relationships between multiple perspectives, e.g., the significance of the three temptations in Matt 4:1-11. Powerpoint slides or video clips can heighten the emotional power of key concepts. Simple stick figure drawings can make complex theological constructs more understandable. Concrete objects can provide riveting images, e.g., the initial display of all American flags at the beginning of a lesson on missions to dramatize how easily a nation can focus on itself and ignore the thrust of the Great Commission. "Word pictures" have the same power. Well chosen verbal illustrations, such as the allusions and parables used so effectively by Jesus, prompt students to form their own visual images. It is for this reason that the use of illustrations of any kind is so important for preaching and teaching. Scripture, nature, and the teacher's own life are just a few rich sources for visuals and illustrations. The more an illustration encapsulates and illuminates a key biblical point, the more effective it will be in encouraging the encoding of that point.

The dangers of information overload. God created the human brain with a limitless capacity for storing memories, a capacity far beyond what will ever be needed by the most learned individuals on earth. It has been suggested that the excess memory capacity may be God's provision for seeing him face to face in the glories of heaven.

Yet despite unlimited *storage* capacity, we have a significantly limited *processing* capacity. Simply put, people can't process too much information at one time! The function of the short-term memory is to keep new information active long enough to be meaningfully and permanently stored in long-term memory. Research consistently demonstrates the loss of information from short-term processing when too much information is presented too quickly.

Bible teachers who understand this fact of human cognition take seriously the maxim, "Less is more." Instead of packing too much content into one lesson, they identify the essential elements of the biblical text, present them clearly, and then provide ample opportunities for rich, meaningful engagement and application. It is sometimes even more effective to anchor a lesson to one central controlling concept in the biblical passage.

The power of active learning. Strategies that encourage students to be actively involved in a lesson and that prompt critical reflection on key points are catalysts to learning. As adult educator Jane Vella has said, "Telling is not teaching." Elementary teachers explain math or reading skills to their students, but the explanation is always followed by extensive periods of practice. Corporate trainers lecture engineers on a new system, but mastery is not assumed until there is hands-on experience.

The same principle applies to the attitudinal learning that is the goal of much Bible teaching. Suppose a Bible teacher tells people what God's Word says on an important lifestyle issue during a lecture segment. Before moving on to the next point, learning research suggests the value of giving students an opportunity to grapple with that issue and what it means for their lives. Instructional methods that promote dialogue, active engagement, and critical reflection stand to significantly increase the depth and permanence of student learning. These kinds of strategies also stand to get learners more emotionally engaged, an important benefit in light of the strong link between the emotions and learning.

Vella advocates frequent use of small group discussions (which she calls "learning tasks") for adult learners. In a "learning task" students receive a clearly defined assignment and any resources needed to complete it, e.g., a short, written case study and directions for each group to apply specific biblical principles to the scenario in the case study. This strategy gives every student an opportunity to be involved. It is not an exercise in "shared ignorance" because the teacher clearly delineates the parameters for the group discussions and then "debriefs" with the entire class which invites even more interaction. "Learning tasks" avoid some of the drawbacks of large group discussions, e.g., the tendency for the teacher and several vocal students to dominant the conversation, and the difficulty of getting some groups out of the habit of a very passive approach to learning.

The importance of questions. Asking good questions is an important technique for maintaining student interest and engagement. Good questions encourage critical thinking and the transfer of Bible content to real-world situations. Teachers who take the time to formulate good questions are rewarded with a window through which to gauge their students' mastery of the material and growth in spiritual maturity. Answers to questions can reveal gaps and deficiencies in the presentation and provide opportunities to explain, integrate, and enrich the content as necessary.

Simple *observational* questions have some value, especially for children ("Who did Nebuchadnezzar see in the fiery furnace?"). *Interpretational* questions go deeper ("Why is the cross a 'stumbling block' to unbelievers?"). *Applicational* questions can get very personal ("In what way has your life been impacted by our study of Moses in Exodus?"). Questions also can equip students to study the Bible on their own ("What is the key point of this passage? What implications can you draw from that point?").

The need for a safe learning environment. Open dialogue requires a supportive and a safe place for learning. Teacher-to-student and student-to-student relationships become very important. Teachers should model transparency and sensitivity and encourage community that extends outside the walls of the classroom. The teacher may sometimes need to model the biblical value of "speaking the truth in love" in correcting a view expressed or attitude displayed. As relationships grow, the teacher should encourage students to take responsibility not only for their own learning, but for the spiritual growth of their classmates as they practice the "one another" commands of Paul's letters. In so doing, Bible teachers have the opportunity to gently counteract the individualism that has crept into a Western understanding of spiritual formation. A maturing class will deepen in its sense of being the people of God.

The challenge of lifelong learning and ministry. The old adage about the value of teaching a man to fish rather than simply giving him a fish dinner can be applied to Christian education in the church. Not every student will be called and gifted for large group Bible teaching, but every believer can and should be able to teach in the sense of informally sharing the Word with believing or unbelieving family, friends, and others God brings into their lives. Christian educator William R. Yount challenges Bible teachers to beware of a mindset of "spoon feeding" students and subconsciously suggesting that they must always rely on the exegetical ability of others for spiritual growth. Ongoing corollaries to Bible study can be activities that gradually encourage students to develop capability for interpreting and applying the Word, to develop their spiritual gifts, and to explore and practice ministry skills.

The importance of the teacher as role model. Learning research has long verified the powerful influence of the respected human model in encouraging people to adopt a new attitude or change an existing one. Bible teachers should embrace this role, recognizing that who they are in Christ is an essential part of their preparation for teaching. Some of the best teaching may take place outside of the classroom as the teacher interacts with students one-on-one, in small groups, or through phone calls, sending cards, or e-mail correspondence.

Transformational Lesson Design for Bible Teaching

When our exegetical study is completed and it is time for the didactic appropriation necessary to craft an effective Bible lesson, the following steps are recommended (see fig. 15.10 for a sample lesson and WJLFP for the template).

Plan the Lesson. Before any strategies are considered, the teacher prayerfully begins with a focus on the learners and their learning.

> *Analyze the teaching assignment and target audience.* Learn as much as possible about the physical and logistical factors in the learning environment. Then consider the motivations, life experience, and cultural, ethnic, and age characteristics of the target audience. For example, the sample lesson (fig. 15.10) is for an adult, middle class, American Sunday school class that has built a level of trust. Analyze your target audience with the goal of designing a lesson that is as relevant as possible for this particular group. Obviously, this kind of analysis is extremely important for teachers working in cross-cultural settings.
>
> *Frame an objective that captures the desired learning outcome.* A helpful format is as follows: "The learners will___ (*insert cognitive, knowledge component*) *so that* they will___ (*insert affective, lifechange component*)." For examples of "knowledge" and "insight" verbs for the "cognitive, knowledge component" see figure 15.5. See the same figure for "attitude" and "skills" verbs for the "affective, life change component." Here is an example for a lesson entitled "How Much are *You* Willing to Risk?" based on Esth 4:1-17:
>
>> "The participants will be able to *describe* specific ways Esther conquered her fear and acted courageously *so that* they are better prepared to *apply* similar strategies in their own lives.
>
> *Write a lesson title.* Work hard to develop a creative title which will awaken interest and capture the essence of the lesson. The process itself can help the Bible teacher hone in on the *big idea* of the lesson.

Figure 15.10. **Bible Lesson**

Text: Esth 4:1-17 (Focus passage: 4:13-17)
Lesson Title: "How Much are *You* Willing to Risk?"
Objective: The participants will be able to describe how Esther conquered her fear and acted courageously so that they are better prepared to apply similar strategies in their own lives.

Introduction *(Strategies to gain attention; provide focus; review as needed)*: Describe: scene in *Fiddler on the Roof* where Russian thugs descend on the wedding of Teyve's eldest daughter—the beginning of the end for Anatevka. Remind students: several thousand years earlier another young woman faced a *huge* trauma as people tried to wipe the Jews out of existence. Ask: In Esther's shoes, what would *we* have done? Focus: We have an enormously encouraging word from the Word today: *Any risk we ever take, God takes it with us!* (This is written on the board.) Review briefly: Main points of Esther 1-3.

Middle *(Big idea/main points of the lesson; opportunities for active involvement)*: Summarize Esth 4:1-12: Mordecai's anguish at Haman's actions and his challenge to Esther; her initial reaction to the risk. Ask: What is risk? List answers on the board. Dictionary: "A *potential* source of danger; a *possibility* of incurring loss or misfortune." Activity: Divide into groups. Ask each group to share areas in their personal and/or professional lives that are the most risky/scary. Debrief: Each group shares one or more ideas. List on the board and discuss. Biblical illustrations: Moses' risk in approaching Pharaoh; Ruth in leaving Moab; Daniel in worshiping God. *Read: 4:13-14-Mordecai's reasoning*: (1) You will die anyway if you don't act (v. 13). (2) If you don't act, God will handle this another way, but you and your family will perish (v. 14a). (3)This may be the very reason God put you where you are (v. 14b). *Read 4:15-17-Esther's response*: (1) Calls for 3 day fast/prayer. (2) Fasts/prays herself. (3) Resolves to step out in faith and trust God implicitly with the results! (v. 16).

Conclusion *(Self-examination, reflection, application, prayer)*: When we face risks in our lives (refer to the previous list on the board), like Esther, our first response may be fear. It is appropriate to consider the potential consequences of doing the right thing. But when you know the action that will honor God the most and bring him the most glory, remember this: *Any risk we ever take, God takes it with us!* Actually, when you get right down to it, *there is no risk* when we serve a God who is sovereign over every detail of the universe and over every detail of our lives! So instead of fear, do what Esther did: Ask others to pray (and fast!). Pray and fast yourself! Then step out in faith and trust God!

Closing prayer: Provide silent time for students to apply lesson content to the challenges in their own lives. Ask God to seal into students (and the teacher) the strong and encouraging truth of his Word discussed today. Give students a handout with the big idea of the lesson and Esth 4:16 printed out to take home and reflect on during the week.

Design the Lesson. Once the objective is written for the target audience and the title created, the three part format below can be used to design a lesson that incorporates the learning principles previously discussed.

Introduction. Work hard to gain the attention and interest of the learners in the first critical minutes of a lesson. Emphasize the *relevance* of the topic. Use a wide variety of strategies from week to week, e.g., an appropriate video clip that leaves the learners in suspense, engaging students in a discussion of their current reactions to the topic of the lesson, a skit or role play, the reading of a dramatic story, or an intriguing visual aid. The more closely these or other motivational methods are conceptually linked to the main idea of the lesson, the more they will "set the stage" for learning. It is also valuable to help students focus on where the lesson is headed. This can be done by explaining the objective in very motivational, applicational terms. Providing an outline of the lesson can also be helpful in this regard. Finally, if there are prerequisite terms, concepts, or information students need in order to understand the new content that will be presented, these should be briefly reviewed.

Middle. This section brings before the students the fruit of the exegetical study covered in earlier chapters of this text. It is here that the main points of the biblical passage are unpacked. Appropriate visuals, whether charts, maps, pictures, video clips, etc., can be used to help students learn and remember these main points. Any visuals should be clearly designed and not distracting.

Especially if time is limited, Bible teachers may do well to use the *"big idea"* strategy of having one major teaching point (see "Basic Message," chapter thirteen). Recalling that people cannot encode a lot of information in a short period of time, this strategy aims for deep engagement with the one central theme of the passage rather than shallow coverage of multiple themes. Note that a teacher using the *big idea* strategy may present several subpoints from the biblical text. However, the subpoints combine to teach the one, clear statement of biblical truth the teacher wants students to "walk away with" and remember.

To further encourage the encoding of the key point or points of a lesson, teachers should avoid a one-way flow of communication during the body of the lesson. While lecturing is a time-honored, valuable tool, overuse precludes the use of interactive strategies that give students time to process ("internalize") key concepts. Small group discussions, case studies, and well worded, thought provoking questions are all effective at this stage. The goal is to prompt students to deeply engage with the text of the teaching passage. These kinds of activities can also build community as students learn together from God's Word. If a student shares a particularly difficult experience, the class could stop and pray before continuing the discussion.

Consider activities that get students physically active. For example, for a lesson on Nehemiah 4, have students on one end of the classroom bounce balloons down the rows until all are at the other end (symbolic of gradually rebuilding the wall). Begin again on the same side, only this time two students ("Sanballat" and "Tobiah") do everything possible to impede the progress of the balloons. Play the game from the same side one last time, but first have students secretly develop strategies to thwart the agitators (e.g., handing, not bouncing the balloons). A game like this is fun, active, visualizes Nehemiah's strategies for facing adversity, causes an emotional response, and involves multiple senses.

Conclusion. Bible teachers praying for life change reserve time to draw the lesson to a close and provide opportunity for self-examination, reflection, and prayer. It takes discipline to avoid ending lessons with, "Oh, we are out of time! Let's pray." The conclusion is a *vital* part of a lesson. It is here the teacher challenges students to put what they have learned into practice. It may be a time for quiet reflection or silent prayer. Musical selections can be used here to good effect. The teacher may suggest "homework," i.e., ways for students to try out what they have learned at home, school, in the office, etc. Attractive handouts to take home can serve as a reminder of the lesson. These kinds of concluding strategies can be prayerfully used by teachers who long for *learning—a change in behavior that is persistent over time*.

Evaluate the lesson. Serious Bible teachers take time after each lesson (normally within 24 hours) for prayerful reflection, noting what went well and areas for improvement. It is helpful to solicit feedback from a spouse or others who attended the lesson and to graciously receive and learn from their comments. Writing notes on lesson plans or in a journal can help teachers steadily improve in the important ministry of Bible teaching. The final moments of the evaluation should be a prayer for the Holy Spirit's continued work in the teacher and students.

Didactic Appropriation: Resources

Materials from Previous Study

All worksheets

Greek is Great Gain

Descriptions in chapter fifteen
Figures in chapter fifteen

Commentaries

Breneman, *Ezra, Nehemiah, Esther*.
K&D

Teaching Theory and Strategies

Vella, *Taking Learning to Task*.
Yount, *Created to Learn*.

Didactic Appropriation: Procedure

I. Survey
II. Analysis
III. Synthesis
IV. Interpretation/Application
V. **Didactic Appropriation**
   A. **Plan the Lesson:** Using the resources noted, plan the lesson using the "Didactic Appropriation" worksheet (See fig. 15.10 for example and WJLFP for template).
      1. *Analyze teaching assignment and target audience.* Consider the teaching environment and logistical requirements. Investigate the characteristics and motivations of the target audience which will bear on your lesson design.
      2. *Frame an objective.* Write an objective for the lesson which includes a cognitive, knowledge goal which will issue in an attitudinal, life change goal (see fig. 15.4.)
      3. *Write a lesson title.* Construct a creative title to awaken interest and capture the main thrust of the lesson.

B. **Design the Lesson:** Use a three part format to structure the lesson. Incorporate the learning principles discussed in this chapter.
   1. *Develop an introduction.* Use a variety of strategies to gain attention and help students understand the potential relevance of the lesson subject matter for their lives. Provide a clear focus and review any prerequisites.
   2. *Develop the middle.* Present the "big idea" and any supporting points. Include interactive learning activities and instructional aids to encourage mental and emotional engagement and active learning. Use visuals and illustrations as appropriate.
   3. *Develop the conclusion.* Draw the lesson to a powerful close and encourage personal application for life change.
C. **Evaluate the Lesson:** Prayerfully reflect on what worked well and what can yet be improved.

Endnotes

1. Fee, *New Testament Exegesis*, 133-54.

2. cf. Robinson, *Biblical Preaching*, 115-37; Liefeld, *New Testament Exposition*, 120-33; Chappell, *Christ-centered Preaching*.

3. The substance of the "Keyword Approach" presented below is from Hamilton, *Homiletical Handbook*. He comments on the origin of the "Keyword Approach" as follows: "The Keyword Approach might well be called the 'Kollerian' method, for it is based on the work of Charles W. Koller (*Expository Preaching*). Koller used the method long before publishing it. The approach has been modified and popularized by Lloyd M. Perry, Faris D. Whitesell, Raymond W. McLaughlin, and other students of Koller, as well as their students" (Hamilton, *Homiletical Handbook*, 57, n. 1).

4. Liefeld, *New Testament Exposition*, 118.

5. Hamilton, *Homiletical Handbook*, 49-51.

6. Shirl S. Schiffman, professor of educational ministries, CIU Seminary and School of Missions, is responsible for the basic content of the "Didactic Appropriation" section of this chapter.

Chapter 16

PERIODIC PREPARATION

Use of a Method for Exegesis and Exposition in Ministry

Making the Method Your Own

Congratulations! You have now covered all of the bases for Immediate Preparation—your weekly adventure in exegesis and exposition of God's Word. At this point the process may still seem overwhelming, but the day will come when its steps will become second nature. You will be able to carry them out without the need for reviewing the recommended resources, procedures, etc. You'll adapt the techniques to your own learning style and ministry needs, and become skillful in knowing which are the most important steps for which passages. Without question, your "Greek Reading" and repeated practice of "A Method for Exegesis and Exposition" are vitally important keys for confident, effective ministry of the Word.

Use of Time

"Fit the task to the time." Give serious thought to how you will schedule your time for "Immediate Preparation" in the context of your total responsibilities. Time is a fixed commodity. Everyone has the same amount of it. Time is not elastic, but we are. A valuable skill to master is learning how to fit your tasks to the time you have. In this case, identify the amount of time you need to reach your goal of thorough, God-honoring sermon or lesson preparation. The exegetical method you have just studied suggests that you maintain your proficiency in New Testament Greek by consistent "Greek Reading" of five lines of the New Testament, fifteen minutes a day, five days a week (see chapter three). Then, "Immediate Preparation" for a Sunday morning sermon is estimated at fourteen to sixteen hours (including eight hours of exegesis) spread across the week.

Scheduling your work. What will a preparation schedule look like for you? Once you know how much study time you need, block out parts of each working day (the mornings are often suggested) and maintain a priority commitment to using them for study of the Word. Go a step further. Break the overall task down into a series of time units. What hours or parts of an hour will you devote to the various steps, e.g., "Survey," the types of "Analysis," etc.? Then you will know how much you can reasonably expect to get done per day. This kind of strategic planning will greatly aid you in responding to the inevitable scheduling adjustments an involved pastor faces during a week. Knowing what it takes to get the various steps done will enable you to carve out time at other points in the week to compensate for study time you rightly diverted to urgent needs of the flock.

Periodic preparation. If your engagement with the Word in study is only during "Immediate Preparation," you can easily get on the path to burn out. If your only time for biblical scholarship is tied to the drumbeat of weekly delivery, you run the risk of never going deeply into God's Word. Never spending time in in-depth study of the Word, you will create a "ceiling" or a "floor" for your own and your congregation's understanding of God's truth. And you can easily run dry in your own excitement and enthusiasm for studying the Bible. It becomes the "same old, same old," for you have not planned to refresh yourself in periodic in-depth study. Such study not only helps you build a rich fund of biblical knowledge and insight, it also refreshes you as through sustained reflection you find new, life-changing insights that you can later share with others.

The antidote is simply to plan ahead and follow a pattern of study which exposes you consistently (weekly) and deeply (periodically) to the Scriptures in the original language.[1] This kind of pattern will help you become a life-long student of the Bible. Over an extended period of time you will be able to increasingly preach or teach out of the riches of an intimate and comprehensive knowledge of God's truth and the wealth of experience. This chapter will discuss the two strategies of Periodic Preparation: Advanced Planning for Preaching and In-depth Study.

Advanced Planning for Preaching

This section is particularly relevant to preachers who normally choose their sermon passages and topics. Bible teachers also may have that responsibility, but frequently teach according to a curriculum scope and sequence decided by another. With this in mind, the material below is aimed at the senior pastor role.

Plan a Year's Preaching Program

Each June (or thirteen months prior to the period to be planned) set up the preaching program (series titles, sermon topics, and preaching portion) for the period July-June a year hence. For example, in June 2007, plan for the period July 2008 to June 2009. This means you will plan at least twelve months of preaching at a time. This process should also involve the continuing mastery of the English Bible through Synthetic Book Studies (described below). Follow these steps.

Block out the calendar. On a sheet of paper or with a calendar software program, place in the Sunday dates for July of the next year through June of the subsequent year. Leave enough room to enter information for preaching and/or teaching responsibilities of each week (e.g., Sunday morning and evening and Wednesday night). Identify Christian year holidays (Christmas, Easter) and any other important dates, e.g., Mother's Day, annual missionary conference, vacation time.

Bracket the weeks and months according to natural breaks in the Christian and secular year: public school year end to summer vacation end; public school start up to Thanksgiving; Thanksgiving to Christmas; January to Easter; Easter to public school year end. This will give you the blocks of weeks or months that may be devoted to one or more sermon series (see fig. 16.1). It is best to preach expository sermons in a series within the context of the each preaching passage's basic literary unit, i.e., the Bible book. Further, the listener is more effectively strengthened when one sermon builds upon another in a coherent fashion.

Select sermon series subject areas. Prayerfully consider the areas of the whole counsel of God to which you believe God is guiding you to lead your people. Review what you have preached on in the past year and the needs of your congregation. Use the following principles[2] in choosing your sermon series subject areas:

- *Christian year.* Whatever your liturgical tradition, the Christian year should be used to advantage. At the very least, a Christmas series running from the Sunday after Thanksgiving through Christmas and a series leading up to Easter, running during part or all of the period beginning in January, can be employed with good results.
- *Types of series.* Bible book studies and doctrinal preaching strengthen the congregation. Series on congregational needs, which you have observed or members bring to your attention, or on the trends of the times, enable the preacher to emphasize relevant application.
- *Whole counsel of God.* Seek to preach as equally from the Old Testament as from the New.

Figure 16.1. **Sample 2008–09 Preaching Program (Partially Complete)**

2008	MORNING	
	Topic/Title	Preaching Portion
July 6		
13		
20		
27		
August 3	VACATION	
10	VACATION	
17		
24		
31		
	PHILIPPIANS	Phil
September 7	Stand Firm	1:1-2, 27-30
14	A Body Has to Communicate	1:3-11
21	A Gospel Evaluated Life	1:12-18a
28	Living is Christ	1:18b-26
October 5	A Mind Like Christ's	2:1-11
12	Shining Stars	2:12-18
19	Two Models of Concern	2:19-30
26	True "All Rightness"	3:1-9
November 2	That I May Know Him	3:10-16
9	Heaven's Citizen Walk	3:17–4:1
16	Qualities Making for Peace	4:2-9
23	Having Enough	4:10-14
30	Missionary Support Dividends	4:15-23
December 7		
14		
21	*Christmas*	
28	*New Year's*	

Figure 16.1. (*continued*)

2009	MORNING	
	Topic/Title	Preaching Portion
	ROAD TO THE CROSS: MARK	Mark
January 4	Beginning of the Gospel	1:1-15
11	His Authority to Forgive Sins	2:1-12
18	Take Heed How You Hear	4:1-20
25	Faith Based Compassion	5:21-43
February 1	His Authority over Nature	6:30-52
8	Faith in Unexpected Places	7:24-30
15	*Missions Conference*	
22	Suffering then Glory	8:27–9:1
March 1	To Be Served or To Serve?	10:35-45
8	His Authority over God's Things	11:1-19
15	Whose Authority is His Authority?	11:27–12:12
22	His Redemptive Sacrifice	14:12-26
29	His Submission to the Father's Authority	14:32-42
April 5	Palm Sunday: The King's Place	15:21-41
12	Easter: An "Awful" Experience	16:1-8
19	THE FUTURE: After Death	Luke 16:19-31
26	Events before the End	Rev 6:1-11
May 3	Events at the End	Rev 13
10	Christ's Return	Rev 19-20
17	Last Judgment	Rev 20:11-15
24	Hell	Mark 9:42-48
31	Heaven	Rev 22:1-5
June 7		
14		
21		
28		

See figure 16.1 for examples: "Book Study of Philippians," "What the Future Holds: Biblical Eschatology."

Choose the weekly sermon topics and their preaching portions. Construct two types of series: topical-Doctrine, Congregational Needs, or Contemporary Trends and Bible Book Studies.

Topical studies:
- *Develop weekly sermon topics.* Consult secondary sources: theology texts, pastoral ministry resources, contemporary writings and periodical articles to identify the components of the subject area. For example, if the series is on issues in bio-ethics, research until you are satisfied that you have a fairly comprehensive grasp of the field. For bio-ethics, research will identify abortion, euthanasia, genetic engineering, artificial insemination, *in vitro* fertilization, organ transplants, stem cell research, nano-technology as some of the basic areas to be covered in the series. Decide how long the series should be and assign a topic to each week.
- *Identify a Scripture passage as each topic's preaching portion.* Such a passage should speak to the issue either by precept, spiritual truth, or principle drawn from example in historical narrative. Since it is to be the basis for an expository sermon, the preaching portion should be a literary unit of one or more paragraphs which deals with one broad subject and manifests a logical unity and a single purpose[3] (cf. fig. 16.1, "Heaven," Rev 22:1-5).

Bible book study series (see fig. 16.1):
- *Identify preaching portions.* In the light of the number of weeks you have scheduled for preaching on the Bible book, and with the aid of synthetic book study results (see below): book charts, outlines, or sentence paragraph summaries, choose the weekly preaching portions for your book series. In general, if possible, the preaching portion should not exceed fifteen lines of Greek text. This is of manageable size both for translation and mechanical layout. The portions should be relatively equal in length but also take into account the book's structure.
- *Decide on a sermon topic/tentative title.* Read over the preaching portion, if possible with the aid of the sentence paragraph summaries, and decide on a sermon topic/tentative title that expresses the passage's content.

Synthetic Study of Bible Books

This exercise can be very helpful in identifying the preaching portions for a Bible book study series. And it enables you to become intimately acquainted with the book you are going to preach. Carrying out a synthetic study in advance of preaching on a book (as well as at other times) will provide the foundational Bible knowledge essential for further fruitful in-depth study. In sum, it is an excellent way for you to fulfill your calling as a life-long student of the Scriptures.

Mastery of the preacher. The synthetic study of a Bible book has two main goals. The first goal to be mastered by the text's content. Read the text prayerfully and repeatedly. Read it independently, without study aids, and as a literary unit, i.e., continuously in one sitting. The preacher should read and re-read the text until it has "become a part of the (his) very being."[4]

Mastery of the book. The second goal is to seek to master a Bible book's content. You want to get a feel for its atmosphere and approach, to discover emphases, highlights, and clues for understanding the inter-relationships of various parts. You aim to crystallize in your mind the book's overall theme or purpose, as well as to uncover the books' organizational structure, its patterns and movements of thought.

Synthetic Study: Resources

English Translation

NIV
ESV
NASB

Study Bible

NIV Study Bible
NIV Reformation Study Bible

Commentaries

Fee, *Philippians*.
Hawthorne, *Philippians*.
O'Brien, *Philippians*.
Silva, *Philippians*.

Synthetic Study: Procedure

I. **General Instructions**
   A. **Use a Favorite Translation.** Choose, for example, the *NASB* or *ESV* or *NIV*.
   B. **Pray before Each Reading.** Affirm to God your implicit trust in his Word. Declare your desire that the Holy Spirit lay bare your soul so that by this Word you may identify and correct wrong thinking and acting. Ask the Holy Spirit to illumine your mind concerning the nature and excellence of the things of God in this Bible book. Pray during the reading as the Spirit prompts you to respond to his Word.
   C. **Read the Bible Book at One Sitting.** See figure 16.2 for estimates of reading times for books. The estimates are based on a reading rate of 200 words per minute which works out to ten pages per hour in the *NIV*.
   D. **Read the Bible Book Independently.** Do not refer to secondary aids like Bible dictionaries, handbooks, commentaries, even notes in a study Bible.
   E. **Read the Bible Observantly.** Make notes after a complete reading. You may want to place "pencil pricks" in the margin during your reading to identify important items that you will want to return to and reflect on.
   F. **Read the Bible Repeatedly, Three to Five Times.** Pore over the book's content until it possesses you, becomes part of your very being. A good sign that this has happened is that a basic outline of the book's content begins to emerge. You are able to talk through the book's flow of argument.

II. **Specific Instructions for Reading and Observation**
   A. **Reading One and Two: General Impressions** (see fig. 16.3)
      1. *Read the English text.* With an English text (*NASB* or *ESV* or *NIV*) as your only source, read the Bible book continuously in one sitting. Read it independently, disregarding all editorial features of the translation: section and paragraph headings; chapter, paragraph, and verse divisions.
      2. *Observe while you are reading.*
         a. *General impact on you.* How did the book's content personally impact you? Describe your initial reactions and impressions. You might want to aim for at least as many observations as there are chapters in the book.

Figure 16.2. **Time Values for New Testament Books.**
Time values for reading at one sitting at a pace of two hundred words per minute, ten pages per hour.

BIBLE BOOK	PAGES IN NIV	TOTAL TIME IN HOURS
Matthew	37	4
Mark	17	2
Luke	28	3
John	22	2
Acts	27	3
Romans	12	1
1 Corinthians	11	1
2 Corinthians	7	1
Galatians	4	½
Ephesians	4	½
Philippians	3	½
Colossians	3	½
1 Thessalonians	2	½
2 Thessalonians	2	½
1 Timothy	3	½
2 Timothy	2	½
Titus	2	½
Philemon	1	½

      b. *Atmosphere of the book as a whole.* Atmosphere refers to the interaction between the author, the audience, and the book's purpose. What is the "mood" of the book which emanates from the relationship between the author and the audience given the circumstances at the time of writing. What is their attitude toward the book's purpose?
      c. *Highlights.* What are the key passages? What are key words and phrases often indicated by repetition?
  B. **Readings Three through Five: Focused Insights**
    1. *Read a third time looking for the book's structure.*
      a. *Observe and note down turning points in the book.* Look for clues like changes in subject matter or persons; changes

Figure 16.2. *(continued)*

BIBLE BOOK	PAGES IN NIV	TOTAL TIME IN HOURS
Hebrews	9	1
James	3	½
1 Peter	3	½
2 Peter	2	½
1 John	3	½
2 John	1	½
3 John	1	½
Jude	1	½
Revelation	14	1 ½

      from one personal, church or community problem to another; key transitional phrases—especially introductory or summary words like "therefore," "finally," "behold"; and key affirmations.
   b. *Observe and note down patterns and movements of thought throughout the book.* This requires thinking backward and forward in the book. For example, how does each paragraph relate to the paragraphs immediately preceding and following?
   c. *Name the major divisions.* Based on the *turning points,* identify and name the book's isolated blocks.
2. *Read a fourth time looking for patterns in repeated themes.* Observe and note down *repeated themes.* Be sure to note down the chapter, verse and a brief indication of content of each occurrence.
3. *Read a fifth time to isolate the main theme(s) or purpose(s).* Determine the book's overall theme or purpose. Sometimes the writer explicitly states it. Especially check the beginning and the end of the book for any "purpose" statements.

Figure 16.3. **Synthetic Study**

Book Philippians

GENERAL IMPRESSIONS

Reading # One

General Impact on You:

Chapter One: As for Paul, so for me, the gospel should ever be my reference point in responding to life in positive and negative circumstances (Phil 1:5, 12, 16, 18, 27).
Chapter Two: Christ's self-giving, humble service for others must ever be my standard as I seek to promote unity. It will show that I am truly interested in the things of Christ (Phil 2:4-5, 6-11, 21).
Chapter Three: I have not yet arrived. I must press on to know Christ–the most valuable thing in the world (Phil 3:8-11, 12-16).
Chapter Four: May I learn the secret of "Christ sufficiency," that through Christ I have enough (Phil 4:11-13).

Atmosphere as a Whole:

Author and Purpose: Though Paul is in prison, he writes with confident zeal (Phil 1:20-21) to Christians at Philippi, for whom he has strong affection (1:7-8; 4:1). He wants to encourage them in firmness in the faith (1:27-30), unity (2:1-18), and true righteousness (3:1-11). And he wants to thank them for their financial support (4:10-20).
Audience and Occasion/Purpose: The Philippians love and respect Paul are concerned to hear news about Paul and Epaphroditus (Phil 2:19-30). They have supported him (1:5; 4:10-20). They face opposition from without and disunity from within, and need encouragement and direction (1:28; 3:2; 2:3-4; 4:2-3).

HIGHLIGHTS: Key passages; key words and phrases

Key Passages–Phil 1:27-30, themes for entire book; 2:5-11, Christ Hymn; 3:7-11, goal of Christian life; 4:17-20, benefits of missionary support.
Repeated Themes–joy (Phil 1:4, 18, 25; 2:2, 17-18, 29; 3:1; 4:1, 4, 10); gospel (1:5-7, 12, 27; 2:22; 4:3, 15); faith (1:25, 27, 29; 2:17; 3:9).

Figure 16.3. (*continued*)

SYNTHETIC STUDY*

Book <u>Philippians</u>

STRUCTURE

Reading # <u>Three</u>

Turning Points:

Patterns of Thought:

Major Divisions:

SYNTHETIC STUDY*

Book <u>Philippians</u>

REPEATED THEMES & OVERALL THEME/PURPOSE

Reading # <u>Four and Five</u>

Patterns of Themes (Scripture reference and content)

Overall Purpose

*Results for Philippians represented in figures 16.4-6.

III. **Specific Instructions for Presentation of Synthesis**
  A. **Chart Form**: Use a sheet of paper not larger than what may be duplicated. The chart or outline could serve later as a teaching aid. Using the "Synthetic Study" notes and constantly referring to the text:
   1. *Place book's theme.* Locate theme at a prominent place on the chart.
   2. *Represent progression of thought.* Visually, with the use of color and space, represent progression of thought through major units and important subunits. As much as possible, use the wording of Scripture to represent the book's content.
   3. *Fill in as much detail as necessary.* Give attention to detail, though emphasize the visual representation of the book's larger relationships.
   4. *Validate your chart.* See Bible study aids (study Bible or commentary) to make sure you have not misunderstood the book's flow of thought.
  B. **Outline**: See instructions in chapter thirteen.
  C. **Sentence Paragraph Summaries**: Using the "Synthetic Study" notes and constantly referring to the text:
   1. *Summarize content.* State the content of each Greek text paragraph in one sentence.
   2. *Be comprehensive and concise.* As much as possible, use the wording of Scripture to represent the paragraph's content comprehensively and concisely.
   3. *Validate your summaries.* See Bible study aids (study Bible or commentary) to make sure you have not misunderstood each paragraph's content.

See figure 16.4 for a chart and figure 16.5 for an outline on Philippians. See figure 16.6 for a set of sentence paragraph summaries. It is from such a chart, outline, or set of summaries that the preacher then identifies the preaching portions for a Bible book study series. See figure 16.1 for an example of the preaching portions and topics/titles of such a series.

In-Depth Studies

As part of your ongoing professional development, carry out appropriate selected "In-depth Studies" to continually prime the pump of your own fountain of biblical knowledge and wisdom. Researchers in scientific fields know the benefit of stepping back from day to day life in the

Figure 16.4. **Sample Chart: Philippians**

1:1-3 Salutation

Thanksgiving for Phil Church
(1:3-8)

1) Joyful Thanksgiving
2) Depth of Relationship
3) Partnership in Mission
4) Basis: God's Continual Work

Prayer's Themes (1:9-11)

1) Object: Love may Abound
2) Purpose: Approve the Excellent
3) Result: Pure & Blameless
4) Cause: Filled with Righteousness

"Experiencing the same conflict which you saw in me and now hear to be in me"

NOW

Organizational Verses

1:27-30

"Only conduct yourselves in a manner worthy of the Gospel of Christ"

"Stand Firm

In One Spirit, with One Mind"

IF THEN: "Let Love Abound"

Paul's Imprisonment 1:12-26	Christ's Humiliation 2:1-18
1) What if imprisonment? (1:12-14) 　　GOSPEL is furthered! 2) What if, while imprisoned, strife in church? (1:15-18) 　　CHRIST is proclaimed! 3) What if imprisonment ends in judgment/death? (1:19-25) 　　CHRIST is exalted!	1) Exhortation to Unity through (2:1-5) 2) Example: CHRIST (2:6-11) 　　Humiliation through 　　Obedience (2:6-8) 　　Exaltation by God (2:9-11) so then: 3) Exhortation to Unity Concluded (2:12-18)

TIMOTHY genuinely concerned (2:19-24)
EPAPHRODITUS longs for them (2:25-30)

THEMES Concluded: 4:1-9　　　　STAND FIRM THEN: "Live in harmony"

Figure 16.4 *(continued)*

4:21-23 Conclusion

Exhortation to Phil Church (4:10-20)

1) Joy for their Giving (4:10-14)
2) Thankfulness for their Faithfulness (4:15-18)
3) Promise of Blessing (4:19-20)

"Striving together for faith of Gospel in no way alarmed by opponents"

FINALLY "Approve Excellent Things"

Paul's Self-Renunciation
3:1-21

1) Beware of opponents (3:1-3)
2) Paul's example (3:4-16)
 –past Jewish worthlessness regarding Christ (3:4-7)
 –present pursuit to know, gain, be found in Christ (3:8-11)
 –future hope to lay hold of Christ (3:12-16)
Therefore
3) Follow Paul's example and not that of opponents (3:17-21)

"Whatever is true . . . honorable . . . let your mind dwell on these things."

Figure 16.5. **Sample Outline: Philippians**

Overall Theme and Outline: Paul writes the Philippians to express his affectionate thankful relationship with them and to encourage them to conduct themselves properly by standing firm in unity, contending for the faith of the gospel (Phil 1:3-4, 7-8; 27-28; cf. 1:9-11).

1:1-11	I.		Opening
1:1-2		A.	Salutation
1:3-11		B.	Thanksgiving and Prayer (Book's main themes: affection, prayer requests–love, knowledge, blameless life, fruit of righteousness)
1:12-2:18	II.		Stand Firm in Love (1:27-30 key verses for book)
1:12-30		A.	Firmness in the Face of Opposition
1:12-18			1. Paul's Present Circumstances: Prison but Christ Preached
1:19-26			2. Paul's Evaluation of Circumstances: Me to Live is Christ
1:27-30			3. Command to Stand Firm
2:1-18		B.	Call to Loving Unity
2:1-11			1. Have the Mind that was Jesus'
2:12-18			2. Apply Humility as Unity
2:19-30	III.		Past, Present, and Future Contacts
2:19-24		A.	Timothy
2:25-30		B.	Epaphroditus
3:1-4:1	IV.		Stand Firm in the Knowledge of True Righteousness
3:1-9		A.	True Righteousness: by Faith
3:10-16		B.	Knowledge of Christ is the Goal
3:17-21		C.	Pattern Your Lives as Citizens of Heaven
4:1-9	V.		Final Exhortations
4:1-7		A.	Be United, Rejoice, Pray
4:8-9		B.	Think Wholesomely, Imitate Paul
4:10-20	VI.		Thankfulness for Care
4:10-14		A.	Paul's Evaluation of Economic Circumstances: Contentment
4:15-20		B.	The Philippians' Continuing Care
4:21-23	VII.		Closing

Figure 16.6. **Sample Sentence Paragraph Summaries: Philippians**

1. Phil 1:1-2–Paul and Timothy greet the Philippian church, its congregation, overseers and deacons, with standard Christian greetings from the Father and the Lord Jesus Christ.

2. Phil 1:3-11–After Paul joyfully and confidently thanks God for his sustaining grace in them and for their partnership in support of the gospel, both during his current imprisonment and in his ministry, he asks God to develop discerning, knowledgeable love in them so they will be filled with righteousness and glorify God at the judgment.

3. Phil 1:12-14–He assures them that the gospel has progressed during his imprisonment both because of his witness throughout the imperial guard and because his example has emboldened many others to witness.

4. Phil 1:15-26–Although some of this evangelism may be done out of envy and partisan motives, Paul rejoices whenever the gospel is preached because he is confident that all this witnessing will lead not to his death and departure to heaven but to his deliverance and necessary return to ministry in Philippi and elsewhere, even though martyrdom and heaven would be better for him personally.

5. Phil 1:27-30–He exhorts them to constancy and unity in their adherence to the Christian patterns of behavior inherent in the gospel, in spite of his absence and the opposition and suffering they face.

6. Phil 2:1-11–He exhorts them to unity and Christ-like behavior in their attitudes toward one another and their treatment of one another, by focusing their attention on the humiliation of Christ's incarnation and the sure prospect of his exaltation as Lord over all.

7. Phil 2:12-18–He urges them to cultivate their salvation actively and to trust God to produce through them a dynamic, faithful and joyous Christian witness in this world's darkness.

8. Phil 2:19-24–He informs them of his intention to send Timothy to them immediately and commends him for his unique, selfless pursuit of their welfare.

9. Phil 2:25-30–He explains that he sent Epaphroditus back to them because of Epaphroditus' own desire to assure them that he had recovered from near death and Paul commends him for his useful ministry.

Figure 16.6 (*continued*)

10. Phil 3:1–Paul encourages them to rejoice and indicates that his repetitious instructions are for their protection.

11. Phil 3:2-11–Paul exhorts them to watch out for the Judaizing legalists who will attempt to focus their attention on merit gained by human effort and says, "Even though I have many things I might brag about, I completely discount all of them and put my confidence of resurrection completely in the righteousness God gives me through faith in Christ."

12. Phil 3:12-16–He counsels them to exhibit maturity by maintaining the same attitude which he displays when he ignores the past and keeps pressing forward toward the goal of being like Christ.

13. Phil 3:17–4:1–Paul adjures them to firmly resist those enemies of the cross who glory in the pursuit of human desires and earthly possessions and to stand fixed in the hope of their heavenly exaltation and glorification.

14. Phil 4:2-7–He entreats them to keep peace between Euodia and Syntyche, to rejoice, to forbear with all men in view of Christ's return, to trust God and to pray so that they will be protected by God's peace of heart and mind.

15. Phil 4:8-9–He promises them God's presence if they fix their attention on positive values and practice the things he has taught and modeled.

16. Phil 4:10-14–Paul praises them for their concern and material support and assures them that he is by the power of God able to live contentedly in circumstances of both abundance and want.

17. Phil 4:15-20–Paul rehearses the history of their faithfulness in meeting his material needs in a generous and liberal way and assures them that their giving will result in God's supply for their own needs according to his wealth in Christ.

18. Phil 4:21-23–Paul closes with a benediction commending them to the Father and to the Lord's grace, sending greetings from all the believers, especially those of Caesar's household.[5]

laboratory to read in the wider field of professional literature or to give themselves the luxury of non-pressured creative thought on a complex problem. New insights or a deeper understanding of a problem can result from these breaks in the routine.

Preachers can also benefit from periodic mini-sabbaticals (or maybe micro mini-sabbaticals) when they can immerse themselves in an area of study which will enrich a sermon series coming up later. There are two kinds of "In-Depth Studies" you can undertake: General–"Survey" or Commentary Reading; or Specific–related to Introductory Matters, genre, literary feature, or content.

General In-Depth Studies

To help you more intelligently choose which features of a passage to study in-depth or to gain a better understanding of the basic interpretational issues for a passage, you may want to consider one of these options.

Conduct a survey on a particular passage. The student of the Word can prepare the way for his "Immediate Preparation" by surveying the text at length and well in advance of the "week before" preparation. This will enable him to thoroughly identify matters for further study and these can become an ongoing agenda for whenever he studies the passage. See chapter five for instructions.

Read a commentary on interpretational issues. Read a comprehensive (not exhaustively thorough) commentary on a passage you plan to preach on (e.g., commentaries in the following series: New International Commentary on the New Testament, Eerdmans [NICNT]; Expositor's Bible Commentary, Zondervan [EBC]). This general orientation to the background, content, and interpretational issues of a passage will provide helpful orientation for when you pursue "Immediate Preparation."

Specific In-depth Studies

Based on the exegetical features of a passage and the type of sermon you plan to preach, choose an in-depth study, which holds promise for significantly enhancing your understanding. It also should be an investigation you could not normally pursue during "Immediate Preparation" because it would take too much time. Consistent practice of this form of professional development will not only make each sermon better, it will build up a fund of Bible knowledge and insight. This resource will continue to pay rich dividends in the lives of the preacher and hearers. There are four basic kinds of in-depth study: introductory matters; genre, literary feature, and content studies. You might want to start off with introductory matters the first time you preach from a given book.

Specific In-Depth Studies: Procedures

A. **Introductory Matters**: With the aid of a New Testament introduction, Bible survey, or Bible encyclopedia[6] investigate the following areas of background concerning your book (see fig. 16.7):
   1. *Author.* Who was he? What was he like? What were his circumstances in writing? What was his relation to his audience?
   2. *Date and place.* When did he write it? What is the relation of its time of writing to other key events in NT history? Where was he located?
   3. *Audience.* To whom did he write? Where were they located? What were they like spiritually, ethnically, and in terms of their current circumstances?
   4. *Composition.*
      - *Occasion and Purpose.* What was the occasion for the work? Why did he write it?
      - *Composition methods.* How did he write it? What literary form, literary features such as sources, large subgenre, style were involved?
      - *Content.* What did he write? What are the general tone and the distinctive doctrines or ideas in the work?
      - *Integrity and authenticity.* Is it one work? Does it have integrity? What is the extent of its textual authenticity? Are there any extended portions of the text not present in the earliest and best manuscripts?

B. **Indepth Study selected according to Genre**
   1. *Epistle*: If studying part of the *doctrinal argument*, develop a mechanical layout and closely trace out the line of argument via grammatical and rhetorical features. Or study a key theological term(s). See chapters seven and nine through eleven.

      When dealing with ethical sections, especially a series of brief commands/prohibitions or a list of vices and virtues, do word studies. Do historical background on ancient practices if one ethical issue is dealt with in an extended fashion.
   2. *Gospels-Acts* (see chapter eight and "Additional Genre & Literary Form Analysis Procedures" at WJLFP): For *historical*

Figure 16.7. **Sample Introductory Matters: Philippians**

Book Philippians

a. Authorship: Who wrote it? (Author) When and Where did he write it? (Date and Place of Origin)

    CONCLUSION: Paul, the apostle, from prison in Rome during the first imprisonment AD 62-63, after Philemon, Colossians, Ephesians.

Identity: Paul

> External Evidence: Polycarp; Marcion's canon; "one of the letters about whose canonicity there appears to have been no dispute" (Carson and Moo, *Introduction to New Testament*, 508).
>
> Internal Evidence: a) Explicit claim: Phil 1:1;
> b) Content and Features: Pauline style; the situation "rings true" to Pauline circumstances (Carson and Moo, *Introduction to New Testament*, 499).

Arguments for Place and Date: Rome, first imprisonment, A.D. 62-63.

> External Evidence: Anti-Marcionite Prologue so identifies provenance.
>
> Internal Evidence: a) Mention of imprisonment (1:7, 13, 17); Praetorian guard and Caesar's household (Phil 1:13; 4:22), and ease in deploying Timothy and Epaphroditus (2:19, 25) squares with the house arrest conditions of the first Roman imprisonment (Acts 28:16, 30-31).
> b) An established church encouraged by his preaching could well be the strong church at Rome (Phil 1:14/Acts 28:11-15/Romans).
> c) Only in Rome could there be a definitive outcome of judicial proceedings against a Roman citizen, as Paul now expects, whether death or release (1:20; 2:17). Expectations of rejoining the Philippians (1:25-26; 2:23-24) square with the first imprisonment.

Figure 16.7 *(continued)*

b. <u>Audience</u>: To whom did he write it? (Destination, Readers) Characteristics: Non-Christian or Christian; Jewish or Gentile (if mixed, which predominates?)

CONCLUSION: a predominantly Gentile Christian church founded by Paul in Philippi on his second missionary journey (Acts 16:11-40; Phil 1:1). Philippi was a city of Macedonia founded by Alexander the Great's father and turned into a Roman colony by Octavius.

Internal Evidence: a) Explicit Claim: Phil 1:1, "all the saints in Christ Jesus in Philippi";
b) Gentile Christian—Gentile names, 4:2-3; termed the "true circumcision," 3:3; qualities of Gentile culture presented as desirable, 4:8;
c) "citizenship" imagery used, 1:27; 3:20 relevant to a Philippi, a Roman Colony;
d) sent support to Paul, 4:15; 2 Cor 11:9; cf. Acts 18:5.

c. <u>Composition</u>: Why did he write it? (Occasion and Purpose/Theme)

Occasion: a) Paul is aware of some specific problems in the church in the areas of lethargy, unity, and Judaizing false teachers (Phil 1:27-2:18; 4:2; 3:2-4, 18);
b) Timothy and Paul are planning to visit Philippi (2:19-24);
c) A gift has arrived with Epaphroditus and sickness and service has delayed his return to them (2:25-30).

Purpose: a) To exhort to wholehearted service (Phil 1:27-30; 2:12-18); counteract a tendency to divisiveness (2:2-5; 4:2); warn against Judaizers (3:1-11);
b) To explain his circumstances (1:12-26);
c) To prepare the Philippians for the visits of Timothy and himself (2:19-24);
d) To commend Epaphroditus to them and explain his delay (2:25-30);
e) To thank the Philippians for their monetary gift (4:10, 14, 18).

narrative, study the historical, cultural and geographical factors that are background to the account. If there are questions about the historical accuracy or authenticity of an episode or its details, do historical criticism.

For a gospel (whether narrative or teaching portion) which has parallels in other gospels, do source, form and redaction criticism, controlled by a confidence in and demonstration of the text's historical reliability. This will serve as a foundation for understanding the distinctive contributions of the gospel writer.
    3. *New Testament prophecy*. Analyze the background and meaning of apocalyptic features and symbolism in your passage (see chapter eight).
C. **Indepth Study selected according to Literary Feature** (See "Additional Genre & Literary Form Analysis Procedures" at WJLFP)
    1. *Old Testament quotations in the new.* Investigate the text form, introductory formula, and function of OT quote(s) in the passage in order to uncover the NT writer's hermeneutical method and how the quote advances his purposes.
    2. *Parables/Gospel teaching portions*: Analyze the historical/cultural background details and the literary structure of parables/gospel teaching (see chapter eight).
D. **Indepth Study according to Content**
    1. *Interpretation problems.* Some passages (e.g., 1 Cor 11:1-16; Matt 19:1-12; Heb 6:1-12) bristle with difficulties for understanding and application. A good way to handle them is to consult detailed commentaries or read periodical articles in scholarly journals. In a nearby theological library the preacher should consult *New Testament Abstracts* (*NTA*). This listing of recently published articles and books on New Testament subjects has a helpful Scripture reference index for each year volume. The American Theological Library Association (ATLA) has a data base of articles, book chapters, and reviews, which can be searched by topic and Scripture passage. The preacher should work back in time by five-year increments as he searches for helpful articles.
    2. *Textual critical problems.* If the explanation in Metzger's *Textual Commentary* is unclear or unconvincing and the text problem occurs at a key point in the passage, the preacher should do his own text critical analysis. (See "Methods and Aids for Textual Criticism" at WJLFP.)

Endnotes

1. Adams, *Preaching with Purpose*, chapter thirteen.

2. See Perry (*Manual for Biblical Preaching*, 139-45) for an extensive discussion of these principles.

3. Robinson, *Biblical Preaching*, 53-56; Perry, *Biblical Sermon Guide*, 17-18.

4. Gray, *Master the English Bible*, 17.

5. Wright, "Course Materials."

6. Carson and Moo, *Introduction to New Testament*; Gundry, *Survey of New Testament*; ZPEB.

Appendix: Greek Grammar Guides

In doing "Literary Analysis: Syntax–Grammar," you need to be able to identify the function of various grammatical features in your passage. A given grammatical form may have more than one function, e.g., the seven uses of the adverbial participle. Therefore, you need to be able to ask the right questions in order to come up with the right answer about how the NT writer is using the grammatical form in your passage. The following sets of Descriptive Outlines and Form/Function Charts should aid you in this.[1]

Resources
(listed in order of increasing grammatical detail)

Larkin, "Grammar in Head Chart."
Harvey, *Greek is Good Grief*.
DBW
Robertson, *Grammar of Greek Testament*.

Structure

Conjunctions

I. **Clauses**
   A. **Definition**: A clause is a group of words which has a subject and verb and is used as part of a sentence.
   B. **Types**: There are two types of clauses.
      1. *Main (independent) clause.* A group of words which express a complete thought and could be a sentence by itself. In Greek, most main clauses are connected to one another by coordinate conjunctions, resulting in one of several logical relationships (e.g., "The boy hit the ball, *and* the girl caught it" shows a *continuative* relationship; see below for discussion of conjunctions).
      2. *Subordinate (dependent) clause.* A group of words which does not express a complete thought and must be attached to a main clause by a subordinate conjunction or a relative pronoun resulting in one of three syntactical functions.
         a. *Noun clause.* A subordinate conjunction introduces a clause, which functions as a noun (subject, object, complement,

appositive) in the main clause (e.g., I know *that the boy hit the ball* has a noun clause [in italics] functioning as a *direct object*).
    b. *Adverbial subordinate clause*. A subordinate conjunction introduces a clause, which modifies the action of the verb in the main clause (e.g., The boy hit the ball *because he was a good batter* contains an *adverbial causal* clause [in italics], which describes why he could hit the ball).
    c. *Adjectival (relative) clause*. A relative pronoun most frequently introduces this type of clause, which limits or defines a noun (e.g., I know the boy *who hit the ball* contains an *adjectival relative* clause [in italics], which describes "boy").

II. **Conjunctions (General)**
  A. **Definition and Types**. A conjunction is a function word which connects words or word groups. There are two types of conjunctions. *Coordinate conjunctions* connect words, phrases, clauses, sentences, or paragraphs of equal value (e.g., Jack went up the hill, *but* Jill stayed at the bottom). *Subordinate conjunctions* connect subordinate (dependent) clauses to main (independent) clauses (e.g., Jack went up the hill, *although* Jill stayed at the bottom).
  B. **Special Note**. Although there are (a few) exceptions, a conjunction normally functions as either a coordinate or a subordinate conjunction. You will learn as a part of vocabulary building whether a conjunction is a coordinate or subordinate.

III. **Coordinate Conjunctions**: Coordinate conjunctions relate equal grammatical units to one another. Those units can be words, phrases, clauses, sentences, or paragraphs. There are nine possible logical relations between the grammatical units.
  A. **Continuative** ("and"): connects parallel items - (strong to weak) τέ, καί, δέ.
  B. **Adversative** ("but"): contrasts parallel items - (strong to weak) πλήν, ἀλλά, δέ.
  C. **Disjunctive** ("or"): distinguishes between items - ἤ, εἴτε, οὐδέ, οὔτε, μηδέ, μήτε.
  D. **Inferential** ("therefore"): introduces a conclusion from what precedes - (strong to weak) ἄρα, διό, ὥστε, οὖν.
  E. **Explanatory** ("that is, for"): introduces an explanation of what precedes - γάρ, δέ, καί.

F. **Transitional** ("now, then"): changes the topic of discussion - δέ, οὖν.
G. **Emphatic** ("indeed"): adds a parallel thought stressing the truth of what precedes - ἀλλά, οὖν.
H. **Ascensive** ("even"): introduces a final addition or point of focus - δέ, οὖν.
I. **Correlative** ("on the one hand . . . on the other hand "): paired conjunctions which express various relationships -
   μὲν . . . δέ "one the one hand . . . on the other hand"
   καί . . . καί, τὲ . . . καί "both . . . and"
   ἤ . . . ἤ "either . . . or"
   οὔτε . . . οὔτε, μηδὲ . . . μηδέ "neither . . . nor"
   εἴτε . . . εἴτε "whether . . . or".

IV. **Subordinate Conjunctions**: Subordinate conjunctions *relate a dependent clause to* a main clause as either a component (substantival [noun] clause) or a modifier of its verb (adverbial clause) or of one of its nouns (adjectival [relative] clause).
   A. **Substantival (noun) clause conjunctions**. These conjunctions introduce clauses functioning as a noun in one of five ways: 1) subject; 2) predicate nominative; 3) direct object; 4) indirect discourse; 5) apposition.

   Ὅτι and ἵνα introduce such clauses most frequently (e.g., John 13:35; 10:7), though they can also introduce adverbial clauses (John 10:1; 1 John 4:19).
   B. **Adverbial clause conjunctions**. Adverbial subordinate clauses have eight possible relations of to main clauses.
      1. *Comparative* ("as"): presents an analogous thought - ὡς, καθώς, ὥσπερ.
      2. *Temporal* ("after, while, before"): limits the action by time.
         a. Antecedent ("after"). Action of the subordinate clause occurs before action of main clause - ἀφ' οὗ.
         b. Coincident ("while"). Action of the subordinate clause occurs at the same time as the main clause - ὅτε, ὅταν.
         c. Subsequent ("before"). Action of the subordinate clause occurs after the action of the main clause - πρίν.
      3. *Purpose* ("in order that"): states the aim of the action, whether positive ("in order that") - ἵνα or ὅπως + subjunctive mood; or negative ("lest") - ἵνα μή + subjunctive mood.
      4. *Result* ("so that"): states the consequences of the action - ὥστε, ἵνα.

Figure A.1. **Coordinate Conjunctions by Logical Function**

Conjunction	Continuative	Adversative	Disjunctive	Inferential	Explanatory	Transitional	Emphatic	Ascensive	Correlative
ἀλλά		❶					②		
ἄρα				❶			②		
γάρ				②	❶		③		
δέ	❹	❶			③	❷		⑤	
διό				❶					
εἴτε ... εἴτε									①
ἤ			❶						
ἤ ... ἤ									①
καί	❶	⑥		③	②		④	⑤	
καί ... καί									❶
μὲν ... δέ									❶
μέντοι		①					②		
μηδέ, οὐδέ								①	
μήτε ... μήτε									①
οὖν		④		❶		❷	③		
οὔτε ... οὔτε									①
πλήν		❶		②			③		
τέ	①								
τὲ ... καί									①
τοιγαροῦν				①					
τοίνυν				①					
ὥστε				❶					

NOTE: Numbers indicate frequency of function, #1 being the most frequent. Dark circled numbers indicate the most frequently used conjunctions for the function.

5. *Causal* ("because"): states the reason for the action - γάρ, ὅτι, διότι, ἐπεί.
6. *Conditional* ("if"): states the condition under which the action will be realized.
   a. *First class.* The "if" clause is assumed to be true for argument's sake - εἰ + indicative ... any mood.
   b. *Second class.* The "if" clause is assumed as *not* true for argument's sake - εἰ + past tense indicative ... ἄν + past tense indicative.
   c. *Third class.* The "if" clause is uncertain as to fulfillment, but still likely - ἐάν + subjunctive ... any tense or mood.
   d. *Fourth class.* The "if" clause is possible as to fulfillment, but remote - εἰ + optative ... ἄν + optative.
7. *Concessive* ("although"): states the condition in spite of which the action will be realized.
   a. *First class.* The speaker views the condition as a fact - εἰ καί + indicative ... indicative.
   b. *Second class.* The speaker views the condition as possible, but doubtful - ἐάν καί + subjunctive ... indicative.
   c. *Third class.* The speaker views the condition as strongly improbable - καὶ ἐάν + subjunctive ... indicative; καὶ εἰ + indicative ... indicative.
8. *Local* ("where"): limits the action by place - ὅθεν, ὅπου, οὗ.

C. **Adjectival (Relative) clause conjunctions.** Relative pronouns introduce clauses which describe, explain, or restrict the noun modified in a definite or indefinite way.
   1. *Definite relative clause*: refers to a specific antecedent and contains a verb in the indicative mood. The pronoun agrees with its antecedent in gender and number, but its case is determined by its function in its own clause - ὅς, ἥ, ὅ.
   2. *Indefinite relative clause*: may refer to an unspecified individual, group, event, or action (i.e., it has no antecedent) using a verb in the subjunctive mood plus the particle ἄν or ἐάν. Or, it may focus on a whole class ("generic") and point to general sense, using ὅστις, ἥτις, ὅ τι or to quantity, using ὅσος. Or it may point to quality, the nature/essence of the antecedent, using οἷος.

Figure A.2. **Classification of Subordinate Conjunctions by Syntactical Function**

Conjunction	Adverbial								Noun
	Comparative	Temporal	Purpose	Result	Causal	Conditional	Concessive	Local	
γάρ					✓				
διότι					✓				
ἐάν						✓			
ἐὰν καί							✓		
εἰ						✓			
εἰ καί							✓		
ἐπεί		②			①				
ἕως		✓							
ἵνα			①	③					②
καθώς	①	③			②				
καὶ ἐάν						✓			
καὶ εἰ						✓			
ὅθεν				①				②	
ὅπου					②			①	
ὅπως			✓						
ὅτε		✓							
ὅτι					②				①
οὗ								✓	
πρίν		✓							
ὡς	①	②							
ὥσπερ	✓								
ὥστε				②	①				

NOTE: Numbers indicate frequency of usage, #1 being the most frequent.

Verbs

Tense

I. **General**: Tense expresses the verb's kind (and time) of action. *Kind* of action (also called "Aspect") is the primary element. *Time* of action (past, present, or future) is explicit only in the indicative mood.[2]

There are three main kinds of action:
- *Progressive* (also called "Internal" or "Incomplete") presents the action as in progress without regard to its beginning or end - present tense, imperfect tense.
- *Summary* (also called "External" or "Simple") presents the action as viewed as a whole without regard to its being in progress or its completion - aorist tense and future indicative.
- *Completed-Stative* (also called "Perfective-Stative") presents the action as completed, but with continuing results - perfect tense and pluperfect indicative.

II. **Progressive Action Tenses**
  A. **Present Tense**
  1. *Basic use: progressive* (or "descriptive"). This use describes action which is in progress or in a state of persistence (Matt 8:25 ἀπολλύμεθα).
  2. *Other common uses*
      a. *Instantaneous* (or "Aoristic"). This use expresses action which is completed at the moment of speaking. It occurs only in the indicative mood (Acts 16:18 Παραγγέλλω σοι).
      b. *Iterative.* This use expresses action which occurs repeatedly at intervals (1 Cor 15:31 καθ᾽ ἡμέραν ἀποθνῄσκω).
      c. *Customary* (or "Habitual"). This use expresses actions which habitually occur or which may be reasonably expected to occur (Matt 7:17 πᾶν δένδρον ἀγαθὸν καρποὺς καλοὺς ποιεῖ).
      d. *Gnomic.* This use expresses a general truth, something that is true at all times (1 John 3:8 ὁ ποιῶν τὴν ἁμαρτίαν ἐκ τοῦ διαβόλου ἐστίν).
  3. *Special uses*
      a. *Historical.* This use expresses a past event with the vividness of a present occurrence. It occurs in narrative material (John 1:29 Τῇ ἐπαύριον βλέπει τὸν ᾽Ιησοῦν ἐρχόμενον πρὸς αὐτόν).

b. *Extending-from-Past-to-Present* (or "Durative"). This use expresses action begun in the past and continuing into the present. It is usually associated with an adverb of time (John 15:27 ἀπ' ἀρχῆς μετ' ἐμοῦ ἐστε).
c. *Futuristic.* This use describes an event which has not yet occurred but is quite obviously about to take place (John 20:17 *Ἀναβαίνω πρὸς τὸν πατέρα μου*).
d. *Perfective.* This use expresses the continuation of existing results through present time (Gal 1:6 *Θαυμάζω ὅτι οὕτως ταχέως μετατίθεσθε*).
e. *Conative* (or "Tendential"). This use expresses an action intended or attempted, but not completed (Gal 5:4 οἵτινες ἐν νόμῳ *δικαιοῦσθε*).

B. **Imperfect Tense**
1. *Basic use: progressive* (or "descriptive"). This use expresses action which is in progress or in a state of persistence in past time (Mark 12:41 πολλοὶ πλούσιοι *ἔβαλλον* πολλά).
2. *Other common uses*
   a. *Ingressive* (or "Inceptive"). This use highlights the beginning of an action or an action on the verge of occurring (Matt 5:2 *ἐδίδασκεν* αὐτοὺς).
   b. *Iterative.* This use expresses repeated action in past time (Matt 27:23 οἱ δὲ περισσῶς *ἔκραζον* λέγοντες, Σταυρωθήτω).
   c. *Customary.* This use expresses action which regularly or ordinarily occurred in the past (Luke 3:10 Καὶ *ἐπηρώτων* αὐτὸν οἱ ὄχλοι).
3. *Special uses*
   a. *Instantaneous* (or "Aoristic"). This use expresses simple action in the past (John 5:19 . . . *Ἀπεκρίνατο* οὖν ὁ Ἰησοῦς καὶ *ἔλεγεν* αὐτοῖς).
   b. *Pluperfective.* This use expresses action in progress prior to the action occurring in the narrative (Mark 6:18 *ἔλεγεν* γὰρ ὁ Ἰωάννης τῷ Ἡρῴδῃ).
   c. *Conative* (or "Tendential"). This use expresses an action intended or attempted, but not completed (Luke 1:59 καὶ *ἐκάλουν* αὐτὸ . . . Ζαχαρίαν).

APPENDIX: GREEK GRAMMAR GUIDES

III. Summary Action Tenses

A. Aorist Tense

1. *Basic use: summary action* (or "constative"). This use views the action in its entirety without any emphasis on its beginning or end (Rom 5:14 *ἐβασίλευσεν* ὁ θάνατος ἀπὸ ʼ Ἀδὰμ μέχρι Μωϋσέως).
2. *Other common uses*
   a. *Ingressive* (or "Inceptive"). This use accents the beginning of the action (2 Cor 8:9 δι' ὑμᾶς *ἐπτώχευσεν*).
   b. *Consummative* (or "Culminative"). This use accents the conclusion or existing results of the action (Phil 4:11 ἐγὼ γὰρ *ἔμαθον* . . . αὐτάρκης εἶναι).
3. *Special uses*
   a. *Gnomic*. This use expresses a "universal" or "timeless" truth (John 15:8 ἐν τούτῳ *ἐδοξάσθη* ὁ πατήρ μου).
   b. *Epistolary*. The writer assumes the position of the reader and uses the aorist to look back at the time of writing as a past event (Phil 2:28 σπουδαιοτέρως οὖν *ἔπεμψα* αὐτόν).
   c. *Dramatic* (or "Immediate past"). This use refers to an event which happened in the recent past. It is often accompanied by an adverb of time (Matt 9:18 ʼΗ θυγάτηρ μου ἄρτι *ἐτελεύτησεν*).
   d. *Proleptic* (or "Futuristic"). This use states a present reality with the certainty of a past event for emphasis. It occurs in the indicative mood (John 13:31 Νῦν *ἐδοξάσθη* ὁ υἱὸς τοῦ ἀνθρώπου).

B. Future Tense

1. *Basic use: summary action* (or "predictive"). This use expresses a summary action expected to occur in the future (John 14:26 ἐκεῖνος ὑμᾶς *διδάξει* πάντα).
2. *Another common use: imperatival*. The second person future may be used to express a command (Matt 1:21 καὶ *καλέσεις* τὸ ὄνομα αὐτοῦ ʼ Ἰησοῦν).
3. *Special uses*
   a. *Deliberative*. The first person future may be used in questions expressing uncertainty (John 6:68 Κύριε, πρὸς τίνα *ἀπελευσόμεθα*;).
   b. *Gnomic*. This use states a fact or action which may be rightfully expected under normal circumstances (Gal 6:5 ἕκαστος γὰρ τὸ ἴδιον φορτίον *βαστάσει*).

c. *Progressive*. This use describes an action in progress in future time (Phil 1:18 ἐν τούτῳ χαίρω. ἀλλὰ καὶ *χαρήσομαι*).

IV. **Completed-Stative Action Tenses**
   A. **Perfect Tense**
      1. *Basic use: intensive* (or "resultative"). This use expresses a present state resulting from a completed action (Col 3:3 καὶ ἡ ζωὴ ὑμῶν *κέκρυπται* σὺν τῷ Χριστῷ ἐν τῷ θεῷ).
      2. *Another common use: extensive* (or "consummative"). This use accents the completed action rather than the continuing results (2 Tim 4:7 τὸν καλὸν ἀγῶνα *ἠγώνισμαι*, τὸν δρόμον *τετέλεκα*, τὴν πίστιν *τετήρηκα*).
      3. *Special uses*
         a. *Aoristic* (or "Dramatic"). This use expresses an action completed in the past but conceived in terms of the present for the sake of vividness. It occurs primarily in narrative material (John 1:15 Ἰωάννης μαρτυρεῖ περὶ αὐτοῦ καὶ *κέκραγεν* λέγων ...).
         b. *Gnomic*. This use expresses a generic or proverbial occurrence (John 3:18 ... ὁ δὲ μὴ πιστεύων ἤδη *κέκριται*).
         c. *Proleptic* (or "Futuristic"). This use refers to a state resulting from an antecedent action which is future from the time of speaking (Rom 13:8 ὁ γὰρ ἀγαπῶν τὸν ἕτερον νόμον *πεπλήρωκεν*).
         d. *Perfect with present force*. Certain verbs (e.g., οἶδα) occur exclusively in the perfect but are used like present tense verbs (Mark 10:19).
   B. **Pluperfect Tense**
      1. *Basic use: intensive* (or "resultative"). This use accents a past state resulting from a previous action. Both the action and the resulting state end in past time (Acts 1:10 ἄνδρες δύο *παρειστήκεισαν* αὐτοῖς).
      2. *Another common use : extensive* (or "consummative"). This use accents a completed action which had results continuing up to some time in the past (John 9:22 ἤδη γὰρ *συνετέθειντο* οἱ Ἰουδαῖοι).

Voice: Voice is that property of a verb which expresses how the subject relates to the action or state described. Three kinds of voice are possible. In the *active voice* the subject performs, produces, or experiences the action. In the *middle voice* the subject produces or experiences the action in such as way as to participate in the results. In the *passive voice* the subject is acted upon by the action described.

I. **Active Voice**
   A. **Normal Use: Simple Active.** The subject performs or experiences the action (Luke 16:15 ὁ δὲ θεὸς *γινώσκει* τὰς καρδίας ὑμῶν).
   B. **Other Uses**
      1. *Stative active.* The subject exists in the state described by the verb. This kind of active voice includes linking verbs and verbs that are translated with an adjective in the predicate (John 1:1᾽ Ἐν ἀρχῇ *ἦν* ὁ λόγος).
      2. *Causative active.* The subject is the ultimate source/cause of the action. The causative idea is often part of the verb itself, especially verbs which end in -οω and -ιζω (John 19:1 Τότε οὖν ἔλαβεν ὁ Πιλᾶτος τὸν ᾽Ἰησοῦν καὶ *ἐμαστίγωσεν*).
      3. *Reflexive active.* The subject acts upon him/herself. The reflexive pronoun is used as the direct object (Mark 15:30 *σῶσον* σεαυτόν).

II. **Middle Voice**
   A. **Common Uses**
      1. *Indirect middle* (or "intensive"). This use of the middle voice accents the subject's role in producing the action (Heb 9:12 αἰωνίαν λύτρωσιν *εὑράμενος*).
      2. *Deponent middle.* This use of the middle voice occurs when a verb has no active form but is active in meaning (e.g., ἔρχομαι).[3]
   B. **Other Uses**
      1. *Direct middle* (or "reflexive"). This use of the middle voice refers the results of the action directly to the subject with reflexive force (Matt 27:5 καὶ ἀπελθὼν *ἀπήγξατο*).
      2. *Permissive middle.* This use of the middle voice accents the subject's interest in the results of the action (1 Cor 6:7 διὰ τί οὐχὶ μᾶλλον *ἀδικεῖσθε*).
      3 *Reciprocal middle.* This use of the middle voice represents an interchange of action among plural subjects (John 9:22 *συνετέθειντο* οἱ ᾽Ἰουδαῖοι).

III. **Passive Voice**
   A. **With Agency Expressed**
      1. *Ultimate agent* (or "direct"). This form of the passive voice uses ὑπό + the genitive. The agent is the person who is ultimately responsible for the action (Acts 22:30 *κατηγορεῖται ὑπό τῶν Ἰουδαίων*).
      2. *Intermediate agent*. This form of the passive voice uses διά + the genitive. The ultimate cause has affected the subject through an intermediate agent (Matt 1:22 τὸ *ῥηθὲν ὑπὸ κυρίου διὰ τοῦ προφήτου*).
      3. *Impersonal means*. This form of the passive voice uses ἐν + the dative or the instrumental dative alone. There is often an implied agent who uses the noun in the dative as his/her instrument (Heb 9:22 *ἐν αἵματι πάντα καθαρίζεται*; cf. Eph 2:5).
   B. **Without Agency Expressed**. There are several reasons why a passive verb might not have an explicit agent.
      - The agent is often obvious from the context.
      - The focus of the passage is on the subject.
      - With some verbs, no agency is implied.
      - The verb is functioning as an "equative" verb.
      - The implied agent is generic (e.g., "someone, anyone").
      - An explicit agent would make the sentence too complex.
      - The agent might be suppressed for rhetorical effect.
      - God is the obvious agent (labeled the "divine passive").[4]

Mood: Mood is that property of a verb which "a speaker uses to portray his or her affirmation as to the certainty of the verbal action or state (whether an actuality or potentiality)."[5]

I. **Indicative Mood**: the speaker presents the action as real/certain.
   A. **Basic Use: Declarative Indicative**. Verb makes a statement (John 1:1 *Ἐν ἀρχῇ ἦν ὁ λόγος*).
   B. **Other Uses**
      1. *Interrogative indicative*. Verb asks a question (John 1:38 Τί *ζητεῖτε;*).
      2. *Cohortative indicative* (or "imperatival"). Verb gives a command in the second person of the future tense (Matt 19:18 Οὐ *φονεύσεις*).
      3. *Conditional indicative*: In a subordinate conditional clause introduced with the conjunction εἰ, the verb is in the indicative mood. See above for conditional subordinate clauses in the section on conjunctions (cf. 1 Cor 15:44).

II. **Subjunctive Mood**: the speaker presents the action as objectively probable.
   A. **Independent (Main) Clause Uses**
      1. *Hortatory subjunctive.* The first person plural subjunctive urges the listener(s) to join the speaker in the action (Heb 4:14 κρατῶμεν τῆς ὁμολογίας).
      2. *Deliberative subjunctive.* The subjunctive in a question weighs a course of action (Matt 6:31 λέγοντες, Τί *φάγωμεν*;).
      3. *Emphatic negation.* οὐ μή + the aorist subjunctive places special stress on a negative proposition (John 10:28 καὶ οὐ μὴ ἀπόλωνται εἰς τὸν αἰῶνα).
      4. *Prohibitive subjunctive.* μή + the second person aorist subjunctive demands that the listener not begin an action (Matt 6:31 μὴ οὖν *μεριμνήσητε*).
   B. **Dependent (Subordinate) Clause Uses**
      1. *Conditional subjunctive.* ἐάν with a verb in the subjunctive mood introduces a condition. See conditional subordinate clauses under section on conjunctions (cf. John 8:36).
      2. *Purpose/Result.* The subjunctive with the conjunction ἵνα frequently states the expressed aim or the result of the action of the verb in the main clause. For *positive purpose*, use ἵνα + subjunctive, and for *negative purpose*, use ἵνα μή + subjunctive. See purpose subordinate clauses under section on conjunctions (cf. 1 John 5:13; 2:1). Other uses:
         a. *Result.* ἵνα + subjunctive (Rom 11:11 μὴ ἔπταισαν ἵνα πέσωσιν;).
         b. *Purpose-Result.* Wallace[6] argues that ἵνα + the subjunctive may also be used to indicate *both* the intention of an action *and* its certain accomplishment (Phil 2:10 ἵνα ἐν τῷ ὀνόματι ᾿Ιησοῦ πᾶν γόνυ *κάμψῃ*).
      3. *Indefinite.* Some subordinate clauses use the subjunctive to state general cases related to the action of the verb in the main clause.
         a. *Relative.* ὅς ἄν + subjunctive (Mark 9:37 ῎Ος ἂν ἓν τῶν τοιούτων παιδίων *δέξηται*).
         b. *Temporal.* ὅταν + subjunctive (Matt 6:5 Καὶ ὅταν *προσεύχησθε*).
      4. *Substantival* (or "Content"). The subjunctive is sometimes used with ἵνα to introduce a subordinate clause which functions as a noun. The clause may function as a subject, a predicate nominative, a direct object (the example below), or in apposition (Matt 12:16 ἐπετίμησεν αὐτοῖς ἵνα μὴ φανερὸν αὐτὸν *ποιήσωσιν*).

III. **Optative Mood**: the speaker presents the action as subjectively possible but doubtful.
   A. **Basic Use: Voluntative Optative**. Optative expresses a wish (1 Pet 1:2 χάρις ὑμῖν καὶ εἰρήνη *πληθυνθείη*).
   B. **Other Uses**
      1. *Potential optative*. Optative expresses perplexity or possibility (Luke 3:15 ... διαλογιζομένων ... μήποτε αὐτὸς *εἴη* ὁ Χριστός).
      2. *Conditional optative*. Optative expresses a future condition which is not likely to be fulfilled. See conditional subordinate clauses under section on conjunctions (1 Pet 3:14 ἀλλ' εἰ καὶ *πάσχοιτε* διὰ δικαιοσύνην).

IV. **Imperative Mood**: the speaker presents the action as intended but dependent on the volitional response of the person addressed.
   A. **Basic Use: Command**. The imperative demands that the addressee undertake an action using the following tenses:
      1. *Present tense*. The command demands that an action be undertaken continually or repeatedly (John 5:8 καὶ *περιπάτει*).
      2. *Aorist tense*. The command demands that the action be undertaken immediately (John 5:8 *ἆρον* τὸν κράβαττόν σου).
   B. **Other Uses**
      1. *Prohibition*. Negative command demands that the addressee refrain from an action.
         a. The use of μή + the present imperative in a prohibition demands that an action in progress be stopped or forbids a repeated action (Phil 4:6 μηδὲν *μεριμνᾶτε*).
         b. The use of μή + the aorist subjunctive in a prohibition demands that an action being contemplated not be started or forbids a summary action (Matt 6:31 μὴ οὖν μεριμνήσητε).
      2. *Request* (or "entreaty"). Imperative has the force of an urgent request from a subordinate to a superior (Luke 17:5 Πρόσθες ἡμῖν πίστιν).
      3. *Permission*. Imperative gives consent from a superior for an action desired or contemplated by a subordinate (Matt 26:45 Καθεύδετε [τὸ] λοιπὸν καὶ ἀναπαύεσθε).

Verbal Mode

Participles: A participle is a declinable verbal adjective which combines the descriptive power of an adjective with the action aspect of a verb. A participle's tense primarily expresses the *kind* (not time) of action. The time of action in participles is (generally) relative to that of the main verb. The uses of participles fit into four main categories.[7]

I. **Substantival Use**: the participle may function in any way a noun does:
   - Subject
   - Predicate nominative
   - Direct object
   - Indirect object
   - Object of preposition
   - Noun in apposition

   The substantival participle usually is accompanied by a definite article which precedes it and agrees with it in gender, case, and number (John 5:10 ἔλεγον οὖν οἱ ᾽Ιουδαῖοι τῷ *τεθεραπευμένῳ* [indirect object]).

II. **Adjectival Use**: the particple modifies a noun in one of the following ways.
   A. **Attributive adjective**: The participle attributes some fact or quality to the noun. It usually follows the noun it modifies, and usually (but not always) has a definite article.
      1. *Ascriptive attributive* (article-participle-noun). The adjectival participle attributes a quality to the noun modified (Rom 3:25 διὰ τὴν πάρεσιν τῶν *προγεγονότων* ἁμαρτημάτων).
      2. *Restrictive attributive* (article-noun-article-participle). The adjectival participle highlights a distinctive characteristic of the noun it modifies (Col 1:25 τὴν οἰκονομίαν τοῦ θεοῦ *τὴν δοθεῖσάν* μοι).
      3. *Ascriptive attributive* (noun-participle). When used without the definite article the adjectival participle assigns a general quality to the noun it modifies (John 4:10 καὶ ἔδωκεν ἄν σοι ὕδωρ *ζῶν*).
   B. **Predicate adjective**: The particple makes a statement about the subject. It is not accompanied by a definite article (Heb 4:12 *Ζῶν* γὰρ ὁ λόγος τοῦ θεοῦ).

III. **Adverbial Use**: the participle modifies the action of another verb.
   - It never has a definite article
   - It usually is in the nominative case
   - It usually is best translated as a finite verb in a subordinate clause introduced by the appropriate conjunction (see below).

   It may modify the verb in one of several ways (listed in order of greatest to least frequency).

A. **Manner** ("... -*ing*"): The participle describes the emotion, attitude, or style in which the action takes place(Heb 13:13 ἐξερχώμεθα . . . τὸν ὀνειδισμὸν αὐτοῦ *φέροντες*).
B. **Means** ("*By* . . ."): The participle describes the physical or mental means by which the action takes place (Matt 6:27 τίς δὲ ἐξ ὑμῶν *μεριμνῶν* δύναται προσθεῖναι ἐπὶ τὴν ἡλικίαν αὐτοῦ πῆχυν ἕνα;).
C. **Time**: The participle describes an event before (aorist tense = "*After* . . ."), during (present tense = "*While* . . ."), or after (future tense = "*Before*...") which the action takes place (Matt 2:10 *ἰδόντες* δὲ τὸν ἀστέρα ἐχάρησαν χαρὰν μεγάλην σφόδρα).
D. **Cause** ("*Because*..."): The participle describes the cause, reason, or ground on which the action takes place (Rom 5:1 *Δικαιωθέντες* οὖν ἐκ πίστεως εἰρήνην ἔχομεν πρὸς τὸν θεόν).
E. **Condition** ("*If*..."): The participle describes the condition under which the action takes place (Gal 6:9 θερίσομεν μὴ *ἐκλυόμενοι*).
F. **Concession** ("*Although*..."): The participle describes the condition in spite of which the action takes place (Heb 5:12 καὶ γὰρ *ὀφείλοντες* εἶναι διδάσκαλοι . . . πάλιν χρείαν ἔχετε τοῦ διδάσκειν ὑμᾶς τινὰ).
G. **Purpose** (or "Telic"; "*In order to* . . ."): The participle describes the aim for which the action takes place[8] (Matt 27:49 ἴδωμεν εἰ ἔρχεται Ἠλίας *σώσων* αὐτόν).

Sometimes the participle describes the actual outcome or **Result** ("*So that*...") of the action (Luke 4:15 αὐτὸς ἐδίδασκεν ἐν ταῖς συναγωγαῖς αὐτῶν *δοξαζόμενος* ὑπὸ πάντων).

H. **Attendant Circumstance** (or "Circumstantial"; "*and* . . ."): The participle describes an event loosely related to, but often logically preceding the action of the main verb (Matt 9:18a ἰδοὺ ἄρχων εἰς *ἐλθὼν* προσεκύνει αὐτῷ).[9]
I. **Absolute Use** : It defines the circumstances in which the action of the verb in the main clause occurs, but its subject differs from the subject of the main clause. It usually is adverbial of *time*. In form,
    - It never uses a definite article.
    - It occurs with a noun or pronoun in the same case.
    - The noun or pronoun is translated as the subject of the participle, and the participle is translated as a verb in a subordinate clause.
A *genitive absolute* has the participle and its subject in the genitive case (Matt 9:33 καὶ *ἐκβληθέντος* τοῦ δαιμονίου ἐλάλησεν ὁ κωφός).

IV. **Verbal Use**: The participle either stands alone as the main verb in its clause or it is so closely related to the verb that it becomes a part of the primary verbal idea in the clause. The three uses are:
   A. **Imperatival**: The participle gives a command or prohibition. It never has a definite article and is clearly unrelated to a main verb or to a noun (1 Pet 3:1 γυναῖκες, *ὑποτασσόμεναι* τοῖς ἰδίοις ἀνδράσιν).
   B. **Complementary**: The participle completes the thought of another verb. It never has a definite article and will agree in gender, case, and number with a noun or pronoun in the clause of which it is a part. It occurs most frequently with verbs of cognition, perception, beginning, continuing, or ceasing (Eph 1:16 οὐ παύομαι *εὐχαριστῶν*).
   D. **Periphrastic**: The participle occurs with a form of the verb εἰμί and emphasizes duration. The tense of εἰμί expresses the *time* of action; the tense of the participle expresses the *kind* of action. It never has a definite article (Eph 2:8 τῇ γὰρ χάριτί ἐστε σεσῳσμένοι διὰ πίστεως).

Infinitive: An infinitive is a verbal noun, which combines the designative power of a noun with the action aspect of a verb. Its tense expresses the *kind* (not time) of action. It has four main uses:

I. **Adjectival**: An adjectival infinitive modifies a noun or adjective, usually a word denoting time, fitness, readiness, ability, power, authority, need, or hope. It is usually not accompanied by a definite article, but it may sometimes occur with a genitive definite article (τοῦ). It may modify a *noun* (John 1:12 ἔδωκεν αὐτοῖς ἐξουσίαν τέκνα θεοῦ *γενέσθαι*) or an *adjective* (Mark 1:7 οὐκ εἰμὶ ἱκανὸς κύψας *λῦσαι*).

II. **Substantival**: A substantival infinitive functions as a noun in one of three basic roles–subject, object, or appositive. It is usually (but not always) accompanied by a neuter definite article (τό).
   A. **Subject**: The infinitive is that of which something is said or asserted (Rom 7:18 τὸ γὰρ *θέλειν* παράκειταί μοι).
   B. **Object**: The infinitive receives or completes the action of the verb as:
      1. *Direct object*. This is the most common use (Phil 2:6 οὐχ ἁρπαγμὸν ἡγήσατο τὸ *εἶναι* ἴσα θεῷ).
      2. *Complementary object*. This use often occurs with verbs of beginning, wishing, being able to, willing, being about to, or being obligated to (Acts 1:1 ὧν ἤρξατο ὁ Ἰησοῦς *ποιεῖν* τε καὶ *διδάσκειν*).

C. **Appositive**: The infinitive explains or describes another noun more fully (Jas 1:27 θρησκεία καθαρὰ καὶ ἀμίαντος ... αὕτη ἐστίν, *ἐπισκέπτεσθαι* ὀρφανοὺς καὶ χήρας).
D. **Indirect discourse**: The infinitive is the object of a verb of mental perception or communication and expresses the content or the substance of the thought or communication (Mark 12:18 Σαδδουκαῖοι πρὸς αὐτόν, οἵτινες λέγουσιν ἀνάστασιν μὴ *εἶναι*).

III. **Verbal**: A verbal infinitive functions as the main verb in a sentence to give a command or a prohibition. This use of the infinitive is very rare. It never has a definite article and is clearly unrelated to a main verb or to a noun (Phil 3:16 εἰς ὃ ἐφθάσαμεν, τῷ αὐτῷ στοιχεῖν).

IV. **Adverbial**: An adverbial infinitive modifies the action of another verb. It is usually introduced by a conjunction (ὥστε), a preposition + an article, or the genitive definite article τοῦ.
   A. **Purpose** (*"In order that..."*): The infinitive states the aim for which the action in the main clause takes place. Forms:
   - infinitive alone
   - τοῦ + infinitive (80% purpose; 20% result)
   - πρὸς τό + infinitive
   - εἰς τό + infinitive
   - ὥστε + infinitive (20% purpose; 80% result)

   (Phil 1:10 εἰς τὸ *δοκιμάζειν* ὑμᾶς τὰ διαφέροντα).
   B. **Result** (*"So that..."*): The infinitive states the consequences of the action in the main clause. Forms:
   - ὥστε + infinitive (80% result; 20% purpose)
   - τοῦ + infinitive (20% result; 80% purpose)

   (1 Thess 1:8 ὥστε μὴ χρείαν *ἔχειν* ἡμᾶς λαλεῖν τι).
   C. **Time** - The infinitive describes an event before, during, or after which the action in the main clause takes place.
   1. *Antecedent* (*"After..."*). The action of the verb takes place after the action of the infinitive (μετὰ τό + infinitive; Matt 26:32 μετὰ δὲ τὸ *ἐγερθῆναί* με προάξω ὑμᾶς εἰς τὴν Γαλιλαίαν).
   2. *Simultaneous/contemporaneous* (*"While..."*). The action of the verb takes place at the same time as the action of the infinitive (ἐν τῷ + infinitive; Matt 13:4 καὶ ἐν τῷ *σπείρειν* αὐτὸν).
   3. *Subsequent* (*"Before..."*). The action of the verb takes place before the action of the infinitive (πρίν or πρὶν ἤ + infinitive; πρὸ τοῦ + infinitive; Mark 14:30 πρὶν ἢ δὶς ἀλέκτορα *φωνῆσαι* τρίς με ἀπαρνήσῃ).

D. **Cause** (*"Because of. . ."*): The infinitive states the ground on or the source out of which the action in the main clause takes place.(διὰ τό +infinitive;ἐκ τοῦ +infinitive; Matt 13:5 εὐθέως ἐξανέτειλεν διὰ τὸ μὴ *ἔχειν* βάθος γῆς).
E. **Means** (*"By. . ."*): The infinitive states the way in which the action is accomplished (ἐν τῷ + infinitive; Acts 3:26 ὁ θεὸς τὸν παῖδα αὐτοῦ ἀπέστειλεν αὐτὸν εὐλογοῦντα ὑμᾶς ἐν τῷ *ἀποστρέφειν* ἕκαστον ἀπὸ τῶν πονηριῶν ὑμῶν).

Case

I. **General**: Case is that property of a noun which indicates how it relates to other words in a sentence. There are four case *forms*, which can represent eight case *functions*.

II. **Nominative Case**: The nominative case form includes the functions of designation (nominative) and address (vocative).
   A. **Designation** (Nominative)
      1. *Subject.* A noun in the nominative specifies that which produces the action (John 3:35 ὁ *πατήρ* ἀγαπᾷ τὸν υἱόν).
      2. *Predicate nominative.* A noun in the nominative expresses a definition or description of the subject with verbs of being (εἰμί, γίνομαι, ὑπάρχω; 1 Thess 2:20 ὑμεῖς γάρ ἐστε ἡ *δόξα* ἡμῶν καὶ ἡ *χαρά*).
      3. *Apposition.* A noun in the nominative follows another noun in the nominative to describe or explain it more fully (2 Cor. 10:1 Αὐτὸς δὲ ἐγὼ *Παῦλος* παρακαλῶ ὑμᾶς).
   B. **Address** (Vocative)[10]: The most frequent use is direct address, in which the vocative expresses the person (or thing) to whom a statement is addressed (Rom 2:1 ἀναπολόγητος εἶ, ὦ *ἄνθρωπε*).

II. **Genitive Case**: The genitive case form includes the functions of description (genitive) and separation (ablative).
   A. **Description** (Genitive) with
      1. *Action nouns.* The noun in the genitive modifies another noun containing a verbal idea (e.g., love, blasphemy, faith). The simplest way to identify "action nouns" is to ask whether the noun has a verb as a cognate (e.g., ἀγάπη has as its cognate verb ἀγαπάω).
         a. *Subjective genitive.* The noun in the genitive denotes what *produces* the action in the action noun (1 John 2:16 ἡ ἐπιθυμία τῆς *σαρκός*).

      b. *Objective genitive*. The noun in the genitive denotes what *receives* the action in the action noun (Matt 12:31 ἡ δὲ τοῦ πνεύματος βλασφημία).
2. *Non-Action nouns*. The noun in the genitive modifies a noun, which does *not* contain a verbal idea, in one of the following ways:
      a. *Descriptive genitive*. This genitive describes the noun modified in a loose manner (category of last resort[11]; 2 Cor. 6:2 ἰδοὺ νῦν ἡμέρα *σωτηρίας*).
      b. *Possessive genitive*. This genitive denotes who or what owns the noun modified (Matt 26:51 τὸν δοῦλον τοῦ *ἀρχιερέως*).
      c. *Partitive genitive*. This genitive denotes the whole of which the noun modified is a part (Rev 11:13 τὸ δέκατον τῆς *πόλεως*).
      d. *Attributive genitive*. This genitive denotes a specific attribute/quality of the noun modified (Rom 6:6 τὸ σῶμα τῆς *ἁμαρτίας*).
      e. *Genitive of apposition*. This genitive denotes a particular instance of the general category designated by the noun modified (Rom 4:11 σημεῖον ἔλαβεν *περιτομῆς*).
3. *Verbs (or adjectives)*. The noun in the genitive modifies or limits a verb (or an adjective) in an indirect way. Several categories to consider: genitive of *price, place, means, agency, reference, association* and *time*.[12] The genitive of time denotes the *kind* of time within which the action occurs (John 3:2 οὗτος ἦλθεν πρὸς αὐτὸν *νυκτός*).

B. **Separation** (Ablative)
1. *Ablative of comparison*. This genitive follows an *adjective* and denotes comparison (John 14:28 ὁ πατὴρ μείζων *μού* ἐστιν).
2. *Ablative of separation*. This genitive follows a *verbal form* and denotes the point of departure (Eph 2:12 ἀπηλλοτριωμένοι τῆς *πολιτείας* τοῦ Ἰσραὴλ).
3. *Ablative of source*. This genitive follows a *noun* and denotes that from which the noun modified arises (Rom 15:4 διὰ τῆς παρακλήσεως τῶν *γραφῶν*).

III. **Dative Case**: The dative case form includes the functions of personal interest (pure dative), position (local dative), and means (instrumental dative).
A. **Personal Interest** (Pure Dative of . . .)

1. *Indirect object.* This dative denotes "to" or "for" whom the verb's action is done (Matt 13:3 ἐλάλησεν *αὐτοῖς* πολλὰ ἐν παραβολαῖς).
2. *Interest.* This dative denotes whether a person was favorably or unfavorably affected by the verb's action (Matt 23:31 μαρτυρεῖτε *ἑαυτοῖς*).
3. *Reference.* This dative denotes the idea of "interest" as applied to things (Rom 6:2 ἀπεθάνομεν τῇ *ἁμαρτίᾳ*).

B. **Position** (Local Dative of . . .)
1. *Sphere.* This dative denotes a location whether spatial (John 21:8 οἱ δὲ ἄλλοι μαθηταὶ τῷ *πλοιαρίῳ* ἦλθον) or logical (Matt 5.2 μακάριοι οἱ καθαροὶ τῇ *καρδίᾳ*).
2. *Time.* This dative denotes a point in time within a succession of events (Matt 20:19 καὶ τῇ τρίτῃ *ἡμέρᾳ* ἐγερθήσεται).

C. **Means** (Instrumental Dative of . . .)
1. *Association.* This dative denotes the person (occasionally thing) accompanying the subject (1 Cor 4:8 ἵνα καὶ ἡμεῖς *ὑμῖν* συμβασιλεύσωμεν).
2. *Means.* This dative denotes the impersonal means producing the verb's action toward a certain end (Eph 2:8 τῇ γὰρ *χάριτί* ἐστε σεσῳσμένοι).
3. *Cause.* This dative denotes the motive or occasion producing the verb's action (Gal 6:12 μόνον ἵνα τῷ *σταυρῷ* τοῦ Χριστοῦ μὴ διώκωνται).

IV. **Accusative Case**: The accusative case form has the function of limitation/extension of the verb's action.
A. **Substantival Uses**
1. *Direct object.* This accusative specifies that which receives the action (John 8:46 *ἀλήθειαν* λέγω).
2. *Double accusative.* This is the use of two accusatives with verbs that require more than one object (or other qualifying accusative) to complete their meaning. Types:
a. *Person + thing.* The person receives the thing (John 14:26 ἐκεῖνος *ὑμᾶς* διδάξει *πάντα*).
b. *Object + complement.* The second accusative asserts something about the first (John 15:15 οὐκέτι λέγω *ὑμᾶς δούλους*).
3. *Subject of an infinitive.* The infinitive's subject will always be in the accusative (1 Thess 1:8 ὥστε μὴ χρείαν ἔχειν *ἡμᾶς* λαλεῖν τι).
B. **Adverbial Uses**: The noun in the accusative may modify or limit a verb's action in an indirect (oblique) way, as:

1. *Measure*. This accusative denotes either duration of time (Matt 4:2 νηστεύσας *ἡμέρας* τεσσεράκοντα καὶ *νύκτας* τεσσεράκοντα) or extent of space (Luke 2:44 ἦλθον ἡμέρας *ὁδὸν*) in which the action occurs.
2. *Accusative of reference*. This accusative denotes that with reference to which the action occurs (Rom 16:6 ἥτις *πολλὰ* ἐκοπίασεν εἰς ὑμᾶς).

The Rest

The Article

I. **Definition:** Articles are words used with nouns to limit, individualize, or give definiteness.

II. **Basic Use: With Nouns/Substantives**. The article points out a specific person or object.
   A. **Individualizing**: The article identifies a particular person/object belonging to a larger class.
      1. *Simple Identification*. The article points out a particular person or object (category of last resort,[13] Matt 5:1 ἀνέβη εἰς τὸ ὄρος).
      2. *Relation to Context*. Uses:
         a. *Anaphoric*. The article points back to a noun previously mentioned (John 4:7, 15 Ἔρχεται γυνὴ ἐκ τῆς Σαμαρείας ἀντλῆσαι ὕδωρ . . . λέγει πρὸς αὐτὸν ἡ γυνή).
         b. *Deictic*. The article points out an object or person which/who is present at the moment of speaking (John 19:5 ' Ἰδοὺ ὁ ἄνθρωπος).
      3. *Reputation*. Uses:
         a. *Well known*. The article points out a well known object which is
            - not mentioned in the context.
            - not considered to be the best in its class.
            - not one of a kind (Matt 13:55 οὐχ οὗτός ἐστιν ὁ τοῦ τέκτονος υἱός;).
         b. *Par excellence*. The article points out a noun which is "in a class by itself," even though there are many other such persons/objects in the same category (John 1:21 ' Ο προφήτης εἶ σύ;).

4. *Quality*. Uses:
   a. *Abstract*. The article points out a noun which represents a concrete application of a quality (Matt 7:23 ἀποχωρεῖτε ἀπ' ἐμοῦ οἱ ἐργαζόμενοι *τὴν* ἀνομίαν).
   b. *Monadic*. The article points out a unique person or object (Matt 4:1 ὁ ' Ιησοῦς ἀνήχθη εἰς τὴν ἔρημον ὑπὸ τοῦ πνεύματος πειρασθῆναι ὑπὸ *τοῦ* διαβόλου).
B. **Generic**: The article distinguishes one class from another (Eph 5·25 *Οἱ* ἄνδρες, ἀγαπᾶτε τὰς γυναῖκας).

III. **As a Pronoun**
   A. **Personal Pronoun**: with certain conjunctions (μέν, δέ) to indicate that the subject has changed (Matt 15:26 *ὁ* δὲ ἀποκριθεὶς εἶπεν).
   B. **Alternative pronoun**: with the correlative conjunctions μέν . . . δε. In this use the singular is usually translated "the one . . . the other"; the plural is usually translated "some . . . others" (Acts 17:32 *οἱ* μὲν ἐχλεύαζον, *οἱ* δὲ εἶπαν).
   C. **Possessive pronoun**: in contexts where the idea of possession is obvious (Eph 5:25 Οἱ ἄνδρες, ἀγαπᾶτε *τὰς* γυναῖκας).
   D. **Mild relative pronoun**: When the article precedes a genitive phrase, a prepositional phrase, or a participle which is used to modify a noun, it may be translated as a relative pronoun (John 5:44 τὴν δόξαν *τὴν* παρὰ τοῦ μόνου θεοῦ οὐ ζητεῖτε).

IV. **As Substantiver** (With Other Parts of Speech): The article can be used to turn other parts of speech into a noun, i.e., an adverb, adjective, participle, infinitive, genitive word/phrase (Gal 5:24 *οἱ* δὲ τοῦ Χριστοῦ [' Ιησοῦ]), prepositional phrase (Eph 6:22 ἵνα γνῶτε *τὰ* περὶ ἡμῶν), particle, clause (Eph 4:9 *τὸ* δὲ ' Ανέβη τί ἐστιν).

V. **As a Function Marker**: The definite article denotes the following grammatical functions[14]:
   - the restrictive attributive position of an adjective,
   - the case of an indeclinable noun,
   - a substantival or adjectival function for a participle,
   - relationship of a demonstrative pronoun to a noun, and
   - most importantly, to point out the subject of a sentence with a "to be" verb when word order is not decisive (John 1:1 θεὸς ἦν ὁ λόγος).

VI. **Special Use: The Granville-Sharp Rule.** When two (or more) nouns are linked by καί and only the first noun has the article, the nouns are united in some way.
   A. **With Singular Personal Non-proper Nouns:** Both nouns refer to the same person (theologically significant, Titus 2:13 τοῦ μεγάλου θεοῦ καὶ σωτῆρος ἡμῶν Ἰησοῦ Χριστοῦ; cf. 2 Pet 1:1).
   B. **With Plural Impersonal and/or Proper Nouns:** The article indicates a contextually-defined coherent unit but does not necessarily mean that both nouns have identical referents. The terms may be related as follows[15]:
   - Distinct groups, though united (Matt 3:7),
   - Overlapping groups (Luke 14:21),
   - First group subset of second (Luke 14:3),
   - Second group subset of first (1 Cor 5:10), or
   - Both groups identical (John 20:29).

VII. **Absence:** The absence of the article ("anarthrous" construction) may indicate indefiniteness, quality, or definiteness (see fig. A.3).
   A. **Indefiniteness:** An anarthrous noun with indefinite meaning refers to a member of a class, without specifying which member (Matt 13:31 ὃν λαβὼν *ἄνθρωπος* ἔσπειρεν ἐν τῷ ἀγρῷ αὐτοῦ).
   B. **Quality:** An anarthrous noun with a qualtitative meaning places stress on quality, nature, or essence (John 1:4 ἐν αὐτῷ *ζωὴ* ἦν).
   C. **Definiteness:** An anarthrous noun with a definite meaning places stress on individual identity. Ten instances[16] presented in three large categories, in which an anarthrous noun has potential for being definite are (see fig. A.3):
   - *Items will be definite*: proper names, ordinal numbers, monadic "one of a kind" nouns, pronominal adjectives.
   - *Little difference in meaning* with or without article: abstract nouns, generic nouns.
   - *Items may be definite*: object of a preposition, predicate noun before copula, complement before object, genitive construction.

Particles, Pronouns, and Prepositional Phrases

I. **Particles:** A particle is a function word which has one of three basic uses.
   A. **Emphasis:** The particle places the stress on either some word in a sentence or the sentence as a whole. Three common emphatic particles are ἀμήν, γέ, ναί.

Figure A.3. **Semantic Meaning of the Non-Use of the Definite Article**

INDEFINITE				
QUALITATIVE				
DEFINITE	*"will* be definite"			
	Proper Names	Ordinal Numbers "_th"	Monadic "One of a Kind" Nouns	Pronomial Adjectives like πᾶς, ὅλος point to a class as a whole or distributively
	"little difference in meaning whether with or without the article"			
	Abstract Nouns (Qualitative-Definite)		Generic Nouns	
	"may be definite"			
	Object of a Preposition	Predicate Noun before copula	Complement before object in Object + Complement Construction	Genitive construction– both head noun and genitive modifier will have the same force, whether indefinite, definite or qualitative

B. **Negation**: The particle denies the reality of a fact.
   1. *οὐ + indicative*. Because οὐ is used to negate alleged factual statements, it generally occurs with the indicative mood.
   2. *μή + moods other than indicative*. Because μή is used to negate potential statements, it generally occurs with the subjunctive, optative, and imperative moods as well as with participles and infinitives.

3. οὐ μή *combination*. The special combination οὐ μή is used with the subjunctive mood to communicate emphatic negation.
4. *Negative particles in questions.*
   a. *Expecting "yes" answer.* A question which begins with a form of οὐ expects a "yes" answer (Matt 13:55 *οὐχ* οὗτός ἐστιν ὁ τοῦ τέκτονος υἱός;).
   b. *Expecting "no" answer.* A question which begins with a form of μή expects a "no" answer (Matt 12:23 *Μήτι* οὗτός ἐστιν ὁ υἱὸς Δαυίδ;).
C. **General Sense**: The particle ἄν adds a sense of indefiniteness or potentiality to a construction. It generally occurs with the subjunctive mood, but it is also used with the indicative and optative moods in conditional sentences. See examples in subjunctive mood section under verbs.

II. **Pronouns**: A pronoun is a word which takes the place of a noun while pointing to a place in the text where the noun occurs (its "antecedent"). Pronouns may function substantivally or adjectivally with the following uses (see fig. A.4):
A. **Substantival Uses**
   1. *Emphasis.* The pronoun gives special prominence to the subject or to a noun.
      a. *Subject focus.* The pronoun gives special prominence to the subject of the sentence (John 1:20 *Ἐγὼ* οὐκ εἰμὶ ὁ Χριστός).
      b. *Contrast.* The pronoun compares or contrasts two different subjects (Mark 1:8 *ἐγὼ* ἐβάπτισα ὑμᾶς ὕδατι, *αὐτὸς* δὲ βαπτίσει ὑμᾶς ἐν πνεύματι ἁγίῳ).
      c. *Identity.* The pronoun emphasizes the individuality of an articular noun or an anarthrous proper name. The pronoun is translated using a form of "-self" (Mark 12:36 *αὐτὸς* Δαυὶδ εἶπεν ἐν τῷ πνεύματι τῷ ἁγίῳ).
   2. *Reference.* The pronoun points backward (or forward) to a specific antecedent.
      a. *Previous reference.* The pronoun points back to an antecedent already mentioned (Rom 6:8 εἰ δὲ ἀπεθάνομεν σὺν Χριστῷ, πιστεύομεν ὅτι καὶ συζήσομεν *αὐτῷ*).
      b. *Switch reference.* The pronoun signifies a change in subject to someone or something which has been mentioned previously (Mark 4:36-38 καὶ ἀφέντες τὸν ὄχλον παραλαμβάνουσιν αὐτὸν ὡς ἦν ἐν τῷ πλοίῳ, καὶ ἄλλα πλοῖα ἦν μετ' *αὐτοῦ*. 4.37 καὶ γίνεται λαῖλαψ

Figure A.4. **Classification of Pronouns by Use**

| | Substantival ||||||| Relation ||
| | Emphasis ||| Reference ||| Relation |||
	Subject Focus	Contrast	Identity	Previous	Switch	Conceptual	Possession	Participation	Mutuality
ἀλλήλων									✓
αὐτός*	✓	✓	✓	✓	✓		✓	✓	
ἐγώ, σύ	✓	✓		✓	✓		✓	✓	
ἐκεῖνος**	✓		✓	✓		✓			
ἐμαυτοῦ								✓	
οὗτος**	✓		✓	✓		✓			

*Also Adjectival–Identity
**Also Adjectival–Proximity

μεγάλη ἀνέμου καὶ τὰ κύματα ἐπέβαλλεν εἰς τὸ πλοῖον, ὥστε ἤδη γεμίζεσθαι τὸ πλοῖον. 4.38 καὶ *αὐτὸς* ἦν ἐν τῇ πρύμνῃ ἐπὶ τὸ προσκεφάλαιον καθεύδων).

    c. *Conceptual reference.* The pronoun refers to a phrase or a clause (Eph 2:8 τῇ γὰρ χάριτί ἐστε σεσῳσμένοι διὰ πίστεως· καὶ *τοῦτο* οὐκ ἐξ ὑμῶν, θεοῦ τὸ δῶρον).

3. *Relation.* The pronoun is linked in a special way to another element in the sentence.
    a. *Possession.* The genitive form of a pronoun designates ownership (Matt 26:51 *αὐτοῦ* τὸ ὠτίον).
    b. *Subject participation.* The pronoun indicates that the subject is also the object of the verb's action (Phil 2:7 ἀλλὰ *ἑαυτὸν* ἐκένωσεν).

Figure A.4. (*continued*)

	Substantival				Adjectival					
	Identity	Quality	Quantity	General Sense	Description	Quality	Quantity	Proximity	Identity	General Sense
οἷος						✓				
ὅς, ἥ, ὅ					✓					
ὅσος							✓			
ὅστις				✓						✓
ποῖος		✓				✓				
πόσος			✓				✓			
τίς, τί	✓									
τις, τι				✓						✓

    c. *Mutuality*. The pronoun expresses an interchange between two or more groups (John 13:34 ἀγαπᾶτε *ἀλλήλους*).
4. *Question*. The pronoun introduces a question related to:
    a. *Identity*. The pronoun may introduce a question related to identity ("Who?" "Whom?" "What?"; Mark 8:27 *Τίνα* με λέγουσιν οἱ ἄνθρωποι εἶναι;).
    b. *Quality*. The pronoun may introduce a question related to quality ("What sort?"; Mark 12:28 *Ποία* ἐστὶν ἐντολὴ πρώτη πάντων;).
    c. *Quantity*. The pronoun may introduce a question related to quantity ("How much?"; Luke 16:7 Σὺ δὲ πόσον ὀφείλεις;).
5. *General Sense*. The pronoun introduces a member of a class without further identification (Matt 16:24 Εἴ *τις* θέλει ὀπίσω μου ἐλθεῖν, ἀπαρνησάσθω ἑαυτὸν).

B. **Adjectival Uses**
 1. *Description*. The pronoun introduces a clause which describes, clarifies, or restricts the antecedent (Rev 1:1 ’Αποκάλυψις ’Ιησοῦ Χριστοῦ *ἣν* ἔδωκεν αὐτῷ ὁ θεός)
 2. *Quality*. The pronoun introduces a clause which expresses a qualitative aspect ("such as," "of such kind as") of the antecedent (Matt 24:21 ἔσται γὰρ τότε θλῖψις μεγάλη *οἵα* οὐ γέγονεν ἀπ’ ἀρχῆς κόσμου).
 3. *Quantity*. The pronoun introduces a clause which expresses a quantitative aspect ("as much as," "as great as," "as many as") of the antecedent (Matt 13:44 καὶ πωλεῖ πάντα *ὅσα* ἔχει).
 4. *Proximity*. The pronoun points out an object as either near or far
    • in the context,
    • in the writer's mind, or
    • in space/time (Matt 3:9 δύναται ὁ θεὸς ἐκ τῶν λίθων *τούτων* ἐγεῖραι τέκνα τῷ ’Αβραάμ).
 5. *Identity*. The pronoun emphasizes the individuality of an articular noun. The pronoun is translated "same" (note: attributive position; Phil 2:2 τὴν αὐτὴν ἀγάπην ἔχοντες).
 6. *General Sense*. The pronoun adds an undefined quality to a common noun (Rom 8:39 οὔτε *τις* κτίσις ἑτέρα δυνήσεται ἡμᾶς χωρίσαι ἀπὸ τῆς ἀγάπης τοῦ θεοῦ).

III. **Prepositional Phrases**: A prepositional phrase is a group of words which includes a preposition and its object.
 A. **Basic Uses**: Prepositional phrases fulfill three basic functions.
    1. *Adverbial*. Most frequently, prepositional phrases modify verbs, participles, or infinitives (Gal 1:18 ῎Επειτα *μετὰ* ἔτη τρία ἀνῆλθον εἰς ’Ιεροσόλυμα).
    2. *Adjectival*. Occasionally, prepositional phrases modify nouns. When used adjectivally, the prepositional phrase is usually in the attributive position (i.e., preceded by an article; Rom 11:21 εἰ γὰρ ὁ θεὸς τῶν *κατὰ* φύσιν κλάδων οὐκ ἐφείσατο).
    3. *Substantival*. Only when a prepositional phrase is preceded by an article and there is no noun that it modifies, does it function substantivally (Gal 3:7 Γινώσκετε ἄρα ὅτι οἱ ἐκ πίστεως, οὗτοι υἱοί εἰσιν ’Αβραάμ).
 B. **Semantic Nuances**: A particular preposition governing an object in a particular case may take on one of several semantic nuances. See figure A.5 which correlates the most common prepositional phrases (preposition + case) with the possible semantic nuances each phrase might assume.

Figure A.5. Prepositional Phrases by Semantic Nuance

Preposition + Case	Direction	Position	Relation	Agency	Means	Cause	Association	Purpose
ἀνά + acc	✓							
ἀντί + gen			✓			✓		
ἀπό + gen	✓			✓		✓		
διά + acc						✓		
διά + gen	✓			✓	✓			
εἰς + acc	✓							✓
ἐκ + gen	✓			✓	✓			
ἐν + dat		✓			✓			
ἐπί + acc	✓							
ἐπί + gen		✓						
ἐπί + dat		✓				✓		
κατά + acc	✓		✓					
κατά + gen		✓						

1. *Direction.* The prepositional phrase indicates the direction of the verb's action with reference to the preposition's object.
   a. *Away.* "out of, from the side of, up, down."
   b. *Toward.* "to, unto, up to, to the side of, upon, into, through."
   c. *In the vicinity of.* "along, about, around, throughout, beyond."
2. *Position.* The prepositional phrase indicates the place of the prepositional object with reference to the verb's action.

Figure A.5. (*continued*)

Preposition + Case	Direction	Position	Relation	Agency	Means	Cause	Association	Purpose
μετά + acc			✓					
μετά + gen							✓	
παρά + acc	✓							
παρά + gen	✓							
παρά + dat		✓						
περί + acc	✓							
περί + gen			✓					
πρό + gen		✓						
πρός + acc	✓							✓
πρός + dat		✓						
σύν + dat							✓	
ὑπέρ + acc		✓						
ὑπέρ + gen			✓					
ὑπό + acc		✓						
ὑπό + gen				✓				

a. *Anterior.* "before, above, over."
b. *In the vicinity of.* "by, beside, at, on, upon, among, in, within."
c. *Posterior.* "from, down, under."

3. *Relation*. The prepositional phrase indicates a logical or temporal relationship.
   a. *Equation*. "as."
   b. *Addition*. "besides."
   c. *Displacement*. "for, in exchange for."
   d. *Advantage*. "for, in/on behalf of."
   e. *Disadvantage*. "against, contrary to."
   f. *Reference*. "about, concerning, with reference to, pertaining to, with respect to."
   g. *Time*. "after, while, in the time of."
4. *Agency* ("by"). In conjunction with passive verbs the prepositional phrase can indicate the subject of the verb's action.
5. *Means* ("by means of"). The prepositional phrase indicates the immediate cause of the verb's action.
6. *Cause* ("because of, on account of"). The prepositional phrase indicates the ultimate cause of the verb's action.
7. *Association* ("with"). The prepositional phrase indicates logical or person accompaniment.
8. *Purpose* ("for, for the sake of, for the purpose of"). The prepositional phrase indicates the goal of the verb's action.

Endnotes

1. The substance of this appendix is taken from Harvey, *Greek Grammar Guides*; cf. Harvey, *Greek is Good Grief*.

2. In recent grammatical discussion Porter (*Verbal Aspect*) and Fanning (*Verbal Aspect*) have disagreed whether tense has a temporal feature at all. Porter says it has only aspect, while Fanning continues to maintain that it has a temporal feature in the indicative (see Porter and Carson, eds. *Biblical Greek Language*, for full discussion).

3. Recent grammatical discussion has called into question the usefulness of the deponency category (Pennington, "Deponency in Koine Greek," 55-76). Rather, such verbs, when their lexical meaning is studied carefully, can be categorized as true Middles, particularly indirect Middles, the action of the verb affecting the subject.

4. DBW, 435-38.

5. DBW, 445.

6. DBW, 473.

7. Wallace (DBW, 616) prefers to divide participles into two main categories: "adjectival" and "verbal" with subcategories, "dependent" and "independent" under each. The equivalent to the categories used here are: "dependent adjectival"=adjectival participle; "independent adjectival"=substantival participle; "dependent verbal"=adverbial participle; "independent verbal"=verbal participle.

8. Wallace (DBW, 635-36) makes the following points related to tense use in purpose participles: a) adverbial participles in the future are *always* purpose; present tense can be purpose; b) a perfect tense participle will never be purpose; and c) aorist participles of purpose are quite rare.

9. Wallace (DBW, 642) suggests five features which most frequently characterize an adverbial participle of attendant circumstance:
- the participle is in the aorist tense,
- the main verb is in the aorist tense,
- the main verb is in the imperative or indicative mood,
- the participle precedes the main verb, both in word order and in time of event, and
- the passage is frequently in narrative literature.

10. Grammarians debate whether the vocative is a legitimate case form (e.g., DBW, 66-67).

11. DBW, 79.

12. Wallace (DBW, 122-30) notes each use is fairly rare.

13. DBW, 216.

14. DBW, 238-42.

15. DBW, 278.

16. DBW, 245-54.

BIBLIOGRAPHY

Abbott-Smith, George. *A Manual Greek Lexicon of the New Testament.* 3rd ed. Edinburgh: T. & T. Clark, 1999.

Adams, Jay E. "Does This Apply to You?" In *Truth Apparent: Essays on Biblical Preaching,* 76-81. Phillipsburg, NJ: Presbyterian and Reformed, 1982.

———. *Preaching with Purpose: The Urgent Task of Homiletics.* Grand Rapids: Zondervan, 1982.

———. "Using the Original Languages in Preaching." In *Truth Apparent: Essays on Biblical Preaching,* 29-31. Philipsburg, NJ: Presbyterian and Reformed, 1982.

Aland, Barbara, Kurt Aland, Johannes Karavidopoulos, Carlo M. Martini, Bruce M. Metzger, and Allen Wikgren, eds. *The Greek New Testament.* 4th rev. ed. Stuttgart: United Bible Societies, 1993.

Aland, Kurt. *Synopsis Quattuor Evangeliorum.* 15th ed. New York: American Bible Society, 1996.

Alexander, T. Desmond and Brian S. Rosner, eds. *New Dictionary of Biblical Theology: Exploring the Unity and Diversity of Scripture.* Downers Grove, IL: InterVarsity Press, 2000.

Allison, Dale C., Jr. "Apocalyptic." In *DJG* 17-20.

Anderson, Leith. Ministries: "Excellence in Preaching." *Christianity Today,* September 17, 1982, 54.

"Apocalypse, Genre of." In *DBI* 35-37.

Archer, Gleason L. et al. *Three Views on the Rapture: Pre; Mid; Post-Tribulational?* rev. ed. Grand Rapids: Zondervan, 1996.

Archer, Gleason L. and Gregory Chirichigno. *Old Testament Quotations in the New Testament.* Chicago: Moody Press, 1983.

ATLA data base. Accessed September 12, 2007. Online: http://www.ciu.edu/library/databases-a.php.

Bailey, James L. and Lyle D. Vander Broek. *Literary Forms of the New Testament: A Handbook.* Louisville, KY: Westminster John Knox, 1992.

Bailey, Kenneth E. *Poet and Peasant and Through Peasant Eyes: A Literary-Cultural Approach to the Parables of Luke.* Grand Rapids: Eerdmans, 1980.

Balch, David. *Let Wives Be Submissive: The Domestic Code in 1 Peter*. Chico, CA: Scholars, 1981.

Balz, Horst and Gerhard Schneider, eds. *Exegetical Dictionary of the New Testament*. 3 vols. Grand Rapids: Eerdmans, 1990-93.

Barclay, William. "The New Testament and the Papyri." In *The New Testament in Historical and Contemporary Perspective: Essays in Memory of G. H. C. Macgregor*, edited by Hugh Anderson and William Barclay, 57-81. Oxford: Basil Blackwell, 1965.

Barker, Kenneth L. and Donald W. Burdick, eds. *Zondervan NIV Study Bible*. fully rev. ed. Grand Rapids: Zondervan, 2002.

Barrett, C. K., ed. *The New Testament Background: Selected Documents*. New York: Harper & Row, 1961.

Basinger, David and Randall Basinger, eds. *Predestination and Free Will: Four Views of Divine Sovereignty and Human Freedom*. Downers Grove, IL: InterVarsity Press, 1985.

Bateman, Herbert W., IV, ed. *Four Views on the Warning Passages in Hebrews*. Grand Rapids: Kregel Academic & Professional, 2007.

Bauer, Walter, William F. Arndt, F. W. Gingrich, revised and edited by Frederick W. Danker. *A Greek-English Lexicon of the New Testament and Other Early Christian Literature*. 3rd ed. Chicago: Univ. of Chicago Press, 2000.

Bauer, Walter, William F. Arndt, F. W. Gingrich, revised and augmented by F. W. Gingrich and Frederick W. Danker. *A Greek-English Lexicon of the New Testament and Other Early Christian Literature*. 2nd ed. Chicago: Univ. of Chicago Press, 1979.

Baumann, J. Daniel. *An Introduction to Contemporary Preaching*. Grand Rapids: Baker, 1972.

Beale, Gregory K. *The Book of Revelation: A Commentary on the Greek Text*. NIGTC. Grand Rapids: Eerdmans, 1999.

———. and D. A. Carson, eds. *Commentary on the New Testament Use of the Old Testament*. Grand Rapids: Baker Academic, 2007.

Beitzel, Barry J. *The Moody Atlas of Bible Lands*. Chicago: Moody Press, 1985.

BibleWorks CD-ROM. BibleWorks Version 7.0. Norfolk, VA: BibleWorks LLC, 1992-2005.

Bibloi CD-ROM. Silvermountain Software Version 8.0. Cedar Hill, TX: Silvermountain Software, 2004.

Black, David A. *Learn to Read New Testament Greek*. Nashville: Broadman, 1993.

———. *Using New Testament Greek in Ministry: A Practical Guide for Students and Pastors*. Grand Rapids: Baker, 1993.

Blass, F., A. Debrunner, and R. W. Funk. *A Greek Grammar of the New*

Testament and Other Early Christian Literature. Chicago: Univ. of Chicago Press, 1961.

Blomberg, Craig L. *Interpreting the Parables*. Downers Grove, IL: InterVarsity Press, 1990.

———. *Jesus and the Gospels: An Introduction and Survey*. Nashville: Broadman & Holman, 1997.

Bock, Darrell L. "Lexical Analysis: Studies in Words." In *Interpreting the New Testament Text: Introduction to the Art and Science of Exegesis*, edited by Darrell L. Bock and Buist M. Fanning, 135-53. Wheaton, IL: Crossway, 2006.

———. *Luke 1:1–9:50, 9:51–24:53*. 2 vols. BECNT. Grand Rapids: Baker, 1994, 1996.

———. "Opening Questions: Definition and Philosophy of Exegesis." In *Interpreting the New Testament Text: Introduction to the Art and Science of Exegesis*, edited by Darrell L. Bock and Buist M. Fanning, 23-32. Wheaton, IL: Crossway, 2006.

———., ed. *Three Views on the Millennium and Beyond*. Grand Rapids: Zondervan, 1999.

———. and Buist M. Fanning, eds. *Interpreting the New Testament Text: Introduction to the Art and Science of Exegesis*. Wheaton, IL: Crossway, 2006.

Bolt, John. "An Emerging Critique of the Postmodern, Evangelical Church: A Review Essay." *CTJ* 41 (2006) 205-21.

Borland, James A. "Reports Relating to the Fifty-eighth Annual Meeting of the Society." *JETS* 50 (2007) 211-16.

Botterweck, G. Johannes, Helmer Ringgren, and Heinz-Josef Fabry, eds. *Theological Dictionary of the Old Testament*. 15 vols. Grand Rapids: Eerdmans, 1974–2006.

Bradley, David G. "The *Topos* as a Form in the Pauline Paraenesis." *JBL* 72 (1953) 238-46.

Breneman, Mervin. *Ezra, Nehemiah, Esther*. NAC. Nashville: Broadman & Holman, 1993.

Brenton, Lancelot C. L. *The Septuagint with Apocrypha, Greek and English*. Peabody, MA: Hendrickson, 1986.

Broadus, John A. *On the Preparation and Delivery of Sermons*. Edited by Jesse B. Weatherspoon. new and rev. ed. New York: Harper and Row, 1944.

Bromiley, Geoffrey W., ed. *The International Standard Bible Encyclopedia*. 4 vols. rev. ed. Grand Rapids: Eerdmans, 1979-88.

Brown, Colin, ed. *The New International Dictionary of New Testament Theology*. 3 vols. Grand Rapids: Zondervan, 1975-78.

Bruce, F. F. *The Epistle to the Galatians: A Commentary on the Greek Text*.

NIGTC. Grand Rapids: Eerdmans, 1982.
——. "Interpretation of the Bible." In *EDT* 565-68.
Brunt, John C. "More on the *Topos* as a New Testament Form." *JBL* 104 (1985) 495–500.
Bullinger, E. W. *Figures of Speech Used in the Bible: Explained and Illustrated.* repr. Grand Rapids: Baker, 1968.
Buttrick, George A., ed. *Interpreter's Dictionary of the Bible: An Illustrated Encyclopedia.* 4 vols. Nashville: Abingdon, 1962.
Callahan, James P. *The Clarity of Scripture: History, Theology and Contemporary Literary Studies.* Downers Grove, IL: InterVarsity Press, 2001.
Carson, D. A. "Unity and Diversity in the New Testament: The Possibility of Systematic Theology." In *Scripture and Truth*, edited by D. A. Carson and John D. Woodbridge, 65-95. Grand Rapids: Zondervan, 1983.
Carson, D. A. and Douglas J. Moo. *An Introduction to the New Testament.* 2nd ed. Grand Rapids: Zondervan, 2005.
Chapell, Bryan. *Christ-centered Preaching: Redeeming the Expository Sermon.* 2nd ed. Grand Rapids: Baker Academic, 2005.
Chapman, David W. and Andreas J. Köstenberger. "Jewish Intertestamental and Early Rabbinic Literature: An Annotated Bibliographic Resource." *JETS* 43 (2000) 577–618.
Charlesworth, James H. ed. *The Old Testament Pseudepigrapha.* 2 vols. Garden City, NY: Doubleday, 1983-85.
"The Chicago Statement on Biblical Inerrancy." In *Inerrancy*, edited by Norman L. Geisler, 493–502. Grand Rapids: Zondervan, 1980.
Clark, Gordon H. "Special Divine Revelation as Rational." In *Revelation and the Bible: Contemporary Evangelical Thought*, edited by Carl F. H. Henry, 25-41. Grand Rapids: Baker, 1958.
Comparetti, Domenico and Girolamo Vitelli. *Papiri Greco-Egizii.* 3 vols. Milano: U. Hoepli, 1905-15.
Coogan, Michael D., Marc Z. Brettler, Carol A. Newsom, and Pheme Perkins, eds. *The New Oxford Annotated Bible with the Apocryphal/Deuterocanonical Books, New Revised Standard Version.* 3rd ed. New York: Oxford Univ. Press, 2001.
Craddock, Fred B. "Commentaries in Use–Three Appraisals: The Commentary in the Service of the Sermon." *Int* 36 (1982) 386-88.
Culpepper, R. Alan. *Anatomy of the Fourth Gospel: A Study in Literary Design.* Philadelphia: Fortress, 1983.
Culy, Martin, gen. ed. *Baylor Handbook on the Greek New Testament.* Waco, TX: Baylor Univ. Press, 2003–.
Danby, Herbert, trans. *The Mishnah.* Oxford: Oxford Univ. Press, 1993.

Doriani, Daniel M. *Putting the Truth to Work: The Theory and Practice of Biblical Application.* Phillipsburg, NJ: P&R, 2001.
Doriani, Paul M. "A Pastor's Advice on Maintaining Original Language Skills." *Presb* 19 (1993) 103-15.
Doty, William G. *Letters in Primitive Christianity.* Philadelphia: Fortress, 1973.
Douglas, J. D. and Merrill C. Tenney, eds. *New International Dictionary of the Bible, Pictorial Edition.* Grand Rapids: Zondervan, 1987.
Durusau, Patrick. *High Places in Cyberspace: A Guide to Biblical and Religious Studies, Classics, and Archaeological Resources on the Internet.* 2nd ed. Atlanta: Scholars, 1998.
Dyrness, William. *Themes in Old Testament Theology.* Downers Grove, IL: InterVarsity Press, 1979.
Eadie, John. *A Commentary on the Greek Text of the Epistle of Paul to the Philippians.* repr. Grand Rapids: Baker, 1979.
Edgar, C. C. *Zenon Papyri in the University of Michigan Collection.* Ann Arbor, MI: Univ. of Michigan Press, 1931.
Ellis, Karl C. "The Nature of Biblical Exegesis." *BSac* 137 (1980) 151-55.
Elwell, Walter A., ed. *Baker Theological Dictionary of the Bible.* Grand Rapids: Baker Academic, 2001.
———., ed. *Evangelical Dictionary of Theology.* Grand Rapids: Baker, 1984.
Erickson, Millard J. *Christian Theology.* Grand Rapids: Baker, 1989.
Evans, Craig A. *Ancient Texts for New Testament Studies: A Guide to the Background Literature.* Peabody, MA: Hendrickson, 2005.
———. *Mark 8:27–16:20.* WBC. Nashville: Thomas Nelson, 2001.
———. and Stanley E. Porter, eds. *Dictionary of New Testament Background.* Downers Grove, IL: InterVarsity Press, 2000.
Fanning, Buist M. *Verbal Aspect in New Testament Greek.* Oxford: Clarendon Press, 1990.
Fee, Gordon D. *New Testament Exegesis: A Handbook for Students and Pastors.* 3rd ed. Louisville, KY: Westminster John Knox, 2002.
———. *Paul's Letter to the Philippians.* NICNT. Grand Rapids: Eerdmans, 1995.
Feinberg, John S. "Truth: Relationships of Theories of Truth to Hermeneutics." In *Hermeneutics, Inerrancy, and the Bible,* edited by Earl D. Radmacher and Robert D. Preus, 3-50, Grand Rapids: Zondervan, 1984.
Ferguson, Sinclair B., David F. Wright, and J. I. Packer, eds. *New Dictionary of Theology.* Downers Grove, IL: InterVarsity Press, 1988.
Finegan, Jack. *The Archeology of the New Testament: The Life of Jesus and the Beginning of the Early Church.* rev. ed. Princeton, NJ: Princeton Univ. Press, 1992.
———. *The Archeology of the New Testament: The Mediterranean World of the Early Christian Apostles.* Boulder, CO: Westview, 1981.

Forlines, F. Leroy. *The Quest for Truth: Answering Life's Inescapable Questions.* Nashville: Randall House, 2001.
France, R. T. *The Gospel of Mark: A Commentary on the Greek Text.* NIGTC. Grand Rapids: Eerdmans, 2002.
Friberg, Barbara and Timothy Friberg, eds. *Analytical Greek New Testament.* Grand Rapids: Baker, 1981.
Funk, Robert W. "The Apostolic *Parousia*: Form and Significance." In *Christian History and Interpretation: Studies Presented to John Knox,* edited by W. R. Farmer, C F. D. Moule and R. R. Niebuhr, 249-68. Cambridge: Cambridge Univ. Press, 1967.
———. *Language, Hermeneutic, and Word of God: The Problem of Language in the New Testament and Contemporary Theology.* New York: Harper & Row, 1966.
Gardiner, Alan. *The Theory of Speech and Language.* 2nd ed. Oxford: Clarendon Press, 1951.
Geisler, Norman L. "Explaining Hermeneutics: A Commentary on the Chicago Statement on Biblical Hermeneutics Articles of Affirmation and Denial." In *Hermeneutics, Inerrancy, and the Bible,* edited by Earl D. Radmacher and Robert D. Preus, 889–904. Grand Rapids: Zondervan, 1984.
Gianotti, Charles R. *The New Testament and the Mishnah: A Cross-reference Index.* Grand Rapids: Baker, 1983.
Goodacre, Mark. "New Testament Gateway" Web site, http://www.ntgateway.com (accessed August 23, 2007).
Gramcord GNT/HMT/LXX Ultimate Bundle CD-ROM. Vancouver, WA: GRAMCORD Institute, 2007.
Grassmick, John D. *Principles and Practice of Greek Exegesis: A Classroom Manual.* Dallas: Dallas Theological Seminary, 1976.
Gray, James M. *How to Master the English Bible: An Experience, A Method, A Result, An Illustration.* Chicago: Moody Press, 1951.
Green, Joel B. *The Gospel of Luke.* NICNT. Grand Rapids: Eerdmans, 1997.
———. and Scot McKnight, eds. *Dictionary of Jesus and the Gospels.* Downers Grove, IL: InterVarsity Press, 1992.
Greenlee, J. Harold. *An Exegetical Summary of Philippians.* Dallas: SIL International, 2001.
Grenz, Stanley J. *Theology for the Community of God.* Grand Rapids: Eerdmans, 2000.
Grudem, Wayne A. *Systematic Theology: An Introduction to Biblical Doctrine.* Grand Rapids: Zondervan, 1994.
Guelich, Robert A. *Mark 1–8:26.* WBC. Dallas: Word, 1989.
Gundry, Robert H. *Mark: A Commentary on His Apology for the Cross.* Grand Rapids: Eerdmans, 1993.

———. *A Survey of New Testament.* 4th ed. Grand Rapids: Zondervan, 2003.
Guthrie, Donald. *New Testament Theology.* Downers Grove, IL: InterVarsity Press, 1981.
Hamilton, Donald L. *Homiletical Handbook.* Nashville: Broadman, 1992.
Han, Nathan E. *A Parsing Guide to the Greek New Testament.* Scottdale, PA: Herald, 1971.
Harvey, John D. *Greek Grammar Guides.* rev. Columbia, SC: CIU Bookstore, 2000.
———. *Greek Is Good Grief: Laying the Foundation for Exegesis and Exposition.* Eugene, OR: Wipf & Stock, 2007.
Harvey, John D., Don N. Howell, Donald L. Hamilton, Joan E. Havens, William J. Larkin, W. Kenneth Phillips, and Shirl S. Schiffman. "Faculty Discussion of Time Requirements in Sermon Preparation." CIU-SSM, Spring term 2001.
Hatch, Edwin P. and Henry A Redpath. *A Concordance to the Septuagint.* 2nd ed. Grand Rapids: Baker, 1998.
Hawthorne, Gerald F. *Philippians.* WBC. Waco, TX: Word, 1983.
———. and Ralph P. Martin, eds. *Dictionary of Paul and His Letters.* Downers Grove, IL: InterVarsity Press, 1993.
Hayes, John H. and Carl R. Holladay. *Biblical Exegesis: A Beginner's Handbook.* 3rd ed. Louisville, KY: Westminster John Knox, 2007.
Hemer, Colin J. "Towards a New Moulton and Milligan." *NovT* 24 (1982) 97–123.
Henry, Carl F. H. *God, Revelation and Authority.* vol. 4, *God Who Speaks and Shows: Fifteen Theses, Part Three.* Waco, TX: Word, 1979.
The Holy Bible, English Standard Version. Wheaton, IL: Crossway Bibles, 2001.
The Holy Bible: New International Version. Grand Rapids: Zondervan, 1978.
Hornblower, Simon and Antony Spaworth, eds. *The Oxford Classical Dictionary.* 3rd ed. Oxford: Oxford Univ. Press, 1996.
House, Paul R. *Old Testament Theology.* Downers Grove, IL: InterVarsity Press, 1998.
Hunt, Arthur S. and C. C. Edgar. *Select Papyri.* 5 vols. LCL. Cambridge, MA: Harvard Univ. Press, 1959.
Hunter, Archibald M. "Grammar and Godliness." In *Gleanings from the New Testament*, 26-29. Philadelphia: Westminster, 1975.
Johnson, Alan F. *Revelation.* vol. 12, EBC. Grand Rapids: Zondervan, 1981.
Johnson, Cedric B. *The Psychology of Bible Interpretation.* Grand Rapids: Zondervan, 1983.
Josephus, Flavius. *Works.* 10 vols. LCL. Cambridge, MA: Harvard Univ. Press, 1926-65.
Kaiser, Walter C., Jr. "Hermeneutics and the Theological Task." *TJ* 12 (1991) 3-14.

———. "Legitimate Hermeneutics." In *Inerrancy*, edited by Norman L. Geisler, 115-42. Grand Rapids: Zondervan, 1980.
———. "Narrative." In *Cracking Old Testament Codes: A Guide to Interpreting the Literary Genres of the Old Testament*, edited by D. Brent Sandy and Ronald L. Giese, Jr., 69-88. Nashville: Broadman & Holman, 1995.
———. "A Neglected Text in Bibliology Discussions: 1 Corinthians 2:6-16." *WTJ* 43 (1981) 301-19.
———. *Toward an Exegetical Theology: Biblical Exegesis for Preaching and Teaching*. Grand Rapids: Baker, 1998.
———. *Toward an Old Testament Theology*. Grand Rapids: Zondervan, 1978.
Keener, Craig. "Family and Household." In *DNTB* 353-68.
———. *The IVP Bible Background Commentary: New Testament*. Downers Grove, IL: InterVarsity Press, 1993.
Keil, Carl F. *Biblical Commentary on the Old Testament Books of Ezra, Nehemiah, Esther, Job*. vol. 4, K&D. Peabody, MA: Hendrickson, 1996.
———. and F. Delitzsch. *Biblical Commentary on the Old Testament*. 10 vols. repr. Peabody, MA: Hendrickson, 1996.
Kittel, Gerhard and Gerhard Friedrich, eds. *Theological Dictionary of the New Testament*. 10 vols. Grand Rapids: Eerdmans, 1964-76.
Königliche Museen zu Berlin. *Aegyptische Urkunden aus den Königlichen Staatlichen Museen zu Berlin: Griechische Urkunden*. 9 vols. Berlin: Weidmann, 1895–1937.
Köstenberger, Andreas, gen. ed. *Whatever Happened to Truth?* Wheaton, IL: Crossway, 2005.
Kohlenberger, John R. *The Greek New Testament UBS^4 with NRSV and NIV*. Grand Rapids: Zondervan, 1993.
———. *The NIV Interlinear Hebrew-English Old Testament*. 4 vols. Grand Rapids: Zondervan, 1987.
Koller, Charles W. *Expository Preaching Without Notes*. Grand Rapids: Baker, 1962.
Kubo, Sakae. *A Reader's Greek-English Lexicon of the New Testament and a Beginner's Guide for the Translation of New Testament Greek*. Grand Rapids: Zondervan, 1975.
Kuhn, Karl G. *Konkordanz zu den Qumrantexten*. Göttingen: Vandenhoeck & Ruprecht, 1960.
Ladd, George E. *A Theology of the New Testament*. 2nd ed. edited by Donald A. Hagner. Grand Rapids: Eerdmans, 1993.
Lampe, G. W. H. "The Evidence in the New Testament for Early Creeds, Catechisms, and Liturgy." *ExpTim* 71 (1959-60) 359-63.
———. *A Patristic Greek Lexicon*. Oxford: Clarendon Press, 1961.
Larkin, William J., Jr. *Acts*. IVPNTC. Downers Grove, IL: InterVarsity Press, 1995.

———. "Additional Genre and Literary Form Analysis Procedures." Available at WJL faculty webpage at www.ciu.edu.

———. *Culture and Biblical Hermeneutics: Interpreting and Applying the Authoritative Word in a Relativistic Age.* Eugene, OR: Wipf & Stock, 2003.

———. "Exegetical Worksheets." Available at WJL faculty webpage at www.ciu.edu.

———. "Greek Grammar in the Head Chart." Available at WJL faculty webpage at www.ciu.edu.

———. "In-Depth Word Study: Introduction and Aids." Available at WJL faculty webpage at www.ciu.edu.

———. "Methods and Aids for Textual Criticism." Available at WJL faculty webpage at www.ciu.edu.

———. "Rhetorical Features Chart." Available at WJL faculty webpage at www.ciu.edu.

LaSor, William Sanford. *Handbook of New Testament Greek: An Inductive Approach Based on the Greek Text of Acts.* 2 vols. Grand Rapids: Eerdmans, 1973.

Lenski, Richard C. H. *The Sermon: Its Homiletical Construction.* Grand Rapids: Baker, 1968.

Liddell, Henry, Robert Scott, Henry S. Jones, Roderick McKenzie, P. G. W. Glare. *A Greek-English Lexicon*, 9th ed. with *Revised Supplement*. Oxford: Clarendon Press, 1996.

Liefeld, Walter L. *New Testament Exposition: From Text to Sermon.* Grand Rapids: Zondervan, 1984.

Lightfoot, J. B. *Saint Paul's Epistle to the Philippians.* London: Macmillan, 1885.

Lillie, William. "The Pauline House-tables." *ExpTim* 86 (1974-75) 179-83.

Loeb Classical Library. Cambridge, MA: Harvard Univ. Press.

Loh, I.-Jin. and Eugene A. Nida. *A Handbook on Paul's Letter to the Philippians.* New York: United Bible Societies, 1977.

Longacre, Robert E. *The Grammar of Discourse.* 2nd ed. New York: Plenum, 1996.

Longenecker, Richard N. *New Testament Social Ethics for Today.* Grand Rapids: Eerdmans, 1984.

Louw, Johannes P. "Discourse Analysis and the Greek New Testament." *BT* vol. 24, no. 1 (1973) 101-18.

———. "The Greek New Testament Workbook." *BT* vol. 30, no. 1 (1979) 108-17.

———. and Eugene A. Nida, eds. *Greek-English Lexicon of the New Testament Based on Semantic Domains.* 2 vols. New York: United Bible Societies, 1988.

Luc, Alex T. "Old Testament Theology Course Materials." Columbia, SC:

CIU-SSM, 2007-08.
Lührmann, Dieter. "Neutestamentliche Haustafeln und Antike Ökonomie." *NTS* 27 (1981) 83-97.
Lust, J., E. Eynikel, and K. Hauspie. *A Greek-English Lexicon of the Septuagint*. 2 vols. Stuttgart: Deutsche Bibelgesellschaft, 1992-96.
Malte, Eric C. "Preaching from the Greek New Testament." *CTM* 25 (1954) 656-62.
Marshall, I. Howard. *The Gospel of Luke: A Commentary on the Greek Text*. NIGTC. Grand Rapids: Eerdmans, 1978.
———. "Introduction." In *New Testament Interpretation: Essays on Principles and Methods*, edited by I. Howard Marshall, 11-18. Grand Rapids: Eerdmans, 1977.
———., ed. *Moulton and Geden Concordance of the Greek New Testament*. 6th ed. London: T & T Clark, 2002.
———. *New Testament Theology: Many Witnesses, One Gospel*. Downers Grove, IL: InterVarsity Press, 2004.
Martin, Ralph P. *Carmen Christi: Philippians ii.5-11 in Recent Interpretation in the Setting of Early Christian Worship*. Cambridge: Cambridge Univ. Press, 1967.
———. and Peter H. Davids, eds. *Dictionary of the Later New Testament and Its Developments*. Downers Grove, IL: InterVarsity Press, 1997.
Martínez, Florentino García. *The Dead Sea Scrolls Translated: The Qumran Texts in English*. 2nd ed. Grand Rapids: Eerdmans, 1996.
Mayer, Günter. *Index Philoneus*. Berlin: Walter De Gruyter, 1974.
McQuilkin, J. Robertson. "Problems of Normativeness in Scripture: Cultural Versus Permanent." In *Hermeneutics, Inerrancy, and the Bible*, edited by Earl D. Radmacher and Robert D. Preus, 217-40. Grand Rapids: Zondervan, 1984.
Meeks, Wayne A. "Why Study the New Testament?" *NTS* 51 (2005) 155-70.
Melick, Richard R. *Philippians, Colossians, Philemon*. NAC. Nashville: Broadman,1991.
Metzger, Bruce M. *A Textual Commentary on the Greek New Testament: A Companion Volume to the UNITED BIBLE SOCIETIES' GREEK NEW TESTAMENT (Fourth Revised Edition)*. 2nd ed. Stuttgart: United Bible Societies, 1994.
Montefiore, Claude G. and H. Loewe, eds. *A Rabbinic Anthology*. repr. New York: Schocken, 1974.
Moulton, James H. and George Milligan. *The Vocabulary of the Greek Testament: Illustrated from the Papyri and Other Non-literary Sources*. repr. Grand Rapids: Eerdmans, 1974.
Mullins, Terence Y. "Disclosure as a Literary Form in the New Testament." *NovT* 7 (1964-65) 44-50.

———. "Formulas in New Testament Epistles." *JBL* 91 (1972) 380-90.
———. "Greeting as a New Testament Form." *JBL* 87 (1968) 418-26.
———. "Petition as a Literary Form." *NovT* 5 (1962) 46-54.
———. "Topos as a New Testament Form." *JBL* 99 (1980) 541-47.
———. "Visit Talk in New Testament Letters." *CBQ* 35 (1973) 350-58.
Neufeld, Vernon H. *The Earliest Christian Confessions*. Grand Rapids: Eerdmans, 1963.
New American Standard Bible. updated ed. Anaheim, CA: Foundation, 1995.
New King James Version Holy Bible. Nashville: Thomas Nelson, 2006.
New Testament Abstracts database. Accessed September 12, 2007. Online: http://www.ciu.edu/library/databases-a.php.
New Testament Study Group–CIU-SSM. "Survey of Time Distribution in Sermon Preparation." Columbia, SC. Spring term 2001.
Newman, Barclay M. *A Concise Greek-English Dictionary of the New Testament*. London: United Bible Societies, 1971.
Nichols, J. Randall. *Building the Word: The Dynamics of Communication and Preaching*. San Francisco: Harper & Row, 1980.
Nicole, Roger R. "The Biblical Concept of Truth." In *Scripture and Truth*, edited by D. A. Carson and John D. Woodbridge, 287-98. Grand Rapids: Zondervan, 1983.
Nida, Eugene A. *Componential Analysis of Meaning: An Introduction to Semantic Structures*. The Hague: Mouton, 1975.
———. "Establishing Translation Principles and Procedures." *BT* vol. 33, no. 2 (1982) 208-13.
Noll, Stephen. "Reading the Bible as the Word of God." *Churchman* 107 (1993) 227-53.
O'Brien, Peter T. *The Epistle to the Philippians: A Commentary on the Greek Text*. NIGTC. Grand Rapids: Eerdmans, 1991.
Original Languages Library CD-ROM. Logos Bible Sofware Verson 3.0. Bellingham, WA: Logos Research Systems, Inc., 2006.
Packer, J. I. "Infallible Scripture and the Role of Hermeneutics." In *Scripture and Truth*, edited by D. A. Carson and John D. Woodbridge, 325–56. Grand Rapids: Zondervan, 1983.
———. "Upholding the Unity of Scripture Today." *JETS* 25 (1982) 409-14.
Pate, C. Marvin, ed. *Four Views on the Book of Revelation*. Grand Rapids: Zondervan, 1998.
Paul, Ian. "Metaphor." In *DTIB* 507-10.
Pennington, Jonathan T. "Deponency in Koine Greek: The Grammatical Question and the Lexicographical Dilemma." *TJ* n.s. 24 (2003) 55-76.
Perry, Lloyd M. *Biblical Sermon Guide: A Step-by-Step Procedure for the Preparation and Presentation*. Grand Rapids: Baker, 1970.
———. *A Manual for Biblical Preaching*. Grand Rapids: Baker, 1965.

Perschbacher, Wesley J. *A New Analytical Greek Lexicon*. Peabody, MA: Hendrickson, 1990.
Perseus Digital Library. Somerville, MA: Tufts University. Accessed September 12, 2007. Online: http://www.perseus.tufts.edu/.
Peterson, Eugene H. "Foreword." In *More Light on the Path: Daily Scripture Readings in Hebrew and Greek*, by David W. Baker and Elaine A. Heath, 5-6. Grand Rapids: Baker, 1998.
———. The Unbusy Pastor." *Leadership* 2 (Summer 1981) 70-76.
Philo. *Works*. 12 vols. LCL. Cambridge, MA: Harvard Univ. Press, 1929-62.
"Poetry, Hebrew." In *IDB* 3:829-38.
Polhill, John B. *Acts*. NAC. Nashville: Broadman, 1992.
Poovey, William A. *Letting the Word Come Alive: Choosing and Studying the Text*. St. Louis, MO: Concordia, 1977.
Porter, Stanley E. "Greek of the New Testament." In *DNTB* 426-35.
———. *Verbal Aspect in the Greek of the New Testament: With Reference to Tense and Mood*. New York: Peter Lang, 1989.
———. and D. A. Carson, eds. *Biblical Greek Language and Linguistics: Open Questions in Current Research*. Sheffield, England: JSOT Press, 1993.
Porter, Wendy J. "Creeds and Hymns." In *DNTB* 231-38.
Pratt, Richard. *NIV Spirit of the Reformation Study Bible*. Grand Rapids: Zondervan, 2003.
Rahlfs, Alfred and Robert Hanhart, eds. *Septuaginta*. 2nd ed. Stuttgart: Deutsche Bibelgesellschaft, 2006.
Ramm, Bernard. *Protestant Biblical Interpretation: A Textbook of Hermeneutics*. 3rd ed. Grand Rapids: Baker, 1970.
Raschke, Carl. *The Next Reformation: Why Evangelicals Must Embrace Postmodernity*. Grand Rapids: Baker Academic, 2004.
Rengstorf, Karl H., ed. *A Complete Concordance to Flavius Josephus: Unabridged Study Edition*. 2 vols. Leiden: Brill, 2002.
"Revelation, Book of." In *DBI* 713-16.
Reymond, Robert L. *A New Systematic Theology of the Christian Faith*. Nashville: Thomas Nelson, 1998.
Ricoeur, Paul. "Biblical Hermeneutics." *Semeia* 4 (1975) 29-148.
———. *Interpretation Theory: Discourse and The Surplus of Meaning*. Fort Worth, TX: TCU Press, 1976.
Robertson, Archibald T. *A Grammar of the Greek New Testament in the Light of Historical Research*. Nashville: Broadman, 1934.
———. *The Minister and His Greek New Testament*. New York: George H. Doran, 1923.
Robinson, Haddon. *Biblical Preaching: The Development and Delivery of*

Expository Messages. 2nd ed. Grand Rapids: Baker, 2001.
Rogers, Cleon L., Jr. and Cleon L. Rogers III. *A New Linguistic and Exegetical Key to the Greek New Testament*. Grand Rapids: Zondervan, 1998.
Ropes, James H. *A Critical and Exegetical Commentary on the Epistle of St. James*. ICC. New York: Charles Scribner's Sons, 1916.
Ryken, Leland, James C. Wilhoit, and Tremper Longman III, eds. *Dictionary of Biblical Imagery*. Downers Grove, IL: InterVarsity Press, 1998.
Sailhamer, John H. *Introduction to Old Testament Theology: A Canonical Approach*. Grand Rapids: Zondervan, 1995.
Sanders, Jack T. *The New Testament Christological Hymns: Their Historical Religious Background*. Cambridge: Cambridge Univ. Press, 1971.
———. "The Transition from Opening Epistolary Thanksgiving to Body in the Letters of the Pauline Corpus." *JBL* 81 (1962) 348-62.
Sandin, Robert T. "The Clarity of Scripture." In *The Living and Active Word of God: Studies in Honor of Samuel J. Schultz*, edited by Morris Inch and Ronald Youngblood, 237-53. Winona Lake, IN: Eisenbrauns, 1983.
Schweizer, Eduard. "Traditional Ethical Patterns in the Pauline and Post-Pauline Letters and Their Development (Lists of Vices and Housetables)." In *Text and Interpretation: Studies in the New Testament Presented to Matthew Black*, edited by Ernest Best and Robert McL. Wilson, 195-209. Cambridge: Cambridge Univ. Press, 1979.
Scott, J. Julius, Jr. "On the Value of Intertestamental Jewish Literature for New Testament Theology." *JETS* 23 (1980) 315-23.
Silva, Moisés. *Biblical Words and Their Meaning: An Introduction to Lexical Semantics*. 2nd ed. Grand Rapids: Zondervan, 1994.
———. "The Case for Calvinistic Hermeneutics." In *An Introduction to Biblical Hermeneutics: The Search for Meaning*, by Walter C. Kaiser, Jr. and Moisés Silva, 251-70. Grand Rapids: Zondervan, 1994.
———. *Philippians*. 2nd ed. BECNT. Grand Rapids: Baker Academic, 2005.
Smith, Jay E. "Sentence Diagramming, Clausal Layouts, and Exegetical Outlining: Tracing the Argument." In *Interpreting the New Testament Text: Introduction to the Art and Science of Exegesis*, edited by Darrell L. Bock and Buist M. Fanning, 73-134. Wheaton, IL: Crossway, 2006.
Soncino Classics Collection for Windows CD-ROM. Version 3.0.8. Brooklyn, NY: Soncino, 2005.
Soulen, Richard N. *Handbook of Biblical Criticism*. 2nd ed. Atlanta: John Knox, 1981.
Sproul, R. C. *The Last Days according to Jesus*. Grand Rapids: Baker, 1998.

Stein, Robert H. "The Benefits of an Author-Oriented Approach to Hermeneutics." *JETS* 44 (2001) 451-66.

——. *An Introduction to the Parables of Jesus*. Philadelphia: Westminster, 1981.

Stiller, Brian C. *Preaching Parables to Postmoderns*. Minneapolis, MN: Fortress, 2005.

Stott, John R. W. *Between Two Worlds: The Art of Preaching in the Twentieth Century*. Grand Rapids: Eerdmans, 1982.

Stowers, Stanley K. *The Diatribe and Paul's Letter to the Romans*. Chico, CA: Scholars, 1981.

Strack, Hermann L. and Paul Billerbeck. *Kommentar zum Neuen Testament aus Talmud und Midrasch*. 6 vols. 7th ed. München: C. H. Beck'sche, 1978.

The Strongest NASB Exhaustive Concordance. Grand Rapids: Zondervan, 2004.

Sweet, Leonard. *Post-Modern Pilgrims: First Century Passion for the 21st Century World*. Nashville: Broadman & Holman, 2000.

Swindoll, Charles R. *Laugh Again*. Dallas, TX: Word, 1992.

Tenney, Merrill C. *Interpreting Revelation*. Grand Rapids: Eerdmans, 1985.

——. "The Meaning of the Word." In *The Bible–The Living Word of Revelation*, edited by Merrill C. Tenney, 11-27. Grand Rapids: Zondervan, 1968.

——., ed. *Zondervan Pictorial Encyclopedia of the Bible*. 5 vols. Grand Rapids: Zondervan, 1975-76.

Thesaurus Linguae Graecae (TLG®) CD-ROM. Version E. Irvine, CA: Univ. of California, Irvine, 2000. Accessed September 12, 2007. Online (available by subscription): http://ptolemy.tlg.uci.edu.

Thielman, Frank. "The New Testament Canon: Its Basis for Authority." *WTJ* 45 (1983) 400-410.

——. *Philippians*. NIVAC. Grand Rapids: Zondervan, 1995.

Thiessen, Henry C. *Introductory Lectures in Systematic Theology*. Grand Rapids: Eerdmans, 1975.

Thomas, Robert L. "A Hermeneutical Ambiguity of Eschatology: The Analogy of Faith." *JETS* 23 (1980) 45-53.

——. "The Principle of Single Meaning." *MSJ* 12 (2001) 33-47.

——. *Revelation 1-7: An Exegetical Commentary*. Chicago: Moody Press, 1992.

——. *Revelation 8-22: An Exegetical Commentary*. Chicago: Moody Press, 1995.

——. and Stanley N. Gundry, eds. *A Harmony of the Gospels with Explanations and Essays*. Chicago: Moody Press, 1978.

Thompson, Michael B. "Teaching/Paraenesis." In *DPL* 922-23.

Toussaint, Stanley D. "A Method of Making a New Testament Word Study." *BSac* 120 (1963) 35-41.
Tov, Emanuel, ed., *Dead Sea Scrolls Electronic Library CD-ROM*. rev. ed. Leiden: Brill, 2006.
Traina, Robert A. *Methodical Bible Study*. Grand Rapids: Zondervan, 2002.
Turner, Nigel. *Christian Words*. Nashville: Thomas Nelson, 1982.
———. *Style*. vol 4, *A Grammar of New Testament Greek*, edited by James H. Moulton, Edinburgh: T. & T. Clark, 1976.
Van Gemeren, Willem, ed. *The New International Dictionary of Old Testament Theology & Exegesis*. 5 vols. Grand Rapids: Zondervan, 1997.
———. *The Progress of Redemption: The Story of Salvation from Creation to the New Jerusalem*. Grand Rapids: Baker, 1988.
Vanhoozer, Kevin J., ed. *Dictionary for Theological Interpretation of the Bible*. Grand Rapids: Baker Academic, 2005.
———. "Lost in Interpretation?" In *Whatever Happened to Truth?* edited by Andreas Köstenberger, 93-129. Wheaton, IL: Crossway, 2005.
Vella, Jane. *Taking Learning to Task: Creative Strategies for Teaching Adults*. San Francisco: Jossey-Bass, 2001.
Wallace, Daniel B. *Greek Grammar Beyond the Basics: An Exegetical Syntax of the New Testament*. Grand Rapids: Zondervan, 1996.
Warfield, B. B. "Revelation." In *International Standard Bible Encyclopedia*, edited by James Orr, 4:2573-82. Grand Rapids: Eerdmans, 1939.
Webb, William J. "A Redemptive-Movement Hermeneutic: Encouraging Dialogue Among Four Evangelical Views." *JETS* 48 (2005) 331-49.
Weima, Jeffrey A. D. "Letters, Graeco-Roman." In *DNTB* 640-44.
———. *Neglected Endings: The Significance of the Pauline Letter Closings*. Sheffield, England: JSOT Press, 1994.
Wenham, John W. *Elements of New Testament Greek*. Cambridge: Cambridge Univ. Press, 1965.
White, John L. *The Form and Function of the Body of the Greek Letter: A Study of the Letter-Body in the Non-Literary Papyri and in the Apostle Paul*. Missoula, MT: SBL, 1972.
———. "Introductory Formulae in the Body of the Pauline Letter." *JBL* 90 (1971) 91-97.
———. "Saint Paul and the Apostolic Letter Tradition." *CBQ* 45 (1983) 433-44.
White, Reginald E. O. *A Guide to Preaching: A Practical Primer of Homiletics*. Grand Rapids: Eerdmans, 1973.
Whitesell, Faris D. *Power in Expository Preaching*. Westwood, NJ: F. H. Revell, 1963.
Wigram, George V. *The Englishman's Greek Concordance of the New Testa-*

ment: *Coded with the Numbering System from Strong's Exhaustive Concordance of the Bible*. Peabody, MA: Hendrickson, 1996.

———. *The Englishman's Hebrew Concordance of the Old Testament: Coded with the Numbering System from Strong's Exhaustive Concordance of the Bible*. Peabody, MA: Hendrickson, 1996.

Wilder, Amos N. *Early Christian Rhetoric: The Language of the Gospel*. London: SCM, 1964.

Wiles, Gordon P. *Paul's Intercessory Prayers: The Significance of the Intercessory Prayer Passages in the Letters of St Paul*. Cambridge: Cambridge Univ. Press, 1974.

Wright, Christopher J. H. *The Mission of God: Unlocking the Bible's Grand Narrative*. Downers Grove, IL: InterVarsity Press, 2006.

Wright, Paul O. "Course Materials." Columbia, SC: Columbia Graduate School of Bible and Missions, 1984-85.

Wuest, Kenneth S. *The Practical Use of the Greek New Testament*. Chicago: Moody Press, 1946.

Yoder, Perry B. *From Word to Life: A Guide to the Art of Bible Study*. Scottdale, PA: Herald, 1982.

Yount, William R. *Created to Learn: A Christian Teacher's Introduction to Educational Psychology*. Nashville, Broadman & Holman, 1996.

Zerwick, Max and Mary Grosvenor. *A Grammatical Analysis of the Greek New Testament: Unabridged*. 5th ed. Rome: Biblical Institute Press, 1996.

www.ingramcontent.com/pod-product-compliance
Lightning Source LLC
Chambersburg PA
CBHW071148300426
44113CB00009B/1129